£17·60

THE PRESENCE OF RENÉ CHAR

THE PRESENCE OF

RENÉ CHAR

MARY ANN CAWS

Princeton University Press
Princeton, New Jersey

Copyright © 1976 by Princeton University Press
Published by Princeton University Press, Princeton, New Jersey
In the United Kingdom: Princeton University Press, Guildford, Surrey
All Rights Reserved
Frontis: René Char. (Photo: Jacques Robert)
Library of Congress Cataloging in Publication Data will
be found on the last printed page of this book
Publication of this book has been aided by a grant from the Louis A. Robb
Fund of Princeton University Press
This book has been composed in Linotype Times Roman
Printed in the United States of America
by Princeton University Press, Princeton, New Jersey

for a Vaucluse of the mind

ACKNOWLEDGMENTS

The generosity of the John Simon Guggenheim Memorial Foundation, of the Senior Fulbright-Hays Program, and, at a later period, of the National Endowment for the Humanities was largely responsible for the released time and the travel necessary to this work.

My very warmest thanks to Henri Peyre, Michael Riffaterre, Albert Sonnenfeld, and Micheline Tison-Braun; to François Chapon and Hanna Charney; to Jerry Sherwood of Princeton University Press; to Tina Jolas and Peter Caws.

To René Char, my deep and continuing gratitude for his welcome, for the inner relevance of his discussions, and above all for the possibilities offered of participating with him in the space of his work.

My grateful acknowledgment to Editions Gallimard for permission to quote in their entirety the following poems of René Char: "Léonides," "Calendrier," "J'Habite une douleur," "Le Visage nuptial," "Redonnez-leur," and "Le Loriot" from *Fureur et mystère*, © Gallimard, 1962, "Toute vie. . . ," "Contrevenir," "Transir," "Front de la rose," "Le Taureau," and "Homme-oiseau mort et bison mourant" from *Les Matinaux*, © Gallimard, 1950, and "Tracé sur le gouffre," "Lutteurs," "L'Ouest derrière soi perdu," "Dyne," "Permanent invisible," and "Ni Eternel ni temporel" from *Le Nu perdu*, © Gallimard, 1971; to José Corti for "Sommeil fatal," "Tréma de l'émondeur," "L'Amour," "A l'Horizon remarquable," and "Transfuges" from *Le Marteau sans maître*, © Librairie José Corti, 1934; to René Char for "L'Anneau de la licorne," from *La Nuit talismanique*, © Editions d'Art Albert Skira, 1972; to Editions Gallimard for "Evadé l'archipel" and "Reception d'Orion," © Gallimard, 1975.

ACKNOWLEDGMENTS

Also to Insel Verlag, Frankfurt, for permission to quote from Rainer Maria Rilke, *Gesammelte Werke*, © 1930, and for English translations, to W. W. Norton: *Duino Elegies* (tr. Spender and Leishman), © 1939, *Sonnets to Orpheus* (tr. M. D. Herter Norton), © 1942 and *Letters of Rainer Maria Rilke*, © 1947; to the University of Michigan Press for quotations from Friedrich Hölderlin, *Poems and Fragments* (tr. Hamburger), © 1967; to the SCM Press for Martin Heidegger, *Being and Time* (tr. Robinson and Macquarrie), © 1963.

All reproductions of manuscripts with thanks to René Char.

LIST OF
ABBREVIATIONS

All the quotations are taken, unless otherwise specified, from the following volumes, many containing previously published works. Throughout this book, the place of publications in French is Paris, of those in English, New York, unless otherwise stated.

Arsenal (privately printed). 1929 (A)

Le Tombeau des secrets (privately printed). 1930 (TS)

Dehors la nuit est gouvernée, preceded by *Placard pour un chemin des écoliers*. GLM, 1949 (D)

Le Soleil des eaux. Gallimard, 1951 (SE)

Pour nous, Rimbaud. GLM, 1956 (PNR)

Poèmes et proses choisis. Gallimard, 1957 (PPC)

Cinq poésies en l'honneur de Georges Braque. Geneva, 1958 (CB)

Commune présence. Gallimard, 1964 (CP)

Flux de l'aimant. GLM, 1965 (FA)

Retour amont. Gallimard, 1966 (RA)

Fureur et mystère. Gallimard, coll. Poésie, 1967 (FM)

Les Matinaux, followed by *La Parole en archipel*. Gallimard, coll. Poésie, 1969 (LM)

En Trente-trois morceaux. GLM, 1970 (E)

Le Marteau sans maître, suivi de *Moulin premier*. Corti, 1970 (MM)

Recherche de la base et du sommet. Gallimard, coll. Poésie, 1971 (RBS)

Arrière-histoire du poème pulverisé. Jean Hugues, 1972 (AHPP)

Le Nu perdu. Gallimard, 1972 (NP)

La Nuit talismanique. Skira, coll. Sentiers de la Création, 1972 (NT)

Aromates chasseurs. Gallimard, 1975 (AC). (First version in *Argile*, no. 1, 1974.)

Sur la poésie. GLM, 1974 (SP)

Prefaces: *Exposition Picasso*: 1970-72 Avignon (May 23 to September 23, 1973) (P)

Hommage à Joseph Sima: Château de Ratilly (June 23 to September 16, 1973) (S)

CONTENTS

THE PRESENCE OF

RENÉ CHAR

Ce qui vient au monde pour ne rien troubler
ne mérite ni égards ni patience.
Fureur et mystère

PREFACE

Que le risque soit ta clarté. (AUSC)

This study of the work and thought of René
Char has a double focus: it concentrates on
the texts as given and also on a manner of experiencing them
appropriate to a poet whose work is vast in scope and complex in nature. The interpretation is prefaced by a reasonably
"objective" account of certain figures divorced from their
wider context and a parallel investigation of the role of the
fragmentary in Char's poetic theory. The phonetic ambiguity of a few recurring elements is then made the basis for a
temporary distortion of their semantic content, as an experi-
ment in one perspective which might even be called a deliberate obsession, this deviant interpretation justified by the
crucial position of the ambiguous within the theory: the ex-
perimental distortion proves its value in the progressive shifting of perception and of expression from the outward and
the stated toward the subjective and the suggested. The major
part of the essay, concerned with a broader context, nevertheless finds an inward path, where the elements and figures are
restored to an overall structure, individual images situated
within developing themes, and these themes, within an inclu-
sive cycle of seasons and of vision. Finally, by a vertical
effort equally of the poet and the reader, the transition is
accomplished from the archipelago of verbal fragments—
La Parole en archipel—into a constellation of the mind.

Thus the approach of the book varies according to the
stage of perception reached—by turns the point of reference
in the text is phonetic or thematic, the method informally
structural or impressionistic, analytic and centered on the
particular, or more descriptive in its windings. The reading, in
its intermittent alterations of direction and its obstinate fidelity to the whole, is based on a prolonged immersion in the
entirety of the published corpus and on certain unpublished

manuscripts, as well as invaluable conversations and correspondence with the poet, both in regard to this commentary
and to the translations of his poems, a shared work complementary to this one.

This essay in correspondence is openly partial and yet deliberately interior, as if one were to see and to speak from the
inside of a poetic universe, by choice. The question once
posed by the poet to himself—"Why this path rather than
another?"—can only find an intuitive answer, but that, says
Char, is the essence of poetry. This path, in its divergent
ways, seemed the least reductive. Rather than dealing with
exterior situation[1] and biographical chronology, we have
preferred here to limit ourselves to the work as given and,
in particular, to interpretations of the texts in their possible
bearing on a theory of reading.

This path begins from the fragment and then widens. One
of Char's metaphors describes the eventual aim: those who
raise to the brim of the well the bucket plunged to the depths
cause the ripples to spread out from each new disturbing of
the water. These seekers of water are said to carry branches
as their sign: their word outlasts the night, although the
branches may themselves be on the point of breaking. Speak-

---

[1] We shall rarely allude to the circumstances of the text, although
they have of course left their mark upon it—and, occasionally, upon
our reading. The poem, attached to its moment, always goes past it.
Georges Poulet's comments about his general interpretation of the
words "crispés" and "horizon clos" in *Feuillets d'Hypnos*—extending
beyond the specific wartime climate of anxiety to which Char alludes
in his original choice of the words—illumine a certain way of seeing
the relationship between circumstances and poem. For eventually the
images and the vocabulary transcend the limits of circumstance.
"Néanmoins, entre la circonstance et celui qui choisit de l'épouser, il
y a une convenance, et qui subsiste—dans le poème comme dans
l'esprit du poète—quand d'autres événements lui ont succédé. C'est ce
choix éternel d'un resserrement en apparence occasionnel que j'ai
voulu ici marquer." (*L'Arc*, 1963, no. René Char).
  As for the situation of the poet, see the material readily available in
the special numbers of *L'Herne*, *L'Arc*, *Liberté*; and, for diverse interpretations in a wide range of tendencies, see the works of Blanchot,
Dupin, Mounin, Rau, Barelli, etc.

ing of the title of the collection *L'Age cassant*, René Char points out that the term "cassant" is applied to the branches of some fruit trees, as if to portend the heaviness of the fruit to come or in witness to what has been. We could hope for no better situation for this essay than to be in an "Age cassant," abundant of yield and nonetheless, or therefore, fragile in its bearing.[1a]

The essay attempts to show a persisting "presence" within a fleeting "passage"—as the poet would have it—to keep the visible and the verbal within the "combustible invisibility" of a distance only sensed by its intermittent flash, characteristic of a meteoric trace. A brief sentence of Mallarmé concerning another passage, Rimbaud's, illustrates the paradox of the two terms and our aim, to signal, in its passing, "l'oeuvre filante" or the meteoric work: "Éclat, lui, d'un météore, allumé sans motif autre que sa présence, issu seul et s'éteignant. / He, the flash of a meteor, lit with no other motive than its presence, born alone and fading out."[2]

In view of the singular nature of René Char's poetry, which it is the essential task of these pages to convey, the attitude adopted in the main body of the work is one of participation rather than of explanation. In this case, and for reasons intrinsic to this reading and suggested above, the approach shifts drastically, after an introduction to the essential character of the poetry, from a preliminary and exterior analysis of images and techniques toward a more involved study of themes in their variations and their continuity, and at last to an effort one might perceive as interior, willingly inscribed within the same universe as that of the poet—an effort to follow the motion of the texts in their arduous verticality. Thus, for instance, the image of the mountain is absorbed deliberately within the essay itself, whose style and whose sense are meant ideally to answer the inital image the poet has chosen.

[1a] "Fruits ennemis. / L'arbre souffle des fruits si lourds, qu'il ne les peut retenir: il les perd ou il se brise." (Valéry, *Oeuvres*, Ed. Pléiade, 1962, I, 577) [V]

[2] The quotation from Mallarmé is taken from his "Arthur Rimbaud," Stéphane Mallarmé, *Oeuvres*, edn. Pléiade, 1945, p. 512.

The final attitude reflects less a refusal of appropriate critical gesture than a belief that the most valid response to this poet's work is other than explanatory, that dialogue is finally possible only along a path chosen by the poet, of which, as he says, the poem forms one half and the commentary the other, in a new and double creation whose "mystery is to be left intact."

Because the poetry of René Char is at once an expressive speech and a presence watching in silence, we have tried to invoke here, insofar as possible, a response and a question, an utterance at moments open and at others reticent, a relation between the offered word of the texts and another word half-hidden. It is this individual reading whose long and constant path this essay recounts, in its shifting approach and in its interrupted wake: "Leur parole reçoit existence du fruit intermittent. . . . / Their speech receives existence from the intermittent fruit. . . ." (NP,31) (JG)

The numerous cross-references—to critics, sources, and, most important, to kindred poets such as Hölderlin and Rilke,[3] to Pascal, Nietzsche, Heidegger, to Rimbaud and Mallarmé— will be placed in the notes, so that the commentary may be seen whole, but with its proper supports.

A few passages cited principally for their content, are given only in English; in other cases, the original is given with an English version. Where the French serves as an epigraph, of essential brevity, or where it is easily grasped from the context, or has been translated elsewhere in the essay, it is given alone. Titles are translated not in the text, but in the lengthy index. The translations of Char's poetry are identical with those in the Princeton University Press edition; exceptions to this rule are marked with an asterisk, *. The translations are mine, except those marked (JG) for Jonathan Griffin.

[3] As in the case of Heidegger and Hölderlin, we have chosen to place the German original and an English translation in the notes; the version of Rilke used by Réne Char is that of J. F. Angelloz, Aubier, 1943.

6

Alternate readings of words in the text—phonetically justified in spite of the orthography—are placed in brackets to
indicate the divergence. In the quotations from unpublished
manuscripts, parentheses, ( ), mark discarded earlier versions and brackets, [ ], the words or phrases added. Elsewhere, brackets around a phrase in quotation marks signal
alternate readings of a word in the texts, phonetically justified, but opening into a different semantic field.

For René Char, the necessary attitude toward poetry is one
of passionate intuition. With that intuition as our final goal
for an ideal coherence, we have nevertheless used a variety
of approaches, in the belief that the greatest poetry demands
them all from the reader who would not reduce it to univocity.
Our advance follows a roughly chronological order, from *Le
Marteau sans maître* to *Aromates chasseurs*, written over
forty years later, as well as an "ordre insurgé," from the exterior aesthetic of the pre-war poems through the "furious"
poems of the Resistance, back to the dense interior of "Le
Visage nuptial" and the quiet lighting of the still earlier
Artine as it is reflected in the recent *La Nuit talismanique*.
In brief, we have attempted to describe a poetic universe of
multiplicity and profundity by all the varied methods we
could manage, while fully convinced that no one reading—
however diverse its technique or keen its sensitivity—could
ever suffice.

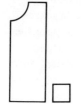

VOICE AND PATH:
VOIX/VOIE

A. Part and Passage: "solitaire et multiple"

Vous serez une part de la saveur du fruit.

(FM,95)

In a poetry said to be composed like a verbal archipelago, as in the title: *La Parole en archipel*, how is the reader to enter into a single text, without betraying its integrity or its relation to the others? Perhaps only by considering it already a paradox: closed off, and yet open to correspondence, like so many points of a moving network changeable and lasting, stretched from island to island, or, in another figure, from summit to summit. The notions of "passeur" and "passage" will recur throughout this essay, which begins by an analysis of parts—images, procedures, terminology—and then selects various passages, choosing its own relation to the archipelago of texts.

From his reading of early Greek philosophers René Char retains a certain affection for the fragment with no apparent frame, the element at once independent and in series. He pictures Heraclitus, the philosopher and the poet of the fragment, placing over our lips his finger whose nail has been torn off: to the sign there remains an essential mystery[1] and a certain risk of misinterpretation, for what assures the transition from one fragment to the next, from a text in a

---

[1] The poet's succinct comment on the difficulty implied in the sign and in the showing, on the relations of exchange and discretion, replaces to advantage any lengthier discourses: "Il n'y a pas, je crois, de 'signe trop bavard', mais un doigt essentiel, à l'ongle arraché, ce doigt-là est 'riche' de sa blessure. Qui montre est ensanglanté de par la qualité même de ce qu'il désigne et reçoit en échange. Les lèvres sont la plaie préférée des dieux, elles sont source du silence pur aussi, quelquefois." (Correspondence with the author, hereafter quoted indirectly.)

8

group of texts toward the following one, when no order is specified? How is one not to betray the fragment even while desiring a "passage?" The special fascination of René Char consists precisely in this relation underlying each reading, like a question implicit yet ceaselessly posed. We have opted for a *spatial* conception as opposed to the more temporal one which would be that of a musical composition. "Parcourir l'espace, mais ne pas jeter un regard sur le Temps. L'ignorer. Ni vu, ni ressenti, encore moins mesuré. A la seconde, tout s'est tenu dans le seul sacré inconditionnel qui fut jamais: celui-là. / To traverse space, but never to glance at Time. To be unaware of it. Neither seen, nor felt, much less measured. To the second, everything was included in the only unconditional sacred ever to have been: that one."[2] Such notions as dénouement and conclusion will not find their place here, since the essential vision to be retained is that of a perspective open and opening, more unsettling than harmonic.

Yet as the reader and the poet meet within the space of the text, a "common presence" confers permanent value upon it. The poet naming himself a "passeur" will take aboard only those with whom this present or this presence can be shared; thus the passage from one moment to the next is a passage in common. The crossing between elements is carried out in a tacit agreement between the poet and the reader, across the waters separating the island fragments of the archipelago corresponding to the participation of the reader in each part of the text. The trace left, like a wake, can then be followed by the next reading, or not. That wake is constituted, during the crossing, by the recurrence of images or words whose poetic charge accumulates with the review of each fragment in the arduous work of remaking the text.

---

[2] René Char is clearly closer to the world of painters than to that of musicians, the spatial vision imposing its particular character even on the moral conception. There is here, as always, another point of view. In his article "Clarté de René Char," *Critique* (juin, 1965, no. 217, p. 52), Roger Laporte says the opposite: ". . . cette dimension temporelle plus importante que la spatiale."

This essay rests on the firm conviction that in each poem of René Char a place must be made for the possibility of a multiple reading at the heart of a convergence, verbal and intellectual. Each reader, following his unique path, may say of his partial and necessarily fragmentary reading that it tries to locate, not the origin, but the center.

"C'est le peu qui est réellement tout. Le peu occupe une place immense. / The little is really all, the little occupies an enormous space." (NT,62) Now a prolonged fidelity to the fragment supposes an immediate refusal of anything that could be read as a rigid formal structure. The poet, who chooses not to establish himself, will remain always on his guard against an easy accumulation and an untroubled ordering. "Wisdom is not conglomerate, but in the creation and in the nature common to us, finding our number, our reciprocity, our differences, our passage . . ." (LM,76): hence the shared presence of the reader, the poet, and the text, each differing and of a different order. Homogeneity likely to yield a facile or a flattened relief would submerge the specific profile in favor of a general topology, wherein an essential individuality would always be lost—thus Char's sarcastic attack on those who prefer a "ville sans pli," a town completely open, undifferentiated in its surface as in its heart. The fragment must remain distinct, like the word, like the person. None of these must repeat, none is seen as weighted with a past. This poetry chooses the exceptional over the like.

Furthermore, for René Char, the weave of the work is luminous, each thread bearing a specific light. "Imitate as infrequently as possible those who suffer from the enigmatic malady of making knots." (LM,79) What guarantees the cohesion of the fragments is often visible only inside the fragment itself: ". . . will what we are make us blossom forth in a bouquet?" (LM,153) The word as archipelago ("notre parole, en archipel" [LM,193]) itself is a fragment become the whole as it becomes the title *La Parole en archipel*.

Since each fragment is entire, not just the model of a totality located above it or beyond it, each is the battlefield between the two opposed if interdependent forces of its impulse. These "punctual and tumultuous mirages" (FM,70) in whose description we already notice an opposition, form the structural basis of the fragment. Of this "exalting alliance of contraries" the poet says—apropos of Heraclitus—that it alone provokes "the shifting of the abysses which carry the poem along in such an antiphysical way," (FM,69) through an act which he qualifies by the adjectives "dissolvante" and "solitaire." Dissolving: no knot remains within the poetic field as a willful obstacle. Alone: what could find an appropriate place in such an abyss or alongside the poet entirely given over to his "métier de pointe?" The work becomes a "commune présence" only when it has been worked out, and even then the echo of the singular is not absent: ["comme une présence . . ."].

The reading works out its own order, one not always apparent, for it takes the risks imposed by an interior necessity for its guide and principle. Its unique aim is finally to become a fragment among the other fragments, part of the common constellation: "J'appartiens. / I belong." (LM,158)

B. Illumination: "mille éclats distants"

.   .   .   .

Éclats de notre jeunesse, éclats pareils à des lézards chatoyants tirés de leur sommeil anfractueux; dès lors pressés d'atteindre le voyageur fondamental dont ils demeurent solidaires. (NT,93).

1. *Fragmentation*: "le terme épars"

In comparing his poetic work to a walking stick split apart, the poet forces, by this simple metaphor, the support on which he leans to furnish from its own substance the fragments which will be then, each one in turn, the support, the guide, and again—by a metonymic displacement—the path.

11

Guiding, showing, preparing, and seducing, he is a troubler of repose: "We are passersby *concentrating* on our passing, thus sowing disquiet, inflicting our ardor, speaking our exuberance." (LM,80) The explosion he summons within the fragment generates different senses and divergent paths. Between the particles the passage may be imperceptible, if the poet does not choose to illuminate it.

a. *Pulverization.*

The clearest expression of an illuminating fragmentation is found in *Partage formel*: the work "partagée," is both shared by poet and reader and divided by their passage through it, is traversed, like another alchemical fire, by *"the water of consecration, penetrating always nearer to summer's heart"* (FM,65). The passage leads from daily drought and insignificant dust to the explosion of a celestial Pleiades, this definitive constellation retaining both the brief presence and the "return upland," the *Retour amont* of the meteor. It is marked by contrary stages, whether it takes for itself the furious sign of alchemy or love: *Fureur et mystère.* Opposite tensions mark the path toward the explosion, like that of Valéry's "Grenade," at once grenade and pomegranate, exploding in the fragments of a poem *éclaté*: "Traverser avec le poème la pastorale des déserts, le don de soi aux furies, le feu moisissant des larmes. . . . Par une nuit, faire irruption à sa suite, enfin, dans les noces de la grenade cosmique. / Traversing with the poem the pastoral of deserts, the gift of oneself to the furies, the fire of tears as it moulds. . . . Finally one night to irrupt in its following, in the nuptial celebrations of the cosmic pomegranate." (FM,76)

As in the conclusion of the epic love poem, "Le Visage nuptial," the sand is redeemed from its granular separation and sterility ("This is the sand dead, this the body saved") by a passionate convergence of elements like this one. Here, the dust of particles is transcended into a stellar pattern, after a passage by fire; the "poème pulvérisé" is a name not just for one collection, but for a process necessary to the eventual flowering of the poem, or of the work. "La lave adorable dissout la roche florissante. / The adorable lava [which can be gilded] [lava "dorable"] dissolves the flourishing rock." (MM,107) In alchemical teaching, gold can come from the transmutation of dust by water. In Char's poetry, the abundance of liquid images—of fountains, of tears, of quick streams—redeems a preliminary fragmentation. *Le Poème pulvérisé*: the image obsesses. "Une poussière qui tombe sur la main occupée à tracer le poème, les foudroie, poème et main. / A dust falling on the hand tracing out the poem strikes poem and hand with lightning." (LM, 133) Yet the dust does not result from laziness or absence: "Salut, poussière mienne. . . ." (AUSC,14) The last of these three words designates this unique "mine," distinct and singular, like the text, even in ruins. The first word remains nonetheless as the context permitting a hesitation: a "salut" of greeting as a poet hails his own fragmentation? Or "salut" in the sense of salvation, as the dust, like a latent alchemical miracle, redeems the rest? Or the recognition of the limits of a path turned to powder as only a walking stick splintered to pieces, the individual fragments now too small to be illuminating flashes. "Essaime la poussière / Let dust swarm." (MM,146) A prolifieration ("essaim," literally, a swarming) scattered along the road? Or then, an invocation to multiplicity: ["Et sème? . . . / And sow?"] Or a description of the intertwining of sentiments, even among the smallest of particles: ["Et s'aiment? . . . / And love each other?"] Distributed and disseminated, the fragments move beyond a momentary dust to a nuptial convergence of all meanings.[3]

[3] In Rilke another convergence beyond the fragments is marked by the one word *staub*, meaning both dust and pollen, so that the transporting of dimensions one into the other is suggested. Rainer Maria Rilke, *Duino Elegies*, tr. Spender and Leishman, Norton, 1956, pp. 48-49. (DE) Poets, like "bees of the infinite," transform the visible into the invisible, the fragment into the whole. (See note 16, p. 159, on Rilke.)

13

Finally, there appears a reflection destroyed, this reading more melancholy than the others, and of more importance for the consideration of the poet's own "marginal" image within his figures: "Whether or not it wishes, resisting it or not, every marginal creature traces a common path, then pulverizes its reflection. This second gesture of diffusing impels tragedy on its way." (RBS,174) Like the path encouraged or just growing from the flowering of fragments upon it, according to the two senses of the verb "pousser," this tragic crescendo is felt as inevitable. The relation of fragment to fragment on the most destructive level will, however, be redeemed by the light-giving alchemical dust, the "poussière éclairante" which reappears in our later discussion of alchemy. Gradually the dust accumulates in clusters, pebbles, fragments, and in an archipelago of stepping-stones, to become a constellation of texts, returned upland.

b. *Intermittence, Succession*

> Ceux-là retiendront la fumée qui auront oublié
> le nuage de la brûlure. (MM,127)

The illumination of the poem cannot be other than partial, intervalent. The corresponding images are like so many parts of a larger whole, eventually gathered up into a constellation, verbal and conceptual. Among the multiple flashes, two in particular show in the pattern of their recurrence the transforming power characteristic of them all, the "fruit intermittent" and the "hirondelle successive." Both the intermittent fruit (or flower) and the swallow succeeding itself in its own flight return under different guises, figuring the discontinuous which is so evidently privileged in its paradoxical enduring within Char's work.

For within the realm of this poetry, the apparently lasting has no lasting power, the ordinarily continuous, no continuity. This contrary light rends and fertilizes all it clarifies, splitting the object asunder before it can be comprehended, so that it may reproduce, and inflicting on the text an uncomfortable modality, through a series of lacerating images: the wounded

14

field, says Char, is the most prosperous of all. An appropriate reading would perhaps resemble a luminous ploughing of this verbal land. In consequence, even the harvest, of a primary importance, may lack the utility it is generally thought to have, since the fruit gathered or the crop harvested will often display a poisonous effect, almost always a disturbing one. In "Fontis," the "très haut fruit couchant qui saigne / the lofty fruit setting, bleeding" has within it all the macabre splendor of Apollinaire's setting sun, beheaded. Those are no ordinary grapes that the harvester gathers there; nor are the texts of René Char without a darker side. The brighter image of the harvest and the fruit will recur, but this preliminary warning serves to indicate the other more obscure slope of a mountain whose "temperate slope" may be perceived in isolation. The incendiary radiance torturing the text reveals a diamantine beauty of an intense inconstancy. The intermittent flash that alone is permitted encourages a reading often ill at ease, whose evident profit might seem sporadic.

Nevertheless, the contrasting image of the "successive swallow," while it suggests the reappearing trace of this flash, related to the flight of the meteor, is at the same time a spiral whose form unites, as both the "aile" and the "rondelle" are phonetically enclosed within the "hirondelle." One of the verbal islands included in the archipelago dedicated to the snake ("A la Santé du serpent") declares: "Dans la boucle de l'hirondelle un orage s'informe, un jardin se construit. / Within the swallow's swirling a storm makes its inquiries, a garden takes its shape." (FM,194)

The circling of the bird implies a continuous and yet a momentary trace, luminous and not imprisoning. The occult power of the circle (as in the image of the self-consuming snake, Ouroboros), or of the ring, is a further sign to a possible path through these texts. The work slips by in a meteoric trace.

Meteorites, traditionally sacred, are for the maritime Dayaks of Sarawak stones of light, "*pierres de lumière*," bearing their

15

sacred power of fire to earth, where they will fertilize even the rocks.[4] Conceived in flashes, "l'oeuvre filante" grants an illumination essentially rapid. The meteoric passing confers its intensity on the flash: "Étincelle nomade qui meurt dans son incendie. / Nomad spark dying in its fire." (FM,204) The text explodes into fragments, dispersing like the novae, those stars the poet calls "night-larks" ("alouettes de la nuit"), brief but enduring in the memory and in the title of a poem. "Premier rayon qui hésite entre l'imprécation du supplice et le magnifique amour. / First ray hesitating between imprecation of torture and magnificent love." This fire made of minimal elements is often alluded to: seen as "parcelles" (of the mountains, of forest branches), as ashes or dust of an alchemical hearth, always inextinguishable for its vital spirit—in the light of a windowpane, of reality, or of the "absolute" itself.

vitre inextinguible (FM,59)

. . . .

l'inextinguible réel incréé (FM,65)

. . . .

cet absolu inextinguible (FM,68)

Distinct and particular meditations are illuminated by the brief burst of aphoristic light characteristic of the separate texts called *A la Santé du serpent* or *A une Sérénité crispée*—those series written in honor of, and in dedication to, an attitude. Each part has a separate intensity, as if there reigned an interior will to difference and yet to coherence.

Neither proverbs, in the common sense of the term—which would ill-befit the poet "created for rare moments"—nor aphorisms in the classic sense (although often compared to them), nor moralistic maxims, these thought-fragments, resembling the Latin *epigrammata*, are traces of illumination, even of conflagration. "L'énigme a fini de rougir. / The enigma has finished blushing" (LM,119): modest remains of

---

[4] Mircea Éliade, *Forgerons et alchimistes*, coll. Homo sapiens, Flammarion, 1956, p. 18.

devouring nuptial fire, the ashes are the paradoxical and traditional source for the rebirth of a phoenix. A "regain guérisseur" is thus attributed to the poetic "fer" and the "lyre," the incendiary ["faire"] and ["lire"], transforming the poem, which is pulverized and transfigured: "The quantity of fragments tears me apart." (FM,32) Fragmentation affects the poet also, prefiguring his later disintegration into the universe, like so many stars of a constellation. "Créer: s'exclure. Quel créateur ne meurt pas désespéré? Mais est-on désespéré si l'on est déchiré? Peut-être pas. / Creating: excluding oneself. What creator does not die desperate? But is one desperate if torn apart? Perhaps not." (RBS,152)

Like the sharp-edged stones left by primitive man from his art and his tool-making ("éclats"), René Char's own work often strikes with a hard and angular force. Each intervalent light intensifies the whole by its renewing action: the discontinuous energy of the *éclat* here is always charged with the illumination of the *éclair*. By this light one should now read these apparently splintered thoughts, recognizing their disquieting power, each illuminating and unique because the text chooses itself to be not only virgin (even when its act is repeated), but "sans redite," a virtue the poet attributes to man and denies to the gods. (NP,117)

Corresponding to the discontinuous illumination is an asymmetrical arrangement, whose force increases by its oblique situation, *en biais*. A certain imprudence of non-equilibrated forms is prepared here: "l'asymétrie est jouvence. / Asymmetry is youthfulness." (NP,79) Even the very expression of that asymmetry might be seen to imply at once its contrary, since under the apparently tranquil phonetic surface could lie hidden the opposite statement ["la symétrie est jouvence . . ."]. That the asymmetry so strongly dominates is in itself an asymmetrical realization. Or again, in a sentence whose self-referential nature covers an irony of the same sort: "Nous avons cette particularité parfois de nous balancer en marchant." (LM,78) The term "se balancer" implies three elements: the physical movement from one

17

side to the other like a response to a mental contradiction, the act of setting in motion a moving body by a lateral shifting, and finally, by a slight transformation, a suggestion that one might as well overturn ("balancer") the whole movement, poetic or personal, by jettisoning the self in the forward advance. Char's most characteristic statements, and his most subtle, are set obliquely, swayed by contrary impulses.

Moreover, he says, the poem or fragment is "born of the summons of becoming and the anguish of retention," (FM, 169) made up of apparent knowledge and of "subtle substance," as of the bird's coming and going and the tree growing upward, yet deeper by its roots. A juncture of wisdom and concrete workmanship, of the future glimpsed and the present passing, Char's poetry declares itself continually to be at the outermost limit of the two states. It can only be envisaged as a complex double motion, the tools of its *faire* serving a parallel destruction, where the gesture and the instrument will always disappear one within the other, as Char says in an essay on the artist Miró. (FA) "A certain aspect of the real proceeds by pure ellipsis, superposition, the junction of images each one of which is revealed in the moment when it plunges into the other. Thus the end becomes beginning and appetite, Miró's form, a chain of advents, of prenuptial lust. (RBS,90) From these "advents" the poem is then built, like the canvas, in durability yet in fragmentation, from an interchange of perspectives and by an alternation of techniques already glimpsed in Char's first major collection, *Le Marteau sans maître*: "Les régimes des aspects alternent." The concern for junction, convergence, and meshing recurs throughout his thought: "dimensions" are said to share their fruits, seasons to grow by the inclusion of other seasons, forms by the absorption of other forms.

2. *Cutting and Closure*

Like the instrument joined to the gesture of Miró, the sharper knife and lightning perfectly match the incisive techniques,

18

the illuminating, embellishing reduction: "l'enlèvement, l'embellissement," and the instant élan: "Être du bond. N'être pas du festin, son épilogue. / Be of the leap. Not of the banquet, its epilogue." (FM,138) The imperative ("être") is also a definition of being ("l'être"): this being devoted only to the leap holds in itself all the qualities of knife, lightning, flash, simplicity, brevity.[5] A simple path furnishes the basis for a complex outlook: the "rampart" made of twigs was to be called, in one of the first versions of this series: "Le Parapet de brindilles." A fragile summit from which to keep watch, lest we become too confident. Witness to a faith in the fragment, the "rempart de brindilles" may serve as protection against verbal proliferation, against the weight of nature and human forces as well as the unpredictable future; for what is only in twigs will never say too much, and can perhaps offer the most modest, most tenuous path, that befitting the "matinal" poet.

The multiple allusions in *Le Marteau sans maître* to the act of pruning repeat a title later suppressed: "Leçon sévère" (which may indicate not only what it seems to but also "a lesson, these verses": ["leçon, ces vers"]), and by the phrase "l'élan coupé des arbres / the cut-off burst of trees"—that is, those gestures in which our dealings with the natural world are closely related to the formal technique of ellipsis. They are equally associated with the luminous brevity of the spark or the flash; for instance, in the recurring emphasis Char places on leave-taking or leave-giving, and in the gesture of burning, particularly in the writings after 1944 although announced previously by brief signals, like bonfires taking on a progressively larger meaning. Pruning, twigs, and bonfires: all the heavy symbolism of destiny, death, birth, and rebirth can here be reduced to the simplest image.

Now the almond, on the other hand, represents, in resumé, the qualities of flowers and fruits: slow formation,

---

[5] On the idea of the *éclat*, see Maurice Blanchot, *La Bête de Lascaux*, G.L.M., p. 15: "éclats de poème ou le poème semble réduit au tranchant du pur éclat, à la coupure d'une décision."

depth of substance, isolation, and then gift. The burgeoning of flower and fruit after the hidden development—as in the image of the chrysalis recurring repeatedly in *Le Marteau sans maître*—is perfectly exemplified by the enclosure of the almond within its hard and lasting walls. Even its name has already a gravity comparable to that of a word like "profound" as in this phrase, complete in itself: "L'éclat de la fleur profonde. / The flash of the deep flower." If the flower is deep by extension, thrusting its roots into our understanding, the almond has the same dimension of beauty, although still concealed. Its solitude responds to our own, its verbal resonance serving as the juncture of two essential concepts; whether this juncture is intentional or unconscious on the part of the poet may not concern us in our reading:

> amante
> profonde
> ⟩ amande ("le plus enclos des amours/
> the most enclosed of loves.")
> (RBS,155)

In the light of this possibility, the other uses of the image, considered together, can be seen as another developing fruit, partly a product of chance, at once enclosed and offering, a stellar fragment gradually flowering dense and profuse in a pattern illustrative of other formations finding the same path: "Parois de ma durée / Walls of my enduring" (FM,58); "L'amande croyable au lendemain neuf. / The almond believable in the fresh day to come." (FM,59); "L'heure la plus droite c'est lorsque l'amande jaillit de sa rétive dureté et transpose ta solitude / The hour is at its most upright when the almond springs forth from its stubborn hardness and transposes your solitude." (FM,136); "Je ne suis pas seul parce que je suis abandonné. Je suis seul parce que je suis seul, amande entre les parois de sa closerie. / I am not alone because I am abandoned. I am alone because I am alone. An almond between the walls of its enclosure." (LM,159) This quadruple concordance in its accruing intensity enables the shell at once separating inside from outside and assuming within itself all duration ("dureté" including the sound of both qualities: hard and enduring) to appear in correspondence with the freshness of the future, the almond now to be read in reverse, with its sign half-confused:

"(len) demain" ⟷ "amande."

When the almond bursts forth through its walls, effecting the verbal and poetic transposition of its isolation like an "exploded solitude," the implications are many:[6] erotic, within the cycle of the couple, seasonal, within the natural cycle, related to fruit and flower, and initially self-referential, related to the fragment and to the reading of fragment. Each flash, composed of a single term, is placed in a ferocious, absolute isolation, describing or revealing its own peculiar intimacy: each can be seen as situated on a threshold between violence and fruition, the "last blood and first loam." (NP, 16)

Within the enclosure of each text, solitary like the bitter green almonds which the poet pictures in *La Nuit talismanique*, the separate words find their echo: "Syllabe d'écho, amante courable." The expression "amante" recalls the almond by a near-echo: "amante/amande." The *fruit commun* as the product of a shared but enigmatic text will in all probability never have our rhythm, nor even that of the poet: "Our words delay in coming to us, as if they contained, separated, a sap sufficient to remain closed all winter. . . . Our voice runs from one to the other; but each avenue, each grating, each thicket, pulls it close, holds it, questions it. Everything

---

[6] The almond tree, first to flower in the spring, is a sign of renascence: "Symbole de l'essentiel caché, du secret, l'amande est aussi *le mystère de la lumière* dans la mystique chrétienne." From J. Chevalier and A. Gheerbrant, *Dictionnaire des symboles*, Laffont, 1969, pp. 22-23. (Quoted in Jean-Pierre Cauvin, *Henri Bosco et la poétique du sacré*, Klincksieck, 1974, p. 222. [HB] In connection with the symbol, Cauvin points out that the family motto of the Livande in Bosco's *L'Antiquaire* is: "La fleur est toujours dans l'amande.") The epigraph for our chapter "The Cycle of the Warring Couple" retains the double image within an amorous closure, suggested phonetically by the noun "amarre," where we might see a telescoping of "amande amère."

conspires to slow it down." (LM,93) The inevitable tension between poet and word is reflected in this text about texts, and under it runs a sadness, only suggested.

It is above all of the poem that many of Char's poems will speak, and of the poet-poem, in a voice sometimes muted but nonetheless epic in tone, to be heard all along the path which merges with it, for the resonance of the "voix" also a "voie" is a serious one. Another "hallucinated order" (NP, 54) will eventually join the "insurgent order" of aphoristic illuminations which the poet will follow and will lead. Each of these texts is active in its own flowering and fruition as well as in convergence, each is certain in its quiet as in its overt statement: "To make sure of one's own murmurings and to direct action toward its completion in the word aflower." (NP,69)

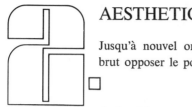

AESTHETIC: *FER/FAIRE*

Jusqu'à nouvel ordre, à la poésie courtisane,
brut opposer le poème *offensant*. . . .

□ (MM,133)

A. LE MARTEAU SANS MAÎTRE

In Char's first major volume, *Le Marteau
sans maître* (1927-1934),[1] the basis is established for a lasting attitude toward poetry, centered on
essential and—at first sight—contrary tendencies. In this universe of a poetry embattled by its own contradictions, "les
mots à forte carrure s'empoignent sur le pont élastique / the
robust words tackle each other on the elastic bridge" (MM,
90) and the poet's attitudes demonstrate a similarly combative stance.

The first element apparent in these poems—which present
themselves as "hammered out"—is the abundance of breath
and of strength, in direct relationship with the *timbre* of the
voice proclaiming them: "la force de chanter à tue-tête / the
strength to sing at the top of his lungs" takes its source in
the physical and psychic energy represented by a "poitrine en
avance sur son néant / chest in advance of its own nothingness" in turn corresponding with the "poitrine athlétique" of
the universe (MM,67). Hence the significance of the strongest
verbs, many of them related to the acts of crossing, chasing,
escaping, climbing, passing, saving. Char's poetry is deliberately active, morally committed. But this vigorous enunciation
does not determine a parallel profusion of speech; rather the

---

[1] With the title image of the hammer, are also associated the hammer and anvil of the ear, and what is implied thereby; what hears
without rhythm, what is understood beyond rhythm. For the beating
of the heart with no master, a text in the *Rougeur des matinaux*
echoes *Le Marteau sans maître*, not without discord: "Quand nous
disons: *le coeur* (et le disons à regret), il s'agit du coeur attisant
que recouvre la chair miraculeuse et commune, et qui peut à chaque
instant cesser de battre et d'accorder." (LM,78)

23

contrary. Its origin is to a great extent located in an equally strong control, in the principle already alluded to, of "enlève-ment-embellissement" associated with the figures of "L'Émon-deur," "L'Élagueur," and "L'Écumeur de mémoire," in their respective gestures of pruning, trimming, and skimming, each of which reduces some *materia prima* in order for the inner form to issue forth. Whereas this principle might generally be taken to apply to a stylistic abbreviation, the initial choice underlying the reaction of the writer consists perhaps in the preliminary refusal to retain everything offered to the memory as the possible material for the writing itself. To be sure, the availability of material is at times menaced from without—as in the later texts from this same volume, where the roads of memory have been "covered with the infallible leprosy of monsters" or again, "frozen." But this undercurrent of pessimism, which will endure, is held in balance by what could more properly be called a distant vision than a precise hope. The poem "Sommeil fatal" presents itself against a background of mountain grasses which are seen as withering throughout periods of recollection or of sleep:

> Les animaux à tête de navire cernent le visage de la femme que j'aime. Les herbes de montagne se fanent sous l'ac-calmie des paupières. Ma mémoire réalise sans difficulté ce qu'elle croit être l'acquis de ses rêves les plus désespérés, tandis qu'à portée de ses miroirs continue à couler l'eau introuvable. Et la pensée de cendres?[a] (MM,51)

Here a certain realization and a certain reflection are deepened within a current freed in its flow by means of ambiguous interrogation. The cycle could begin anew, as the ships seen in the first line lead toward a mysterious water, discovering only, in the ashes, the proof of the memory and

---

[a] Ship-headed animals surround the visage of the woman I love. Mountain grasses wither under the eyelid's lull. My memory attains the knowledge it seemingly acquired in its most desperate dreams, while within the reach of its mirrors water unfathomable still flows. And the thought of ashes?

of the dream finally destroyed. Or does the mirrored and remembered water triumph even over the "thought of ashes?"

As for the poet, he retains the consciousness of these paths of dream or memory as of an ocean traversed, and it is of this abundant source—abbreviated, intensified, crystallized— that he forms his inflammatory language by the opposition of water and fire. This is a fitting description of a man whose lesson of economy, of measure, and of keeping, has been taught him from the beginning, in the shade of a tree well-pruned.

But writing must be tempered. As in the later prose poems of "Le Devoir," where a child plunges his eyes in the "hearth of red smelting," or "Fréquence," where the "narrow night of metal" underground is brought to light, there appears the profile of the "équarisseur," the man of the quarry (in both senses), who alone is able to make of the mud and slime a squared-off stone appropriate to a hard moral lesson: "Nous nous galvanisons dans les cendres. . . . / We are galvanised in the ashes. . . ." (MM,85) Personal determination stands out in relief against the poetic theory. The poet in his "secret rage," behind his mask, takes the force of the hammer and the anvil present by implication in the title to cast his own peculiar poetic being—its plural languages ignited. In *Le Marteau sans maître* he already utilizes a whole vocabulary of fire: the "knot of metal," (MM,73) the "central fire," (MM,67) the unifying conflagration, (MM,71) and above all, the image of the phoenix renascent in the flame and in the text ("the red bird of metals," MM,82) nourished by "specks of ashes." (MM,127)

Yet it must not be assumed, in speaking of those "messengers of a frenetic poetry," that the omnipresent frenzy or the ardent forging results in a clear poetry. It is often, at first sight, opaque: "Let us remain obscure" (LM,154) or earlier, "Cloud, go first. . . ." For in the most untouched or the most enveloped poem, René Char's intense disquiet can be sensed most vividly. It is formative rather than debilitating, and the reader comes to share it as such. In "Robustes météores," this

development takes place within the tight chrysalis: if it is opened too soon to the air, the vertiginous qualities of this poetry might be threatened by an exterior adulteration. The poet's commentary for "J'habite une douleur," a poem which has kept its "marrow" untouched, may serve us as a warning, as if the chrysalis were to reform: "L'intacte chrysalide a recouvré ses propriétés agissantes de vertige. / The intact chrysalis has recovered its active properties of vertigo." (MM,99) The chrysalis must be respected, must never be completely exposed.

B. WEAPON

In a first sketch of *A une Sérénité crispée*[2] we read, scratched out, an interrogation and a decision, both of major importance: "Must we choose between the dart and the hammer? The dart." The implications of the choice are multiple, and significant throughout the entire work; related to the bee-sting, to the beam of the star and the brilliant flash, to the iron opening the weeping rose, the instrument chosen for attack penetrates instead of flattening. Both are the chosen weapons of the gods: of Thor[3] whose iron gloves for holding the hammer find their echo in the initial sense of the "fer," and whose belt of strength links him to Orion, the hunter and the constellation presiding over the conclusion of this essay; and of Jupiter (as well as Cupid): "L'essaim, l'éclair et l'anathème, trois obliques d'une même sommet. / The swarm, the flash, and anathema, three obliques of a single summit." (LM,79) The hammer finally gives momentum to the flash, as of a dart sent from a summit.

---

[2] Bibliothèque littéraire Jacques Doucet. Fonds René Char–Yvonne Zervos. No. 724 (AE-IV-14). (We refer to this manuscript by the letters AUSC:A. The published versions of this work differ greatly. Here we refer often to the Gallimard edition of 1950, but also to the original manuscript, to see the source.) All the references marked AE come from this source, consulted and quoted with the poet's permission.

[3] For whom the little town of Le Thor, near the poet's home in the Vaucluse may be named: "Le Thor s'exaltait sur la lyre de ses pierres."

All the self-destructive force of the blinding beam is thus gathered in the difficulty of the poem, intended to be a passage fully as wounding as that of love: "Derrière cette persienne de sang brûle le cri d'une force qui se détruira elle seule parce qu'elle a horreur de la force, sa soeur subjective et stérile. / Behind blinds of blood burns the cry of a force which will alone destroy itself, having a horror of force, its subjective and sterile sister." (FM,77) The chosen destruction insists upon the awakening of a common passion: "Enfin, si tu détruis, que ce soit avec des outils nuptiaux. / Finally, if you destroy, let it be with nuptial tools." (LM,81) Illumination itself takes the form of a cry or a dart, in testimony to an emotional strength, amorous and fertilizing: "Love tracing a furrow is preferable to an adventure which humiliates, a wound preferable to a bad temper." (RBS,163) A wounding probe is to be chosen in the place of a more massive, imprecise force, or an experience less painful and less serious, bearing in consequence no fruit.

Now the passage from *Le Marteau sans maître* to *Aromates chasseurs*, written over forty years later, suggests the figure of Orion, for in the latter volume his bow and arrow replace the earlier hammer for a more precise hunting, as the poet finally gives chase only to himself. And yet the arrow serves more and more as a subtle interiorization of the hammer's force, turned at last against the self. *Le Marteau sans maître* was originally necessary for the shattering of the common mold, the vigorous production of individual fragments. The title conveys a heart beating without exterior forces in their captivating influence, and also, by a phonetic play, a ["marteau sans mètre / hammer without meter"], since the will is never in complete control. And by another phonetic extension, this hammer already ambivalent in its use touches the limits of human suffering, or again of human love: the "marteau/martyrisé."[4] Whereas on its own,

<hr />

[4] Here the poem is also a woman, and hammered by the poet. Cf. Georges Blin (preface to *Commune présence*, Gallimard, 1966), and Diana Festa-McCormick (on "A ***," *French Review*, special issue on contemporary poetry, 1973). To this title, compare Rimbaud's

the light exactitude of a weapon without the hammer's force diverges into less favorable paths, such as "the dart of ideologies," this double strength of the dart and the hammer inspires the following thought, where the destructive countenance appears alongside the nuptial countenance in the poet become himself the only master: "We are ungovernable. The only master propitious to us is the Flash, now illuminating us, now cleaving us asunder." (LM,15) And so the entire work, in its precision and its interpretation, places itself under the intermittent sign of the *éclair*, a cleaving brilliance both formal and erotic. The word illuminates and rends, clarifies and yet leaves obscure.

C. The Hidden

L'idéal, disait cet imbécile, ce serait une ville sans plis.[5]

1. *Pleat, Fold*

Like the ellipsis, difficulty is fruitful. The "offending" poem has rarely a simple access. The poetry of René Char does not unfold entirely, does not lend itself completely to an *explication* or unpleating. The pleat ("le pli") is depth and silvering

---

"Rêve pour l'hiver," dedicated to an unknown person, "A ***." Subsequently, the poet added: "Elle." (OR,75) In this connection, we might note the modification of the title "Élise" to that of "Marthe" for this poem on the fountains, which reappears in one of the cycles; the interest of such a modification easily transcends the biographical reference to a childhood friend. Consciously or not, what is *chosen* simply on the level of the text ("élise" = elected) apparently gives way at the outset to what is modeled, worked, *martelé*. For example, the "Sept parcelles de Luberon"; and in "Le Visage nuptial," "La parcelle vermeille franchit ses lentes branches. . . ."

[5] Ms. 4912. This text, important for the revelation of an attitude, is formed gradually: after this first and barest version, we read: "Ce serait de construire une ville sans plis! Cette espèce de hanneton tonsuré!" (AUSC:A) Next: "l'imbécile" becomes a "prestidigitateur," and the verbal anathema develops: "Pénétrez, ventres plats, dans la ville-monceau." (Last version in a torn-up notebook called "brièvement d'un cahier") (no. 725, AE-IV-14), here referred to as AUSC:B.

to the poem, a mirror which retains its own mystery: "Accumulate, then distribute. Be, in the mirror of the universe, the densest, most useful and least apparent part." (FM,127)

The "pli" becomes in its turn a "repli," folding in upon itself, secretly protecting in a privileged space the "contracted fruit of a great unfinished prelude . . . ," (RBS,171) forbidding the poem or its work to end in *exposition*.[6] The almond, one of the primary images in this poetry, teaches us a particular closure: "Les commodités (de la connaissance) sont mortelles." (AUSC:A) The commodious is unwelcome to the poet, like too close a knowledge. Underlining the uncomfortable moral distance of this writing, which cherishes its obstacles, Char entitles a group of essays about his friends: *Grands Astreignants ou la conversation souterraine*. It is not by chance that Antonin Artaud is the first to figure in that subterranean correspondence of difficult artists, instead of among *Les Matinaux* as was first intended.[7]

Yet the "grands astreignants" like "les grandes interdites" in *La Nuit talismanique*, like all the larger-than-life abstract and concrete personalizations who figure in these works (those heroes of slow gestures who come to read their fate on the lap of Artine): the automaton, the violet man, the calumniator as well as the tree-pruner, the quarterer, and the other figures of severity so intimate a part of the aesthetic—all these are at once mysterious and comprehensible, dominating the texts by their presence slightly to the side of any daily lighting without denying it altogether. We think here of

[6] Compare Rilke on the flower and the secret fruit: "Feigenbaum, seit wie lange schon ists mir bedeutend, / wie du die Blüte beinah ganz überschlägst / und hinein in die zeitig entschlossene Frucht, / ungerühmt, drängst dein reines Geheimnis. / . . . / . . . Wie aber verweilen, / ach, uns rühmt es zu blühn, und ins verspätete Innre / unserer endlichen Frucht gehn wir verraten hinein. // Fig tree, how long it's been full of meaning for me, / the way you almost entirely omit to flower / and into the seasonably-resolute fruit / uncelebratedly thrust your purest secret . . . But we, we linger, / alas, we glory in flowering; already betrayed / we reach the retarded core of our ultimate fruit." (DE, 54-55)

[7] No. 717-723 (AE-IV-13).

29

L'Homme qui marchait dans un rayon de soleil, a play semi-allegorical in style in which the sail-maker falls in love with "la passante"; and of those transparents, the "lunisolar vaga-bonds"—all these are passersby.[8]

The epigraph to the "Rengaines d'Odin le Roc" (that is, of Woden, father of Thor with his hammer and his lyre of stones) sings the interplay of the parts of the text: "What fascinates you at moments in my verses is the future, darkness sliding from before the dawn, while the night is already in the past tense." (LM,31)

The dividing line ("ligne de partage," as Yves Bonnefoy uses these words in *L'Arrière-Pays*)[9] is also the zenith of the horizon where two limits touch. At this line of sharing, two elements meet and are doubled in an ephemeral encounter beyond a simple alternation: "*Aoûtement. Une dimension franchit le fruit de l'autre. Dimensions adversaires.*" (FM, 19) The brief and intense crossing over is another form of the pleat, stressed both by the poet's imagery and its sparse form. In one fruit, or in one season ("August ripening"), the other will not be lost, neither its flavor nor its memory. "One dimension crosses the fruit of the other": the extraordinary use of the verb *franchir* in the writing of René Char betrays an exceptional vigor, as does another dominant verb, *jaillir*. Together they mark also the moment at which one element leaves or joins a second, a spatial figuring of the "ligne de partage" in action and a formal realization of the amorous meeting of two opposed beings. Corresponding examples abound, among which the slow and profound initial de-

---

[8] On the passerby and the "neutral" of the unknown in René Char, see Maurice Blanchot in *L'Arc*, no. René Char, 1963. (For another commentary on a revealing detail of grammar, see Jean-Pierre Richard, *Onze études sur la poésie moderne*, Seuil, 1964, p. 91: the remark applies specifically to the images of storm and of garden in Char's work, but generally, to an attitude. "Le *et* s'y fait *à la fois*, l'*entre* y devient *tour à tour*.")

[9] Skira, 1972. This *partage* encounters the essential notion of the threshold: see Yves Bonnefoy's *Dans le leurre du seuil*, Mercure de France, 1975 (fragments previously published in *L'Ephémère*, nos. 11 and 19/20).

scription in "Le Visage nuptial": "La parcelle vermeille franchit ses lentes branches à ton front, dimension rassurée. / The crimson foliage traverses its slow branches at your forehead, dimension reassured." (FM,58) In our subsequent discussion of the threshold, all the weight of this earlier crossing should be felt, even if it is not stated. At another crossing, in "Biens égaux," an unadorned departure marks, and with the same verb, "franchir," the revelation of an essential nature precisely at the moment of exit, over the most rough-hewn threshold: "Te voici nue et entre toutes la meilleure seulement aujourd'hui où tu franchis la sortie d'un hymne raboteux. / Here you are naked and among all the best only today when you traverse the exit of a rough-hewn hymn." (FM,173) Nevertheless the memory of the crossing remains clear: "L'homme qui emporte l'évidence sur ses épaules / Garde le souvenir des vagues dans les entrepôts de sel // The man bearing evidence on his shoulders / Keeps the memory of waves in the storehouses of salt." (MM,52) Within the memory stored, the motion of the waves continues. The fold, in its doubled fabric,[10] and the almond shell guarding the enclosed space represent the crossroads of meeting. Each element participates in its opposite, as the "visage nuptial" is seen to be an inner countenance and an inner crossroads, a sharing of two personalities on the deepest level.

However, the will-to-the-fragment remains in evidence. The "unfinished prelude" will not flower into a symphony,

---

[10] Clearly, the pleat here is equivalent to the margin, the space around or inside which protects the private depth. Compare with the image of the pleat in the work of Paul Éluard: in both authors the connotation is no less poetic than erotic. As Mallarmé's fan contains the pleat and the unfolding, so the "volet de buis" that Char places in the center of his poetics is both retraction and enduring pleat folding back upon itself, but also the opening of the summits in their "comprimante splendeur," and yet is simultaneously the spiritual *envolée* of the text fragmented but holding. In a preliminary version of *L'Arrière-Histoire du poème pulvérisé* (no. 738, AE-IV-13) we read this exclamation scratched through: "Poèmes soufferts, poèmes des larmes. / Leurs volets frappent mon visage!" Thus the poem opens out and in, with its own explication and implication.

and in this pleated poem the "grand prévoyants" themselves, accustomed to seeing ahead, see only the (re)beginning, and the poet, another summit for starting out again. "Isn't the poet this mountaineer who balks constantly, and whom the repeated assault on the summits puts constantly back on his feet?" (AHPP) The text imposes an always partial knowledge. "J'appartiens": the credo of the reader become part and partner will remain nevertheless at the margin of knowledge and understanding ("à l'orée de la connaissance"), where the ear ["l'oreille"] is almost permitted to hear the implications which occupy the whole place of the poem.

2. *Enigma: "l'éclair nourri"*

> Qui croit renouvelable l'énigme, la devient. Escaladant librement l'érosion béante, tantôt lumineux, tantôt obscur, savoir sans fonder sera sa loi. Loi qu'il observera mais qui aura raison de lui; fondation dont il ne voudra pas mais qu'il mettra en oeuvre. (NP,130)

"Il ne faut pas que ma lyre me devine. . . . / My lyre must not find me out." (LM,154) And again, "On exile une lyre." (NP,44) Poetry must protect its margins. The word imposes its own laws of distance, of mystery, and of understanding. And the poet with "future eyes" (NP,32) openly admits his attachment to a prophecy, lit by an illumination far from clear: "We are not a direct will, but the derouted instrument of a perfidious wanting placed between obscurity and ourselves, between vigor, desire and the loyal solar term." (NP, 105) Between what is said—in fragments and maxims—and what is silent—in the more complex poems—another vocabulary can be sensed, anticipated, only half-revealing. Here no questions are asked as to the origins of the language, which imposes itself, understood only from a distance. The announcement of sense is clear or confused according to the moment it chooses to make itself heard: "*Levé avant son sens, un mot nous éveille, nous prodigue la clarté du jour, un mot qui n'a pas rêvé.* / *Risen before its meaning a word wakes us, lavishes on us the brightness of day, a word that has not dreamed.*" (NP,115) (JG)

In the "Mirage des aiguilles"—already a title-mirage where the mountain peaks disappear within the text in its lament of the flat—Char's condemnation will weigh heavily against those who fear obscurity, who cover over any trace of "oblique fires," who prefer to think of the "jaundiced laughter" of shadows as only a dimmer clarity, who flee enigma and the thought of death. This poem stands as a bitter invective against too-facile political solutions, against those who prefer (as in an early version of *A une Sérénité crispée*) a town "without pleats," who long to unknot every mystery: "Aucun viatique précieux n'embellit la gueule de leurs serpents déroulés. . . . Ils se sont établis et prospèrent dans le berceau d'une mer où l'on s'est rendu maître des glaciers. Tu es prévenu. / No precious viaticum embellishes the mouth of their uncoiled snakes. . . . They have settled and they prosper in the cradle of a sea where glaciers have been mastered. Be warned." (NP,17) If the poet drank "To the Health of the Snake," it was in part because of his enigmatic coiling. Here uncoiled, the snake no longer moves. And the poem, once completely disentangled, would lose its essential radiance: one of the lessons of *Le Marteau sans maître* and of alchemy itself,[11] is that of the enigmatic.

But always lacking, always at fault in the face of the enigma, which of us will ever be deserving of any philosopher's stone? "Comment, faible écolier, convertir l'avenir et détiser ce feu tant questionné, tant remué, tombé sur ton regard fautif? / How, feeble schoolboy, should one convert the future and rake out this fire interrogated and stirred up so often, which has caught your offending gaze?" (NP,17) This path cannot be surely said to lead anywhere, neither toward a place of our desiring (and what can desiring signify if desire itself, like the will, is recognized as "involuntary?") nor to-

[11] Alchemical images abound in the works of Char, or in the Work: we shall return to this in "The Cycle of Alchemy."

ward a *convergence des multiples* (NP,29) of opposed elements at once amorous and fratricidal? ". . . toute l'étendue montrée du feu, tenue du vent; l'étendue, trésor de boucher, sanglante à un croc. / . . . all the sweep revealed by the fire, held by the wind; the sweep, the butcher's hoard, bleeding on a hook." (NP,18) The road leading from this lacerated mirage to the following text, "Aux Portes d'Aerea," is an arduous one.[12] Time is banished from the text; moreover, or therefore, the search for the lost city of Aerea—supposed by Pliny and Strabo to be situated somewhere on a height between Orange and Avignon—is a doomed one. It too is only, perhaps, a mirage, an impossible past lost within the perpetual present and destined to a future oblivion. "Mais le présent perpétuel, le passé instantané sous la fatigue maîtresse, ôtèrent les lisses. / Marche forcée, au terme épars. . . . Visée par l'abeille de fer, la rose en larmes s'est ouverte. // But the perpetual present, the instantaneous past, under masterful exhaustion, removed the bindings. / Forced march, to the scattered ending. . . . Target of the iron bee, the rose in tears has opened." (NP,19) (JG)

In the opened lists: "lisses," ["lices"] ensues a jousting where the erotic and efficacious iron probe ("fer") or the verbal "faire"—like the dart in its precision—will finally attain its object in the poem. Similarly, as in "Le Visage nuptial," the flint instruments used for climbing mountains have left their trace, plunging into the soft earth, leaving behind only the tears of a beauty past, or presently wounded, a source discovered afresh. For the transfers in this poetry are not only formal: often an interior melancholy is transferred to an exterior figure seen against the landscape, a rose weeping, an animal wounded and fleeing, a bird felled. Compare, from

[12] The poem's original title suggested the legendary presence of the town: "Apparition d'Aerea." (Mechthild Cranston, in her "Violence and Magic: Aspects of René Char's Surrealist Apprenticeship," *Forum for Modern Language Studies*, Vol. x, no. 1, Jan. 1974, p. 6, note 4, discusses the metallic images such as "l'abeille de fer" here in their relation to the surrealist poems.) *Apparition* reminds us of the "apparitions d'Artine."

the poem "Versant" of *Le Marteau sans maître*, the lines: "Quel carreau apparu en larmes / Va nous river / Coeurs partisans?// What windowpane appeared in tears / Will rivet us / Partisan hearts?" (MM,93) which might also be translated: "What crossbow appeared in its weeping. . . ." The question posed has no answer, which permits the multiple response of a "verbe en fleur," like an outward flowering.

D. Crossing, Distance

. . . .

—Laisse dormir ton ancre tout au fond de mon sable.
Sous l'ouragan de sel où ta tête domine,
Poète confondant, et sois heureux
Car je m'attache encore à tes préparatifs de traversée.

(PPC,149)

Often, a detail in the manuscripts gives us the key to an attitude: the poet's preference, originally stated in regard to one road: "c'est *cela* et non cet autre," has been scratched out from the text in manuscript, as if every path were destined to disappear behind him. The poet speaks of the solitary seeking and of the threshold not to be crossed or then instantly murderous: "Because what we were looking for could not be discovered by the many, because the life of the mind, a single-threaded life unlike that of the heart, is only fascinated, in the temptation of poetry, by a sovereign and unapproachable object which shatters just when, having crossed the space between us, we are on the point of touching it." (RBS,45)[13] This is perhaps the most significant statement made by the poet about his essential distance from the group mentality of even the most individual of surrealist

[13] But here a paradox is present to the mind of the poet. "Le combat de l'esprit sépare. . . . Je ne suis pas séparé. Je suis *parmi*. D'où mon tourment sans attente." Later the paradox will reappear, briefly.

gatherings. It is not only in the sky of Provence that "La constellation du Solitaire" is stretched out. (LM,146; SP,23) "J'ai cherché dans mon encre ce qui ne pouvait être quêté; la tache pure au-delà de l'écriture souillée. / I looked in my ink for that which could not be sought: the pure spot beyond the soiled writing." (RBS,174) We might juxtapose this passage with the following ones, by a phonetic similarity, serving as a bridge, "tache" leading to "tâche": "Le poète n'a pas de mission; à tout prendre, il a une tâche. / The poet has no mission; taking all with all, he has a task." (RBS,152) Or again: "la tâche de la poésie . . . ," (RBS,163) and the clear restatement: "ouvrir dans l'aile de la route, de ce qui en tient lieu, d'insatiable randonnées, c'est la tâche des Matinaux." (LM,96)[14] The task is at once pure and difficult; it guides us toward this passage left white, or heated to whiteness (thus pure by its emptiness) in the "ferme distance." (LM,19)

Nevertheless, in another paradox of the double reading we undertake as loyal partner and opponent, the poem, refusing to link elements in any ordinary fashion, simply unravels. The work *unifiliare*, of one thread, like the mind, and yet *filante*, shooting by like the meteor, is also slipping away, burning out like the wick of a candle. ("Tu es une fois encore la bougie où sombrent les ténèbres autour d'un nouvel insurgé, Toi sur qui se lève un fouet qui s'emporte à ta clarté qui pleure. / You are once again the candle where the shadows are engulfed around a new insurgent, over you is lifted a whip flaring up at your brightness weeping." (NP, 42) The original thread, visible or not, remains the essential element in the poem: the poet meditates on the word, in a passage moving from ellipsis to ellipsis: "After the horrible and insipid verb: 'to liquidate,' here, copiously used, is the

[14] (Zarathustra speaks for all the men of morning: "Do I then strive after happiness? I strive after my *work!* . . . This is *my* morning, *my* day beginneth: *arise, now, arise, thou great noontide!*"), *The Philosophy of Friedrich Nietzsche*, Random House (Modern Library) 1954, p. 367. [N]

36

word 'fil.' A small word, right in the saliva and the demonstration, but how dry it is! Word of agony: *We climb back up the slope.*" (RBS,166-167) The frequent recurrence of vertical preoccupations is no accident: "Isn't the poet this mountaineer. . . ?" The words used are by preference words with many senses, "mots à étages," veiled or open. "Nous remontons la pente": the passage of the text is never anything but a climb, a difficult "return upland," glimpsed in an essential convergence of views. From the mountain—which is, as one would already have gathered by intuition, an interior one—there will always be "Toujours plus larges fiançailles des regards," (MM,140) wider unions of elements seen, yet in whose sweep the distance will be understood and retained, even increased: "Supprimer l'éloignement tue. / To suppress distance is mortal." (RBS,183) In this severely mountainous vision, linking is never rendering identical, lest one "slip into the inanity of indistinction suppressing all illumination. . . ." In its vow of irregularity and disharmony, that statement, originally found in the torn-up notebook of *A une Sérénité crispée* and frequently quoted, is an indication of the way one would choose also to read René Char.

Ultimately the poet prepares his own crossing, plunging the poem into the *source* at once the image of origin and of rebirth by water—both implicitly included in the title "Les Premiers instants," where the adjective refers to the earliest moments but also to the fresh recreation—and to the river of oblivion which is also that of tempering, the Lethe of a long alchemical preparation described in *Le Marteau sans maître*, that smelting hearth, "foyer de fonte rouge" where the child plunges his eyes, for a more difficult vision where fire and water merge. The present immersion baptizes the future and consecrates the past: "Ce qui aura lieu baigne, au même titre que ce qui a passé, dans une sorte d'immersion." (AUSC, 38) Yet here the *passeur* is also, no less so than the reader, a *passant*—we think of Mallarmé's description of Rimbaud, already quoted: "ce passant considérable."

37

Nous sommes des passants *appliqués* à passer (LM,80)

. . . .

les passants profonds (LM,203)

. . . .

nous sommes . . . les passants. (LM,125)

The enthusiasm of the poet consecrated to his task redeems in part the passing of love and life along with the fragile landscape:[15]

. . . .

Terre sur quoi l'olivier brille,
Tout s'évanouit en passage.[b] (FM,172)

Moreover, the unguided passage is alone worth making. The injunction:

"Laissez filer les guides maintenant . . . / Let the reins go now . . ." (PPC,281) corresponds to the leave given to the escort at the outset of the poem "Le Visage nuptial."

A final leave-taking was implied all along in the vocation of the *matinaux*, of the visionaries in whose number the

---

[15] As in the poetry of Rilke, so in that of Char, only a "maison mentale" is not passing: "Nirgends, Geliebte, wird Welt sein, als innen. Unser / Leben geht hin mit Verwandlung. Und immer geringer / schwindet das Aussen. Wo einmal ein dauerndes Haus war, / schlägt sich erdachtes Gebild vor, quer, zu Erdenklichem / völlig gehörig, als ständ es noch ganz im Gehirne. // Nowhere, beloved, can world exist but within. / Life passes in transformation. And ever diminishing, / vanishes what's outside. Where once was a lasting house, / up starts some invented structure across our vision, as fully / at home among concepts as though it still stood in a brain." (DE,60-61)

Absence is the corollary to the presence of poetry, and its indispensable partner. Rilke: "Und wir: Zuschauer, immer, überall, / . . . / Wer hat uns also umgedreht, dass wir, / was wir auch tun, in jener Haltung sind / von einem, welcher fortgeht? Wie er auf / dem letzten Hügel, der ihm ganz sein Tal / noch einmal zeigt, sich wendet, anhält, weilt–, / so leben wir und nehmen immer Abschied. // And we, spectators, always, everywhere / . . . / Who's turned us round like this, so that we always, do what we may, retain the attitude / of someone who's departing? Just as he, / on the last hill, that shows him all his valley / for the last time, will turn and stop and linger, / we live our lives, forever taking leave." (DE,70-71)

[b] Land where the olive glitters / All fades away in passage.

poet is counted: "The poet does not retain what he discovers; having transcribed it, he soon loses it. In that resides his novelty, his infinite, and his peril." (LM,147) Around the poet whose ambition is to become a "vivant de l'espace" (MM, 123) a place will always be made for absence, for an essential liberty finding its metaphor in the air "which I feel always about to be lacking for most beings . . . ," (LM,92) as the reader maintains inviolate the space stretching between fragments as well as the margin between the text and its author, between the poet and himself. Although the poetic presence is more than once called "commune," only the passage can be so, definitively.

That solitude has been felt from the beginning of this essay, which it haunts. It is doubtless essential to poetry: we have only to read the conclusion of *Pour nous, Rimbaud*,[16] quoted more fully later. For the present work is dedicated both to passage and to presence. "In poetry, we only inhabit the place we leave. . . ." To the most devoted companion, both attentive and self-effacing, who might wish himself to be, above all else, a "passant profond," René Char has already given his own credo, buried in the context of an early poem, tempered in another current for a later birth:

Comme je m'approche, je m'éloigne[c] (MM,29)

And it is here that the poet takes his final leave of us. Although Char speaks to another poet, it is not only "For Rimbaud," but also for us: "Like Nietzsche, like Lautréamont, after having required everything of us, he asks that we 'send him away.' Final and essential requirement. How could we satisfy ourselves with him, who was satisfied with nothing?" (PNR,16) Such a drastic leave-taking was already prepared by a severe detachment: "In poetry, you only inhabit the place you leave, you only create the work from which you

---

[16] "Pour nous, Rimbaud" (1956) reprinted as preface to Rimbaud, *Poèmes*, Coll. Poésie, Gallimard pp. 14-15. (PNR)

[c] As I come near, I take my distance. (From "L'Ambition," one of the seven poems in the rare text of 1930, *Le Tombeau des secrets*, privately printed, TS, 15.)

39

detach yourself, you only obtain the lasting by destroying time. But everything you hold by means of rupture, detachment, and negation, is obtained only through another. . . . / The bestower of freedom is only free in others. The poet only enjoys the freedom of others." (PNR,15)

To give happiness without sharing it: "We belong to no one. . . ."[17] (FM,87) This is, for us, the hardest teaching of a solitary poet, whose solitude implies our own: "Et nous, réclamant notre part d'éloignement, nous ne sommes qu'en différence. / And we, claiming our share of distance, we are only in our difference." ("Le Dos houleux du miroir," exhibition Zao Wou-Ki at the Galerie de France, 1975)

[17] Rilke: "Denn mein / Anruf ist immer voll Hinweg . . . / . . . Wie ein gestreckter / Arm ist mein Rufen. Und seine zum Greifen / oben offene Hand bleibt vor dir / offen, wie Abwehr und Warnung, / Unfasslicher, weitauf. // . . . For my call / is always full of 'Away!' . . . / . . . Like an outstretched arm is my call. And its clutching, upwardly open hand is always before you / as open for warding and warning, / aloft there, Inapprehensible." (DE,62-65) And the final injunction: "Sei allem Abschied voran. / Be in advance of all parting." (SO,94-95)

40

LOYAL ADVERSARY:
LYRE/LIRE

Qui appelle encore? Mais la réponse n'est point donnée. (NT,74)

Each valid reading requires the convergence of intuitions, the reader's with the poet's and then with those of other readers, in a *Partage formel*. Its guiding motto might well be the two-line statement given a consistently ambiguous resonance—perhaps not by accident —in its title, "Lyre." In view of the proliferation of this image, one might suppose that the association between the sound of poetry (its "lyre") and its reading (its "lire") is intended to impress itself on the reader's understanding: "Lyre sans bornes des poussières, / Surcroît de notre coeur // Limitless lyre of dusts / Increase of our heart." (FM,205) Char's brief later commentary on this "pulverized" text, published in *L'Arrière-Histoire du poème pulvérisé*, is revealing in the present context of our discussion. In the first version of the responding verses, the title is followed by a question mark, as befits the presentation, in which the scene is at least double. But the sense is optimistic, if one takes this version as a first stage, transcended in the definitive text.

"Lyre?"[1]
Lyre nuptiale. Lyre sans merci.
Du ciel tombe une plume d'aigle.
Introuvable.
(Rarement trouvée.)[a]

One of the texts in the first version of *Arsenal*, "Flexibil-

[1] No. 738 (AE-IV-18). The word "Introuvable" is crossed out.

[a] "Lyre?" / Nuptial lyre. Merciless lyre. / From the sky falls an eagle feather. / Unfindable. / (Rarely found.)

ité de l'oubli," has already suggested the orphic identification of lyre and poem:[2]

Pour moi qui avance en chantant
Sur instrument à cordes.[b]

The lyre as the instrument of Orpheus and thus associated with love in its loss, is often present in the poet's consciousness, as the manuscripts show. In the struggle for expression the instrument can do battle with itself, as in the phonetic ambiguity of "Poésie, cette lutte matinale. [which can be read also as "luth matinal"] / Poetry, that matinal struggle [or "lute"]." That the strings of the lute are heard only by the ear listening for them[3] is as it should be, in this poetry of an "Écoutant" (NT,9), but the demand for expression and realization can be far more strident:

[2] No. 684 (AE-IV-4). The presence of Orpheus will guide us. But elsewhere, in the text for the artist Sima ("Se rencontrer paysage avec Joseph Sima"), this presence is already infused with its ending: "Il n'y a pas de pouvoir divin, il y a un vouloir divin éparpillé dans chaque souffle: les dieux sont dans nos murs, actifs, assoupis. Orphée est déjà déchiré." (S) Thus the poet will be finally disaggregated in the universe, "éparpillé." Rilke's *Sonnets to Orpheus* (New York, 1942, tr. M. D. H. Norton 32-3) provide a somber and luminous background: "Nur wer die Leier schon hob / auch unter Schatten, / darf das unendliche Lob / ahnend erstatten. // Only one who has lifted the lyre / among shadows too, may divining render / the infinite praise." Heidegger (*Existence and Being*, Regnery, 1949, pp. 284-285) discusses Hölderlin's use of the lyre in "The Blind Singer" and elsewhere: this discussion is not foreign to René Char.

[b] For me as I go singing / On a stringed instrument.

[3] The following passage provides an example of a reading listened for, and itself about reading: the italicized words fit into a pattern of reference and half-reference: "Bientôt s'effondrerait le roulis de sa lyre . . . / Un corbeau rameur *sombre déviant* de *l'escadre* / Sur le *muet silex* de midi *écartelé* / Accompagnait notre *entente* aux mouvements tendres / . . . / Notre rareté commençait un règne // Soon the rolling of its lyre would cease / . . . / A crow, somber rower, swerving from the fleet / On the mute flint of quartered noon / Accompanied our understanding with tender movements / . . . / Our rarity was opening a reign." (FM,61) Here, and in the following passage, we italicize the terms which indicate the doubled sense of our reading, half-permitted by the poet, that "lyre de la mort / lyre of death" (or: of love, "l'amour"). For the sound of reading on this second level is muted,

. . . .

. . . le guetteur qui sourit

Quand sa lyre profère: "Ce que je veux, sera."ᶜ (FM,171)

. . . .

Yet the poet is frequently obscure even to his own vision: ". . . le poète comme l'araignée construit sa route dans le ciel. En partie caché à lui-même, il apparaît aux autres, dans les rayons de sa ruse inouïe,⁴ mortellement visible. / . . . the poet like the spider builds his road in the sky. Partly hidden to himself, he appears to others, in the beams of his ruse unheard [or, unheard of], mortally visible." (FM,76) The sense requires for its deciphering the understanding of a reader accepting willingly his fraternal involvement in the web.

"L'étoile furtive de la pluie s'annonce. Frère, silex fidèle, ton joug s'est fendu. L'entente a jailli de tes épaules. / The furtive star of the rain proclaims itself. Brother, faithful flint, your yoke has cleft in two. Understanding has sprung from your shoulders." (FM,32) These faithful companions, the poet and his reader, are just as surely "loyal adversaries" or equal enemies: similar and opposed, they share a fidelity to their common struggle, against the text that has become theirs together, only to move in its turn beyond them both. The frequent images of the yoke, of the shoulder opened, split apart, or cleft asunder appear as subtle but evident indications of this uncomfortably intimate relationship, where the poet precedes and engenders, often without knowing, and sometimes against his will, his mute, burdensome, and faithful partner:

---

made opaque in its deviation from an ordinary framework, or "cadre." It is at once somber, and threatened with submersion, "sombre" used adjectivally, and also as a verb ("sombrer" = to sink, thus "un rameur sombre" = a rower sinks, or a somber rower). From the flint, however silent now, can be struck the spark of noon light, as the silex breaks open the text "écartelé." Yet the poetry is never to lose its part of mystery, and the somber figure of the rower always accompanies us.

ᶜ . . . the watcher smiling / When his lyre speaks: "What I wish, shall be."

⁴ We hear another voice: "La blessure inouïe dont je voudrais guérir." Pierre Reverdy, *Main d'oeuvre*, Mercure de France, 1949 p. 335.

43

. . . . . .

Cet enfant sur ton épaule
Est ta chance et ton fardeau.

. . . . . .

Violente l'épaule s'entr'ouvre;
Muet apparaît le volcan.[d] (FM,172)

. . . . . .

To the reader thus engendered, the text may reveal a luminosity manifold in aspect, but destined to bear no further fruit, that is: "Est apparu un multiple et stérile arc-en-ciel. / A multiple and sterile rainbow appeared." (LM,185) But on occasion, the poet as "scout" or light-bringer ("éclaireur") not only chooses to clarify—"Il fut midi à mon poème / It was noon by my poem"—but also to consider his thought fertile. The poem "Fontis" appearing at the close of the collection *La Parole en archipel*, gathering it finally into one cluster of thought, renders homage to the harvest and the implied fruition of pain:[5]

. . . .

Le rosaire de la grappe;
Au soir le très haut fruit couchant qui saigne
La dernière étincelle.[e] (LM,206)

The radiance itself is identified with a natural image of human profundity: ". . . sans l'angoisse tu n'es qu'élémentaire." (RBS,165) More important still, from the anguish, a fruit may be reborn: ". . . la grappe desséchée de Dionysos, —qui sait?—demain reverdissante. / . . . the withered cluster of Dionysos—who knows?—tomorrow becoming green once more." (RBS,165)

[d] This child on your shoulder / Is your fortune and your burden / . . . / Violent the shoulder parts asunder; / Mute the volcano appears.

[5] On the relation of pain and fruition, see Rilke: "Sollen nicht endlich uns diese ältesten Schmerzen / fruchtbarer werden? / Ought not these oldest sufferings of ours to be yielding / more fruit by now?" (DE,22-23) and a later discussion of fruit in its ripening.

[e] The rosary of the cluster; / In the evening the lofty fruit setting, bleeding / The last spark.

For the poem itself is flower and fruit held in common.[6]
One of the "Deux poèmes ornés d'ipomées" (two brief manuscript texts originally placed between petals of the flower ipomoea) the poem itself is a source of illumination, taking within its circle the past unfolding and the future distance:

> Comment rejeter dans les ténèbres notre coeur antérieur
> et son fruit de retour?
> Un poème qui devient gloire s'éloigne pour toujours du
> poète, de cette lyre de la mort.[f]

The poet singing of death sings also, by implication, of love. The verbal charge accumulating between the related concepts of "la mort" and "l'amour" presently extends to our reading of all the love poems in their deep ambivalence. For example, in the invocation: "Chante ta soif irisée / Sing your irised thirst" (FM,129) we may read, at the same time, the association implicit there and elsewhere:

$$\text{iris} \longleftrightarrow \text{Eros}$$

The verbal material of this poem refuses the limits of one precise significance. (It will perhaps be noticed that we began

[6] On the concept of the "common," see in particular, Victor R. Turner, *The Ritual Process: Structure and Anti-Structure* (London, Routledge, 1969). He explains how the feeling of communitas asserts itself against the rigid form of the structure, its incursions especially evident on the edge where the marginal is situated (and so the notion of marginality that Char represents through the images of the wolf and the snake joins the notion of the common fruit, of the "partage"). "Communitas breaks in through the interstices of structure, in liminality; at the edges of structure, in marginality; and from beneath structure, in inferiority." His comments on "passage" are equally relevant in this context: ". . . the immediacy of communitas gives way to the mediacy of structure, while in *rites de passage*, men are released from structure into communitas only to return to structure revitalized by this experience of communitas." For a work on "liminality" approximately equivalent to the notion of threshold, to which we shall return later in connection with several texts, Turner refers us to the publications of Van Gennep.

[f] How to cast into the shadows our former heart and its returning fruit? / A poem becoming a halo departs forever from the poet, that lyre of death.

45

with the simple homonym of the "lyre/lire," to develop gradually more complex readings, more open to disagreement.) One look does not suffice, even to the ellipsis. Only multiple readings, parallel and free—since the reader must remain so —can give the margin around the poem the depth it deserves: "But who will establish around us that space, that density really made for us. . . ,"[7] (RBS,173) so that the poem will eventually detach itself from the poet, freeing them both. "Le poème donne et reçoit de sa multitude l'entière démarche du poéte s'expatriant de son huis clos. / The poem gives and receives from its multitude the complete progress of the poet in his voluntary departing from his situation *in camera*." (FM,77)

A. Margin

> Chaque poème s'accompagne de sa marge confidante (AHPP,14)

Char's poetry is more changeable in rhythm than that of most contemporary poets: it moves often with great interior rapidity, hurtling past the logical stages like the formal equivalent of the expression "être du bond," but occasionally, in a grave unhurried manner, suiting the poet's conviction that the work should not be pushed "to advance more quickly than its own movement"; the poet is drawn to certain beings not yet fulfilled: "Those who inspire a tender compassion . . . bear within themselves a work they are in no hurry to deliver." (S.) Once this deeper and enclosed word is proffered, it shows a special strength for its long accumulation within. Thus

---

[7] Rilke: "Wer zeigt ein Kind, so wie es steht? Wer stellt / es ins Gestirn und gibt das Mass des Abstands / ihm in die Hand? . . . / Who'll show a child just as it is? Who'll place it / within its constellation, with the measure / of distance in its hand?" (DE,44-45). Poetry demands its space, whether terrestrial or stellar, or in the "entre-deux." The poet, says Heidegger of Hölderlin, but also of all poets, "is one who has been cast out—out into that *Between*, between gods and men. But only and for the first time in this Between is it decided, who man is and where he is settling his existence." (EB,312)

the feeling, upon reading the "fragments" in series, of an energy violating the space between the texts: or, in a reverse image, as if the fragment had absorbed the margin. The poem-island, endowed with contradictory impulses, may spread out even while it is enclosed, like a fruit of long meditation, first the poet's and then the reader's.

In every case, what is to the side of the text is illumined or illumines, whether it be a gloss or a post-commentary (for instance, the "rapid relation" of the poem seen afresh by the poet) as in the *Arrière-Histoire du poème pulvérisé*,[8] where "each poem is accompanied by its confident margin" or whether, as in the complex texture of *Contre une maison sèche*, a wall—of a house or a tomb—sends back in a verbally illuminating reflection a response called clairvoyant, or, as in *La Nuit talismanique*, Char's own illustrations respond to the text which dominates and controls them. (Thus the startling difference in effect between this volume and the numerous correspondences of Char's poems with the illustrations of other artists, where the resonance is double, visual and verbal.)

Opposed examples might be given from two other generations of twentieth-century poets. In the poetry of Max Jacob, the white margin marks the distance between the poem in prose and all it is not. To be "situé," as he said, the prose poem was to be isolated or "perched" in such a fashion that the separation between it and ordinary language (or "ordinary" poetry) was inviolable. The framework, visible in the ironic style, for instance, was always to function as framework, a barrier desired and never overcome. To take a contrary example, in the poetry of André du Bouchet, where words are distant from each other, their interrelations rare (the more so as space engulfs them), the gaze is initially drawn to the vacancy around the sparse lines. Never does the text intrude on the empty place, which remains, even appearing to absorb the text.

[8] Referred to later as AHPP.

47

On the contrary, we might advance the hypothesis that in the densest writing of René Char, one first notices the margins of thought; yet the evident paucity of verbal matter composing each fragment rather encourages the expanse of the place of reading and the slowest measure. Only on successive readings is the real monumentality of the work realized.

B. Ellipsis, Compression

D'omission en omission (RBS,155)

The "émondeur d'arbres," or pruner of trees, furnishes a natural model for the poet of brief speech, whose preferred technique of ellipsis is aimed at eventual fruition: it is from the imposition of human measure that natural abundance seems to come. Thus, in one of the psychological reversals customary to this poetry, it is from the limits of gardens that forests are born. "Abundance will come," according to the title of a group of poems; that these words which have the sound of a proverb were found, as it were, in a man's name, in no way diminishes their effect. (See the first note in "The Cycle of Alchemy.") The title occurs in the collection *Le Marteau sans maître*, which is not without significance: the time of plenty will come only after the initial forging and the primary suppression have taken place.

Difficulty and even pain attach to the harvest: "But the word revoking, under the word unfolding, has appeared once more . . . so that together they may make us suffer." (LM, 159) The choice of a path is finally justified, for in this work, "nothing is frankly unfruitful." The impulse toward density encourages quintessence rather than quantity: "We are the contracted fruit. . . ." (AUSC,37) René Char's most characteristic statement is made up of contrary elements and reverse constructions, of logical developments turned inside out, it finds its form and its meaning within an exiguous and compressed space: "notre comprimante splendeur" ("A ***"), placed always in the most active form, modifying all about it.

48

Brief but adequate, the compact text will take its luminosity from its paradoxical tension, its intensity from its compression. A single example suffices to illustrate the whole, its necessary brevity opening out into a three-fold extension: "Le point fond. Les sources versent. Amont éclate. / The point melts. The springs pour out. Upland bursts forth." (NP,48) The background against which these three statements are inscribed has implied in it the following suppositions. First, that a fevered vision, or a passionate one—which, according to Char, is always required of poetry, explicitly or implicitly—can affect a simple geometric figure just as if it were a material substance: thus the point melts when it is observed. Second, that natural elements can work as the agents of a figurative abundance within language itself: thus the sources, or springs, pour forth at the moment they are seen, nourishing the text in all its rich sparseness. And third, that a purely topological description may function as the instrument of an explosion, symbolic and real, when that which is upland from us breaks out like a sudden illumination.

Several other cases of ellipsis may serve as models for the way of reading we have chosen. The brief text "Tréma de l'émondeur" is, from its abrupt beginning, placed off-balance:

Parce que le soleil faisait le paon sur le mur
Au lieu de voyager à dos d'arbre.[g] (MM,20)

The conjunction has nothing to join: the passage lacks either a beginning for the sentence or then an end—that is, were it to be considered prose. But this short-circuit of a poem is also a way of reading, where the explanation is given to a non-existent phenomenon, or an answer to a question posed differently each time.

"L'amour" declares itself ambiguously:

Être
Le premier venu.[h] (MM,31)

[g] Because the sun was playing the peacock on the wall / Instead of traveling on a tree's back.
[h] Being / The first-comer.

49

Is this "being" a verb? A noun? But the lack is already implied in the title, of which the poem is the definition. Are we enjoined to a rapidity, in order to win? Or is the first-coming the result of a simple accident? A first version[9] read:

> L'
> N'attends rien de toi-même
> Qui ne soit passé par moi-même
> AMOUR
> C'est ne rien entendre à toi-même.[i]

If the ellipsis and the consequent ambiguity are not noticed in the syntax, as in the cases just cited, they may be present even in the most minimal trace of punctuation. The following example is the final line of a prose poem entitled: "Rapport de marée": "Bien-aimée, derrière ma porte? / Beloved, behind my door?" (LM,139) A possible ellipsis in the title is also possible, by implication: for the "mariée," a bride whose adventure is perhaps recounted along with that of the "marée" or tide, could be seen as the verbal source of the interrogation. Without the question mark, one would of course accept the remark as a simple statement of a presence (loved) behind a door. But the mark forces another, ambiguous reading, in which the status of the beloved is questioned: Beloved? behind my door? or then: Beloved. Behind my door? The ending of the poem opens a door to a meaning wilfully concealed.

In an early version of *A une Sérénité crispée* (AUSC:A),[10] the deliberate working-out of ellipses is obvious, for instance,

---

[9] Consulted in a copy of *Arsenal* given to Paul Eluard, No. 684 (AE-IV-4); verified in the copy at the Bibliothèque Nationale (Res. Mye. 515).

[i] Expect nothing from yourself / Which hasn't passed through myself. / LOVE / It's understanding nothing about yourself.

[10] Compare with this title the phrase, "Je me gouvernais dans une véhémence sereine," and Heidegger's remarks on Hölderlin's theory of the Serene as a highness, a clarity, and a joyousness. "The Serene preserves and holds everything in tranquillity and wholeness." (EB,271)

in the successive versions of the following maxim: "Le poète doit rosser sans ménagement son aigle comme sa grenouille s'il veut ne pas gâter sa lucidité. / The poet must ruthlessly thrash his eagle as well as his frog if he wishes not to spoil his lucidity." The first versions show a progressive compression; first a tightening of the vocabulary: ". . . la part de notoriété que sa poésie lui concède (accorde) s'il veut *maintenir saine* sa lucidité. / . . . the share of notoriety which his poetry concedes (accords) him if he wants to *keep* his lucidity *healthy*." The expressions which we italicize for emphasis are replaced by severer ones in the later versions of the text: ". . . la part de notoriété que sa poésie lui *octroie* s'il veut *ne pas gâter* sa lucidité. / . . . the share of notoriety which his poetry *grants* him if he wants *not to spoil* his lucidity." The image of the eagle, added here, lifts the maxim to a symbolic plane. Also, this image possibly prepared by the idea of notoriety permits a slight word-play in the next-to-last version: ". . . l'aigle dont la notoriété de sa poésie le vole. [*sic*] / . . . the eagle which the notoriety of his poetry takes from him." In the final version, the addition of a more modest animal, a frog, makes by its contrast with the eagle a violent opposition between high and low: in alchemy, these two signify earth and air (spirit). The image of the eagle dominates the whole, stressing the difficult struggle between self and public, not without an echo of Jacob battling his angel.

Char's conception of poetic work is directed toward the active and the accurate, against passivity and imprecision. His is a "métier de pointe," roughly, a profession of the point. The iron-worker or the artisan of the word hammers and forges, but precisely. The simplest text may develop its unique resonance only through a whole series of combats undertaken like so many blows on the anvil by the "hammer with no master." Such work manifests a contradiction, and also a struggle against it: "In the center of poetry, a contradictor awaits you. He is your sovereign. Fight loyally against him." (RBS,165) The eagle, victor as well as vanquished, is necessarily at the heart of the poem.

51

C. DISPLACEMENT, REVERSAL

Qu'est-ce que nous réfractons? (NT,63)

The basis for construction is often a conscious ambiguity. The essential texture of Char's poetry is complex, set in an active equilibrium of interdependent tensions: semantic, phonetic, and structural. The following examples run counter to ordinary experience and ordinary vision. The first shows a one-way conceptual transfer. The poem "Sur les hauteurs" concludes, between parentheses, with what purports to be an explanation:

.   .   .   .

(Il y avait un précipice dans notre maison.
C'est pourquoi nous sommes partis et nous sommes établis
ici.)[j] (LM,45)

The paradoxical quality lies in the *displacement* of characteristics generally applicable to the exterior landscape toward an interior one, as if refuge were to be sought from the dangers of the latter on the exposed summits ("On the Heights"). The parentheses surrounding this "explanation" reenforce the interior menace, as if its acceptance were a matter of course.

The second example will recur in the discussion, for it implies the counter-logical but nonetheless human perception enforced in the reader. "Une rose pour qu'il pleuve. / A rose so it may rain." (FM,199) The future result necessitates the return to a cause not yet evident, all links of ordinary causality being suppressed in the text. The flowering which might be encouraged by the rain becomes, here, the prelude to the rain itself, as if the proof of its falling were alone able to summon the precipitation desired. The succession of natural elements is perceived as an "ordre insurgé," revolutionizing the natural order by a poetic action.

---

[j] (There was a precipice in our house. / That's why we left and settled here.)

D. Multiplicity, Plurivalence

Chacun appelle (NT,77)

Within certain expressions a multiple reading may develop, yielding what we might more properly call differing angles of vision than differing meanings. Two examples, each important for its relevance to the reading itself, will serve as guides to a subsequent discussion of plurivalence and then of semantic and syntactic convergence and divergence, in their alternating aspects.

1) "Tu as la densité de la rose qui se fera. / Yours is the density of the rose in its making." (NP,82) Is it the density of the flower that will form, or the flower itself? Or both at once? Since this last probable answer excludes nothing, we would always choose it as permitting the greatest range, our primary criterion for the poetic:

   a) la densité (de la rose) qui se fera
   b) la densité (de la rose qui se fera)
   c) (la densité de la rose) qui se fera

Upon rereading, the poem unfolds its multiple content within its apparently simple form.

A heightened or extended perception immediately extends in its turn the language of description. In *Flux de l'aimant*, the essay on Miró already quoted, a color envisions its own multiplication just because it is brilliant. In similar fashion the rose in the above phrase is defined not in the generic sense but in the figurative one, by the quantity of its petals and the intensity of their color. This bud or this text in its potential density will blossom forth subsequently—a product of future readings, like an "intermittent" flower. As a natural description, the fragment only implied, wholly in bud, is also a metatextual reference to the compact poem itself, in its future unfolding.

2) A second expression whose density is equally dependent on a multiple reading also treats a subject that it formally

reflects. The ambiguous fragment, like a stone one can turn about in any sense, for contradictory or harmonic visions, is frequently a product of Char's lapidary work; here it is stressed by the poet himself, in the punctuation: "Cette part jamais fixée, en nous sommeillante, d'où jaillira DEMAIN LE MULTIPLE." (LM,105) Is it tomorrow that is multiple and will spring forth? In that case, the three capitalized words would be grouped together; or does "tomorrow" signify exactly the moment where the multiple will suddenly be realized? Or the evident but ambiguous source is read as an interrogation, separated from the preceding context, as can be all three interpretations: "d'où jaillira, en effet, l'avenir? / From where, indeed, will this multiple morrow come?" The phrase just quoted might be called a metapoetic emblem: in the poem-fragment, multiple and multiplying, meanings and paths lead to one another in echo: "In the poem's cloth there should be found an equal number of hidden tunnels, of harmonic rooms, along with future elements, sunning harbors, deceptive trails, and existing elements calling to each other. The poet is the ferryman of all that in its order." (AUSC,44)

Now the image of a ferryman, a "passeur," is inextricably linked to the idea of a passerby: "Les passants que nous sommes. . . ." (FM,216) In the name of these two essential concepts of the trail and the ferryman, the poem will develop its new order. Or, more suddenly, like a path exploding from its exploration: the rod striking it which flies in fragments from the impact ("bâton éclaté") is at once the walking-stick of the passerby and the baton of the orchestra leader (thus the "chambres d'harmonie"), and still again the pointer of the guide to these tunnels leading from poem to poem.[11] Here the path discovers its divergent echoes, plays out all its future possibilities on repeated risks. "Et l'avenir est fécondé / And the future is fecundated." As the fragment is to be read in several senses, its formal isolation permits a depth redoubled by the readings and reinforced by the margin; the diverse senses, corresponding to the star and its rays or to the flower

---

[11] Compare with the drover's stick summoning the poet in "La Faux relevée."

whose petals point in different directions, are all justified, even if occasionally divergent from the poet's reading. The following statement applies equally to poet and reader: "One cannot begin a poem without some error about oneself and the world. . . ." (LM,146) These errors, all fertile, generate the poem's radiance in a constellation made up of plurivalent words whose original meanings are forgotten: "amnesiac words." (LM,146) Luckily, we have often no way of knowing which interpretation the poet would have chosen, for, as a willing creator of labyrinths, admittedly "confusing" by his nature, he would not choose to have us choose between meanings. Each reading is the source of the next, each poses an "impossible solution" like that of the painting haunting much of Char's work, Georges de La Tour's "Madeleine à la veilleuse," described in a poem by that name.

Within the field of syntax alone the range of examples is great. Often one cannot interpret the subject, which remains in suspension, permitting all senses. In the poem "Allégeance," for instance, the central figure occupying the space of the poem, and of the poet's imagination, is undefined as to gender: "Dans les rues de la ville il y a mon amour." We may know "my love" to be a woman by some evidence exterior to the text, but within the poem itself, the expression retains its mystery completely, allowing full rein to our perception— which remains at a distance. In each reading, the poem is written afresh, the reader perhaps unconsciously placing his own imprint upon the pronoun and thus upon the text.

In an unsettling fashion, the pronoun may be unattached to any definite person or thing. "Le Mortel partenaire" begins: "Il la défiait, s'avançait vers son coeur. . . . Il pesait du regard les qualités de l'adversaire. . . . / He challenged it, advanced toward its heart. . . . His look surmised the qualities of the adversary. . . ." (LM,121) In the first version of the text, the second pronoun was tied down to a specific referent: "Il marchait sur la vie / He moved against life." (no. 760, AE-IV-22) The interest of the final version is heightened by this ambiguous introduction, an enigma accentuated by the more general conclusion, deliberately and

55

admittedly secretive: "Certains êtres ont une signification qui nous manque. Qui sont-ils? Leur secret tient au plus profond du secret même de la vie. / Certain beings have a meaning which escapes us. Who are they? Their secret resides in the depths of the very secret of life." (LM,122)

A concise example of multi-layered reading occurs in *Le Marteau sans maître*:

Les grands chemins
Dorment à l'ombre de ses mains

Elle marche au supplice
Demain
Comme une traînée de poudre.[k] (MM,25)

The central pronoun whose absent referent gives "her" character to the poem is surrounded with echoes on the phonetic as well as the semantic levels, these echoes accentuated by the rhyme. Thus the "chemins" are the antecedent of this slow and yet explosive walking, compared not directly to gunpowder but rather to its trail, the attention we pay to her walking underlined by the slight temporal discordance between the senses of "is walking" and "tomorrow." All of this bears the trace of what might be a revolutionary advance, the powder spilling along the path from the hands, the ["mains"] indicated indistinctly in the words "che*min*" and "de*main*" if the accentuation is slightly modified: ["deux mains" / "two hands"]. But now the accessory terms describing this still absent "elle"—unflattering, as in "traînée de poudre," which we might read as a heavily made-up prostitute, or then the opposite, as the pulverized trail of a meteor —themselves evaporate finally, becoming nothing but dust, a dispersal more powdery than dangerous within the play of words.[12] And this dispersal distracts our attention from the indefinite point retaining its enigmatic centrality.

[k] The high roads / Sleep in the shade of her hands // She walks to her torment / Tomorrow / Like wildfire.

[12] Compare the association of trail and powder in the following fragment: "Qu'elle le veuille ou non, s'en défende ou non, toute créature à l'écart trace un sentier commun puis en pulvérise la réflexion. Ce second geste de répandre pousse en avant la tragédie." (RBS,174)

1. Semantic

Frequently, the poem or a part of it seems to gravitate around a double meaning, evident or not, which determines the rest of the reading. The range of possibilities is great, and depends entirely on the reader's consciousness of the ambiguity, which the poet may or may not have chosen.

Even within the most minimal of expanses, the simplest word can become, by a multiple stress—of the text itself, the context, or another text—the center of the poem. In "La Liberté," the pronoun "elle" offers a double interpretation ("she?" "freedom?"): "Elle est venue par cette ligne blanche pouvant tout aussi bien signifier l'issue de l'aube que le bougeoir du crépuscule. / It came along this white line that might signify dawn's emergence as well as dusk's candle." (FM,52) And in the corresponding final expression, the ambiguous "ligne blanche," which retains the swan ("cygne") is also the sign ("signe") of the text: "cygne sur la blessure, par cette ligne blanche. / swan on the wound, along this white line."

In similar tone, the following poem presents the form and the idea of an hourglass, with a central device for inverting it:

> Toute vie qui doit poindre
> achève un blessé.
> Voici l'arme,
> rien,
> vous, moi, réversiblement
> ce livre
> et l'énigme
> qu'à votre tour vous deviendrez
> dans le caprice amer des sables.[1] (LM,84)

The image of a wound, "blessé," determines the reading of a ["larme"], this tear replacing its possible cause: "l'arme" or the weapon, a single visible drop, fallen to the following line,

[1] Every life which must dawn / finishes off a dying man. / Here is the weapon, / nothing, / you, me, reversibly / this book, / and the enigma / which in your turn you will become / in the sands, bitter caprice.

where it becomes nothing: "rien." This book ("ce livre") which offers itself ["se livre"] can be read in two directions, in a reversible deciphering, laterally from "vous" to "moi," from the poet to the reader or vice versa; the enigma is then posed in this pictogram of a text which can be turned upside down for still another deciphering, that is, from bottom to top.

The title of the following poem, "Le Tout ensemble," serves also as a description for an ideal interpretation: everything together, in echo:

> Faucille qui persévérez dans le ciel désuni
> Malgré le jour et notre frénésie.
> Lune qui nous franchis et côtoies notre coeur,
> Lui, resté dans la nuit.[m] (LM,49)

· · · · · · · · ·

Here the "Lui" can be read as an invocation to the moon to continue its shining ["luis"] or even as in the first edition of this poem (1950)—when the line read not as a direct address to the moon, but as a more distant description—in third-person form: "Lune qui franchit et côtoie notre coeur." The phonetic suggestion might have operated in the same way:

$$\text{Lui} < \begin{matrix} \text{Luis} \\ \text{Luit}^{13} \end{matrix}$$

A few readings have a particularly dense texture because of a possible correspondence with other poems. In the following lines of "Robustes météores," there may pass through the poem or at least through the reader's mind the memory

---

[m] Sickle persevering in the disunited heaven / Despite the day and our frenzy / Moon crossing us and skirting our heart, / Remaining there in the night.

[13] The intricacies of this particular word- and concept-play which Robert Cohn has pointed out in the work of Rimbaud function also for René Char; the communion between Mallarmé's eulogy of Rimbaud ("Éclat, lui, d'un météore") and the central theme of our present work scarcely needs more illumination than this. (*Arthur Rimbaud*, Princeton University Press, Princeton, 1974.)

of a line from Breton's *Second manifeste*: "Cet été le bois est du verre / This summer the wood is glass," so that he might see in the forest worm this other glass which, added to the approximate and half-suggested sounds like ["le ver"] and ["l'hiver"]—the winter of the cocoon—enriches the present poem:

Dans le bois on écoute bouillir le ver
La chrysalide tournant au clair visage
Sa délivrance naturelle[n] (MM,21)

. . . .

Ver/vers/verre: to the worm turning into butterfly and to the verse of the poem there is added a glass clarifying the future in preparation for the final illumination; it is just the conjunction of these three senses that will effect the liberation from winter and with it, the possible clarification of the whole text after its first confusing chiaroscuro. In a later discussion of *Artine* and *La Nuit talismanique*, this poem will find another place, in the light of its varied meanings, by then accumulated within our own reading.

In an action contrasting with that of the robust meteors of the title in their spectacular natural falling, the trees are felled by the sharp instruments of men to yield the eventual flame, a firewood illumination, through a violent undoing of nature for human ends—thus, a forced liberation of the wood's potential, within the limits of the fireplace: "Levez-vous bêtes à égorger / A gagner le soleil // Rise up beasts to slaughter / To reach the sun." (MM,21)

In another example, "Hommage et famine," a poem written partly in honor of a woman's comprehension, beginning: "Femme qui vous accordez avec la bouche du poète . . . / Woman tuned to the mouth of the poet," (FM,51) has as its title, re-read, the veiled announcement of a couple:

Homm(age) et fam(ine) → [Homme et femme]

[n] In the wood we listen to the worm boiling / The chrysalis turning toward a clear face / Its natural deliverance.

59

The dark children mentioned in the last part of the poem, "ces enfants sans clarté" who will speak later, after the poem, or whose future utterance the poem is, by an implied cyclical motion, are perhaps to be found within the homage and the famine in their contrary directions. Thus the real title also speaks within the apparent one, as if an eventual clarity were to have been gained inside the surface text.

Finally, a vigorous aesthetic, relying on the force of a personality felt within the briefest and seemingly lightest of poems, defines itself by an explosive implication within a breathing later characterized by the poet as "aggressive." The second line of "Les Poumons" can be interpreted in several ways:

L'apparition de l'arme à feu
La reconnaissance du ventre.° (MM,35)

Is it a menace, so that once one has recognized the stomach, the shot will be fired? Or an ironic reference to a possible suicide? Or a fat bourgeois stomach protecting itself with gratitude ("Reconnaissance" carrying the double sense of recognition and appreciation)? For there is again the possible trace of a tear, ["larme"] in "l'arme." Or an erotic allusion, to that which can go off, and to that into which it can be fired ("ventre" taken here in a sense which this partial explanation should sufficiently explain)?

The power of the word as firearm, or the "fer continu" of the text forged, whether a continuous iron or continuous effort, depends partly on a reading corresponding to the vigor and the constancy of the *faire*, recognized as continuously difficult.

2. *Syntactic*

Occasionally two readings must be followed in order for the whole to be seen. This dilemma is familiar, for instance, in

° The appearance of the firearm / The thanks of the stomach. Originally printed in *Le Tombeau des secrets*, and entitled "La Respiration." (TS,20)

the careful ambivalence of Pierre Reverdy's poetry, where the position of a word enables it to be read in either of two directions, and forces it to be read eventually in both.

A poem called "Singulier," singular indeed in both senses of the word—unique in René Char's early poetry and odd in its effect on the reader—offers one of the simplest and most efficacious examples:

.   .   .   .

Elle mange à sa faim et plus
Haute est l'estime de ses draps.

Nomade elle s'endort allongée sur ma bouche.[p] (MM,26)
.   .   .   .

Since the word "plus" would have to be pronounced in one or other of two ways according to the sense attributed to it, we would have to decide on one before reading the poem aloud, a decision obviously impossible to make.

The central word can set in balance two lines, as in the above example, or two far larger masses. The prose poem "J'habite une douleur" turns and turns again about the word both single and simple, the "Pourtant/However" situated at its center.

.   .   .   .

. . . Plus tard, on t'identifiera à quelque géant désagrégé, seigneur de l'impossible.
Pourtant.
Tu n'as fait qu'augmenter le poids de ta nuit.
.   .   .   .

Il n'y a pas de siège pur.[q] (FM,178-9)

According to the direction in which this reservation is oriented, the poem changes its sense completely. Either the first

[p] She eats to her content and more / Lofty is the esteem of her sheets. / Nomad she falls asleep stretched out on my mouth.
[q] . . . Later they will identify you with some disaggregated giant, lord of the impossible. / However. / You have only increased the weight of your night. / . . . / There is no untainted seat.

paragraph predicts it, or it controls the second paragraph, or then both. Occupying a line alone, it is not linked by its context to anything beyond itself, except possibly to the conclusion, which would then finish a sentence beginning with the end of the first part, followed by the reservation, the first part of the second long mass, and finally the conclusion as to the impossibility of it all. Since we shall return to the poem at some length later, we will limit our remarks here to the simplest structure, divorced from the meaning, in a reading deliberately fragmentary, befitting the analysis of parts and fragments which forms the initial step of our path. Thus the poem reads, along its barest trajectory, either from the observation of the impurity essential everywhere to the image of a stellar giant disaggregated, or then from this nocturnal and radiant "lord of the impossible" back to the initial statement, now seen as an explanation. Although we ordinarily read from initiation to ending, the statement of impossibility and disaggregation here is so strong as to force a subsequent rereading. The poem could be compared to a figure eight in which the narrow middle of that one conjunction acts as a bridge for returning, from the final negation to the statement of a later vision: "plus tard. . . ." Alternation between the verbal masses and this deceptively simple conjunction underlines the tragedy implicit in this poem, where the pain or suffering inhabited by the mind is finally inflicted also upon us, a situation whose specific content is unspoken and presumably unspeakable.

3. *Semantic/Syntactic*

This most frequent sort of double ambiguity can be seen to include many of the more complex texts, from brief expressions to whole poems. A paradigm example might be "les nobles disparus" (MM,110)—those who are now gone are noble, and/or it is the nobles who have disappeared, no more noble for this action: that is, a simple exchange of roles between the adjective and the noun, in which the two slightly different senses do not clash. Most of the terms so doubled fulfill a double function, that of situation and that of meaning. Concentrations of opposed linguistic forces, they serve in general as a center of formal tensions, mirrored by a complexity of theme. The examples given here of this "omnidirectional state" of poetic language are arranged according to their structural complications.

"Front de la rose" (LM,123) announces its ambivalent content in its title: the battlefield of the rose joins the forehead of the rose—that is, the brow of the rose, and of the hill from which the rose of dawn is seen breaking forth—and its summit, or its audacity, "front" bearing all three meanings. And the flower itself, in its redness, sets the forehead blushing, and also by a phonetic rereading, sprinkles it: "la rose!" ["l'arrose!"]. Thus the reading in all its complications is prepared; within the body of the poem itself the recalls of senses are woven into the verbal canvas by interior rhymes, accentuated by the choppy epigrammatic style. Once again we give here, deliberately removed from their context in this first stage, only the particular fragments sustaining this multiple reading:

> . . . nouveaux venus, épris. La rose! . . .
> . . . Le désir resurgit, mal de nos fronts évaporés.[r]

The possible senses of this first line quoted prepare the way for a more subtle working of the last line. After the salutation to beauty where the name of Venus appears by orthographic suggestion, the hint of amorous captivity ["Venus est pris(e)"] is itself taken [prise] in the form of the literal surface, where the "épris" is echoed by a "repris," a subject smitten by love as in surprise and then once again.[14] The exclamation: "La rose!" attracts all the attention—being not only the object of the affection causing the blush, the perspiration, or per-

---

[r] . . . newcomers, in love. The rose! / . . . Desire surges up afresh, disorder of our flighty foreheads.

[14] A preliminary version reads: "nouveaux-venus épris" (*Le Rempart de brindilles*, no. 761, AE-IV-22); the change toward a more ambiguous form, without a hyphen joining the two words, more easily permits this double reading.

63

haps (later) the malady, but it is also to be read in the imperative: lest beauty expire, it must be watered. The perspiring forehead is simultaneously a symptom of malady, brought about on the formal level by the odd placing of the comma, since normally, if present at all, it would follow "mal," forcing the reading of an adverb "surges forth badly, from our giddy brows." From the sickness evident in the face, even on the brow or the face of the text, the evidence evaporates. With it disappears the effect of the phonetic suggestion, leaving only an ellipsis sensed and never located.

La rose! → [l'arrose → eau] → fronts évaporés.

The enigmatic prose poems of *Abondance viendra* yield a profusion of double readings and approximate ambivalences, such as "Le leader[15] a tiré la vermine éclatante / The leader pulled [or attracted, as "attirait" has almost the same sound] the dazzling vermin," phonetic echoes ("la lave") and semantic repetitions, partially disguised: ("lacé . . . pédestres," where the pedestrian foot is an absent link for the lacing) together with the ellipses and other techniques. Here are the beginning and the conclusion of "Domaine" (MM, 110-11):

Tombe mars fécond sur le toit de chagrin.

. . . .

Faut-il *malgré* se réjouir?[8] (MM,110-11)

The contrast of the "tombe" (read not now as the verb "fall" but as the noun "tomb") with the concept of fecundity invites a closer look at another reading, where the memory of Valéry's "Cimetière marin" ("toit/toi") haunts the tomb on the surface; yet the imperative of the verb: "Tombe! mars fécond / Fall! fecund March" cannot be discarded. And the final ellipsis, already taken as a prime example of the tech-

[15] Albert Sonnenfeld suggests also the reading *Lieder*, as in Rilke's epitaph ("lieder / lider," song and eyelids).

[8] Fall fecund March on the roof of sorrow. / . . . / Must we *despite* rejoice?

64

nique, in connection with the motif of the breach, opens onto the infinite of a sense left undefined, by the typographic accentuation of the *malgré* (rejoices despite what?). Or is it a void, left on purpose, where the complete statement would be phrased: "malgré [rien]"? The apparent "closure" of this poem is in fact a formal openness—an interrogation mark—doubled by an omission at its center. The irony of the punctuation is incontestable. For a psychological interpretation of the effect on the reader, compare the statement: "Here is the minute of considerable *danger*: ecstasy in front of emptiness, new ecstasy in front of the fresh emptiness." (RBS,163) In the case of this formal and textual leap, the poet has, so to speak, framed the ellipsis by italicizing it, so that the "vide frais," the perforation freshly made in the text, will remain an obvious gap, serving eventually as a source: "Faire la brêche et qu'en jaillisse la flambée d'une herbe aromatique / Make the breach and may there flash forth from it the sudden flaming of an aromatic herb." (NT,67) The fragrance of these plants of René Char's countryside will return all along the path followed by the present essay.

Occasionally, as in "Front de la rose," the title appears as a preliminary enigma, whose ambiguity is reinforced inside the poem. For example, should the title "Recours au ruisseau" be read in the imperative: "Re-cours au ruisseau / Run back (or: flow back) to the stream"? Or as the formal designation of the source from which the fluid verse should take its substance: "[Ayez] recours au ruisseau / Rely on the stream"? Or is it simply the descriptive statement of this recourse which is the poem? The inextricable verbal meshing of these three possibilities is matched by a parallel interweaving of images in the final line, where gravel appears sparkling in the water as the stars sparkle in the sky. But, by a telescoping technique, one of the two original geographic components will be suppressed in the text, imposing its attributes on the other, with which it is finally identified: "le gravier qui brillait dans le ciel du ruisseau . . . / the gravel sparkling in the sky of the stream. . . ." (LM,61) (Compare

65

the same kind of transfer in "Attenants," one of the *Cinq poésies en hommage à Georges Braque*: "Les prairies me disent ruisseau / Et les ruisseaux prairie.") Under the tranquil appearance of the textual stream also there are revealed multiple levels of reference. The cosmic referent will be absorbed in the matter of the image-source: this compression, at first glance reductive, serves in fact to widen and deepen the interior dimensions of the text. The distinction high/low, which might have been taken in the literal sense, is interiorized and transposed to form the metaphysical background of the space inside which flow the currents and cross-currents of the poem itself, as well as its central image.

E. Convergence

> . . . puisque la raison ne soupçonne pas que ce
> qu'elle nomme, à la légère, absence, occupe le
> fourneau dans l'unité. (FM,39)

To illustrate the ways in which the two principal strategies reinforce each other—these "techniques" or "methods" seen always from the reader's point of view—we shall take a brief example of minimal change from the successive modifications of the second edition of *Les Matinaux*.[16] In the first version, an identification between poet and mountain is clear: "Nous avons en nous, sur notre versant tempéré. . . . / We have in us, on our temperate slope. . . ." No question is asked here; the mountain is localized, explicitly, its interior situation un-

---

[16] Bibliothèque littéraire Jacques Doucet, cote Ms.4912. Certain "préciosités" have been eliminated ("Doléances du feutre" as the title of the poem now called "Hermétiques ouvriers"), as well as some heavy echoes (for example, in "Qu'il vive!," a "navire chaviré" has been modified to a "barque chavirée.") Likewise, some notes and punctuation that needlessly complicated the surface of the text have also disappeared: in "Cet amour à tous retiré," there was an extra stanza in the first edition, followed by a series of suspension marks and an italicized note at the bottom of the page: "Rire énorme, coup de bâton et glas sur moi. . . ." The additional suppression of parentheses around the stanzas simplifies the final version of the poem.

derlined by an implicit repetition. (The passage is reminiscent of the one quoted earlier, in which the precipice within the house forces the inhabitants toward the summits, where they feel more at ease. To the interiorization of the mountain there was attached a certain irony, absent in the passage under discussion.) But in the second version, the convergence of mountain and poet is drawn further inside the text; taken for granted, it is left unsaid: "Nous avons sur notre versant tempéré. . . . / We have on our temperate slope. . . ." In the exchange between poet and nature it is impossible now to say which is likened to the other. The mountain is no more brought to the poet than the poet to the mountain. The text absorbs all else as exterior and interior landscape merge.

However, the textual evidence of the meeting of two or more elements does not subtract from the effect on the reader: the movement of the poem will always appear to be directed from the multiple to the one, that is, exactly the reverse of the movement which we place under the sign of plurivalence. Instead of reading, in the sense of an outward progression, as illustrated above ("Multiplicity, Plurivalence"), we read in this case toward a convergence, a "unité" felt as ineluctable. (As in "L'Absent," where the absent brother is still present, keeping the crucible of unity.) All the possible lines of compression lead toward this center, a compactness invisible yet dominant in each line it controls.

1. *Expressed*

First, there may be a logical progression, some explicit final identification, as evident as an argument in classical logic (although never explicit in the same sense as in a prosaic formulation—any comparison of the "evident" or the "expressed" with the less so is here considered only within the limits of poetry as Char conceives it and develops it). "Le soleil volait bas, aussi bas que l'oiseau. La nuit les éteignit tous deux. Je les aimais. / The sun was flying low, as low as the bird. The night extinguished both of them. I loved them." (LM,158) The relation of the sun to the bird begins as a

67

metaphor, continues as a conjunction, and ends in a union, in the eyes of the narrator appearing at the conclusion of the three observations. Thus the convergence operates little by little, as the length of the elements is reduced.

2. *Implied*

As an intermediate passage between an expressed convergence such as that just exemplified and an interior and suggested convergence, the poem "Jouvence des Névons" shows the work of the poet as it is gradually hidden from view. The first stanza of the poem contains a parallel negative structure (a "ruisseau sans talus" and an "enfant sans ami") to which the second stanza adds another element, openly: "Un rebelle s'est joint / Au ruisseau, à l'enfant, / A leur mirage. . . . // A rebel came to join / The stream, the child, / Their mirage. . . ." (LM,36) In the first edition, from 1950,[17] the poet adds a three-sentence note, of which only the third part is retained in the subsequent edition, figuring there as an epigraph. The two others are suppressed, as if they had made too clear the convergence of the elements: ("L'enfant, le ruisseau, le rebelle ne sont qu'un seul et même être qui se modifie suivant

---

[17] The poet marked the changes in RRF (1950)/Ms. 9358 (H7-IV-27). A comparison of the two versions shows the concision gradually obtained. For example, in the order of the texts: in the first version of *Les Transparents*, Laurent complains because "sa maîtresse n'est pas venue au rendez-vous (où il l'a attendue aussi). (SEC). Dépité, il s'en va (pour de bon)." The material between parentheses was suppressed in the second version as unnecessary. As an example of the minimal detail nonetheless important, we might consider the following passage, where two completely opposed elements are found on the surface of the text, the first perhaps determining the second: "C'est sur les hauteurs de l'été / Que le poète se révolte, / Et du brasier de la récolte / Tire sa torche et sa folie." (LM,25) The poem, entitled "Divergences," shows precisely the role of a divergence within a single letter. The same work can be followed, under its different aspects in the successive versions of *A une Sérénité crispée*, as they appear in the manuscript: see the partial analysis of variants in the chapter called "Trace."
Virginia A. La Charité (*The Poetics and the Poetry of René Char*, University of North Carolina Press, Chapel Hill, 1968) gives a list of variants between printed versions of several works.

les années. Il brille et s'éteint tour à tour, au gré de l'événement, sur les marches de l'horizon. / The child, the stream, the rebel, are only one and the same being modified according to the years. He shines and fades in turn, at the whim of the event, on the steps of the horizon.")[18] And precisely, the sentence kept as epigraph hints at the verbal suppression whose presence is still felt: "Dans l'enceinte du parc, le grillon ne se tait que pour s'établir davantage. / In the limits of the park, the cricket is silent only in order to impose itself the more." (LM,36)

3. *Interior*

In the poem "Marmonnement," the title, "Murmuring," predicts that the word will not be at its clearest in this text. The poet describes here the affection he feels for the wolf, "qu'on dit à tort funèbre, pétri des secrets de mon arrière-pays / wrongly called funereal, moulded with the secrets of my back country."[19] Everything suggests the animal: the secrecy, the harsh geography, the mountain chase, until the middle of the poem where suddenly a doubt penetrates as to the nature of the wolf, as to its identity in the psychological world, as to its name and particularly our understanding of its being: "Loup, je t'appelle, mais tu n'as pas de réalité nommable. De plus, tu es inintelligible. / Wolf, I call you, but you have no nameable reality. Moreover, you are unintelligible." (LM, 131) All at once a transfer is made from the wolf, solitary, self-consuming, ferocious by reputation and named only by humans, to the other sense of the word, not yet named, under the half-disguise of the animal (for the word "loup" signifies

[18] The poet describes the background of this text: since it was wartime, when all the men had left the villages except the old and feeble, who taught the rebellious boys.

[19] The figure of the wolf will return: this marginal being is situated near the center of many texts. In the brief statement written to introduce *Retour amont* (from May, 1966), Char insists that we remain, for the space of our living and our dying, with the wolves ("pour vivre et pour mourir, *avec les loups*"); their land is the barest possible one, that to which our "returning upland" takes us.

a mask as well as a wolf, both senses figuring in an ambiguous line of Paul Éluard: "Mon coeur et mon nom sont des loups."). Now the lack of "nameable reality" and the incomprehensibility reveal at least their reason, when one sense is replaced by, although kept within, the other; for the presence of the mask within the unspeakable reality of the wolf is to be retained, as a second sense partly grasped in the legend masking the wolf, here half-unmasked. "Sincérité du masque," says the poet elsewhere. (RBS,162)

Here the verbal techniques constitute one further mask, shielding the interior essence of the text. For as we look more closely, the poem seems to reveal another level of complexity beneath the surface. Does not the poet, attracted by the notion of the wolf, assume the disguise suggested, only to be himself implicated in its complications? The game appears to unfold further after the acknowledgment of the incomprehensible, or of what will be incomprehensible so long as it will have only its first sense: "Derrière ta course sans crinière, je saigne, je pleure, je m'enserre de terreur. . . . / Behind your maneless running, I am bleeding, weeping; I gird myself with terror. . . ." (LM,131)

The track of this bare or maneless running, as if stripped to its essential element—fear—denies the presence of an ordinary animal, whereas the poet is taken more and more into the text, whose mask, now become his own, he will use as if it were the poem: ["je m'en sers"]. This last, circular image by which he is himself caught as in the "piège à loup" from which he makes the trap of the poem, is doubly marked and masked, the ["trac"] implicit in the trace or "traque," the fear covered by the often deliberate confusion of language although alive forever in the poet's memory.[20] "Traque

[20] A boy watching over sheep for a cruel farmer loses two of them, flees up the Mont Ventoux, and is overtaken by night. He awakes there, guarded by the wolves throughout the time of darkness. Thus the sign marked on the side of the mountain is that of their guardian claws, and of their—and his—running. The memory of this boy, his grandfather, has not left the poet. (Manuscript in *Poems of René Char*.)

70

impitoyable où l'on s'acharne, où tout est mis en action contre la double proie: toi invisible et moi vivace. / Pitiless and unending pursuit, where all is set in motion against the double prey: you invisible and I perennial." This chase after the image and after the prey, whether the other or the self, is to be understood also as a sign of fear, all the more so since the unrolling of the text—or of the chase—is strengthened in intensity by all the literature of romantic texts and heroes, where the masked man simultaneously frightens and elicits pity. What is hunted here is thus a double prey ("double proie"), as the mask, the poet, the prey and the poem uniting them in a trap and a revelation, are all linked ("que sais-je?") in a pitiless language and difficult imagery mirroring the ideas of persecution and escape: "Continue, va, nous durons ensemble; et ensemble, bien que séparés, nous bondissons par-dessus le frisson de la suprême déception pour briser la glace des eaux vives et se reconnaître là. / Go on, we endure together; and together, although separate, we bound over the tremor of supreme deception to shatter the ice of quick waters and recognize ourselves there." The knowledge, clearly, is self-knowledge; the animal pursued is the poet, in whose personal mythology and in whose mind this poem and its profound reason for being have left their ancestral mark. The mumbling text continues a trail of fear, escape, and recognition within the hunter in the ascent of the mountain where (see *La Nuit talismanique*, p. 39) the circle of the sun marks on the mountain the enigmatic trace of the wolf's claws burned into the slope, a branding taken also into the text, only later to be revealed.[21]

The poet had already recommended the rapidity of the leap: "Être du bond," where being and the counsel given to being fuse into one. Like the wolf, his image and the image of his own memory, he bounds over this other wolf disguised by

---

[21] "He who fights with monsters should be careful lest he thereby become a monster. And if thou gaze long into an abyss, the abyss will also gaze into thee." No. 146, *Apophthegms and Interludes, Beyond Good and Evil*. [N,466]

71

name and legend, invisible and still the emblem of the hunted, toward an enduring beyond the waters of the present, into the future state. The ice, a false reflection shattered by the true recognition, is only a trap of Narcissus overcome for the departure for the "initiating summit" of a new beginning.

Behind the deepest texts, there is always this masked convergence of the saying and the hearing, where the reader is present in the same capacity as the poet: "Entends le mot accomplir ce qu'il dit. Sens le mot être à son tour ce que tu es. Et son existence devient doublement la tienne. / Hear the word accomplishing what it says. Feel the word becoming in its turn what you are. And its existence becomes doubly yours." (NP,70)

The reader also may be marked by the profound trace left in René Char by the upland but inward flight—the echo long murmuring in his memory, as in that of the poet. For in the opening out of this text, the recognition in its torment and its privilege is ours as well as his. Indeed the readings and re-readings have this as their primary purpose: "se reconnaître là / to recognize ourselves there."

RANGE: "UNE MONTAGNE DANS LE REGARD"

Qu'à toute réquisition un poème puisse efficacement en tout comme en fragments, parcours entier, *se confirmer*, c'est-à-dire *assortir ses errements*, m'apporte la preuve de son indicible réalité. (MM,141)

A. MEETING

1. *From Question to Question*

C'est qu'il y avait un pourquoi à lever. (P)

The mountainous poem[1] retains its difficulty of approach. The poet's observations will often appear as questions, and his questions as declarations. Several of the most pertinent statements on the situation of text and reader in this regard are to be found in *Seuls demeurent*—a title that is in all respects the necessary double of *La Parole en archipel*, since the word remains alone, in its unique habitation—here we might read: ["seule demeure"]—maintaining also its correspondence, as these fragments endure in the archipelago of the mind.

"Je sais où m'entravent mes insuffisances. . . . Ce soir, la grande roue errante si grave du désir peut bien être de moi seul visible . . . Ferai-je ailleurs jamais naufrage? / I know in what way my insufficiencies hamper me. . . . Tonight the great wandering wheel of desire, so grave, may well be visible

---

[1] As an example, within the text, of the interior mountain residing always at the center of the poet's imagination, we might take the following. In *Le Rempart de brindilles* (no. 756, AE-IV-22), "la chaîne de démentis" is directly suggested by a passage subsequently removed: "Nuit glacier éternel. Montagne de glaces." If the mountain is not always apparent, its presence is nevertheless felt more frequently than we might suppose from surface indications.

only to me . . . Shall I ever be shipwrecked elsewhere?"
(FM,36) Placed in the exact heart of the poem, this wheel
"errante"[2] indicates the difficulty of any unique or univocal
deciphering: its wandering does not detract from the wide
sweep of the wheel nor from the fatality of the desire thus
figured, the expression "grave" here bearing the same sense
as the title "Gravité" for the first in a major group of love
poems, "Le Visage nuptial." Akin in form and function to
the wheel of destiny turning in reverse, whose teeth tear to
shreds those standing in the way of its perverse functioning
(AC, first version), the nocturnal force replaces the lightness
of the day. "I know where . . .": the text begins by a closed
statement, intensely serious. A question turning around, the
meeting of interrogation and of an attainment within the
circle of the text which we might call a ring: this same form
recurs on the level of the image, turning like the wheel of
history or the simple watermill in the following text. Here
a possible answer is formed of the very matter of the interrogation itself within the circle of the poem:

"LÉONIDES"

Es-tu ma femme? Ma femme faite pour atteindre la rencontre du présent? L'hypnose du phénix convoite ta jeunesse. La pierre des heures l'investit de son lierre.

Es-tu ma femme? L'an du vent où guerroie un vieux
nuage donne naissance à la rose, à la rose de violence.

Ma femme faite pour atteindre la rencontre du présent.

Le combat s'éloigne et nous laisse un coeur d'abeille sur
nos terres, l'ombre éveillée, le pain naïf. La veillée file
lentement vers l'immunité de la Fête.

Ma femme faite pour atteindre la rencontre du présent.[a]
(FM,37)

---

[2] Or again, the adjective "errante" might be taken in the original
sense of the word: simply an itinerant going, or turning.

[a] Are you my wife? My wife made to attain the encounter of the
present? The phoenix hypnosis envies your youth. The hour-stone
invests it with its ivy / Are you my wife? The year of the wind where

The complex form of this poem seems to correspond with the rebirth of the phoenix to which "les lions ailés de la moisson / the winged lions of the harvest" in another text may allude, and also to the cyclic images of nature. Harvest ("le pain naïf") and rebirth are linked like death and life presided over by the "zealous lion" ("lion zélé"), a griffin half-hidden in the text or in the dormant gold of a yellow wheat field, awaiting the alchemical transmutation which will wake it.

The waiting is finally resolved by the sentences reborn from questioning, absorbing the question in an oblique answer. This indirect response is made first in the suppression of the question mark, then in the *ritardando* of the rhythm to make way for a reply which is the exact repetition of the first question: "Es-tu ma femme? ma femme faite. . . ? / Es-tu ma femme? . . . / Ma femme faite . . . / . . . / Ma femme faite. . . ." Finally, the identification of the "femme" with the "Fête," which signals the encounter of the couple in the revels[3] as the goal finally attained, assures to the participants an immunity to time's passing. It is acknowledged as definitive, although by a circular path which leads back to the beginning:

fête = ma femme faite (ma femme = Fête)

The text has the formal and thematic characteristics appropriate to rebirth: the old cloud's passing contrasts with the violent youth of the rose, watering the flower in accord with the poet's desire, natural and yet illogical in its reversal of

---

an old cloud battles gives birth to the rose, the rose of violence. / My wife made to attain the encounter of the present. / The combat withdraws and leaves us a bee's heart on our lands, the shadow awakened, the naive bread. The evening gathering streams slowly toward the immunity of the Revels. My wife made to attain the encounter of the present. "Femme" is perhaps nearer to "woman," but that does not fit the line.

[3] Char's language often has a Shakespearean quality. Compare, for instance, this fête with Theseus' opening speech in *A Midsummer Night's Dream*, with its "nuptial hour" (1.1) and its triumph and "revelling" (1.19).

the state of things: "Une rose pour qu'il pleuve / A rose so that it may rain." So that the rose may grow, the cloud weeps, too old for revels. The echoing structure responds to this wish of youthfulness like the phoenix always desiring and constantly fulfilled, contained, by all the age of myth, in the youthfulness of the poem's presence.

Like "Léonides," "Grège" is the double image of a question answered in the ground of a festival both explicit and implicit, verbal and psychological density converging in the brevity of a text.

"Grège"

La Fête, c'est le ciel d'un bleu belliqueux et à la même seconde le temps au précipité orageux. (. . .) C'est le grand emportement contre un ordre avantageux pour en faire jaillir un amour . . . Et sortir vainqueur de la Fête, c'est, lorsque cette main sur notre épaule nous murmure: "Pas si vite . . . ," cette main dont l'équivoque s'efforce de retarder le retour à la mort, de se jeter dans l'irréalisable de la Fête.[b] (LM,59)

Although this poem is part of *Les Matinaux*, inner joy and orderly celebration are shadowed by a circle belonging to death as to life. The motifs of festival and meeting reappear, but in a condensed form which shows a division at the center. Two epochs share the same moment: threshold and risk, hesitation and fever; from the marriage of the contraries there breaks forth once more the "first instant," not of a resurgence (as in the poem entitled "Les Premiers instants"), but of a love, waging battle against death in an equivocal scene. The meeting is here recognized as impossible except within the exterior limits of the text, where the concluding pagan revels, the equivalent of the feast in the preceding poem, are one

[b] The Revels, a sky of bellicose blue and in the same instant, a season of stormy precipitate. . . . The passion against an advantageous order so that a love may spring therefrom. And to exit victorious from the Revels, when this hand on our shoulder murmurs "Not so fast . . . ,"—this hand whose ambivalence tries to delay the return to death—is to cast oneself into the unrealizable Revels.

with those at the poem's outset. Death is, by implication, identified at last with the ritual celebration itself, consuming each victor.

The title already indicates this will of a reveler to gather up everything into one single bouquet: greige the muted color, with the suggestion of raw silk, as well as a psychological atmosphere and also a girl's name, and finally bearing the resonance of fireworks: a "feu grégeois" or Greek fire. A bonfire is born in the revels, containing the idea of death, at once the death of the poem and—since the poem is cyclical—its new beginning. This celebration meets with the revelation afresh from the revels. A poem whose illumination is provided by a mere couple of twigs: a word-color and a word-feast, yielding a textual conflagration where a phoenix is implicit.

Of a similar structure, the poem "Invitation" (LM,140) moves from an initial summons ("J'appelle les amours. . . . / I call the loves . . .") to a summons in echo ("J'appelle les amants. / I call the lovers.") Pursued by summer's scythe, the couples are stilled in the air of evening. To their inaction, embalming the air with its perfume but also with its mortal odor, the finale of the stone-cutter responds, like a pause in the dance or like the hand touching our shoulder in "Grège." The final summons encloses the text, like the return to the revels, so that the inner joy and the outward festival, the death called upon by ritual and temporarily delayed, meet within the ring of the poem's fire. Later, at the moment of *La Nuit talismanique*, the circular dance of the candle flame will make a graphic reply to the summons and the bonfire of this text turning, round.

2. *Oblique Setting*

> Mais peut-être notre coeur n'est-il formé que
> de la réponse qui n'est point donnée? (LM,119)

"Mission et révocation," the last text of *Seuls demeurent*, partly illuminates the theme of the encounter: "Devant les précaires perspectives d'alchimie du dieu détruit . . . j'interroge: 'Commandement interne? Sommation du dehors?' La terre s'éjecte de ses parenthèses illettrées. Soleil et nuit dans un or identique parcourent et négocient l'espace-esprit, la chair-muraille. . . . / Confronting the precarious perspectives of alchemy, of a destroyed god . . . I ask: Internal governing? Exterior orders? The earth ejects itself from its illiterate parentheses. Sun and night in an identical gold traverse and negotiate the space-mind, the flesh-wall. . . ." (FM,82) The alchemical perspective "of a destroyed god" gives way to a tension—between "l'espace-homme" and "la chair-muraille" —but beyond terrestrial limits and either-or interrogations. Knowledge is posed at the moment of speaking, in reply to the question posed: projecting itself beyond the millennial silence which would have kept it in suspense, like a paralyzed future. The "identical gold" in which the daylight and darkness are fused would seem to require a clear answer to the implicit interrogation which will follow upon the one explicit within the text: what will then replace death?

But, says the poet, in his complex universe things do not function only by contraries, and no thought is simple. Within his meditative texts are found often the quietest of answers, or those couched as further questions. From the latter, or those concluding the text, an entire scale of responses can be perceived, generally ambiguous as to sense and heavy with multiple implications, reopening the poem exactly at the instant when the unwary reader might have expected an ending.

A remark, inserted in the first manuscript version of *La Bibliothèque est en feu* and subsequently scratched through,[4] applies to this oblique presentation of the question: "Le poème qui nous attache, a un arrière-pays dont seule la clôture est sombre. Nul pavillon ne flotte longtemps sur cette banquise qui, au gré de son caprice, se donne à nous et se reprend. / The poem which holds us has a back country

[4] First version (no. 792, AE-IV-29). The remark is taken up again later; but here it is the original context which interests us.

whose enclosure only is dark. No flag floats long on this ice-floe which, according to its whim, offers itself to us and then pulls back."

a. *Question and Divergence*

On the simplest level, a fault or slippage may be noticed between the question and what precedes it, as if a transition sentence had been eliminated.

"Rapport de marée," a poem mentioned above in connection with its form, opens with a double question, and concludes with a single one: "Terre et ciel ont-ils renoncé à leurs féeries saisonnières, à leurs palabres subtiles? Se sont-ils soumis? / . . . / Mais, cette fois, nous ne ferons pas route ensemble. / Bien-aimée, derrière ma porte? // Have earth and sky abandoned their seasonal wonders, their subtle parley? Have they given in? /. . . / But this time, we shall not travel together. / Beloved, behind my door?" (LM,139)

This natural couple of the beginning, speaking in an undertone like the "parley" of the text, no more explains its intentions than does the poem itself. The path which the poet will not follow (with us? with her?) or will follow alone, will be either stormy or calm; the person loved either is or is not behind the door, will or will not answer. This question is questionable: might it be only an introduction to another conversation, that one inaudible? In like fashion, the poem is situated at the edge and not in the center of understanding; we assume that the door will not open, that the reader will not step over the threshold.

b. *Question and Return*

Another sort of reading is indicated when the conclusion of the text signals the necessity of a fresh beginning instead of a deliberately unresolved meaning. "Dans la marche" ends in an ambiguous threshold moment, of dawn or dusk: "Pour l'aurore, la disgrâce c'est le jour qui va venir; pour le crépuscule c'est la nuit qui engloutit. Il se trouva jadis des gens d'aurore. A cette heure de tombée, peut-être, nous voici. Mais pourquoi huppés comme des alouettes? / For the dawn, disgrace is the day about to come; for twilight, the night swallowing up. Formerly there were people of dawn. At this moment of falling, perhaps, we're here. But why crested like larks?" (LM,197) Too simple an answer would throw off balance the delicate relationship:[5] the key word "perhaps" serves to block an exact symmetry: moreover, this formal and psychological hesitation is already underlined by doubt in the text.

Like the central word "pourtant" acting as a grammatical lever for the poem "J'habite une douleur"—a poem itself placed at the unstated center of this essay, marked only by our recurring allusions to it—the word "peut-être" functions here as a central source for the psychological nuances in the flux of this text. But these "hesitations," poetic rather than personal, will never be allied with the "incertitudes" the poet loathes: for the mountain larks enter the text to circle in the evening air, forcing a return to an obvious equation (we, like larks, are of the evening slope). "Huppés" because these red feathers of the mountain larks have at their end a dark tuft, as the crimson sky either of dawn ("ce brisant de rougeur") or of sunset ("Ce très haut fruit couchant qui saigne / La dernière étincelle"), makes way for evening, at the somber outer limit of the poem, and of the life, which it represents. Moreover, Char's reader, conscious of how each flash of perception refers to another, for example, the characteristic soaring of the lark recalls the image of the swallow and his swirling flight wherein the storm is formed and the garden is planned. (FM,194) Thus the image of the return or the *renvoi* itself, essential to this reading, and a reminder of its structure, is inserted within the poem's advance.

[5] Another example of an intimate intuition in its spontaneity: the poet tells us that Heidegger, without having to consult him, explained this image by saying one day to Jean Beaufret, his French translator, that not all larks are crested, only those of the mountains. On the slope of the mountain, beings of dawn or of twilight, they announce what they will never see. Like the poet, adds René Char.

c. *Question Opened*

Rather than being inflected toward a possible point of
closure, the question may remain entirely open: "De même
qu'il y a plusieurs nuits différentes dans l'espace, il y a plusieurs dieux sur les plages du jour. /. . . / Meilleur fils du
vieux disque solaire et au plus près de sa celeste lenteur. Cette
envie substantielle se répéta, se répéta puis sa tache se perdit.
/ Nuit à loisir recerclée, qui *nous* joue? / Just as there are several different nights in space, there are several gods on the
shores of day. /. . . / Best child of the old solar disk and
nearest to its celestial slowness. This substantial longing came
again, came again, then its spot vanished. / Night at leisure
re-hooped, who plays *us*?" (NP,95) (JG) The poem's form
corresponds to the daily cycle moving from nocturnal to diurnal rhythms, turning slowly like another disk. The central focus—"plusieurs dieux"—appears on the horizon at the outset,
but furnishes the implied basis for the final question, to which
the answers are as numerous as the gods and nights in Char's
universe. The "tache" or the "tâche" of self-identification with
the celestial body by its preferred offspring fades out by repetition, whether a spot gradually fainter or an effort gradually
weaker, until the final scene (itself apparently recircling)
where in a nocturnal landscape, the leisurely spinning of man
at the low point of his activity is reduced to a record turning
aimlessly, as if on a phonograph—"Cycle bas," (PPC,232)—
or then a revolution in tune with that of the stars, with whose
figures we write our own dreams (see, for instance, "Possessions extérieures"). The text in its entirety reads as a warning
against an unnecessary speed, in favor of a universal rhythm
of an "éparse lenteur," as in *La Nuit talismanique:* "On
a jeté de la vitesse dans quelque chose qui ne le supportait
pas." (NT,85) It is also a celebration of the plurality of
enigma, in a tribute to those gods within us and without us
to be found in "La Flamme sédentaire" (NT,84) and other
texts. We must adjust our cycle to theirs.

Yet the occasional juncture of the slow with the rapid is

frequently invisible and always placed beyond us, in the space of our reading, whose conceptual limit is marked by an interrogation. "Cotes" in *Le Nu perdu* supposes a meeting beyond even the sheaves gathered at harvest and disaster itself, an improbable encounter between two rhythms as opposed as the attitudes of hope and despair: the final question, disquieting, leads again to no answer: "Nous avons les mains libres pour unir en un nouveau contrat la gerbe et la disgrâce dépassées. Mais la lenteur, la sanguinaire lenteur, autant que le pendule emballé, sur quels doigts se sont-ils rejoints? / We have our hands free to unite in a new contract the sheaf and the disgrace exceeded. But deliberation, sanguinary deliberation, as well as the runaway pendulum, on what fingers have they joined?" (NP,65)

The sheaves are left standing, but in a new order, after this "réponse interrogative" as Char calls it later. (AC)

d. *Question Sacrificed*

In a few cases the movement toward the enigmatic seems to reverse itself, from the more veiled to the less so, particularly in texts of a strong moral content where the poet decides to render his thought apparent. The meaning of the following two-line declaration is clear in its definitive version:

"CONTREVENIR"

Obéissez à vos porcs qui existent. Je me soumets à mes dieux qui n'existent pas.

Nous restons gens d'inclémence.[c] (LM,201)

But in the printers' proofs, an expression which had sliced the last sentence in two, rendering it ambiguous, was eliminated by the poet. The first version read:

Nous restons, mes semblables, gens d'inclémence.[6]

[c] Obey your pigs who exist. I submit to my gods who do not. / We remain men for inclemency.
[6] No. 783 (AE-IV-34).

This preliminary version permitted two readings: the "We remain" could have been interpreted as standing alone, linguistically and conceptually separated from the inclement weather and the difficult times by the poet's equals, they also made for harsh moral climates. The apposition could have applied to either of the first subjects, or to both. The final version includes together, as if in one moment, the poet and those he chooses to consider his peers.

B. CALL AND ECHO

Pourquoi ce chemin plutôt que cet autre? Pourquoi celui-ci? Où mène-t-il pour nous solliciter si fort? Chacun de nous hésite quelques secondes au moment de poursuivre sa route. Soudain du fond de l'horizon l'appel silencieux monte et nous prend. Allons. Et que l'inconnu nous adopte. On ne marche jamais en vain.

(From a first version, *De Moment en moment*)[7]

1. *Flint*

"Le muet silex de midi écartelé" (FM,61): a secret source of fire, the flint, silent until split apart at the noontime separation of the day in two, casts an exigent light. As if still covered with earth, it appears beneath the textual surface, hidden often in the center of the poem, although its presence is not forgotten, nor its power. For the flint represents a luminous future, a potential flame trembling under the twigs sometimes dispersed, sometimes gathered in a bundle for burning: "Le silex frissonnait sous les sarments de l'espace / The flint was shivering under the vine-shoots of space." (FM,60)

This will be the key image representing the art of the past, all that has been accomplished with the greatest effort. In another epoch, a flint stylus would have chiseled these texts,

[7] No. 702 (AE, IV-11).

as it traced the heavy but delicate profile of the bisons engraved in the prehistorical grottoes of Lascaux and the Font-de-Gaume, profiting always from the irregularities of the stone walls to accentuate the forms in relief, where certain lines protrude, and others recede. In similar fashion, the best lighting in which to study these texts will be an unequal one, like that cast by a lamp with a wavering flame, or by the candle in *La Nuit talismanique* which guides the last part of this essay, leading it from source and fragment to meditation.

The previous discussion called "Lyre" developed a group of associations between reading and the flint. If the complete sense of the image can only be seized after its potential ramifications throughout multiple readings, a triple pattern can nonetheless be seen to emerge with insistence:

pierre de silex—to inflame
burin de silex—to trace
lampe de silex—to illuminate

The simple evocation of this image charged with a long past calls to the foreground all our ancestral links. The following passage, more discreet than clarifying in its illumination, is taken from *Les Compagnons dans le jardin*, with its implicit invitation for the reader to join the younger poets to whom the poem is explicitly addressed. It gathers several aspects of the image into one single bundle, figuratively placed near the primitive fire: "After the departure of the harvesters, on the high plains of Ile-de-France, scarcely is this small sharpened flint from the earth in our hand before there issues from our memory an equivalent kernel, the kernel of a dawn whose change and whose end we think we shall never see; only its sublime blush and its lifted countenance." (LM,152)

The sharpened flint could have drawn on grotto walls, or in turn made other tools, as certain of Char's poems seem to have been flaked off—"éclaté"—from a larger surface by a hammerstone, as it was suggested above. (The very word *éclat* contains within it a suggestion of this sharp fragment: a "pierre éclatée" might yield a series of Char's aphorisms.) But once taken over by man, without losing its almost magical primitive power, it sets up a net of correspondences, suggesting a timeless and unchanging dream where the red of a flame indicates a future hope more intense than that of the single uncertain dawn which it also includes: "La rougeur des matinaux." The metaphor of the visage is associated with celebration in the chapter on meeting and will then return in the "Cycle of the Warring Couple." Here it might be that of a beast or a man, of a size befitting a great statue, into whose side an immense difficulty is engraved.

Opposed to the facile current of ordinary words, the durable trace of the hardest silex remains throughout Char's work, offering its strength to the verbal ascent of the "Visage nuptial," despite its brief expanse, a model of epic complexity. The primitive struggle marked on the cavern walls of Lascaux and Font-de-Gaume must give its precision and its violence to contemporary poetry: "Il faut réapprendre à frapper le silex à l'aube, à s'opposer au flot des mots. / Seuls les mots, les mots aimants, matériels, vengeurs, redevenus silex. . . . / We must learn again to strike flint at dawn, to stand firm against the flow of words. / Only words, magnetic, material, avenging, become flint once more. . . ." (AC,15)

2. *Passage by the Hand*

The implicit link between the three great *working* images of Char—that is, flint, bread, and iron—is the human hand. A cycle of poems revolves about this image in *Retour amont*, to which we shall return later; at this point in the path it suffices simply to consider the importance of this most concrete and yet abstract container, holding all that is created, harvested, gathered, protected, inflicted, and suffered. The frequent recurrence of the verb "pétrir" translates an attitude: the hand molds the text and the figures peopling the landscape, like the "loup pétri des secrets de mon arrière-pays."

A meditation written, or sculpted, at the Rodin Museum invokes the collective force of these hands whose partisan the poet is, placing himself voluntarily "on their side":

> Toutes les mains sur une pierre,
> Les mains de pourpre et les dociles,
> Pour deux actives qui distillent.
>
> Mains, par temps sublime, que l'air fonde
> au même instant que l'arc.[d] (LM,128)

. . . .

The concluding image of the bow, or of the arch, like that of the bridge reappearing in a capital text of *Aromates chasseurs* and discussed at the end of our study, links, crosses, and causes to correspond; it turns in a half-circle, and is used, like the hands building it, or grasping it, for moments of traversal and of meeting.

3. *Bread, Iron, Furnace*

The elementary image of bread, conveying the poet's care for the everyday, carries a suggestion not unlike that of the hand which serves to knead or sculpt it ("pétrir"). By its own past it suggests the wheat field; by its present, the meaning of work and the value of the simple; and by its extension into the future, the suffering provoked by the prolongation of this work. The three developments of the image are traditional: to put one of them into play is instantly to call upon a whole system of implications. For example, the path linking the bread to the wheat involves the whole family of feelings gathered around the harvest, so that the expression: "pain de lumière" (FM,74) brings with it the radiant August field, which in its turn suggests the burning fruit-dish in the summer heat of *Le Nu perdu*. The images are each linked to the others by the freest of chains, like the diverse and even divergent meanings of one word. Nothing better explains the system of

---

[d] All hands on one stone, / Hands crimson and those docile, / For two active ones, distilling. / Hands, in sublime weather, founded by air at the same moment as the bow.

possible resonances around one central image than a simple remark about the births and the lightning-flashes settling in a fountain, gathering and rippling the waters over the "sour bread" of a poet's imagination of circumstances like the incrustrations about the stick plunged into the water, according to Stendhal's theory of crystallization in *De l'Amour*. "Gravitaient autour de son pain aigre les circonstances des rebondissements, des renaissances, des foudroiements et des nages incrustantes dans la fontaine de Saint-Allyre." (FM,68-9) The eventual meeting of all the poems in one retrospectively shared source and fountain is added to each particular use, in the collective work of poetry. The notion of a nuptial lyre is stretched to become a "lyre commune," in the sense that a fruit is called common, or a reading shared. The bread-maker, at his work of clearing his inner silence, finds a faint echo of the pine tree ("pain/pin"), but it is only an echo.

Sketching in the simplest fashion a partial profile of this image, we might, for example, consider only the ways in which it furnishes a major source for the *Fureur et mystère* of that collection, where the examples already cited were also found; each repetition colors the central image with nuances not apparent at first sight, like the progressive ripplings about the "bread" of the fountain.

Bread and light: in a line of "Le Visage nuptial," at the height or the "roof" of the text, and also signifying here the summit of the act of love, "le pain suffoque à porter coeur et lueur / Bread suffocates bringing heart and light." (FM,60) The image is juxtaposed to an invocation to the streams, so that the renewing power of water and the radiance of bread and all that it signifies shed upon each other a reciprocal gleam. It is also in that sense that we read, in "Léonides": "Le combat s'éloigne et nous laisse un coeur d'abeille sur nos terres, l'ombre éveillée, le pain naïf." (FM,37) Simple bread, in preparation for the revels and the ritual always renewed, therefore naive, or freshly baked, will bring with it the calm luminosity of peace sufficient through the shadows for the rebirth of each image.

87

Bread illuminates also in its breaking and, like the text, by being shared.[8] In Char's work, it signifies a desire for unity to be found once more on the other side of the fatigue earning it, but also the suffering of being broken, as we are broken, "rompu," necessarily by our work. The bread, in two halves or in pieces, arouses an ardent wish for the healing of the parts: "Guérir le pain / Heal the bread," (FM,135) expresses an outgoing impulse toward a human community of individuals grouped around the most essential nourishment, image of a life in common which itself takes part not only in elemental depth but in the widest reach of a ritual celebrated on the level of the daily: "Attabler le vin / Bring the wine to the table." The bread cured from its division and joining the wine at the table shared: a manna continuing life, but, says the poet, bread itself is sick at present; like wheat, like life.

Under the triple aspect—bread = work = light—a breadmaker or lover or builder in his interior silence sees his construction, human or material, finally clarified by the light of August in which "les dimensions" are no longer separate, the fruit of one crossing into the other for another essential sharing. Bread carries illumination here as in the above quotation from "Le Visage nuptial." The spaces traversed in this light lead toward a unity of which freedom is still a vital part, as the "dimensions franchies" are also those formal moments stretching between the sentences like islands or fragments in

---

[8] "Au tour du pain de rompre l'homme, d'être la beauté du point du jour." (FM,194) The elementary simplicity of the image of bread and its division had suggested to us at one moment the possibility of a thought which might be equally simple. But all corresponds: human work and celestial radiance share a time of ashes before the phoenix is renascent: "Ah! aujourd'hui tout se chante en cendres, l'étoile autant que nous." ("Faire du chemin avec. . . ," 1976)

See also Hölderlin's elegy "Brot und Wein," where he "develops his notion of alternating eras or cycles of Day and Night, epiphany and retraction . . . likening history to natural processes." (*Friedrich Hölderlin: Poems and Fragments*, tr. and ed. Michael Hamburger, Ann Arbor, University of Michigan, 1967, p. 609.) Compare with Char's poem "Même si . . . ," on the alternation of day and night (NP,95), discussed also in this chapter.

appearance detached, but in reality joined by their significance: "Dimension rassurée. . . ." In the same text, the initial
image of breathing, work, and self-liberation ("L'homme fuit
l'asphyxie . . . se délivrera par les mains / Man flees asphyxia
. . . he will find freedom by his hands") is retrospectively infused with all the light of exterior and interior construction, as
the mountain is exterior and interior, in the world and in the
vision. The poet's daily work is that of joining, whether the
links are visible or not: "je bats le fer des fermoirs invisibles.
/ I strike the iron of invisible hinges." (FM,19)

Again the homonyms "fer" and "faire" meet like another
pair of invisible hinges themselves, in a verbal correspondence: "fermoirs." For the "faiseur de pain" in his bread-
baking and the poet ("je bats le fer") share in a cooperative
work for which the hearth functions as an image at once
everyday, poetic, and alchemical: as an oven for the baking
of the common bread—thus the poet cuts short his farewells,
"to be there when the bread comes from the oven"—as a
furnace for trying metals and characters, and as the crucible
at the heart of alchemical unity ("L'Absent"). The heat of this
image carries over to that of the iron rod plunged into the
river to harden, the "fer" conveying, by extension, all the
work of passion ("Post-scriptum"). In *Partage formel*, whose
title takes on still another sense in the celebratory sharing of
the work, poetry, which refuses reduction as it refuses the
loss of freshness or the loss of passion, finds a metaphor at
once optimistic and simple in a song of a winter night, a poor
bakery, and a bread of a most modest radiance: "elle chante
la nuit de l'hiver dans la pauvre boulangerie, sous la mie d'un
pain de lumière." (FM,74) A more somber nuance is seen
in the period of the Resistance; the poem "Chant du refus:
début du partisan" sings of the man who made suffering into
bread, in the reddening heat of a slow struggle: "Celui qui
panifiait la souffrance n'est pas visible dans sa léthargie rou-
geoyante." (FM,48) The particular note of this song is prolonged in all the allusions to a heroic duty, whether of the

poet or the child, as he "plunges" his vision into the smelting hearth ("L'enfant . . . plongeait d'un seul trait ses yeux dans le foyer de fonte rouge," in the poem "Le Devoir," FM,43).

This strongest and most vital side of the image of bread is also inscribed under the sign of generosity and willingness, for the bread is "secourable," brings succor, like its maker, the poet. Nor is there here any sense that the longest and hardest work is in any way limited to one gender any more than the other. The ritual symbolized by the well reaches beyond it and beyond the celebrations of any cult but the poetic. The poem "Yvonne," given its real name only after the death of the person whose memory and whose work, in the fullest sense, it commemorates, joins by a day-long giving the well to the fountain of rebirth, matches thirst ("Ô ma Soif anxieuse") to as generous a welcome as that offered in "Bienvenue" or "Seuil": the poem is subtitled: "La Soif hospitalière." By the rim of the well, what was formerly divided is joined again: the beginning and the end of day, as well as man's work and woman's hands: "De l'éveil au couchant sa manoeuvre était mâle." (NP,30) Near the "reflowering" of its waters—the ripples spreading out or blossoming from the dipping of the bucket—daily nourishment quenches a spiritual thirst and an actual hunger. The substance once divided is made whole, taking within itself all the force of water, as if the bread made entire could now in fact bring the wine to the table where it can be shared. The possible depth of daily ritual—protected from maudlin sentimentality by the difficulty of the verbal medium by which it is generally conveyed —reveals through the simplest images another entire landscape, not mountainous, yet sufficient in its own range.

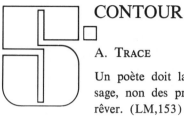

CONTOUR

A. TRACE

> Un poète doit laisser des traces de son pas-
> sage, non des preuves. Seules les traces font
> rêver. (LM,153)

The summit-texts of René Char appear in
profile. They are neither colored nor ample,
but rather, scarce in their density, tightly enclosed. Rarely do
they offer a scene filled with indications sufficient to satisfy
at a first reading: "Congé à vous, mes indices. . . ." A glance
at the construction work may offer a glimpse into the "tunnels dérobés" and the "pistes captieuses" which echo and
summon (RBS,174)—a momentary sighting of the half-
rubbed out trail, of the line half-sketched, or some indication
by which to distinguish the "être qui projette" from the "être
qui retient" (FM,77). As a massive psychological backdrop
against which these formal traces appear in relief, as if made
by stone instruments on the irregular walls of the brief caverns
of texts, one single sentence from *L'Age cassant* may serve,
paradoxically.[1] It shows by a slight modification in form, a
description at once extreme and positive, the exact opposite
of the progression toward an effacement of outline which will
be seen in the subsequent series of examples.

1. *Backdrop*

1º J'ai, je le crois, la respiration agressive. (first version)
2º J'ai de naissance la respiration agressive. (RBS,180)

In the definitive version: "Ever since I was born, I have had
an aggressive respiration," there is neither hesitation, as
in the "I think" of the former one, nor the suggestion of a
momentary situation, which might eventually be altered. It
is by opposition to this aggressive, taut breathing that we

---

[1] No. 878 (AE-IV-7).

91

must read the modifications—sometimes scarcely visible, usually tending toward the ambiguous—seeing the irregular changes as partially effaced frescoes, or fragments like those of Heraclitus, around which others have disappeared or are disappearing. Our aim would be always to give to the *effaced or ambiguous line* its real importance. The two qualities are often associated, particularly for the reader who will retain from the original direction of thought only that which can be deduced from the indication effaced. "The flight line of the poem," says the poet, "should be sensible to all" (FM, 111); but since this "magician of insecurity" (FM,66) voluntarily chooses a position of risk for his work (the risks of incomprehension, of saying little, among others), he will place himself, with the reader, in front of the trace that will never serve as a monument, in order to see therein the "ashes always unfinished." (FM,66) But in the occasional melancholy of his voice, there is neither sentimentality nor resignation: his unrest is his poem.

2. *The Way of the Work*

Upon occasion, brevity requires the longest path. In the first draft of *A une Sérénité crispée* the simple title: "Art bref" went through a number of stages to attain its two monosyllables.

> Bref
> Bref cahier
> Tranche de cahier
> Brièvement, d'un cahier (AUSC:B)

The notebook of work opens toward a unique and complex saying. "La poésie c'est *cela* de préférence à cet autre. / Poetry is *that* in preference to the other." (First draft of AUSC:A)

3. *Ambiguity*

The most obvious form of this search for the ambiguous, or more properly, for an expression in which the ambiguous

92

will not be reduced to the unequivocal, is the transformation of the affirmative to the interrogative. For example, in *Le Rempart de brindilles*[2] (RB:C), the following fragment, worked over repeatedly: 2° "Je crois en Lui: il n'est pas. Je ne m'en rapporte pas à lui: est-Il / I believe in Him: he is not. I don't rely on him: is He?" (LM,118) At first the sense was completely different, the tone far surer: 1° "Je ne crois pas en Lui: Il est. / I don't believe in Him: He is." The distance between the two illustrates the tendency of a certain aspect of Char's work, encouraging a complexity of multiple meanings.

Reworking serves also to reduce the verbose: in "Les Inventeurs" (LM,69), excess verbiage is clearly condemned, by the simple suppression of a single line. The course of future events takes no account of a human, verbal intervention, which adds nothing to the emotion naturally aroused:

1° Oui, l'ouragan allait [bientôt] venir;
il n'y avait pas à douter. Mais cela valait-il la peine que l'on en parlât? [et qu'on dérangeât l'avenir?]
Là où nous sommes, il n'y a pas de crainte urgente.
2° Oui, l'ouragan allait bientôt venir;
Mais cela valait-il la peine que l'on en parlât, et qu'on dérangeât l'avenir?
Là où nous sommes, il n'y a pas de crainte urgente.[a]

The laconic nature of Char's writing is striking. Of two more complex examples, the first concerns the transformation of an observed fact into a question touching on the future. Revealing a laborious and long-meditated process, the text we see as situated at the summit of the series *Lascaux* shows, within the corrections made of the proofs, serious

[2] No. 683 (AE-V-2). The title "Joue et dors" (play and sleep) suggests "Jouets d'or" (golden toys), poems ranged therefore on the side of a lighter inspiration.

[a] Yes, the hurricane was soon to come; / There was no doubting it. / But was it worth mentioning and disquieting the future? / Where we are, there is no pressing fear.

alterations in the poem's resonance. This passage sounds as a prelude, more questioning than tragic, to the texts of *Le Nu perdu* and *Aromates chasseurs*:

"TRANSIR"

Cette part jamais fixée, en nous sommeillante, d'où jaillira DEMAIN LE MULTIPLE.
L'âge du renne, c'est-à-dire l'âge du souffle. Ô vitre, ô givre, nature conquise, dedans fleurie, dehors détruite!
Insouciants, nous exaltons et contrecarrons justement la nature et les hommes. Cependant, terreur, au-dessus de notre tête, le soleil entre dans le signe de ses ennemis.
La lutte contre la cruauté profane, hélas, voeu de fourmi ailée. Sera-t-elle notre novation?
Au soleil d'hiver quelques fagots noués et ma flamme au mur.
Terre où je m'endors, espace où je m'éveille, qui viendra quand vous ne serez plus là? (*que deviendrai-je* m'est d'une chaleur presque infinie).[b] (LM,105)

The poetic motto TOMORROW THE MANIFOLD invoked at the outset of this essay in relation to a technique and a tendency, now reveals its fuller significance, in relation to a history continuing. Of the reindeer age named in this text as its moment, we have almost entirely destroyed the traces just by our living, as, on the walls of Lascaux, the paintings were damaged by our breathing, a thoughtless intrusion of present nature upon a past culture. But the past holds us still by its ancient rites: the astrological signs half-hidden on the cave's

---

[b] This never stilled part, slumbering in us, from which will spring TOMORROW THE MANIFOLD. / The age of the reindeer,—that is, the age of breathing. O window-pane, o hoarfrost, o conquered nature, in flower within, outside destroyed! / Thoughtlessly we exalt and oppose nature and men, nothing less. Meanwhile, terror overhead, the sun is entering the sign of his enemies. / The struggle against profane cruelty, alas, a winged ant's vow. Will it be our renewal? / In the winter sunshine a few bundles of faggots and my fire by the wall. / Earth on which I go to sleep, space into which I wake, who will come when you are no longer there? (*what shall I become* has for me an almost infinite warmth). (JG)

ceiling—or, by transposition, glimpsed on the whitewashed ceiling of the room where "L'Extravagant" lies dreaming— indicate that the moon enters the solar sign ("la lune devient solaire," in a preliminary version, then suppressed)[3] and that the sun changes its sign, in its turn.

A ritual of identification with an ancestral indigence— celebrating the simplicity and bareness which form the principal virtues in *Le Nu perdu*—takes place near the sparse fire of these few bundles of kindling, by the projection of a shadow against the wall. The place seems designated by the traces of a former outline, in a superposition of present man on a figure half-man and half-bird, and of a dying bison. Firelight illuminates the poet's question as to the human future at the close of the text, where the typographical stress responds to the adage stressed at the beginning, communicating to it a warmth, and necessarily, a shadow: "DEMAIN LE MUL-TIPLE⟷ *Que deviendrai-je?*" The text pierced through with cold is nevertheless infused with flame. The rest of Char's work is an answer to this enduring question.

But this question itself leads to the next: "La lutte . . . sera-t-elle notre novation?" First, in the ambiguous suggestion of the adjective become also a verb: "la lutte profane" (the struggle at once profane and profaning) as in the other examples encountered in the work, "la rose violente" (the rose both violent and violating) and the pen making innocent by its own innocence (as if derived from the verb "innocenter"). This passage is by far the most worked over.[4] The first version shows no ambiguity in the simple observation:

[3] No. 736 (AE-IV-17).

[4] No. 762 (AE-IV-22). In view of the importance of this passage within the work of René Char, as a self-examination and as a consideration of the roles of poet and reader in their common innocence and culpability, we give here two of the early versions of this passage, in their entirety: the first, called "mauvais" and scratched out by the poet, announces several future texts. The words in parentheses were marked out in the manuscript; the words in brackets were added subsequently.

No. 758 (AE-IV-22)

1° Prends garde [quelquefois] aux mots auxquels ton esprit con-

1° La lutte contre la cruauté profane n'est plus un voeu de fourmi ailée. Elle est notre novation.[c]

The verb "être," colorless and free of any doubt, forms a sure center for the passage toward a lesser certainty. In a second version, tried out on the same manuscript, the interrogation comes to light in the double role of the word "profane" as a verb-adjective, as the initial negative statement disappears, by a slope which may be a "piste captieuse."

---

fère une infaillibilité de longue haleine, un pouvoir de fine manoeuvre. Ne lâche pas étourdiment quelque proposition dangereuse dont tu n'entends pas précisément le sens [sur les pentes de ton volcan] ni ne mesures soigneusement la portée. Ton lecteur sera (souvent) pratiquement quelqu'un que ta spéculation arme mais que ta plume innocente. C'est (de plus) un campeur imprudent. Hors la poésie et ses phrases passionnées, (elle) la prose absolument libre, parce que chez elle le remède et le mal sont [inséparables] dans la même coulée. (prends garde. Un oeillet n'est pas sans analogie avec une blessure dont le sang mousse. Il suggère de l'accompli.)

No. 762 (AE-IV-22)
2° Hors la poésie et ses phrases passionnées, il te faut [quelquefois] prendre garde aux mots que tu écris [aux panacées que tu prononces], auxquels ton esprit confère un infaillibilité de longue haleine [et la faculté de fine manoeuvre]. Qui sera ton lecteur? Quelqu'un pratiquement que ta spéculation arme, mais que ta plume innocente? Cet oisif [sur ses coudes] à sa fenêtre? Ce campeur imprudent? Ce meurtrier encore sans objet? Tu ne sais pas. Prends garde [quand tu peux] aux mots que tu écris.

The work leading to the definitive version is particularly arduous here, and for good reason. This meditation on writing involves also the notions of fault and of innocence obsessive in all Char's work. The following is the definitive version; the parentheses indicate the changes in proof.

No. 783 (AE-IV-34)
3° Et la faculté de fine manoeuvre? Qui sera ton lecteur? Quelqu'un que ta spéculation arme mais que ta plume innocente. Cet oisif, sur ses coudes? Ce criminel encore sans objet? Prends garde, quand tu peux, aux mots que tu écris, malgré leur ferme distance. (Tu ne sais pas.)

[c] 1° The struggle against profane cruelty is no longer a winged ant's vow. It is our renewal. 2° The struggle against profane cruelty? Alas, a winged ant's vow. This morning it is our renewal.

2° La lutte contre la cruauté profane? Hélas, voeu de fourmi ailée. Ce matin elle est notre novation.

The phonetic repetition apparent in the first version: "ailée / elle est"[5] now has another element inserted between its halves, and that of temporal specification: the present morning marking a new beginning and a future interrogation.

In the final version, inserted in the text quoted above, the question is transferred to the last sentence, the first retaining its ambiguity: is it simply a wish? or a vow? And the question as to a possible beginning is posed in the future, thus preparing the double interrogation of the conclusion, explicit and implicit: "what will come?" leading to: "what shall I become?" an insistent question in Char's meditation.

4. *Distance Shared*

Le Rempart de brindilles establishes a path along a series of what one might call "des brindilles éclatantes," that is, twigs at once radiant in themselves, and potentially on fire, for the illumination of the text and the source of its ardor; they are, moreover, apt to splinter that which they touch, like the "pierres éclatantes." The last prose poem, at the rampart's end, reveals the same procedures we have signaled: transfer of interrogation, insertion or suppression of details to obtain a subtler and more ambiguous effect, a distancing of the text in relation to the reader. The entire passage has been greatly altered, although the perspective taken here—on the rampart as elsewhere—is deliberately selective: "To prefer *that* to the other. . . ."

The passage of particular interest from this viewpoint concerns the reader and the relationship of reader to author. A first version crossed out by the poet, who calls it "mauvais,"

---

[5] Compare Paul Éluard's prose poem in *Capitale de la douleur* (coll. Poésie, Gallimard, 1966, p. 137) entirely formed about the implied phonetic doubles: "ailée/elle est." Thus the lifting of a certain winged presence at midnight gives rise to the poem: "Elle est—mais elle n'est qu'à minuit quand tous les oiseaux blancs ont refermé les ailes. . . . Elle est. . . ."

nevertheless contains several concepts essential to other texts: for instance, a reference to the reader as a "campeur imprudent," that is, one who does not stay, once having come too close. Significant too, the comparison between the blood of a wound coming from a real or figurative struggle, and a flower —"un oeillet n'est pas sans analogie avec une blessure dont le sang mousse. Il suggère de l'accompli. / A carnation is not without analogy to a wound frothed with blood. It suggests something accomplished." Compare, in "Le Mortel partenaire," the red streak traced across the cheek of the second wrestler during the battle, this "raie rose" likened to a lizard in another version. The mark of a rose-colored line, horrible in its delicate exactitude, will return as a frequent leitmotiv, of a force now negative, now again positive: an almost invisible rip at the center of things, disquieting, of uncertain origin and duration, irreparable: "une minuscule plaie. Il est loisible à chacun de fixer une origine et un terme à cette *rougeur* contestable." (LM,23) Or again, it appears as a slash on the opposite face, of the color of future daybreak, silent in the certainty of its trace: "brisant de rougeur . . . où ne sont pas gravés le doute et le dit du présent." (NP,56)

The trace leaves an indelible mark. In "Le Mortel partenaire," a red streak suggests on the level of the image, the flower and the star—whose rays sting like the bee, according to the familiar net of recurrent images—and phonetically, the other side of the mortal flight, like the "rose en larmes" from the probing of the "faire/fer":

raie rose ⟵⟶ éros

This suggestion is reinforced by a sentence in the manuscript version, which is eliminated later: "La rosée et la nuit se laissaient sentir en concert, se concentrant ou s'effaçant selon le (au gré du) quotient des pelouses." Here the green lawns, scene of the concerted struggle, are hidden within the playing of dew and against the night:

rosée ⟵⟶ raie rose ⟵⟶ éros

98

Such tranquility, only hinted at, corresponds paradoxically with the white surface, which is the ground for the struggle, the outstretched sheet against which the night leaves its mark. Subsequently, this mortal struggle inserts itself in the cycle of the amorous and warring couple, in the history of the animal wounded and fleeing, innocent and pursued, like an inescapable image of the poet as he falls prey to his text.

The first version presents a statement over which there hangs apparently not the slightest suggestion of doubt: this statement will reappear, altered:

> 1º Ton lecteur sera souvent soigneusement quelqu'un, que ta spéculation arme, mais que ta plume innocente.[d]

But in another manuscript version of this last "brindille," the following sentence on the subject of innocence poses no question as to the possible reader:

> 2º Et la faculté de fine manoeuvre? Qui sera ton lecteur? Cet oisif, sur ses coudes, à sa fenêtre? Ce meurtrier encore sans objet?

Finally, when the sentence of particular interest here has been added, it appears among many questions in a series whose form itself stresses the strength of this adjective used as a verb:

> Quelqu'un que ta spéculation arme mais que ta plume innocente? . . . Prends garde, quand tu peux, aux mots que tu écris. Tu ne sais pas.

But in this case the doubt will be effaced. For every reader is armed and yet innocent.

[d] 1º Your reader will be often, carefully, someone armed by your speculation, but made innocent by your pen. 2º And the faculty of delicate manoeuvre? Who will your reader be? This idler, propped on his elbows at his window? This murderer still unmotivated? / Someone armed by your speculation but made innocent by your pen? . . . Watch out, when you can, for the words you write. You don't know. 3º And the faculty of delicate manoeuvre? Who will your reader be? Someone armed by your speculation but made innocent by your pen. This idler, propped on his elbows? Watch out, when you can, for the words you write, in spite of their firm distance.

Here we think of Heidegger's meditations on two thoughts
of Hölderlin:[6] that poetry is the most innocent of all occupa-
tions ("unschüldigste")—"Therefore has language, most *dan-*

[6] Martin Heidegger, "Hölderlin et l'essence de la poésie." (QM)
All the quotations from Hölderlin which take Heidegger as a starting-
point come from the edition of Norbert von Hellingrath used by
Heidegger, to which the roman numerals refer. The other quotations
from Hölderlin are drawn from Friedrich Hölderlin, *Sämtliche Werke*,
ed. Friedrich Beissner, Stuttgart, Verlag Kohlhammer, 1951. (HSW)
or from Hamburger, *op.cit.* (FH). Heidegger quotes several passages from Hölderlin (IV,238) on the danger and innocence of language, of the mountain and the valley proper to the poet, adding,
about language, that it must become the property of the community,
that the word must be made common: "Even the essential word, if it
is to be understood and so become a possession in common, must
make itself ordinary." (EB,298-9) It must bear witness to belonging,
to decision, and to existence: "In order that history may be possible,
language has been given to man. . . . It is language which first creates
the manifest conditions for menace and confusion to existence, and
thus the possibility of the loss of existence, that is to say—danger."
We risk the "continual danger for itself" that language conceals, in
order to enjoy its unique openness: "it is that event which disposes
of the supreme possibility of human existence." (EB,300)

Some relationships between Char and Hölderlin have been sketched
by Franz W. Mayer (in the number of *L'Herne* devoted to Char, 1971,
pp. 81-88), in particular concerning the image of the eagle, the theme
of the future, and so on. But here we often attempt to see the correspondence Char/Hölderlin through the perspective of the philosopher Heidegger, in order to bring out this often oblique correspondence, which has its roots rather in a philosophic-poetic thought than
in a specific poetic text.

It seems to us, that in the matter of the rhythm and tone of the
poetic text, Char is often as close to Rilke as to Heidegger. Compare,
for example, the latter's poems on the angel with those of Hölderlin,
and both with Char's on the same topic. Compare in particular Rilke's
poems with the figures of the angel and the unicorn (Meudon, 1905-
06); see our later discussion of the unicorn. In the notes of the
present essay, frequent comparisons will be drawn between Rilke
and Char: for example, concerning the relation between dance and
stillness, fruit and knife-blade, voice and constellation, fountain and
freedom, harvest and offering. For the relationships between Rilke's
own language and French poetry, see R.A.J. Batterby, *Rilke and
France*, Oxford University Press, 1966, especially on the Valéry/
Rilke relationship, and Rilke's translation of "Cimetière marin" as
a determining force in his development at the time of the Duino
Elegies. Another example of the oblique correspondence which in
part governs the present work.

100

gerous of possessions, been given to man . . . so that he might affirm what he is." (EB,273) Heidegger maintains that "it is only language that affords the very possibility of standing in the openness of the existent. Only where there is language, is there world . . ." (EB,300) and adds the following thought on the poet, which seems to us particularly appropriate to Char's work: "This innocent boundary belongs to the essence of poetry, just as the valley does to the mountain: for how could this most dangerous work be carried on and preserved, the poet were not 'cast out' from everyday life and protected against it only by the apparent lawlessness of his occupation?" (EB,309) The theme of innocence and of culpability recurs often in René Char's thought, but insofar as he stresses that the fruit is shared, by poet and reader—where we notice still another correspondence with Hölderlin: "First the fruit must become more common . . ." (H,238) ("Vous serez une part de la saveur du fruit / You will be a part of the fruit's taste" FM,95)—its innocence is shared also. Now the apple, implicit in the reference to fruit, no longer condemns, even if shared. The poem is, as the poet says repeatedly, *incorruptible*, although perishable; its moral force, felt everywhere in his work, is also to be shared, and to be protected against eventual loss.

In the final version, the central interrogation disappears, to become a certainty. We are all armed and thus, potentially criminal, but we are innocent:

3º Et la faculté de fine manoeuvre? Qui sera ton lecteur? Quelqu'un que ta spéculation arme mais que ta plume innocente. Cet oisif, sur ses coudes? Ce criminel encore sans objet? Prends garde, quand tu peux, aux mots que tu écris, malgré leur ferme distance. (LM,119)

Here the useless details, such as the window from which the idler gazed, have disappeared. For we might as easily look down, at our leisure, from the rampart of twigs, without engaging ourselves in any act of sharing. And there are not only murderers to be incriminated: is not the idler also at fault?

101

And the "innocent" reader? This "firm distance" does not protect, after all, against a common ancestral fault, even though the poet does not feel himself guilty. Another thread in the net: later, the fault will be definitively lifted, in an explicit "Aiguevive" after an Aiguemortes, implicit. Living waters are then risen from the dead—but it is not said for whom.

A clear development is felt in the passage from an individual consciousness to the recognition, not of the group, but of "certain beings." The profile of these persons—among whom there are not only poets—remains constant in the work; for those of the same stature share a recognition. "Les grands ne se perpétuent que par les grands. . . . La mesure seule est blessée." (LM,203) These are the unyielding, indomitable beings who refuse to submit: "les insoumis," "les réfractaires. . . ." The theme is stressed also on the level of the formal trace, particularly during this period of a great poetic complexity, the period of "L'Inoffensif," "Le Mortel partenaire," "Front de la rose," all written in 1953. A final example, still centered on the themes of innocence and of the poetic task, is provided, in our reading of our texts, by the ending of "Le Mortel partenaire," added to the manuscript[7] and reworked at length.

In the first stage of the passage,[8] the poet draws from the long meditation on the wrestlers a general conclusion, stated as a moral evidence, so that the individual yields to the global:

1° Ainsi nous sommes. Nous mettons la vie (puissante) au défi.[e] (RB:E)

[7] No. 760 (AE-IV-22) [RB:E].
[8] No. 757 (AE-IV-22) [RB:D].
[e] 1° We are like that. We put (powerful) life to the test. 2° Some beings (with an odd heart) are like that; it is complicated (difficult) to find a name for them and a homage. . . . Their secret resides in the depths of the secret of life which kills them at their command preferring them to others . . . of a more important (less innocent) aspect. 3° Certain beings have a meaning which is lacking to us (escapes us). Who are they? Their secret resides in the depths of life's secret. They approach it (provoke it). Life kills them. Oh labyrinth (source) of extreme love!

(Here, and elsewhere, the parentheses indicate the immediately anterior version.) In a second version, all personal allusion disappears at the conclusion, so that the praise is displaced slightly from the expected path of the text, setting at a certain distance the particularity of those who will become, at the moment of *Le Nu perdu*, the "few beings" whose proud look is always future.

2º Ainsi sont certains êtres (de coeur bizarre) pour lesquels il est compliqué (difficile) de trouver un nom et un hommage.

. . . .

Leur secret tient au plus profond du secret de la vie qui les tue sur leur ordre en les préférant à d'autres . . . d'aspect plus important (moins innocent). (RB:E)

The distinction of these victims is not left in doubt. Noble, they choose their destiny, accepting their privilege and the risk it entails, fully conscious of the fact that nothing in their own appearance would seem to justify it. Here we think of the short text called "Lutteurs," where, in the poet's vision, the humblest immigrant workers are linked to the shining of stars by means of the sweat shining on their foreheads and their hands. They are joined, too, with the "quelques êtres" the poet recognizes as his companions.

But in the final version, the distance is drawn still more distinctly, as if we were never to be part of this group of mysterious beings, as if the qualification "certain" were to be irremediably opposed to the pronoun "nous." Their secret, here, is no longer necessarily felt as ours, as if it were no longer a time for sharing:

3º Certains êtres ont une signification qui nous manque (échappe). Qui sont-ils? Leur secret tient au plus profond du secret même de la vie. Ils s'en approchent (la provoquent). Elle les tue. O dédale (source) de l'extrême amour! (RB:E)

The last change abandons the open image of the fountain

for the complications of the inner maze, as the source becomes a labyrinth, the equivalent of a medieval "ordalie" or testing-ground for heroes. In parallel fashion, along with the psychological distance gradually established, the choppy rhythm hammering out the final version sets a formal distance from the flowing sentences of the former versions. The angular is created slowly, like the flint tools sharpened by other flints, in a series of difficult *éclats*, with an edge ever more precise.

5. *Toward the Text Within*

In one preliminary version of "Le Mortel partenaire," it is only a question of a mortal struggle against life, described with second-order details that will finally disappear to make way for the deeper text, the definitive version whose beginning could refer as well to an amorous warring as to that of the wrestlers in the arena:

> 1° Il marchait sur la vie, s'avançait vers son coeur, comme un boxeur ourlé, ailé et puissant à l'abri derrière la coquille de ses gants, et ramassé bien au centre. . . .ᶠ (RB:E)

> 2° Il la défiait, s'avançait vers son coeur, comme un boxeur ourlé, ailé et puissant, bien au centre. . . . [final version]

The brief initial shock: "il/la" already forms the model for a couple: virginity/experience, or else life/death, an opposition whose resonance remains subtle partly because of the suppression of the adjective "vive" further on in the poem, which has gained in abstraction. Like "the shell of his gloves" which disappears in the first sentence, the change from "pollen" to "first name" here permits a wider reach of meaning, encouraging a more personal meditation on the nature and being of the poem:

ᶠ 1° He strode toward life, advanced toward its heart, like a hemmed, winged and powerful boxer, sheltered behind the shell of his gloves, and concentrated right in the center. . . . 2° He challenged it, advanced toward its heart, like a hemmed, winged and powerful boxer, exactly in the center. . . .

1º Dans l'air volait le pollen des fleurs (voisines) vives d'été. (La rosée et la nuit se laissaient sentir.) La nuit et la rosée nouvelle allaient de concert, se concentrant ou s'effaçant (au gré) selon le quotient des pelouses. Enfin une légère grimace parcourut la joue du second des adversaires et une lézarde rose lui succéda (s'installa).ᵍ (RB:E)

2º Dans l'air de juin voltigeait le prénom des fleurs du premier jour de l'été. Enfin une légère grimace courut sur la joue du second et une raie rose s'y dessina.

All the unessential elements are now removed from the mortal battlefield, leaving occasional traces: for example, "la rosée," a dew suggesting or suggested by the perspiration of the fight, suggests also, by the "rose" included in it, the color of the scratch—therefore, the wound itself. The "pelouses," calm lawns, contrast with the erotic struggle about to ensue: the word implies a playing-field where heads can sway from side to side, like roses in bloom on their stalks—the implied image of a certain leisure sensed also in the rhythm which underlines the irony: for the boxers' heads knock one against the other from the violence, but as if it were in slow motion. Another sentence, later eliminated, read: "à un rythme de coups guère plus rapide qu'un rythme de remarques chez deux promeneurs épris de causerie": the slow rhythm like that of two strollers chatting is finally summarized in the simple words "dodelinant" and "battant," while the image of chatting leads to an insulting remark seemingly made at the end of the poem by one opponent to the other, fighters always equal in their struggle and always together on the same path of opposition, amorous adversaries taken with their battle.

ᵍ 1º In the air the pollen of (neighboring) flowers vivacious from summer. (Dew and night were felt.) Night and fresh dew joined in harmony, intensifying or fading out (at the whim) according to the quotient of lawns. At last a slight grimace ran across the cheek of the second opponent and a rosy crack succeeded it (was installed). 2º In the June air flitted the given name of the flowers of summer's first day. At last a slight grimace ran across the cheek of the second one and a rosy streak was sketched there.

Above and opposite: Manuscript of the poem "Le Mortel partenaire" (March 8, 1953), in *Les Matinaux*. From the Fonds René Char-Yvonne Zervos in the Bibliothèque littéraire Jacques Doucet. (Previously unpublished.)

de l'autre

du secours des paroles qui ~~est~~ ~~fermement~~
où parfaitement ~~augmentaient~~ que je condamne celui-ci
fila, prompt, totale, précise une foudre
qui coucha net, et ~~d'incarnation~~ l'incarnation
l'avait ~~tuée~~, le ~~compagnon~~ combattant,

~~Armée~~ ~~metton~~ mettons la ~~va~~
en puissante au défi.

Ainsi ~~tout certain être~~ ~~de courbasse~~ pour lesquels il est
~~s'efface de~~ ~~ton~~ ~~pour~~ ~~en~~ ~~nous~~ ~~et~~ ~~nos~~ ~~in~~ ~~connus~~ et un hommage.
~~la assentir~~ ~~à renouer~~ ~~de~~ ~~tout~~ ~~secret~~ de
tout secret ~~tient au plus haut~~ ~~profond~~ ~~même~~ de
la vie ~~qui les tue~~. ~~en~~ ~~to~~ ~~apparent~~

~~temps~~ ~~plus~~ ~~se~~
~~tout~~ ~~plus~~ ~~mais~~
~~vibrants~~ ~~s'en~~ ~~fendre~~
~~douce~~
~~plus~~ ~~d'enfant~~
~~si~~
~~mais~~ ~~innocent~~.

→ Certains êtres ont une signification
qui nous ~~échappe~~ manque. Qui sont-ils? Leur secret
tient au plus profond du secret même
de la vie. Ils ~~le~~ ~~provoquent~~ s'en approchent. Elle les tue
mais l'avenir qu'ils ont ~~ale~~ ~~de~~ ~~eux~~ ~~avoir~~ ~~rien~~,
~~définitif~~, les crée. O ~~sourd~~ de l'extrême amour!

L.C. (29-30 mars 53)

The "battants," at once these opponents and "combattants"—a set of swinging doors, metaphoric and violent, are also figures opening onto the poem as the scene of mortal *encounter*: they are thus a model for Char's poetics itself. The connection of form and image, a transfer operating from a rhythmic *ralenti*, a slowing-down of pace to the apparent gentleness of the shock of heads continues to the end of this verbal flow, where the place of honor is left for the "incomprehensible combattant," who had been described in the former version given above as "singulier." This latter word has a double significance, marking the fight as one between the two halves of a singular being, and signaling at the same time his membership in the family of "L'Extravagant" and the other extreme heroes, of whom the poet says, in referring to the inheritance of Rimbaud: "From the extreme adolescent to the extreme man, the distance is not to be measured." (PNR,7) Either way this characteristically ambiguous sentence is read, the emphasis is clearly not placed on the category of age, but on that of the unique. The force of the verbs "franchir" and "jaillir" in the framework of all this poet's writing, so strongly marked by his own personality, has been noted here; to those verbs must be added the adjective "brutal," for it marks the other point of the triangle, and the angular nature of the work. Brutality refreshes this being, as he says openly: "être brutal répare."[9] "L'Absent," one of the

---

[9] The figure of the poet as brutal being recurs in several major texts, determining the tone and explaining the attitude of such poems as "Assez creusé" and "L'Anneau de la licorne." Hölderlin's "Der Zürnende Dichter" is an allied spirit, and his Empedocles, who demands space around him ("Weit will ichs um mich machen / I will have space around me!" FH,290). The poet insisting on an "immensité" made for him and displaying the occasional ferocity of a marginal being, is identical with the poet more quietly dismissing his followers. He requires the same kind of remote and spacious dwelling as Empedocles describes in the third version of Hölderlin's play about this philosopher: "Mir aber ziemt die stille Halle, mir / Die hochgelegene, geräumige // But as for me, / It is the quiet hall that's fitting, one / More spacious, higher up, remote, aloof" (FH,338-9). (The poet's *dwelling* is similar for Hölderlin and Char, cf. note 6, p. 229.)

clearest portraits of the poet himself, begins: "Ce frère brutal. . . ." Difficult poets and the difficult opponents who are their proper companions take their strength in their oppositions: "Nos orages nous sont essentiels / Our storms are essential to us." (NP,124)

Now the poem can be traced in a reduced model—as the work of Heraclitus and of Georges de La Tour shows "l'action contre le réel, par tradition signifiée, simulacre et miniature" (FM,67)—from its initial neutral formulation of fact. "Une lézarde rose lui succéda," by way of a duration where no abruptness is implied: "une lézarde rose s'installa," to a precise act stressed by monosyllabic repetition and alliteration: "une raie rose s'y dessina." (RB:E) This precise cruelty is found elsewhere in the trace of a bleeding animal in Artine's bed, in a rose-tinged animal fleeing over the rock, in the crack of a wall like a gaping wound.

6. *In Search of the Angular*

Char often chooses the most angular words, in correspondence with his attitude of a "being standing." Even his attention to a four-line poem, "Vers l'arbre-frère aux jours comptés," (LM,115) indicates sufficiently his effort toward the angular and the complex. The original title, "Portrait du frère aux jours comptés," was at once more static and less specific. These lines, now directed not only toward a mortal brother but toward the tree similar in its mortality to man, are—by implication and in fact—hammered, chopped, and finally felled like the tree resembling them. *Le Marteau sans maître* is never far from the poet's thought. "Dans le bois on entend bouillir le ver": the worm heard within the forest of

---

In one of Char's plays *Le Soleil des eaux*, the brutality of Apollon (whose name already bears its own illumination, that of the sun god) is given its full heroic weight in particular balance with his tenderness, when after his most violent gesture he extends a crumpled iris that he has picked that morning, "because it was the bluest of them all" (SE). The double nature of eros—noticeable in the images of the "raie rose" in "Le Mortel partenaire" and in the "iris" of *Lettera amorosa* ("iris/éros")—is thus accentuated.

the early poem "Robustes météores" is later to become these *vers* in their double sense: these four lines of verse and their direction toward ("vers/vers"). They are counted, like the time of trees and the days of man.

If we consider the two lines in the center of the "brief harp" of the poem heard in its successive modifications[10] we notice that in almost every case the more general word, or the one which more perfectly matched its neighbor, is altered for a word more precise or lending a greater contrast. The words in parentheses are preliminary versions, stages on the way:

1° Sur l'étendue de mousse et de cailloux à naître (De l'immense rocher) (Enlevés au rocher)

—En suspens de forêt (du sapin) réfractaire aux nuages—

2° Sur l'éperon de mousse et de dalles en germe (Prédites, possibles, promises)

—Façade des forêts (sapins) où casse (couche) le nuage[h]—

The suggestion of pointed moss, and that of a cloud of matter as breakable as porcelain, removes the poem from the domain of the cliché (such as the equation: moss=soft; cloud=gaseous) but without betraying the sense of reality. For seen close up, there are indeed points on the strand-ends of moss, and, seen from a sufficient distance, a cloud dissolving at the middle can indeed be said to have broken in two. It is simply a matter of varying the perspective.

The definitive changes are responsible for a destiny slowly acquired: the word "dalles," taken from the world of culture as opposed to the world of nature, suggests a slight nuance of antiquity, as in ancient tiles. In another example, of all the synonyms of a future birth tried out, "en germe" is the

[10] No. 757-758 (AE-IV-22).

[h] 1° On the expanse of moss and of pebbles to be born (of the immense rock) (Removed from the rock) / suspended in a forest (from the fir) refractory to clouds 2° On the spur of moss and of tiles in seed (predicted, possible, promised) / Façade of the forests (fires) where breaks (lies) the cloud—.

only one to refer specifically to the vegetable world; "à naître," a birth with no reference to the specific form, did not offer the same contrast with "dalles," since it may refer just as well to the world of man.

Two intermediate passages briefly tried out for the same poem were considered and subsequently rejected: "De l'immense rocher" and "Enlevés au rocher." Since the rock would have corresponded to the "pebbles" already present, either expression would have added only one more exterior allusion to this interior and rocky world always present in the difficult mental habitation of the poet. Furthermore, clouds being already suspended by their nature, and linked to the refraction of light, the modification "en suspens . . . réfractaire" → "façade . . . casse" has the advantage of suggesting another element: the world of culture, the stage, the artificial scene, in the same sense as the modification: "cailloux" → "dalle." This scenery prepares the way for the concluding credo again ambiguous: "Contrepoint du vide auquel je crois / Counterpoint of the emptiness in which I believe."

Finally the formerly passive line becomes active, as a stubborn forest describes a state, and the breaking cloud, an action. After the "mélèzes," the "sapins" was a needless specification: the generic category of forests already furnishes a scene sufficiently spacious so that the brief music of the poem can be heard in a counterpoint to emptiness. From the text we cannot discern in which element the poet puts his own belief, so that this text remains open.

B. RELIEF

Je suis pour l'hétérogénéité la plus étendue.
(RBS,44)

Between these moments of the work seen as summits of tension or flashes of complex illumination there appear other texts seemingly easier and more relaxed. The lighter poems (from what the poet calls his "temperate slope") alternate

109

with the prose poems of an exceeding density: otherwise the texture of the poetry as a whole would tend toward the monolithic, lacking a passage. Just as dead or null moments are necessary for a message to be understood, so a communicable series of poems must have some unevenness, some sharp relief. The principle of alternation remains in evidence: "les aspects des régimes alternent." In the recent collection *Aromates chasseurs*, texts with an intensity parallel to that of the prose poems of the summits, those of 1937 and 1953, for instance, alternate with "matinal" poems and political or ethical meditations all joined by the figure of Orion and his stars.

However, the structure of the chain is not always made apparent. One might suppose that it stretches upland on the slope of this interior mountain, or further upstream in this mental river, where there is only a *Retour amont*. In "Recours au ruisseau," the town retraced by the poet in the running water and in the blowing wind, so that it may be wiped out and started again ever higher—this town is shown to be incomprehensible, particularly to the competent and efficient builders who use quite another material for their buildings, made for lasting in another sense. "Sur l'aire du courant, dans les joncs agités, j'ai retracé ta ville. Les maçons au large feutre sont venus; ils se sont appliqués à suivre mon mouvement. Ils ne concevaient pas ma construction. Leur compétence s'alarmait. / On the surface of the current, among the quivering rushes, I retraced your town. The masons came with their broad felt hats; they endeavored to follow my movement. They could not comprehend my poem. Their competence took fright." (LM,61) The masons depart and the poem builds its being, as it must: constructed in the matter of flux itself, it can be effaced and then rebuilt, higher up. The poet has no need of the "gravel sparkling in the sky of the stream," for his matter is entirely other; the few rocks contemplated in the space of *La Nuit talismanique*, etched as this poem is etched, are still associated with the algae and the fluency of this stream. Finally, in the myth of Orion,

110

these rocks will once again form a constellation, like an archipelago reflected in the mirror of the sky, through one of the reversals of vision characteristic of Char's poetry. A few texts, whose construction would be equally "inconceivable" to the masons of poetry, seem at once transparent and dense, crystal-opaque monuments serving as the signposts of passage. The one we choose among others to mark our path here bears a partly ironic title, where the singular noun "faste" lends its ornament and its display to this event recorded ("fastes" in the plural), this textual inscription of the retreat of waters and of time, yet inscribed also in the constancy of a love holding firm even within that flux:

"FASTES"

L'été chantait sur son roc préféré quand tu m'es apparue, l'été chantait à l'écart de nous qui étions silence, sympathie, liberté triste, mer plus encore que la mer dont la longue pelle bleue s'amusait à nos pieds.

L'été chantait et ton coeur nageait loin de lui. Je baisais ton courage, entendais ton désarroi. Route par l'absolu des vagues vers ces hauts pics d'écume où croisent des vertus meurtrières pour les mains qui portent nos maisons. Nous n'étions pas crédules. Nous étions entourés.

Les ans passèrent. Les orages moururent. Le monde s'en alla. J'avais mal de sentir que ton coeur justement ne m'apercevait plus. Je t'aimais. En mon absence de visage et mon vide de bonheur. Je t'aimais, changeant en tout, fidèle à toi. (FM,209)[i]

---

[i] Summer was singing on its favorite rock when you appeared to me, summer was singing apart as we who were silence, sympathy, sorrowful freedom, were sea still more than the sea whose long blue spade was playing at our feet. / Summer was singing and your heart swam far from it. I embraced your courage, heard your confusion. Road along the absolute of waves toward those high peaks of foam where virtues sail, murderous to hands bearing our houses. We were not credulous. We were surrounded. / The years passed by. The

111

The passage is initially made from a season specified in the first two paragraphs, with its recognizable attributes: the spade[11] left on the beach, digging out a long furrow of blueness for the sea and the swimming, the waves and the foam, the rocks where children play under the mother's gaze (the classic echo "mer/mère" is dimly heard), an image where the song of a summer love is so strong as to efface all seasons and all attributes in the last paragraph. But the passage is made also in the opposite direction. The first ephemeral appearance of love, accompanied by the song *à l'écart*, becomes a presence progressively more dominant and absorbing; it triumphs over even physical absence. The exterior details are gradually reduced until the complete disappearance of everything that is not this unforgettable song of the ever faithful *mal-aimé*. A passage leads from the impersonal season toward an understated homage to a fidelity finally acknowledged: "à toi."

Another passage can be taken. Beginning by the waves and the foam of this water on which human love can leave no trace, the poem rises, by a force both structural and psychological, to the summits: the word "pics" is placed in the exact middle of the text, as if it were itself the seascape from which the verbal peaks emerge, a "mer plus encore que la mer." Topologically prepared by the "roc" of the first line, the vision of the peaks appears in a central transforma-

---

storms died down. The world went its way. I suffered to think it was your heart which no longer perceived me. I loved you. In my absence of visage and my emptiness of joy. I loved you, changing in every way, faithful to you.

[11] For a reading of these words, see Georges Mounin (*op.cit.*, p. 2): "L'image de la pelle communique, à la vitesse de la lumière, la vision de chaque vague comme une large pelletée d'eau, son poids, sa retombée éparpillée, le ruissellement de sable d'abord chassé vers la rive puis s'écoulant avec l'eau qui redescend sur le rivage entier vu d'un seul coup comme un immense château de sable unique, à cause de *s'amusait* répondant à *pelle*."

Thus, he continues, the occlusives of the sentence play against the laterals, in alternance.

112

tion suddenly suggested: a seascape entirely flat becomes a mountainous landscape, erected and then effaced:

rocs → hauts pics → passèrent

For directly after the meeting of wave with mountain there is an emptiness hollowed out in the poem, as if the words "où croisent . . . entourés" were only the walls protecting this abrupt elevation from its surroundings, as the empty margin surrounds a text:

route ⟷ pic ⟷ route

From the lofty peak in the center, there is no path that does not descend, a steep decline stressed by the brief and quiet triple blows of a parallel impersonal construction. The love has only to follow the slope already marked: "Les ans passèrent. Les orages moururent. Le monde s'en alla." This bare descent leads to the rubbing-out of the sentimental vision ("ne m'apercevait plus"), the absence of visible happiness, and the retreat of the waters from the poem as from a beach deserted, even by the sea.[12]

Nevertheless, since the text in its double natural and topological character continues to play on both levels—sea and mountain—we might perceive in it the ebb and flow of a temporal tide, seasonal and recurring, inflicting a cyclical sadness with no enduring reason for being. The allusion to a seascape is reinforced by a rereading of the poem's point of departure, where the summer singing on the rocks suggests a mermaid combing her long blue hair ("la mer dont la longue *pelle* bleue," where the word "pelle" suggests the hair of an animal, as in "peau" or the Italian "pelle"): or again,

[12] Among the poems which Heidegger dedicated to Char (see *L'Herne*), the one called "Wege" touches the most nearly on this subject:
"Chemins / chemins de la pensée: ils vont d'eux-mêmes / ils s'échappent. . . . / Chemins allant d'eux-mêmes / Jadis ouverts, soudain refermés, / plus tard. Montrant de l'antérieur / iamais atteint, voué au non-dit. . . ."

the river Lethe ("l'été" = "Léthé"). This forgetfulness is the obvious cause of sadness ("ton coeur justement ne m'apercevait plus") and yet also eventually, of the welcome oblivion to that sadness, in the season beyond the poem. Regardless of the ebbing and flowing of the text and the seasons, or of psychological alteration in the passage of time and feeling ("changeant en tout") the song continues to triumph over silence, imposing its repetitive structure on the surface of the text, whose continuity it reinforces:

> l'été chantait
> l'été chantait
> l'été chantait
>
> .   .   .   .
>
> nous n'étions pas
> nous étions
>
> .   .   .   .
>
> je t'aimais
> je t'aimais

The outline, in echo, prepares a forgetting: the initial triple form is answered by another triple form marking the temporal refusal, and by the other complex of images suggesting psychological diminishment and eventual loss. Nevertheless, after the period of doubt: "J'avais mal," in the final moment, a fidelity as illogical as it is poetic, traced in firm letters against absence and change, is recorded in spite of everything.

C. Transfer, Threshold

> Le plus difficile est de distinguer la brouette du jardinier, le nez du profil, et de n'en tenir qu'*imperceptiblement* compte. (RBS,166)

In spite of several instances of the contrary, where the direction seems to lead toward the easier solution, the threshold is finally the most poetic and difficult of habitations, that of the marginal being—"We can only live in the half-open, exactly on the hermetic dividing line between shadow and light." (LM,196) —in spite of our irresistible urge forward, against which the struggle seems to last a lifetime. And elsewhere, the impossible habitation of the dividing line is again chosen or accepted: "I don't expect anything *finished*, I accept my steering between two unequal dimensions." (LM, 117) This statement was originally an answer to the question: "Comment, quoi? rien de fini?" with the significant change: the original verb "boitiller" (limping) becomes "godiller" (steering), so that the previous involuntary imbalance is altered toward a deliberate and continual action.

The threshold in all its forms is the central architectural figure and the thought of the poetry of René Char, where traversal is continuous, in all senses: verbal, moral, and conceptual. In a universe where the extremes correspond, and dimensions cross over into one another, the image is capital. As a step toward the images and the texts centering on the threshold, we quote only the beginning of "L'Allégresse," one of the clearest examples of meeting, of a reciprocal transfer, seen in images of which we shall speak again later. The correspondence with the more formal meeting and transfer observed in the first part of the study is deliberate; nor is it inappropriate that the references to meeting should recur. "Les nuages sont dans les rivières, les torrents parcourent le ciel. . . . Le temps de la famine et celui de la moisson, l'un sous l'autre dans l'air haillonneux, ont effacé leur différence. Ils filent ensemble, ils bivaquent!" (LM,205)

Contrasting with this passage in the open, with its frank juxtaposition of contraries, and its unambiguous celebration of meeting, the texts situated on a threshold suggest luminous shadows and obscuring lights, without an always visible line of demarcation: these are texts of a reciprocal sensitivity. Only an extraordinary lighting can reveal them: "a lamp unknown to us, inaccessible to us, at the tip of the world. . . ." (FM,50) The following discussion is meant only to open a possible way toward that other more profound passage by

115

a candle held out in *La Nuit talismanique*, the latter volume describing a dimly-lit dwelling partly foreseen in the firelit cavern of the poem "Transir" and for which the figures of *Artine* and of the penitent Magdalen in La Tour's "Madeleine à la veilleuse" serve as the threshold.

At the end of a primordial night, which also marks a new beginning, a temporal correspondent to a spatial threshold, or a sill, the poet establishes his house alone; there he is to receive his peers, dwellers also in the reciprocal forming the intuitive parallel to the space of the *entre-deux*, space of Hölderlin, of Heidegger, of all poets.[13] Here the generosity of a hospitable abode in a poet's imagination predominates finally over the difficulty of access. The poem "Seuil" is a sufficient indication of a lasting attitude: the poet who has endured all seasons, here compared implicitly to Orion, awaits his future companions at the threshold of night's submission to day:

"Seuil"

. . . .

J'ai couru jusqu'à l'issue de cette nuit diluvienne. Planté dans le flageolant petit jour, ma ceinture pleine de saisons, je vous attends, ô mes amis qui allez venir. Déjà je vous devine derrière la noirceur de l'horizon. Mon âtre ne tarit pas de voeux pour vos maisons. Et mon bâton de cyprès rit de tout son coeur pour vous.[j] (FM,181)

This active scene of the poet's imagination is open, by its very form, to risk. The heart has not the limits of the house: "mon âtre . . . vos maisons," nor its possible stability, situated as it is in the "flageolant petit jour." Here we think of the construction erected further and further upstream, always built

---

[13] For the notion of the *entre-deux*, see Heidegger on Hölderlin, discussed elsewhere in these pages.

[j] I have run to the outcome of this diluvian night. Standing firm in the wavering daybreak, with my belt full of seasons, I am waiting for you, my friends who will come. Already I divine you behind the black of the horizon. My hearth's good wishes for your homes never dry up. And my cypress walking stick laughs with its whole heart for you. (JG)

higher. The welcome extended here imports for all of Char's work; it is properly that of a mental dwelling, that of the poem itself.

Accepting the "impossible" and the uncomfortable ambiguous consciousness of a private enigma ("Il m'offrait, à la gueule d'un serpent qui souriait, mon impossible que je pénétrais sans souffrir / He offered me, in the mouth of a smiling snake, my impossible which I penetrated without suffering" [FM,193]) the poet rejects the stabilizing anchor sometimes implied in the ink of writing, moving beyond the play of the "ancre" against the "encre": "J'ai cherché dans mon encre ce qui ne pouvait être quêté: la tache pure au-delà de l'écriture souillée." (FM,174) If the work located at the extremes of consciousness is sullied by its too great violence of junction or disjunction, the more nuanced writing of the threshold will be marked by ignorance of the final verdict.

"CALENDRIER"

J'ai lié les unes aux autres mes convictions et agrandi ta Présence. J'ai octroyé un cours nouveau à mes jours en les adossant à cette force spacieuse. J'ai congédié la violence qui limitait mon ascendant. J'ai pris sans éclat le poignet de l'équinoxe. L'oracle ne me vassalise plus. J'entre: j'éprouve ou non la grâce.

La menace s'est polie. La plage qui chaque hiver s'encombrait de régressives légendes, de sibylles aux bras lourds d'orties, se prépare aux êtres à secourir. Je sais que la conscience qui se risque n'a rien à redouter de la plane.[k] (FM,26)

[k] I've linked my convictions to one another and increased your presence. I've granted a new course to my days, leaning them against this spacious force. I've dismissed the violence limiting my authority. Unobtrusively I've taken the wrist of the equinox. The oracle no longer holds me in sway. I enter: I experience grace, or not. / The menace has become polished. The shore which, each winter, was encumbered by regressive legends, by sibyls whose arms are heavy with nettles, is readying itself for beings it may succor. I know that the conscience which takes a risk has nothing to fear from the smooth.

117

The text is inserted in time and pervaded by a single presence: this time-space is accepted as a global concept in the same terms as is the "chair-muraille" found elsewhere. It must be entered, its threshold crossed, by an active decision: "J'entre: j'éprouve ou non la grâce." An augmentation is declared by an explicit chain ("J'ai lié") and by a generous juxtaposition: "octroyé/adossant."

Of all the long series of texts on leave-taking, this one is perhaps the most serious. For it is not here, as it is in "Le Visage nuptial," an act of bidding farewell to an escort of friends or of witnesses to secure a couple's solitude but rather a demonstration of the necessity for severing a part from the rest over which it is too dominant: the "brutal" part of being and, in particular, of poetic being. The former irregular violence, the bursts of anger like storms refreshing and nourishing a dry land would limit the potential reach of nuance: "J'ai pris sans éclat le poignet de l'équinoxe." Not the hand, nor the arm, but only the wrist: the mediator between the two, the joining element. The expressions of ambiguity, such as the equinox and the entire sentence beginning: "J'entre" continue the complexity of an intermediate situation.

The second stanza examines the notion of risk apparent in the first, in the same balance evident between the two parts of the texts in *Contre une maison sèche*, that is, an upper and a lower, responding: statement or *exemplum*, and explanation, examination, or elaboration, directly below it, in italics. The two equal parts mirror here the equinox and the threshold prior to decision. Certain pages, polished by the ocean's ebb and flow, but oracular and difficult ("sybilles . . . orties") are destined to be read, as the "légende" implies a *legenda*, read however in reverse, in their ebbing, to the point of becoming "régressive." Once more, as in "Fastes," a mountain landscape appears within the seascape, its peaks joining the crests of waves or its slopes rising from the shore. The decision will in general be toward the steeper rather than toward the temperate, gentler slope, the "versant tempéré"; the latter seems, within the space of Char's greatest work to be progressively absorbed by the more abrupt tendency, betraying a conscience preferring its risk and inimical to a long stretch of plateau or plain. To choose the nettles and the rough edges of what is not yet resolved rather than what has been smoothed out, or made plain, involves a constant opposition to the tide that polishes by its cyclical movements; finally, the recession of the sea—and, perhaps, of the too-easy summer —is marked again here, as in "Fastes."

As a parallel to this poem of division and of relationship of sea to shore, the poem "Pénombre" is situated on the threshold of dusk in opposition to "Calendrier," where the initial circular image of the sun yields to that of the night itself slowly recircled. In "Pénombre," the beams of the stars battle in an expression of potential violence replacing that renounced by the narrator.

"PÉNOMBRE"

J'étais dans une de ces forêts où le soleil n'a pas accès mais où, la nuit, les étoiles pénètrent. Ce lieu n'avait le permis d'exister, que parce que l'inquisition des États l'avait négligé. Les servitudes abandonnées me marquaient leur mépris. La hantise de punir m'etait retirée.

. . . .

J'étais dans une de ces forêts où le soleil n'a pas accès mais où, la nuit, les étoiles pénètrent pour d'implacables hostilités.[1] (FM,160)

We recognize this forest; it is described elsewhere as ancient and as always to be born, having the form and the metaphorical value of the almond, like a density enclosed. Here the perspective is vertical, as the stars enter. The visionary now takes precedence over the erotic, the latter only suggested

[1] I was in one of those forests to which the sun has no access, but where stars penetrate by night. This place was allowed existence only because the inquisition of the State had overlooked it. Forsaken easements showed me their scorn. The obsession to chastise was taken from me. / . . . / I was in one of those forests to which the sun has no access, but where stars penetrate by night for a relentless warring.

119

within a horizontal perspective: "Je voudrais me glisser dans une forêt où les plantes se refermeraient et s'étreindraient derrière nous, forêt nombre de fois centenaire, mais elle reste à semer. / I should like to slip into a forest where the plants would close up once more, embracing behind us, a forest many centuries old, but it remains to be sown." (CP,137)

"Pénombre" creates exactly the landscape of an "entre-deux," a realm between two times or seasons or spaces, as well as that between two lights or between gods and men—Hölderlin's "Zweilicht" reconciling day with night-time. (FH, 250) This aspect of a deliberately ambiguous poetry finds its form in the threshold, its image in the equinox, and its psychology in a "université suspensive," as if the balance were to be learned.

The situation is described as marginal: "parce que . . . négligé," and the speaker as a changed man. In "Calendrier," he had dismissed violence and forsaken custom; here again he has forsaken a sort of cruelty and the "servitudes," the laws or constraints he formerly obeyed, the traditional and informal institutions of a former time. (The poet explains his use of "servitudes" here in this way, giving as an example the custom of a certain right-of-way granted, over someone else's land to a spring, for instance.) Only the memory of the lost violence remains, and a present "véhémence sereine" taking its source now in the personal strength of a marginal being rather than in that of custom. A "force spacieuse" energetically marked both place and time in "Calendrier"; here the half-lit scene links the human to the natural: "J'étais l'égal de choses dont le secret tenait sous le rayon d'une aile. / I was the equal of things whose secret fitted under the ray of a wing." The narrator, now self-contained, acquires by a secret intermediary the radiance and the serenity of a bird's flight and repose, and of its minimal intrusion into the universe: compare the poem on the swift, who lives in a narrower space than other beings: "Nul n'est plus à l'étroit que lui." (FM,214) The entry of the stars and their exit, at the outset and the conclusion of the text's own penumbra, is hostile as if by transfer from the former violence of the speaker; their celestial struggle confers an intense radiance on these formal thresholds.

Another and more enigmatic text, whose tone and sensibility differ from those discussed so far, is narrated by an "inoffensive" voice which has not only forsaken violence, but has—at least at a first hearing—a peculiarly weak tone. Whereas the vehement yet serene speaker in a penumbral setting was in correspondence with the night, in its radiance and its violence, this one greets the night's spectacle with diffidence:

"L'INOFFENSIF"

Je pleure quand le soleil se couche parce qu'il te dérobe à ma vue et parce que je ne sais pas m'accorder avec ses rivaux nocturnes.

.   .   .   .

... Il fait nuit. Les artifices qui s'allument me trouvent aveugle.ᵐ (LM,120)

.   .   .   .

The most faithful reader is surprised by this uncharacteristic "poème *offensant*." (MM,133) First, the immediate confession of weeping appears to be at odds with the poetic personality generally felt to be dominant ("les larmes méprisent leur confident"). And so intimate is the communication between the poet's voice and the form of his writing that a corresponding weakness might be sensed in the poem itself; to announce it openly on the threshold only serves to mark its significance. These tears apparently shed at parting seem to conflict with the self-control of the other narrators, with Char's spoken and unspoken exhortations against a nostalgia showing too little restraint, and with his moving observations on the brevity of meeting (see, for instance, the series entitled: "L'amie qui ne restait pas").

ᵐ I weep when the sun sets because it takes you from my sight and I do not know how to get along with its nocturnal rivals. . . . / It is night. Contrivances lighting up find me sightless.*

121

The lover weeps at his inability to "s'accorder," whereas in the long series of heroic texts, the figures of the extravagant one, the partisan, the absent one are only known to sing a "chant du refus," and, in particular, the reaper, the tree-pruner, the carder, the plunderer of memory all represent forces of self-control, as if the refusal song were also to be directed against what is too facile in the singer, as well as in the world.

But now the offending "inoffensif" changes his story, putting all the weight of his sorrow into a nightmare vision, suddenly the contrary of mawkish sentimentality:

Je n'ai pleuré en vérité qu'une seule fois. Le soleil en disparaissant avait coupé ton visage. Ta tête avait roulé dans la fosse du ciel et je ne croyais plus au lendemain.[n]

Avowing the lie, or the exaggeration, the narrator acquires depth; the interrogation contained in the conclusion, of a tone entirely different from that preceding it—far less personal—opens the poem to another order of distinctions not previously evident. This last sentence serves as a formal threshold for a fresh beginning, if we read the text as cyclic: it was in fact added after the initial version.[14] The reversal is therefore deliberate.

Even more than the other texts already considered, this poem is marked from the outset by an obsession with the threshold: the former version quoted above signaled the false opposition between morning and evening, sun and stars, natural fire and artificial contrivances, the fireworks of calculation. For these "artifices qui s'allument" were originally found in the first sentence: "et parce que je ne sais pas m'accorder avec les artifices des faux rivaux." It served in that first ver-

[n] In truth I only wept once. The sun in disappearing had cut off your face. Your head had rolled in the sky's grave and I no longer believed in the morrow.*
[14] This sentence was added, in blue ink, standing out against the black ink of the text as originally conceived: No. 759 (AE-IV-22). All the variants we cite here are taken from this version.

sion[15] as the prelude to a poem on the dialectic of complementaries, which would be wrongly perceived as simple contraries: "les faux rivaux," an expression found in large letters at the top of the manuscript, is sufficient indication. The slow development of the text shows a typical balance and an evolution toward the compressed—for example, the elimination of a phrase whose rhythm was excessively loose, precisely before the harshness of the verb "arracher." This phrase having been eliminated, the sentence juts out in vivid profile against the moderation of what follows. Compare the two versions:

1º Impossible d'aller contre lui, de suspendre son effeuillaison, de gagner quelques secondes sur sa lueur de plus.

2º Impossible d'aller contre son déclin, de suspendre son effeuillaison, d'arracher quelque envie encore à sa lueur moribonde.º

The relief of the poem is shaped by just this alternation; after the sentence made brutal by the verb "arracher," the poem softens again into its liquid sounds, toward a rhythm and images of melting or merging: "Son départ te fond dans son obscurité comme le limon du lit se délaye dans l'eau du torrent par delà l'éboulis des berges détruites. / Its departure melts you in its obscurity as the silt of the bed is diluted in the water of the torrent beyond the crumbling of the destroyed banks." And the explanation of the chosen alternance is given in the poem itself: "Dureté et mollesse au ressort différent ont alors des effets semblables. / Hardness and gentleness with differing resilience have then a similar effect." The

---

[15] No. 759 (AE-IV-22). Written on March 6, 1953. Many of the more difficult poems date from around this period: see the accompanying illustrations of "Le Mortel partenaire," "Front de la rose," and "L'Inoffensif" itself.

º 1º Impossible to go against it, to suspend its shedding, to win some seconds still from its gleam. 2º Impossible to go against its decline, to suspend its shedding to wrench yet another desire from its moribund gleam.

123

following passage is at first slow-paced, in no way predicting final precision; it then increases in nervousness, in direct contrast to the relaxed rhythm of the two preceding sentences:

1° ce n'est plus la douceur nerveuse de ton poignet que je tiens dans ma main mais la branche creuse d'un quelconque arbre mort et déjà débité!

2° ce n'est pas le fuseau nerveux de ton poignet qui tient ma main mais la branche creuse d'un quelconque arbre mort et déjà débité.[p]

The intense effort toward balance and concision is apparent in the alterations of the penultimate paragraph. First, separation provokes a sentimental plaint, as the dying sun removes the person addressed from the narrator's gaze:

1° Le soleil en mourant m'avait séparé de ton visage; ta tête avait roulé. . . .

Next a visual force is gathered directly into a verb divisive in the extreme: "The disappearing sun had split your face. . . ." From now on the speaker or spectator is absent from the sentence:

2° Le soleil en disparaissant avait partagé ton visage; ta tête avait roulé. . . .

But in the final version, the violence of the verb "coupé" ("cut off")—which lends to the conclusion the resonance of Apollinaire's famous "cou coupé" concluding his poem "Zone" with the terrible image of a severed neck—impedes the continuation of the sentence, which now ceases abruptly after the spectacle of the face cut off:

3° Le soleil en disparaissant avait coupé ton visage. Ta tête avait roulé. . . .

[p] 1° What my hand is holding is no longer the nervy gentleness of your wrist, but a hollow branch from some dead, already chopped tree! 2° What my hand is holding is not the nervy spindle of your wrist, but a hollow branch from some dead, already chopped tree. (JG)

At this stage of the work, the lament is interrupted in the middle by an exclamation point: "ton poignet branche d'un quelconque arbre mort et déjà débité!" The deliberate shock of juxtaposing the wrist with a dead, undistinguished, and ignominiously divided thing is signaled by the striking punctuation; this exterior typographical interruption disappears from the second working-out of the text, where the simple word "fuseau," as sharp in tone as in the spindle's profile itself, alone betrays the nervousness. Then the last interrogation is added, a single brief sentence putting all the rest in question with utter simplicity, setting the first mass against the second:

> Lequel est l'homme du matin et lequel celui des ténèbres?

The question seems simple enough: which of these men is the matinal, and which the tenebrous? Or are they both penumbral, like the speaker of the preceding poem? Yet the form of the question itself reveals a progressive complexity and an accumulated doubt as to the single oppositions, contrasting, on the page, with the actual diminution of the visual form, toward the final brief interrogation. To put in balance or in play the forces and matter of the text would seem an occupation proper to a poet of the threshold whose texts are always stretched between the explicit and the implicit, situated on a thin and difficult line, a sill or a "seuil." The texts participate in a penumbra of two dimensions, a partially lunar state[16] where the narrator expresses an uncertainty: "j'éprouve ou non la grâce. . . ."

Of all the texts which seem to take their starting-point in the image of the threshold, in the theme of hesitation, or in

[16] Lévi-Strauss tells how, for the Salish, the moon alone represents the equilibrium between antagonistic forces. "Seule la lune, quand elle éclaire doucement les ténèbres illustre ce *tempérament réciproque* de la lumière et de l'obscurité. Elle est donc *de la nuit* et *du jour*; car l'expérience atteste qu'elle n'est pas exclusivement de la nuit, puisque les nuits les plus nocturnes—parce que les plus sombres—sont celles où elle est absente du ciel." (*L'Homme nu*, Plon, 1971, p. 312.)

125

an analogous structure, one of the most intricate is a "pulverized poem" whose source, says Char, is completely "envelopped." (AHPP)

"J'HABITE UNE DOULEUR"

Ne laisse pas le soin de gouverner ton coeur à ces tendresses parentes de l'automne auquel elles empruntent sa placide allure et son affable agonie. L'oeil est précoce à se plisser. La souffrance connaît peu de mots. Préfère te coucher sans fardeau: tu rêveras du lendemain et ton lit te sera léger. Tu rêveras que ta maison n'a plus de vitres. Tu es impatient de t'unir au vent, au vent qui parcourt une année en une nuit. D'autres chanteront l'incorporation mélodieuse, les chairs qui ne personnifient plus que la sorcellerie du sablier. Tu condamneras la gratitude qui se répète. Plus tard, on t'identifiera à quelque géant désagrégé, seigneur de l'impossible.

Pourtant.

Tu n'as fait qu'augmenter le poids de ta nuit. Tu es retourné à la pêche aux murailles, à la canicule sans été. Tu es furieux contre ton amour au centre d'une entente qui s'affole. Songe à la maison parfaite que tu ne verras jamais monter. A quand la récolte de l'abîme? Mais tu as crevé les yeux du lion. Tu crois voir passer la beauté au-dessus des lavandes noires. . . .

Qu'est-ce qui t'a hissé, une fois encore, un peu plus haut, sans te convaincre?

Il n'y a pas de siège pur. q (FM,178)

---

q Do not leave the task of governing your heart to those affections akin to autumn whose placid demeanor and whose affable death-pangs they borrow. Eyes are early in their narrowing. Suffering knows few words. Prefer to sleep unburdened: you will dream of the morrow and your bed will be light for you. You will dream that your house has window panes no longer. You are impatient to join with the wind, the wind rushing through a year in one night. Others will sing the melodious embodying of substances, flesh personifying no longer other than an hourglass witchery. You will condemn gratitude repeating itself. Later they will identify you with some disaggregated giant, lord of the impossible. / However. / You have only increased the weight of your night. You have returned to high wall fishing, to the dog-days with no summer. Think of the perfect house you will

A single word may serve as a threshold. Thus, around the central word: "pourtant," neutral in appearance, two verbal masses are set in motion, opposed. Eventually the delicate balance triumphs over the hermetic details of the text, giving them a sense by their formal situation, within the whole. The pain and its refusal, evident in the first three sentences, incite the desire for lightness, for the suppression of time as it ordinarily extends ("une année en une nuit"), of sadness and fatigue ("sans fardeau"), of the physical phantasms ("d'autres chanteront...les chairs"), and of verbal excess ("la gratitude qui se répète"). The poem predicts the concern for spiritual austerity which will set the tone for later writings (for example, even the title *Le Nu perdu*) by the open refusal of any other dwelling more commodious than the mental habitation of pain alone. Finally, it is the poem, entire, which furnishes the poet's mental habitation ("la tête habitable") perhaps not only for the moment of its composition. Speaking of it, the poet says: "I was in that moment heavy with a thousand years of poetry and previous distress. . . . I took my head as one seizes a block of salt and I literally pulverized it." (AHPP)

After the ambiguous formal bridge, the conjunction singled out by the text makes of the entire passage one single sentence. The second and more negative part works against the stated desire for lightness by all the weight of night, of return, of feeling, and of imagination tinged with regret:

tu rêveras du lendemain		tu n'as fait qu'augmenter
et ton lit sera léger	**POURTANT**	le poids de ta nuit
tu rêveras que ta maison		songe à la maison parfaite
n'a plus de vitres		que tu ne verras jamais monter

---

never see built. You are raging against your love at the center of a frenzied understanding. When shall it be, the harvest of the abyss? But you have put out the eyes of the lion. You think you see beauty passing above the black lavender. . . . / What has lifted you once again, slightly higher still, without convincing you? / There is no untainted seat.

The only hope would be to harvest regret and sorrow, gathering the abyss for sole nourishment; however the "and yet . . ." is suppressed in the text, leaving no other trace than the suspense marks (". . .") like a second "pourtant" which seems to put into question the sense already reversed a first time. For the conclusion imposes a slight elevation: "Qu'est-ce qui t'a hissé . . . un peu plus haut?" The poem's dwelling has come to resemble the dwelling imagined, although the faint regret of another perfect house that it cannot replace never completely disappears: "sans te convaincre." The verb "hisser" seems to respond to the verb whose action is proven impossible: "monter." Like his brother, the speaker in this text has "recourse to the stream"; this town too will be begun higher up once it has been effaced by the current.

The final statement of the necessary mixture of all things, of the imperfection implicit in every human place, instant, and feeling—even in what appears to be barest, most transparent, and simplest—is tragic only in a first moment and for one who might have believed in simple perfection. Should beauty pass above the black lavender, the sight would blind the observer (as beauty is said to "crever les yeux") and would dazzle even the alchemists' gold dormant in the dreaming lion—or Mercurius, a warm-blooded form of the dragon.

However, this poem so enclosed will find its distant power increasing within the space of the work, lending to other texts a resonance often imperceptible. Like the memory of the rushes ("Recours au ruisseau") whose fragile presence is deeply felt again in one of the last texts of *Contre une maison sèche*—"Nous passerons de la mort imaginée aux roseaux de la mort vécue nûment / We shall pass from imagined death to the reeds of death lived starkly," (NP,125)—here the ornaments of fiction give way to the simplicity of a Pascalian meditation on the fragility of man, in his dignity of thought. So the memory of this lavender and of the girl carrying it as a light and mysterious burden, will never be totally absent from the last sentence of the same collection, the exit from *Le Nu perdu* and the eventual entry into *La Nuit talismanique*:

"Qui, là, parmi les menthes. . . . ." The death that will necessarily triumph at last—as in the verb "prévaudra," at once
powerful and simple—may be already felt, passing now in
the reeds, above the black lavender, although the passage is
not outwardly expressed. It remains thus, in its suggestion,
open to each reader.

D. CIRCLE, CYCLE, WHEEL

> Vous tendez une allumette à votre lampe et
> ce qui s'allume n'éclaire pas. C'est loin, très
> loin de vous, que le cercle illumine. (FM,116)

Within the expanse of Char's work, circular images play
several roles, some traditional, suggesting potential motion,
sensed even in their repose, or the infinite, or the alternations
of fate. For example, "la grande roue" of desire, both grave
and wandering, like chance itself, summons forth the wheel
of fortune in its turning, now sunlit, now shaded. The transition between a clear text such as "Recours au ruisseau" and
the far gloomier one, "Le Masque funèbre," which follows
it, is made by a passage composed of an isolated brief sentence, like a circle revolving from innocence to innocence
slaughtered: *"Le soleil tourne, visage de l'agneau, c'est déjà
le masque funèbre."* (LM,62)

In a brighter mood, the image of a wheel is materialized in
the useful and common wind- or water-mill; only by extension
does the motion become that of consuming and racking. The
boy of ten, standing "enshrined" in the Sorgue river, contemplates the waterwheel ("moulin à eau") in its churning of
smoke-like spray: "Mais quelle roue dans le coeur de l'enfant
aux aguets tournait plus fort, tournait plus vite que celle
du moulin dans son incendie blanc? / But what wheel in the
heart of the watchful child turned more forcefully, turned
more quickly, than that of the wheel in its white consuming?"
(LM,180) And the child grown older transposes to this simplest of spectacles a love now made specific in its joyous

repetition, as the "moulin à eau" is illumined to become, with another light upon it, a "moulin à soleil."

.   .   .   .

Je demeurais là, entièrement inconnu de moi-même, dans votre moulin à soleil, exultant à la succession des richesses d'un coeur qui avait rompu son étau. Sur notre plaisir s'allongeait l'influente douceur de la grande roue consumable du mouvement, au terme de ses classes.[r] (FM, 24)

But in the darker turning of the image, a menace is imposed, precisely by the repetition of the cycle. In *Aromates chasseurs*, a text already cited pictures the wheel of history turning in reverse, endlessly destructive.[17] (AC,7) At other moments, the image of racking becomes interiorized within the man having become his own assassin: "Le pire est dans chacun, en chasseur, dans son flanc." (FM,218) The huntsman hidden in the self serves as fate's own henchman, preparing the final destiny of Orion "chasseur de soi."

The horizon of history is glimpsed only from a subjective viewpoint; from the present we see only the past, and never the future. Approaching our end, we see only a beginning: "Bientôt on ne voit plus mourir mais naître et grandir. Nos yeux sous notre front ont passé. Par contre, les yeux dans notre dos sont devenus immenses. La roue et son double horizon, l'un à présent très large et l'autre inexistant, vont achever leur tour. / Soon we shall see dying no longer but rather birth and increase. Our eyes have dimmed beneath our foreheads. However, our eyes turned backward have grown

---

[r] I remained there, entirely unknown to myself, in your sun-mill, exulting at the riches in succession of a heart which had snapped open its vice. Over our pleasure there stretched out the influential gentleness of motion's great consumable wheel, at the end of its classes. ("Envoûtement à la Renardière")

[17] Compare Char's commentary on Sima: "Pareil à la fumée bleue qui s'élève du safre humide quand les dents de la forte mâchoire l'égratignent avant de le concasser." (S) The distance between man and what surrounds him is not always great.

immense. The wheel and its double horizon, one now wide of span and the other nonexistent, are about to end their turning." Yet it is only by our attachment to the temporal that we can insert ourselves into the curve of the universe, "insoumis et courbé." (NP,65) The image of our own circular clocks seems to bend time to our own shape: "courbera le temps, liera la terre à nous." (LM,117) The adjustment of our own revolution to that of the stars forms in itself a brief cycle of *La Nuit talismanique.*

To the cyclic images and themes—the alchemical cycle, the myth of the eternal return, the "retour amont" and the return of seasons—a cyclic form corresponds. The poem, a brief and intense flash, nevertheless remakes itself, gaining in force as its theme is stated, repeated, and reversed: "J'aime, je capture et je rends à quelqu'un. Je suis dard et j'abreuve de lumière le prisonnier de la fleur. / I love, I capture, and I give back to someone. I'm a sting and I quench the flower's prisoner with light." (LM,68) To which an exactly matching response, is given: "L'étoile me rend le dard de guèpe qui s'était enfoui en elle. / The star gives back to me the wasp sting which had plunged into it." The star is thus blinded by its own radiance, as it might be, in a metaphorical transfer, by the sting of an insect; the latter is said to be in its turn stung by the radiant beam of a flower and thereby lit, then pierced once more by the star it had wounded and illuminated.

Occasionally, under the first superficial form is a form understood to be turning on a deeper level, as a central wheel in a number of poems, including "La Liberté." "Elle est venue par cette ligne blanche pouvant tout aussi bien signifier l'issue de l'aube que le bougeoir du crépuscule. / . . . / D'un pas à ne se mal guider que derrière l'absence, elle est venue, cygne sur la blessure, par cette ligne blanche. // It came along this white line that could signify dawn's emergence as well as dusk's candlestick. / . . . / With a pace unsure only behind absence, it came, a swan on the wound, along this white line." (FM,52) The ambiguity of the white line permits us to read the passage from night to day, the crossing of a threshold

131

toward a pale dawn, or the passage from day to evening, by the image and the light of the candle: within the circle of this flame we become aware either of a double exit, or of the obligatory fresh beginning of the form. And the circle of light reflects also on the subsequent reading of *La Nuit talismanique* and of *Artine*, like an earlier flame lending its depth to that later one.

From the white line, the swan rises in memory of the Mallarméan lake and also in a reflection of the line itself, as the white verse is traced on the wound between the two doors opened—or closed—on the poem. The sign which he also is ("cygne/signe") points equally toward the entrance or the exit, as if the most essential texts permitted a double direction of sense, in their threshold and their outcome.

Now the effect of a poem in circular form is quite different from that of a linear poem. In "Grège" and "Invitation" the form revolves constantly in the same place: the revels continue, the outer festival is always the countenance mirroring the inner joy, and the death of one festival clearly leads to another festive birth, in a way uninterrupted and certain. Similarly, the stone-cutter's finale, playing at a dance to which we are all invited, is not only general but inescapable. In the poem "Allégeance," whose bare and quiet fidelity is opposite to the full orchestration in the epic "Visage nuptial," the form of the poem itself corresponds to an unceasing hidden loyalty. The words "mon amour," situated at the heart of the text, are never specified as to gender, the person loved being completely identified with the love itself and even with its verbal expression (hence the necessary "it" in the translation, so as not to betray that expression). Moreover, this love is lit by the secret it bears, unsuspecting. Its own place is already prepared even in its soaring freedom, by the other freedom. Nor does the weight of that fidelity bind; it only illuminates from a distance.

"Allégeance"

Dans les rues de la ville il y a mon amour. Peu importe où il va dans le temps divisé. Il n'est plus mon amour,

chacun peut lui parler. Il ne se souvient plus; qui au juste
l'aima?

. . . .

Dans les rues de la ville il y a mon amour. Peu importe
où il va dans le temps divisé. Il n'est plus mon amour,
chacun peut lui parler. Il ne se souvient plus; qui au juste
l'aima et l'éclaire de loin pour qu'il ne tombe pas? (FM,
219)[s]

The few words added here at the end give their light not
only to the love but also to the deeper sense of the text. Even
in a divided and divisive time, even from a distance, this
clarifying fidelity protects against despair, lifting the beloved,
the faithful voice, and the poem exactly its echo to a higher
level, where what might have seemed merely pathetic rises
to the tragic redeemed. For solitude, absence, and unknow-
ing are never to be sensed by the one lit from afar, who is
illumined only in ignorance. And yet, one change of tense
alters the whole reach of the poem: for the condition situated first in the past, the love deceived, is finally made the
still present source of a formal and thematic poetic continuum
yielding its own clarity, no less effective than that of love.

l'aima $\longrightarrow$ l'éclaire

So the simplest line becomes continuous. All the circular
forms and images—the recurring flight of the phoenix past
the dust of ashes, the "opaque anneau" (NP,22) ringing the
dispersed elements, the tragic wheel of history and the passionate cycle of a hopeless love matched to time and to
seasons—in their reappearances finally triumph over the
despair of a solitude, illuminating its freedom and, perhaps,
its hidden correspondence.

[s] In the streets of the town goes my love. Small matter where it
moves in divided time. It is no longer my love, anyone may speak with
it. It no longer remembers; who exactly loved it? / . . . / In the
streets of the town goes my love. Small matter where it moves in
divided time. It is no longer my love, anyone may speak with it. It no
longer remembers; who exactly loved it and lights it from afar, lest
it should fall?

133

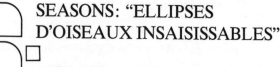

SEASONS: "ELLIPSES D'OISEAUX INSAISISSABLES"

A. The Cycle of Alchemy

> J'admets que l'intuition raisonne et dicte des ordres dès l'instant que, porteuse de clefs, elle n'oublie pas de faire vibrer le trousseau des formes embryonnaires de la poésie en traversant les hautes cages où dorment les échos, les avant-prodiges élus qui, au passage, les trempent et les fécondent. (MM,125-126)

The texts of *Le Marteau sans maître* seem at first glance to be the least approachable of all Char's writing, relating, we might suppose, to his state of mind at the time of its composition. These are books that speak little: *Artine*, written in 1930, is dedicated to silence and, implicitly, to dream ("au silence de celle qui laisse rêveur") and has at its center an image connected to the tradition of a *Mutus liber*: "the book opened on Artine's knees was readable only on dark days." (Although we shall speak at greater length of *Artine* as reflected in *La Nuit talismanique*, as is Georges de La Tour's *Madeleine à la veilleuse*, it will not be in order to "open" the work; what is silent, by the poet's preference should not be so lightly disclosed.)

L'Action de la justice est éteinte, dedicated to André Breton, and *Abondance viendra*,[1] dedicated to Paul Éluard, date,

[1] Char explains the title thus: his great-grandmother had a poor mason working for her, whose only wealth was fourteen children; he was one of the Abondance family. Subsequently Char, in a fit of black humor, named the collection after this richness never to come except in number. By an inexplicable conjunction, he continues, the title *Le Marteau sans maître* is thus linked to the title *Abondance viendra*: the latter volume is the résumé of several elements from preceding texts, and the prefiguration of many elements to come after it. This in part explains, says the poet, its slightly sideways aspect, its singularity ("son aspect à côté.").

respectively, from 1931 and 1933, from the moment of what Char calls the "domaine irréconciliable de la surréalité"; (MM,50) Char's participation in surrealism is limited by his own repeated statements, to the years 1930-34. The difference in attitude between him and those with a longer allegiance to the surrealist movement is sufficiently clear. *Arsenal* (1927-29), written before Char's contact with surrealism, is consecrated, in a fashion only partly ironic, to the theme of liberation proper to the young poet—who is preparing here the arsenal of his weapons and his personal energy for the struggle with language, a preoccupation manifest not only during the surrealist years but before and since.[2] On the other hand, in the collections dated 1930-34, no cohering theme seems more dominant than the alchemical. Within the aesthetic of *Le Marteau sans maître*, discussed earlier, the exhortations to hammer, to reduce, to prune, to consume, and to select, form the apparent source for the later intricate texture of his writing. Yet they can also be seen as instructions for the transformation of disparate parts into a whole at once transparent and golden, a psychological and formal liberation coinciding, in the paradoxical language characteristic of alchemy, with the hermetic work: "L'homme morne et emblématique vit toujours en prison, mais sa prison se trouve à présent en liberté. / Drab and emblematic man still lives imprisoned, but his prison has been given its liberty." (MM,109)

The emblems of alchemical man will never be fully displayed, but their indications suffice to the work. *Abondance viendra* and *Moulin premier* (1934-35) furnish abundant alchemical images familiar to the poet. By entitling one of the longer texts "Crésus," he suggests the image of gold as the key to a poetic wealth. The gold-bearing sands ("placers") of the Pactole river drift throughout like an illuminating dust ("poussière éclairante"). By suggesting elliptically the methods and the aims of the Work, the poet grants us the right to

---

[2] Char reminds us that it was through Paul Éluard's enthusiasm for *Arsenal* that he was presented to the surrealist group: the poems included therein thus pre-date his contact with surrealism.

mention them without detailing them. Certain passages sound like alchemical texts, always written to be read *on the inside as well as on the outside*. We have only to look, in the necessarily dim and therefore appropriate lighting for a *via oscura*, at the references to fountains, to the ocean that is also the mother (the "mer-mère" of the *materia prima*), and to the crossing. Matched to all the images and their transmutations is the highly occult style of a few passages in particular. Certain prose poems of *Abondance viendra* are rendered dense as if by a hidden oracle, speaking in its voice at once "empestée" and marvelous: we might compare their tone to a word at once granting and negating, "la parole qui révoque sous la parole qui déplie." (PPC,169) A brief text from *Moulin premier* exemplifies this language of chiaraoscuro, half-lit by the glow-worm within it: " 'Sans doute, un poème se passant la nuit doit-il être lapidé de vers-luisants. Mais un autre allant le jour? Père amant, voyez-nous jouir, très éprises, le fleuret d'un miroir dans les doigts.' Ainsi s'étalent vos outrances, Novices mouillées de l'arc-en-ciel, follettes du mil, à la criée, mes chères peaux . . . Navigue docile discorde."[a] (*Moulin premier*, LIII,MM,138-9) The passage is badly rendered in language other than its own or any clearer, since it is not meant to be "taking place in daylight." In a later poem, a glow-worm resting in the hand shows the years to come. Here, this poem of night is itself pursued ("lapidé," pelted with stones) and made lapidary by the glow.

The incestuous eroticism of the third line, "Father lover, see us . . . ," is an exposure magnified through the mirror handle held like a fencing foil by the "rainbow-wet novices" in their "outrageous" display of their own pleasure. To the latter the poet extends an ironic salute: "mes chères peaux"

[a] "Doubtless, a poem taking place at night should be pelted with glow-worms. But another, taking place in daylight? Father lover, see us take our pleasure as we are very much in love, the foil of a mirror in our fingers." Thus your excesses are exposed, novices wet from the rainbow, spirits of the millet, auctioned off, my dear skins. . . . Docile discord navigates.

suggesting at once ["pots"]—the nocturnal chamberpot, and ["mes chapeaux"], a compliment ("chapeau!/hats off!") pluralized and personalized. This "poem passing by at night" points our way from the stick in its multiple connotations, to the fingers, and in a divergence (or a "discorde"), from the glow-worm the "vers-luisants"—also these "shining verses" —to the bright mirror, the novae implicit in the sky above, and finally to the rainbow. The path of night, whether watery or bestarred, and the path of day might be seen to converge.

1. *Illuminating Dust*: "poussière éclairante"

We have spoken of the significance of dust ("poussière") in connection with the fragment. But the precise function of this dust that illuminates by its future, shining in spite of, and even because of, the obstacles in its path—this "grain solaire," the product of a *Moulin premier* and the goal of a "pulverizing" poetry—gives force to the expressions of multiplication and transformation, such as "essaime la poussière / let the dust swarm," to the image of fertilizing ashes and that of the trail of powder ready to explode. The hardest matter can flower through its own dissolution, by means of the gold ("or") already implied in an adjective to all appearances innocent: "adorable," containing also the ability to be gilded: ["lava dorable"]. The fire of this suggested volcano mingles with the gold, providing the major source of light to be thrown on the poem.

Such images and formulas expand rapidly within these two collections. The following text on correspondence has already been quoted for its key image of *quarrying*, suggesting the allied figure of the *Équarisseur*—which, by extension, we connect[3] to the later title "Dans la pluie giboyeuse," as the quartered element can be either beast (the quarry) or quarried matter (taken in squares or "carrés"):

[3] The verbal connection here is the reader's own. The Équarisseur is shown explicitly only in a dark perspective, as he hacks apart. He can thus be considered the somber double of the other figures: of L'Élagueur, L'Écumeur, L'Émondeur . . .

137

"Les Rapports entre parasites"

. . . .

Derrière les arbres civilisés, une équipe d'ouvriers équar-
rissait la boue, cette autre pierre précieuse. L'homme re-
stitue l'eau comme le ciel. Pour être logique avec la nature,
il sème des lueurs et récolte des épieux. . . . Mais aucune
indignité ne souille les correspondances. Cette nuit, au faîte
de sa splendeur, mon amour aura à choisir entre deux
grains également sordides de poussière. Les chaînes mag-
nétiques naviguent loin des feux commandés.[b] (MM,108)

. . . .

The transformation and the restitution operated by poetry
seen as the alchemical Work are carried out through common
expressions and simple gestures, which scatter throughout
all the texts seeds of potential clarity, the source of a future
radiance. A speck of "sordid" dust can be a solar speck as
well. Yet the most precious stone, like the most common
word, can easily be disguised within ordinary mud: the quar-
rier as quarterer gives it a shape, that, however, may be visible
only from inside the Work, like another philosopher's stone.

Here, in Char's image, the magnetic chains are subservient
to no command, unguided and unlit by lights of any shore.
Later, allusions to automatic writing, a collective experience
that Char never shared in any serious fashion, will disappear
completely. But an unshakable belief remains in the myriad
gods present in man's own understanding, and it is against
the backdrop of this belief that the alchemy of poetry will be
seen as the part in man transcending his dull reasonableness.
(One day, sharing in the "commune présence" that gives its
title to the last poem of *Moulin premier*, we may harvest even

---

[b] . . . Behind the civilized trees, a team of workers quarried the
mud, that other precious stone. Man restitutes water like the sky. To
be logical with nature, he scatters streaks of light and harvests spears.
. . . But nothing unworthy sullies correspondences. Tonight, at the
peak of her splendor, my love will have to choose between two
equally sordid specks of dust. Magnetic chains navigate far from control lights. . . .

the fruit of suffering, with pain our only dwelling as in "J'habite une douleur.") The title "Rapports . . ." signifies not only a series of relationships clearly stated, parasitical in that each element depends on another, but also between absence and presence, relating to certain distinctions and to the necessity of choosing between them. So that the poem pulverized may flower, "the multiple occult properties derived from poetic phosphorus" (MM,36) should be seen under a fiery magnifying glass capable, in turn, of setting a fire, a "loupe incendiaire" corresponding—according to the law of contraries—to the "loupe noire" of the poem "Eaux-mères," both a *texte matrice* and a *materia prima.*[4]

2. *Corpse, Convulsion, Recreation*: "Cadavre récréatif," "Convulsif ambre jaune"

A second obsessive motif, the recreating corpse, is linked to the coffin, a hollow and potentially maternal object ready for impregnation ("cet objet creux destiné à être longuement fécondé") in the center of the text just cited, whose title can now be read differently: "O mère / Oh mother." (MM,103) The images of tomb and mother appear in another text, "Domaine": "Tombe mars fécond sur le toit de chagrin / (literally) Fall fecund March on sorrow's roof." (MM,110)

First, as one of the fragmentary statements in the text tells us, we must suffer in ourselves the invasion of space: this suggestion sheds a diffuse light upon the next-to-last text of the series *Abondance viendra*, called "Intégration." "Le souffle abdique sur la cendre. / . . . / Grand tronc en activité crois-tu au dénouement par la lèpre? / . . . / Craie . . . j'évoque les charmes de tes épaisseurs voilées, siège de la cabale. Nous fûmes le théâtre d'étranges secousses. . . . Craie,

---

[4] (The title is of course related to the Magna Mater.) The poem is itself generative, for the account of a dream, serving as primary material, provides a simultaneous commentary imposed on the poet's mind in dream, as Char tells us. The commentary or *reflection* is italicized in the text, whose two-level presentation finds a distinct counterpart later in the wall and reflection of *Contre une maison sèche*.

enrôle-moi, cadavre, dans ton principe. . . . // Breath gives up on ashes. / . . . / Tall trunk and vital, do you believe in a scaly undoing? / . . . / Chalk . . . , I call upon the charms of your muffled layers, seat of the cabal. We were the theater for strange quakings. . . . Chalk, enroll me, a cadaver, in your principle. . . ." (MM,112-113) Alluding at once to a corporeal decomposition into dust and, perhaps, to that of the text—for metatextual allusions are to be seen, often, through the reader's eyes, and then, retrospectively, through the poet's—this passage expresses the body's dissolution by means of its own activity, and consequently, through its own choice. The text become object places itself on the same level, participates in the same force as the cabalistic assault, which, like a secret speech and a veiled power besieges the rational. The narrator commits himself fully to the principle of defeat, and, in the act of dissolving the text, undoing it for a later reforming, he accepts the poem's disintegration and thereby, implicitly that of the poet: "se démanteler sans se détruire. / to undo oneself without destruction." The true force of this disintegration resides, paradoxically, in the disintegration of a poem turned to powder, "le poème pulvérisé," only to be remade. The chalk disturbs the blackboard across which these "étranges secousses" are felt; the message then effaces itself completely. As a second "recreative corpse," this poetic dust is at the height of its luminescence during the very act of its decomposition and, like the chalk, the poet and the poem are consumed in and yet illumined by their writing; so too, the reader, in his reading. (And yet, since the calcium carbonate of the chalk comes from sea creatures, we might consider that the *materia prima* of the "Eauxmères" once again furnishes the element for clarifying, in the double act of creation and decreation, like another corpse impregnating the mind from a distance.)

The theme of the recreative corpse that appears openly in "Les Rapports entre parasites" as well as in "Domaine" and, by suggestion, in "Intégration," is illuminated by a "*réserve romancée*" in *Moulin premier*, where a dead body uncovered (a tradition called "the transfusion of the sun") and a resuscitation by water (the son's tears shed on the mother's body) precede a doubled image in the mirror, that of the mother and, beside her, a savage picture or re-creation of a former lover. Her *reflection* is the following, and might be called the story's "reservation": "ne trépane pas le lion qui rêve / don't trepan the dreaming lion." Sleeping lions must be let lie, and their dreams lead to a "recreative" remark at the conclusion of the text: "Et l'avenir est fécondé. / And the future is made fecund." From the hidden reflection of the living being once buried springs a possible future birth.

In this text the sun dying, only to be muted and reborn ("la transfusion du soleil"), represents the beast dreaming, like a yellow-maned king asleep. The mother, restored to life, is the *matrice* of the text and the tomb as a coffin/womb, the vase or Athanor where the work will be done. The procedure interrupted in its operation will be resumed or fecundated by the son, the sun illuminating all elements from inside, drawing contraries into harmony and thus giving birth to the poem. "Féraporte," the family named in the text, suggests "fer-apporte": the bringer of the *fer*, at once the necessary instrument of engendering, the iron of strengthening and the *faire* of the writing. What will be engendered is the poem of the new man, of the son as the golden liberator and the sun as the gold liberated.

Another text from the same series comments, in an echo, on the essential loneliness of each separate element, each fragment enlisted in the chalk's own writing and in its future undoings, "assimilating and appropriating one's future nothingness, fortification, and offering necessarily vain." (MM, 139) We think here not only of the space between the verbal flashes, appropriated by the text, but also of the reverse—of the moment when the poet, taking upon himself the form of the disintegrated poem, will find himself once more in fragments, a "disaggregated giant," shattered into the multiplicity of the poem. Nevertheless, the text finds its own integrality, as "the intact chrysalis" finds its "active vertiginous properties" (MM,99)—the vertigo advocated by surrealism and Breton's "convulsive beauty" suggest the "convulsive ambre jaune" in this collection dedicated, precisely, to André Breton. The chalk shuddering against the board of its undoing is equally a product of these convulsions and an agent of the Work in its "grand pacte d'abondance / great pact of plenty." (MM,105) *Abondance viendra*: the goal of the alchemical and poetic endeavors is this amber called gold by virtue of its color and, elsewhere, noontime, like the brighter slope of the mountain, lit at its summit: "Midi réhabilité / noon rehabilitated." Both the noontime sun in its yellow-white heat—thus the furnace for a "convergence of multiples," having the color of "convulsive amber"—and the nighttime "conjonction d'astres" where poet and the poem undone are reborn, require the most vigorous "return upland" of the Work.

3. *Conjunction, Transmutation*: "Conjonction d'astres"

A third theme, omnipresent and inseparable from its alchemical overtones, that of the marriage between male and female elements (MM,134) as in this meeting or conjunction of contraries, (MM,105) finds its noblest testimony on the human level in *Le Visage nuptial*, but is assumed throughout the entire course of Char's writing.

The scout leading, by his light, the procession into the "commune presence" found as a poem-epilogue to *Le Marteau sans maître* and *Moulin premier*—thus, the "éclaireur" or light-bringer—is also the sun appearing at the window,[5]

---

[5] Compare the light-bringing sun (son) of the "réserve romancée" of *Moulin premier*, discussed in this chapter. The first line of "Commune présence," the poem which concludes *Le Marteau sans maître*, reads: "Éclaireur comme tu surviens tard." The concept is close to these lines of Hölderlin, from "Der blinde Sänger" and "Chiron" respectively, where the light is personified: "Wo bist du, Jugendliches! das immer mich / Zur Stunde weckt des Morgens, wo bist du, Licht! // Where are you, youthful herald who always once / Would waken me at daybreak, where are you, light?" (H,184-185); "Wo bist du, Nachdenkliches! das immer muss / Zur Seite gehn, zu Zeiten, wo bist

the first witness to morning, the bringer of light and, eventually, the agent of the hidden union that ends the early poems only in order to begin another writing, no less hermetic although more humanly illuminating. It is the sun-scout who designates this encounter between the sleeper and his dream, (MM,109) containing the image which is *soror* to his work. In *Moulin premier*, the poet explains: "Here the male image pursues tirelessly the female image, or vice versa. When they succeed in reaching each other, it's the creator's death and the poet's birth." (MM,134) The alchemical themes attracting us to these texts have as their overriding pattern that of certain contraries juxtaposed and interdependent: the "coeur d'eau noire du soleil," (FM,36) or the "soleil et nuit dans un or identique," (PPC,212) both examples of the meeting, or confrontation termed "Confronts" in a poem of 1932. This outwardly visible tension of opposites betrays a central convulsion, as the title of Benjamin Péret's "feu central." Like a participator in some violent rite of passage, the narrator is forced to make his way through this *trying* (as an iron is tried in the flame, within Char's early poems of forging), and then beyond the purely alchemical figures to an arduous description of the poem:

"DOMAINE"

Tombe mars fécond sur le toit de chagrin.

. . . .

Matériaux vacillants, portes, coulisses, soupiraux, réduits, comme je voudrais pouvoir régler mon allure suivant la vôtre.

. . . .

Une allumette bien prise a debouclé le carcan, biceps et coude. Le leader a tiré la vermine éclairante. C'est la lave finale. Régicide, estime-toi favorisé si une langue de boeuf vient de loin en loin égayer ta cuvette.

---

du, Licht? // Where are you, thought-infusing, which at this time / Must always move beside me, where are you, light?" (H,188-189)

Ma maîtresse mouillée, écorchée insultante, je te plante
dans mon cri.

. . . .

Mes songes, hors l'amour, étaient graves et distants.
Faut-il *malgré* se réjouir?ᶜ (MM,110-111).

This final and enigmatic "despite" may be read in relation
to the first line, as if it signified: "Must we, despite the tomb,
rejoice?" Will the gold (*aureum vulgi*) or the gold of understanding (*aureum intellecti*), the new man represented by
the Work, come forth from this chrysalis? ("Dans la forêt
nous écoutons bouillir le ver. . . .") The following lines serve
as a gloss on the theme of the tomb become fecund: by this
series of "matériaux vacillants" or intermediary corridors—
never certain—a passageway can possibly be extended from
the hidden to the open.

"Surviving, I could unburden myself of depressing happiness." An old man willing to play the drabbest of dreamers
("ce dormeur morne") can be resuscitated within a coffin
marked by an "exclusive" legend: DEPOT D'EXCLUS.
Against a scene of tombstones ("passive memories of white
wood") an alchemical regicide takes place, as arson liberates
the new king and the old son is massacred, for transmutation
requires the extreme violence of a metaphoric act. The work
is inscribed through the four elements: an aerial sluice-gate,
steps on the sand or the earth ("fantasmes pédestres"),
matches with their implicitly contained flame, and a final
humid cry as if from molten lava for a wet and fiery washing: "la lave finale." In an essay of 1973 on the artist Sima,
Char describes "a plunge into the conflict of the four ele-

ᶜ Fall fecund March on the roof of sorrow. / . . . / Vacillating
materials, doors, corridors, air-holes, crannies, how I should like to
regulate my pace on yours. / . . . / A match afire has unfastened the
iron collar, biceps and elbow. The leader has pulled forth the illlumi-
nating vermin. It's the final lava. Regicide, count yourself privileged
if an ox-tongue comes now and then to brighten your basin. / My
dampened mistress, flayed and insulting, I set you in my cry. / . . . /
My dreams, outside of love, were grave and distant. / Must we *despite* rejoice?

144

ments absolved in behalf of an elementary book, just born, tired before its opening." (S) But as the forest yields up the wood where the worms and verses are boiling, the book must be opened, for it has served as a tomb imprisoning the word now to be reborn in clarity.

Fire mingles with water in the basin of rebirth: "Une allumette bien prise a débouclé . . . la lave finale," in order to free the "vermine éclairante," at once vermin and verse, clarifying and explosive: "vers-mine." Over the basin, the crucible, or the vase, the ox-tongue chants its half-heard song ("*la la*ve"), deliberately passing through the absurd sign toward the irrational marvelous: "reciter of solfeggio. Bludgeon, you snore for the helix miracle." The poetic tongue, insulting, imploring, this "damp mistress" or then "my wet locks" ("maîtresse mouillée" or "mes tresses mouillées") forms a grotesque image to hold the attention at the center of the cry, and of the understanding.

"A well-dressed society has a horror of flame." (MM,114) The peculiar brute strength of this tongue will not often be perceived in the future works, and yet the ox flayed raw in a Rembrandt canvas that the poet accepts as his unique sun ("seul soleil) at the conclusion of *Le Nu perdu* is only the last in date of an enduring lineage. A convulsive perception is seen to lie at the center of everything mortal, this scandalous and paradoxically resurrective principle or a potentially engendering corpse ("cadavre récréatif")—like the crucible of unity glimpsed in "L'Absent"—within every text.

B. CYCLE OF WATERS

A verte fontaine, fruits souvent meurtris.
(NP,103)

Closely linked to the alchemical inspiration, the fountain acquires, by every one of its appearances, a renewing power still greater. Unlike other less localized images of water, such as "the land of rains," "the quarried rain," and "the quick waters," the general image of the fountain brings the specific themes of offering and bestowing to each text where it is found. As the image of the star lends precision to the motifs of flash and brilliance, so the surging forth of water in its almost miraculous abundance represents the motifs of verbal recreation and renaissance. "The poet torments by means of unfathomable secrets the form and the voice of his fountains." (FM,77) The springtime surge of the Fontaine de Vaucluse represents the force of poetic language, while the water's green represents both Venus and resurrection.

Yet the voice does not always pour forth in simplicity. To quench the deepest thirst, for example—and not only an amorous thirst, omnipresent, which has its own cycle implicit in the present chapter—fire is preferable to rain: "The gradual presence of the sun gives it drink." (FM,188) This paradox on the level of the image befits the constant pattern of warring contraries familiar in the worlds of alchemy and of love. Insofar as form is concerned, a certain kind of structure can contribute a more nourishing flow than another, as if it were to emulate, in its accumulation, the generosity of fountains. Thus, in the poem "Jacquemard et Julia," the peaceful repetition of one expression seems to quench the dryness visible in the poem, assuring, against the constant tendency to fragmentation and dissolution, the gathering of emotional force, like a reservoir for the renewal of language in its diverse currents:

> Jadis l'herbe, à l'heure où les routes de la terre s'accordaient dans leur déclin, élevait tendrement ses tiges et allumait ses clartés. (. . .)
>
> Jadis l'herbe connaissait mille devises qui ne se contrariaient pas. (. . .)
>
> Jadis l'herbe était bonne aux fous et hostile au bourreau. (. . .)
>
> Jadis l'herbe avait établi que la nuit vaut moins que son pouvoir, que les sources ne compliquent pas à plaisir leur parcours, . . . Jadis, terre et ciel se haïssaient mais terre et ciel vivaient.

L'inextinguible sécheresse s'écoule. L'homme est un étranger pour l'aurore. Cependant à la poursuite de la vie qui ne peut être encore imaginée, il y a des volontés qui frémissent, des murmures qui vont s'affronter et des enfants sains et saufs qui *découvrent*.[d] (FM,186-187)

The past knowledge, tenderness, and justice of the grass—as in "Les Trois soeurs," where an unknown child about to be born is sheltered in grass by the seasons as they advance— serve here as the simple source ("les sources ne compliquent pas à plaisir leur parcours") for the present victory over a wasted land until, at the conclusion, a convergence of three strong verbs surges against the prior state of things in which man was not yet destined to the morning. The motion from uncertain trembling to certain battle, toward the final revelation of the spring at the heart of grass, encompassing the space from the initial past tense of the verb to the concluding present is no less significant than the progression from the past tense of the love stated at the outset of "Allégeance" to the present illumination: in both cases the source precedes, and lights from afar the figures of the text, against a future falling "which cannot yet be imagined":

"Allégeance": l'aima ⟶ ne tombe pas
"Jacquemard et Julia": jadis l'herbe ⟶ des enfants qui . . .
découvrent

The rejuvenating power of water is a literary constant, traditionally convincing in the same sense as the ephemeral beauty of the rose. A poem we have quoted in the analysis of fragments shows a complex series of verbal exchanges

[d] Formerly the grass, at the moment when the roads of earth agreed in their declining, gently raised its blades and lit its brightness. . . . / . . . / Formerly the grass knew a thousand mottoes which did not counter one another. . . . / . . . / Formerly the grass had prescribed that night should be of less worth than its power, that springs should not delight in complicating their course. . . . Formerly, earth and sky hated each other but earth and sky lived. / The unquenchable drought slips by. Man is a stranger for dawn. Nevertheless in the pursuit of life which cannot yet be imagined, there are wills trembling, murmurs doing battle, and children safe and sound *discovering*.

147

based on an ambivalent malady and on subsequent *resurgence*.[6] The play of words and concepts forms a difficult text where a metaphysical suffering ("mal") is partially cured by the *flow* of the poem against its fragmentary images and the ambivalence of its expressions: "front," "mal," "souffle," "arrosé," "évaporé":

"FRONT DE LA ROSE"

Malgré la fenêtre ouverte dans la chambre au long congé, l'arôme de la rose reste lié au souffle qui fut là. Nous sommes une fois encore sans expérience antérieure, nouveaux venus, épris. La rose! Le champ de ses allées éventerait même la hardiesse de la mort. Nulle grille qui s'oppose. Le désir resurgit, mal de nos fronts évaporés.

Celui qui marche sur la terre des pluies n'a rien à redouter de l'épine, dans les lieux finis ou hostiles. Mais s'il s'arrête et se recueille, malheur à lui! Blessé au vif, il vole en cendres, archer repris par la beauté.[e] (LM,123)

[6] The motifs of "réviviscence"—a word set by itself in one of the manuscript versions of *A une Sérénité crispée*: AUSC:A, and then the title of a poem—and of renascence meet in the concept of water. They are, in particular, most often associated with the image of a fountain or a spring: the Fontaine de Vaucluse in its springtime increase, in "Les Premiers instants," and with the fountain-mirror of "Marthe," where the presence and the present accumulating are the surface and the depth in which the poet also is reflected, increasingly. Furthermore, the poetic voice is reborn in all the words such as "source," "reconnaître," "revivre," where the event is seconded by, or guided by, the renewed flowing of water; the image of the fountain has a natural association with the spirit of generosity. Compare this vision with that, completely different, of Pierre Reverdy, for whom the fountain seems to be associated with the most useless and dusty forms, and with the least fertile wound, to which there is lacking even the red that would be a sign of life:

Sur le meuble, une plaie livide et des carrés poudreux. Le jet d'eau creuse l'air—la vapeur sort des lignes et le bruit de la mer se calme peu à peu. (*Au Soleil du plafond*, Tériade, 1955, p. 126)

[e] Despite the window opened in the room of long leave, the rose fragrance remains joined to the breath which was there. Once again we are without prior experience, newcomers, in love. The rose! The fields of its moving paths would fan away even death's boldness. No gate to make opposition. Desire surges up once more, disorder of our

The presentation of this forehead, this brow of a hill, or this battlefront ("front/front") is marked by absence; in a previous version[7] instead of the "long congé," the room appeared: "la chambre sans personne." But this deserted room still contains breath and wind: as if the "souffle" were the trace of a recently uttered word. The vacation ("congé") which is also a leave-giving and leave-taking, corresponding to the opening space and the uncompromising dismissal at the outset of "Le Visage nuptial" and, in "Biens égaux," space as "cet absolu et scintillant congé"—suggests the freshness of a discontinuous experience or that of a "new arrival" ("nouveau venu" in the first version). In a secular baptism of beauty, a toast is made to this fresh beginning: "La rose!" ["l'arrose"], in contradiction of the "grill opposing," the corresponding expression, to which it is nevertheless phonetically attached by a rhyme: "nulle grille qui s'oppose." In an early version (PA:F), not yet turned toward the couple,[8] where we read: "Le désir vit, mal de mon front évaporé," the verb "vit" had perhaps suggested, by its nominal homophone [vie] the idea of its opposing partner, "mort" ("l'oubli de la mort") in the sentence which directly followed it ("Le champ . . . mort"). In the definitive version, the formerly neutral or even negative concept of oblivion ("l'oubli") is altered in favor of a strongly positive concept: "la hardiesse," so that the contrast is developed.

By the change in word order, the final accent of the initial paragraph no longer falls upon death, but rather, once the sentence has been put in its final place, upon "le front évaporé," this brow of sentimental battle, whence the sweat has

---

flighty foreheads. / He who walks on the earth of rains has nothing to fear from the thorn, in places finite or hostile. But should he stop and meditate, woe to him! Wounded to the quick, he flies to ashes, archer recaptured by beauty.

[7] No. 783 (AE-IV-34) (PA:F).

[8] Compare this other modification, which deviates from purely personal feeling: "L'expérience que la vie dément, celle que je préfère," (PPC,237) which in a later version yields "celle que le poète préfère."

disappeared or is about to do so. Whether or not the image "évaporé" (either "giddy" or "evaporated") is engendered by the suggested word ["arrose"] from its dampness to its evaporation, and that of the "mal" or evil by the male figure ["mâle"] of the newly arrived, these verbal suggestions are, once heard, inseparable from the poem. It is the song of the comings and goings of a rose—its "champ" and its ["chant"] —whose fragant motion would fan away evil, absorbing within it the explicit breath or the wind implicitly present; from the beginning.[9] "La terre des pluies," an image added after the preliminary sketch of the poem and corresponding to a hidden source of nourishment, confers on the land across which the archer strides a potential fertility. But motion itself is the surest protection against the malady of beauty, seeming to negate fragmentation. Thus through a series of points discontinuous but traversible, through dust or ashes of a shattered whole, the poem, itself identified with the hunter who is the poet, pursues its way toward rebirth or resurgence, like a renascent phoenix, to awaken a waste land.

[9] In one of the Duino Elegies, Rilke combines just the same notions of an empty room, a breath, a departure and an evaporation of beauty "from ember to ember." The juxtaposition of these six elements reminds us of the terms "chambre au long congé," the "souffle," the "fronts évaporés," and the "cendres." "Denn wir, wo wir fühlen, verflüchtigen; ach wir / atmen uns aus und dahin; von Holzglut zu Holzglut / geben wir schwächern Geruch. Da sagt uns wohl einer: / ja, du gehst mir ins Blut, dieses Zimmer, der Frühling / füllt sich mit dir. . . . Was hilfts, er kann uns nicht halten, / wir schwinden in ihm und um ihn // For we, when we feel, evaporate; oh, we / breathe ourselves out and away; from ember to ember / yielding a fainter scent. True, someone may tell us: / 'You've got in my blood, the room, the Spring's / growing full of you'. . . . What's the use? He cannot retain us. / We vanish within and around him." (DE,28-31) In both cases, the central focus of the poem is on beauty. Rilke's Elegy continues here: "Und jene, die schön sind . . ." and in connection with "le champ de ses allées" (read as a "chant" because of Orpheus' singing) and the "Arôme de la rose," see also, in the Sonnets to Orpheus, the following passage: ". . . Ein für alle Male / ists Orpheus, wenn es singt. Er kommt und geht. / Ists nicht schon viel, wenn er die Rosenschale / um ein paar Tage manchmal übersteht? // . . . Once and for all / it's Orpheus when there's singing. He comes and goes. Is it not much already if at times / he overstays for a few days at the bowl of roses?" (SO,24-25)

Manuscript of the poem "L'Inoffensiv" (March 26, 1953), in
Les Matinaux. From the Fonds René Char-Yvonne Zervos in
the Bibliothèque littéraire Jacques Doucet. (Previously unpublished.)

Manuscript of the poem "Front de la rose" (March 8, 1953), in
Les Matinaux. (Previously unpublished.)

The image of the archer, a possible allusion to one of Zeno's paradoxes (containing no figure, but simply his arrow) is absent from the first version, where the poet tries successively: "beauté reprise par la beauté," "passant repris . . . ," and "feu noir . . . ," each of the three terms related to a different aspect of Char's thought. The notion of beauty recaptured by beauty illustrates the correspondence of like elements, as of a flash of thought to an apparently divergent flash, as the passerby illustrates in his walking a constant traversal of the fragments, as the black fire represents the tension holding between alchemical opposites: from illumination to ashes. But the archer, whose arrow exists only in its flight avows his defeat before the object of his desire.[10] And this poem of 1953 itself leads to ashes, in a premonition of the poem "Mirage des aiguilles," dating from almost twenty years later, which concludes by the statement that "The present is only a game or a massacre of archers." (NP,17) (For another interpretation of this "massacre," see above, the section on "Enigma.")

Nevertheless, not all the poems have this malady at their core. Those centered on the fountain, the spring, and the well show a clear conviction: "La source, notre endroit!" (LM,130)[11] The figure of a fountain-maker, or a well-digger recurs, in the poem from which the above exclamation is quoted, and elsewhere. In "Médaillon" (FM,30), he will have his "memory eliminated," an abrupt signal of freshness that links him to the other figures invested with special poetic

[10] Compare "L'Eternité à Lourmarin" (LM,199), written on the death of Albert Camus:

A l'heure de nouveau contenue où nous questionnons tout le poids d'énigme, soudain commence la douleur, celle de compagnon à compagnon, que l'archer, cette fois, ne transperce pas. (LM,199)

In one of Zeno's paradoxes, the separate points, each at rest, are nevertheless overcome by our simple moving, as an arrow really moves, in spite of the intellectual dilemma, toward the target. Here the paradox gives way to pain, as the distance, before only metaphoric, between friend and friend, cannot at present be overcome by any arrow's flight, cannot be vanquished by any mental solution or any metaphoric archer.

[11] See note 6, p. 148.

powers, such as "L'Élagueur," "L'Émondeur," "L'Éclaireur," "L'Équarisseur." Even the waters of his well, said to cover over past crimes by the violent luminosity and sudden freshness implied in their description as a "green lightning" are "saccagés d'un proche sacre / plundered by a near consecration." This violence is allied with the sacred: the poem takes its strength in this image, for the thunderbolts like Jove's are brought close, ravaging a memory which might have hindered by its "discouraging weight" the impulse toward recreation. Often in this harsh universe where cruelty seems to lie near the source of feeling, the fountain is the scene for the most profound mutual recognition of a love, where a wound is deepened by the waters toward an erotic undoing irreversible in its consequences and wide in its reach. (For the more positive generosity of the well seen as "secourable," nourishing, and yet tragic, located at the very heart of joining, see the above comments on "Yvonne: la soif hospitalière," placed, because of the poem's tone and its force, in the discussion of "Bread.")

"Jeunesse" and "Marthe" have their common source in the fountain: both are turned toward the fairer and more generous side of the poet's interior climate.

"JEUNESSE"

Loin de l'embuscade des tuiles et de l'aumône des calvaires, vous vous donnez naissance, otages des oiseaux, fontaines. . . .
Éloge, nous nous sommes acceptés.[f] (FM,25)
.   .   .   .

The freshly born voice of the fountain[12] a hostage to the hovering birds triumphs over the fragmentary, its resurgence

---

[f] Far from the tiles' ambush and the calvaries' alms, you bring yourself to birth, hostages of the birds, fountains. / . . . / Eulogy, we have accepted ourselves.

[12] Rilke's fountain, too, is generous and speaks with a pure entire voice: "O Brunnen-Mund, du gebender, du Mund, / der unerschöpflich Eines, Reines, spricht— // O fountain-mouth, o giving, o mouth that speaks / exhaustlessly one single, one pure thing—" (SO,98-99).

relieving "the nausea of ashes" (like the "mal" of another text), and triumphing over the pain of distance:

. . . .

Le chant finit l'exil. La brise des agneaux ramène la vie neuve.[g] (FM,25)

A former estrangement makes way for the new wind, with the innocence of lambs, furnishing a few fresh strands for the poet's own song, which "transforms everything into prolonged woolen threads." (FM,74)

"Marthe," a poem given the name of a childhood friend, describes a flow of experience which must be left unlimited, like a fountain: the poem, like Martha herself, must be unhampered in its "thirst for departure." So liberty mixes with the source of and the remedy for the very thirst it imparts, speaking for the new moment free from the weight of past ritual, and free too from any future precaution equally imprisoning: "without having to greet each other, to foresee. . . ."

Marthe que ces vieux murs ne peuvent pas s'approprier, fontaine où se mire ma monarchie solitaire, comment pourrais-je jamais vous oublier puisque je n'ai pas à me souvenir de vous: vous êtes le présent qui s'accumule.[h] (FM,191)

. . . .

After the name announced, the sentence flows, increasing its force in three successive waves until the definition including all the rest: "vous êtes. . . ."

The present accumulating in the text also is made of privileged or primary moments. "Les Premiers instants" shows a cascade increasing to the point of denying the very mountain which has given it birth:

[g] Song terminates exile. The breeze of lambs brings back life anew.
[h] Martha, whom these old walls cannot appropriate, fountain where my solitary ruling is reflected, how could I ever forget you for I have not to remember you: you are the present accumulating.

153

"Les Premiers instants"

Nous regardions couler devant nous l'eau grandissante. Elle effaçait d'un coup la montagne, se chassant de ses flancs maternels. Ce n'était pas un torrent qui s'offrait à son destin mais une bête ineffable dont nous devenions la parole et la substance. Elle nous tenait amoureux sur l'arc tout-puissant de son imagination.[1] (FM,213)

. . . .

Victorious not only over a more sterile past but also over "la modicité quotidienne," the dull reasonableness and paucity of the everyday, this one cascading frenzy, as Char describes it elsewhere, adopts the onlooker, conferring on him its own enduring transparency. "Une victoire qui ne prendrait jamais fin": the ashes are overcome, but by a presence which the poet describes as perpetual rather than eternal, thus active in its renewal rather than statically assured. This poem, consecrated to the Fontaine de Vaucluse—whose name underlies the text without being spoken—is the source of the Sorgue, and also of the path returning uphill, the force heading upstream for the "retour amont." Even in that expression, the mountain, always interior, lies at the heart of the spring.

C. Cycle of animals

. . . .

Le chasseur qui vous pousse, le génie qui vous
    voit,
Que j'aime leur passion, de mon large rivage!
Et si j'avais leurs yeux, dans l'instant où j'es-
    père? (LM,102)

To give myths back their value the poet calls his bestiary to-

---

[1] We were watching the water as it flowed, increasing before us. It effaced the mountain suddenly, expelling itself from her maternal side. Not a torrent submitting to its fate but an ineffable beast whose word and substance we became. It held us amorous on the all-powerful arch of its imagination.

154

wards him.[13] Last in the herd, after the graceful deer passing across the wall of the Lascaux cave, comes a beast heavy with a future birth. This image of a "Bonté" unproved, an image of sympathy and wisdom felt but never present in the actual scene, will guide our going in silence, bereft even of a name.

1. The Beast

Il ne fait jamais nuit quand tu meurs,
Cerné de ténèbres qui crient,
Soleil aux deux pointes semblables.

[13] As a backdrop to Char's bestiary, all of Rilke's eighth Duino Elegy, but in particular the following: "Doch sein Sein ist ihm / unendlich, ungefasst und ohne Blick / auf seinen Zustand, rein, so wie sein Ausblick. // . . . But its own being for it / is infinite, inapprehensible, / unintrospective, pure, like its outward gaze." (DE, 68-69) And by contrast, but still in correspondence, from Nietzsche's "Dithyrambes of Dionysos": "Der Wahrheit Freier—du? so höhnten sie / nein! nur ein Dichter! / ein Thier, ein listiges, raubendes, schleichendes, das lügen muss, / das wissentlich, willentlich lügen muss / . . . / Nur Narr! Nur Dichter!" (Friedrich Nietzsche, *Werke*, Berlin, de Gruyter, 1969, vol. VI₃, pp. 375-376)

A few passages from Nietzsche concerning the eagle could easily be placed beside Hölderlin's, as the *correspondants* of Char's imagery: "Oder dem Adler gleich, der lange, / lange starr in Abgründe blickt, / in seine Abgründe . . . / —oh wie sie sich hier hinab, / hinunter, hinein, / in immer tiefere Tiefen ringeln!" (ibid., p. 377).

The wisdom of the bird such as Nietzsche shows it to us in its intimate association with silence and with motion underlies, by its own silent presence, the works of Char: "Vois, il n'y a ni haut ni bas. Toi qui es léger, lance-toi, fuis, reviens. Chante, ne parle plus. / Les mots ne sont-ils pas faits pour ceux qui sont lourds? Les mots ne mentent-ils pas pour celui qui est léger? Chante. Ne parle plus." See the quotation and discussion by Jean-Louis Backès in "Le Gai Saber" (*Critique* No. 251, avril 1968, p. 237; quoted in French).

See the study of James Lawler: "René Char's *Quatre Fascinants*," in *About French Poetry from Dada to Tel Quel: Text and Theory* (ed. Mary Ann Caws, Wayne State University Press, 1974). Also see the poem "L'Oiseau spirituel" illustrated by Braque, in *Exposition Georges Braque/René Char*, Bibliothèque littéraire Jacques Doucet, 1963; and, on the work in common of Braque and Char, Thomas J. Hines, "L'ouvrage de tous les temps, admiré: *Lettera amorosa*/René Char and Georges Braque," *Bulletin du Bibliophile*, no. I, 1973, pp. 40-57.

>Fauve d'amour, vérité dans l'épée,
>Couple qui se poignarde unique parmi tous.[j]
>(LM,106)

Charged with brutal strength, the massive struggle illuminates both our night and the nocturnal struggle of an amorous couple. With his heritage of legend the fighting bull weighs heavily on the more tranquil image of the ox: "Un boeuf au loin . . . nous précédait. La lyre de ses cornes, il me parut, tremblait. Je t'aimais. / An ox preceded us . . . a good way ahead. The lyre of its horns was, I thought, trembling. I loved you." (LM,110)

This trembling, apparent rather than certain, is nevertheless of the same order as that of the violent couple, bestial, mortal, and stabbed together. But in this poem, and in the brief tension of the five-line "Taureau," there can be felt an incipient future force gradually inflecting the current of the work.

The white bull of Provence (Lou Rouan) is said to be seen only once every hundred years: each animal in René Char's bestiary is, like that bull, "unique among all."

2. The Lark, The Swift

"Carillon maître de son haleine et libre de sa route. / Peal of bells, in control of her breath and free to choose her way." (LM,109) "Alouettes de la nuit, étoiles, qui tournoyez aux sources de l'abandon, soyez progrès aux fronts qui dorment. / Larks of the night, stars at the springs of desertion, be progress to the sleeping foreheads"; (FM,203) "Les oiseaux libres ne souffrent pas qu'on les regarde. / Free birds do not permit us to look at them." (LM,154) An exterior and miniature image of an interior freedom, the bird indicates a naked moral force, fragile yet continuing. Strong in a high and tragic flying, soon to be stricken down.

---

[j] It is never night when you die, / Ringed about with shadows that cry, / Sun with the two matched points. / Love's wild beast, truth in the sword; / Nonpareil couple stabbing each other. (JG)

"LE MARTINET"

Martinet aux ailes trop larges, qui vire et crie sa joie
autour de la maison. Tel est le coeur.

Il dessèche le tonnerre. Il sème dans le ciel serein. S'il
touche au sol, il se déchire.

. . . .

Il n'est pas d'yeux pour le tenir. Il crie, c'est toute sa
présence. Un mince fusil va l'abattre. Tel est le coeur.[k]
(FM,214)

The entire reach of the swift's circling is caught within itself,
in one single cry.[14] Trying out a freedom "too wide," like his
wings, his cry loud and desiccating in its joy; the bird's very
presence exceeds. And by this excess of qualities accumulated
in numerous poems which this one touches, the swift will
have sinned against the "modicité quotidienne," reasonable,
measured, and devoid of risk. Spiraling around the house,
of easier access than his own domain, he still rejects the familiar as mediocre conformity, imprisoning, albeit benevo-
lent. ("Of what value is the lace of the tower?") The poem
will never be a product of this imprisonment, against which
Le Marteau sans maître hammered most precisely. And yet,
this marginal flight is easily menaced. Such is the heart—now
a quieter tone of universal doom replaces the singular cry,
as the bird plummets to the earth in the future.

Refusing the look of others, the bird voluntarily depos-
sessed will be defeated by the slenderest weapon, appropriate to his own bareness. Later, particularly in *Le Nu perdu*,

[k] Swift with wings too wide, wheeling and shrieking his joy, around
the house. Such is the heart. / He dries up thunder. He sows in the
serene sky. If he touches ground, he tears himself apart. / . . . / No
eyes can hold him. He shrieks for his only presence. A slight gun is
about to fell him. Such is the heart.
[14] Rilke: "Wie ergreift uns der Vogelschrei . . . / . . . / Schreien
den Zufall. In Zwischenräume / . . . / treiben sie ihre, des Kreischens,
Keile. // How the cry of a bird can stir us . . . / . . . / Cry chance.
Into interstices / . . . / they drive their wedges, wedges of shrieking." (SO,120-121) For the interaction of the bird cry and silence,
see p. 276, note 8.

157

a great value attaches to the sparse, to a chosen poverty; here, the weapon is chosen as suitably matched to its target. Everywhere there is made apparent the spiritual correspondence of poet and bird, the animal nearest to him along with the wolf and the snake—marginal beings, flying and fleeing. "In my country . . . badly dressed birds are preferred to faraway goals." (LM,41) On occasion, Char sends the snake twining about the bird, for example, by a single caption in *La Nuit talismanique* marking the bird in flight as "Le Serpent," or in this poem, where the swift spirals down to his doom like the thin coiling of smoke from the slender gun.

The poem, an already half-closed circle, itself imitates a spiral flight and its descent as the bird falls wounded, to complete the round as if a verbal homage to a liberty finally lost were itself to be threatened. This cry will not go unheard even in the celebration of freedom; the bird's essential tragedy is inescapably our own.[15]

3. *The Bee*

"Elle transporte le verbe, l'abeille frontalière qui, à travers haines ou embuscades, va pondre son miel sur la passade d'un nuage. / Transporting the word, the boundary bee, through hatred or ambush, goes to deliver honey on the fancy of a cloud."* (LM,132) Defined by what it discovers and by the elements it places in correspondence, the bee is mediator for the poem. Like the poet, it serves as guardian of and guide to the passage: for it knows the subtlest transferring of qualities, corresponding, linking, renewing.

Frequenting the white line between dawn and dusk, the bee is the emblem of threshold and of sharing, but also of danger. Armed only with its sting, it lives as an incarnation

[15] For the attachment to "the house" or to one land in their multiple suggestions finally provokes the downfall, both of this circling bird and of the human heart. Rilke's lament is particularly tragic within this context: "Wir sind nicht einig. Sind nicht wie die Zug- / vögel verständigt . . . // We're never single-minded, unperplexed, like migratory birds. . . ." (DE,40-41)

of a stellar flash at once dart and beam, of a correspondence between inner and outer realities as well, like Rilke's bee.[16]

[16] In a letter to his Polish translator, Witold von Hulewicz, from the Greene and Norton translation: "Yes, for it is our task to imprint this provisional, perishable earth so deeply, so patently and passionately in ourselves that reality shall arise in us again 'invisibly.' *We are the bees of the invisible. Nous butinons éperdument le miel du visible, pour l'accumuler dans la grande ruche d'or de l'Invisible.*" (*Letters of Rainer Maria Rilke*, New York, Norton, 1947, vol. II, p. 374.) See also other notes on Rilke's angel (notes 6 and 7, pp. 222-24).

The image of bee and of fruit will always be associated with the exceptional being, who is his own prey and whose own consciousness is his primary nourishment. The few who harbor no dislike of being a "petit nombre," an "aristocratie discontinue" (Valéry, *Variété* III, Gallimard, 1936, pp. 13, 19) [V], like Char's small group of "certains êtres," or of "quelques êtres," are all finally, as Valéry says of Mallarmé, "de ceux qui ne peuvent goûter l'ivresse que de soi. . . ." (V,10) Here the mortal partners are perhaps only one, two shadows linked in the voluptuous struggle of a single being. "Est-il tourment plus pur, division de soi-même plus profonde que ce combat du même avec le Même. . . ?" (V,29): in these words from "Je disais à Stéphane Mallarmé," a split is revealed at the heart of being. Char's "chasseur de lui-même" is linked in his desperate and solitary duet with the self-wounding consciousness always present in Valéry: "Ô dangereusement de ton regard la proie!" (*Poésies*, Gallimard, 1942, p. 63) [P]. In the song of its purest danger ("de soi-même un cri pur comme une arme," p. 17) and its doomed self-delight, coiling and curving, the function of the serpent penetrates the interior of being itself: "Je m'enlace, être vertigineux," (P,56). Observer and prey, snake and snake-like movement are absorbed in the waking consciousness. (See the spiraling *line* ["ô courbes, Méandre"] and also the line, "Ô dangereusement. . . .")

One of Valéry's poems of the frontier between sleep and alertness is entitled "Aurore," which reminds one of Char's poem on dawn and on "La Liberté," with its "cygne sur la ligne blanche." Furthermore, his concept of the frontier or boundary resembles Char's own use of it, in his recurring image of the bee crossing boundaries and mingling elements, or then—not unlike Valéry's own bee—summoned also to arouse ("J'ai grand besoin d'un prompt tourment: . . . cette infîme alerte d'or") ("L'Abeille"). Valéry's Aurora sings the pricking of thorns, in its obvious suggestions: "L'éveil est bon, même dur! / . . . Il n'est pour ravir un monde / De blessure si profonde / Qui ne soit au ravisseur / Une féconde blessure. . . ." (P,88) We are reminded of the "prosperous" or fruitful domain of the wound as in Char's question: "Pourquoi le champ de la blessure est-il tous le

159

．　．　．　．　．　．　．　．　．　．　．

Rivière au coeur jamais détruit dans ce monde fou de
prison,

plus prospere?" (FM,95). Here, the blood come to the surface proves
the fruitfulness of the wound, the possession of the prey, and the
waking. The sting of the bee, the bite of the snake, or the piercing
of the single horn serve equally for the awakening of the self. Compare, in *La Jeune Parque*: "Oh! parmi mes cheveux pèse d'un poids
d'abeille, / Plongeant toujours plus ivre au baiser plus aigu, / Le point
délicieux de mon jour ambigu. . . ." (P,69) Thought, this *ver* and this
vers in both authors, includes all the preceding notions: "Comment
tuer la pensée toujours en travail et renaissant d'elle-même?—Ver
rongeur qui s'engendre de *ce même qui doit être rongé.*" (Valéry,
Cahier viii, p. 469) In the famous lament from "Le Cimetière marin": "Le son m'enfante et la flèche me tue!," (P,151) where the
exclamation point serves also as the arrow of the page pierced, or
the consciousness again wakened and wounded, the arrow is associated with one of Zeno's paradoxes, like the arrow in Char's "Front
de la rose."

Many specific images at the center of Valéry's poetry recur in René
Char, frequently in the lighter poems, taken from the "versant tempéré" of his mountain; but occasionally they develop a more dynamic
thrust, as if from the whole vibrant canvas, the withdrawn or reserved
image becoming suddenly outward in its essential force: thereby the
entire image is modified. Rather than attaching separate footnotes for
each of the dozen capital images in common, we might simply list a
few; the comparison is far less important than that with Mallarmé.
As an example of the difference in tone, we might compare the delicacy of Valéry's "La Ceinture" ("une Ombre à libre ceinture / Que le
soir est près de saisir. / Cette ceinture vagabonde") to Char's descrip-
tions of Orion girded with the belt of seasons, the circle of stars, as if
in fact the difference of gender of the wearer determined the different
effect of the image. The same holds true for the cluster of grapes, the
angel, the pomegranate exploded ("ô grenades entrebaillées . . . / Cette
lumineuse rupture") like Char's "noces de la grenade cosmique," the
swan and the sign (Valéry's "lisse effacement d'un cygne" and Char's
"cygne sur la blessure"), Valéry's "Toi, mon épaule où l'or se joue"
(P,120) and Char's poem "Joue et dors, bonne soif. . . ." All of this
played on the *lyre*, no longer Hugo's (*Toute la lyre*). For both Valéry
and Char, the *lire* is made evident: "Hélas! ô roses toute lyre / Con-
tient la modulation! / Un soir, de mon triste délire / Quant la constellation." (P,121) (See the chapter above marked "Lyre.") Jean
Gaudon has pointed out the frequency of the rhyme "délire/lyre" in
the 18th century poet Jean-Baptiste Rousseau, where it connotes a
movement of passion. The double resonance, like Mallarmé's "mor-
sure/mort süre" is heard in both *lires*; as an example, to compare
with Char's "amande/amante," Valéry's: "Tu vois du sombre amour
s'y mêler la tourmente / L'amant brûlant et dur ceindre la blanche

160

Garde-nous violent et ami des abeilles de l'horizon.[1]
(FM,211)

Each animal image concentrates several qualities newly perceived, if not always openly stated. The reader detects in the second sentence of the following passage the presence of a bee not actually present in text, whose buzzing is heard indistinctly in the noisy vibration of the morning heat: "Bienfaisance des hommes certains matins stridents. Dans le fourmillement de l'air en délire, je monte, je m'enferme, insecte indévoré, suivi et poursuivant. / The good will of men on strident mornings! In the swarming of the delirious air I rise up, I shut myself in, an undevoured insect, hunted and hunting." (LM,150) (JG) These two sentences are mutually nourishing. The poet assumes the rising of the insect and its relationship to the swarm in which he finds himself still individualized: "je m'enferme" makes such an intense affirmation of solitude that we hear implied in it: "je m'affirme." Without allowing itself to be consumed by the multitude, nor by the stridency of the rapacious air (like the "brûlure du bruit" AC,14) this insect teaches ascent, exemplifying how we might occupy our own moment exactly placed in space and time: before, behind, and in the present.

---

amante." (P,111) Doubly significant, Valéry's description of a certain fruit, as quoted by Charles Whiting in his edition of *Charmes ou poèmes* (London, Athlone Press, 1973, pp. 93-94) illuminates also a profound sense of Char's "fruit contracté," his "amande libre" to be juxtaposed with the reflection of Heidegger and Hölderlin quoted later in these pages: "La pensée doit être cachée dans les vers comme la vertu nutritive dans un fruit. Un fruit est nourriture mais il ne paraît que délice. On ne perçoit que du plaisir, mais on reçoit une substance. L'enchantement voile cette nourriture insensible qu'il conduit." (Might not this last word be seen alongside the title of Char's poem "Conduite" with its "fine pluie d'amande"?) Finally, the aromatic herbs perfume both works lightly: Valéry's "vers un aromatique avenir de fumée" (P,28) leads to a clearer identification between the fragrance and an animal gentleness, as in La Pythie's song: "ils m'assoupirent d'aromates / Laineux et doux comme un troupeau." (P,121) See also note 26, p. 311 on *Aromates chasseurs*.

[1] River with heart never destroyed in this world crazy for prison, / Keep us violent and a friend to the bees of the horizon. (JG)

Sharing the resonance and the equilibrium of more explicit formulations, such as "Hôte et possédant"—host, guest, possessor and possessing—or implicit as in the image of Orion, the blinded hunter who is traditionally "his own quarry," the expression "suivi et poursuivant" connects this text to others that construct a parallel experience. As in a canvas of Poussin,[16a] where a blinded hero is groping, in all his dignity; at the boundary of two dimensions, upland and upstream, another "bee of boundaries" completes his work:

"RÉCEPTION D'ORION"

Qui cherchez-vous brunes abeilles
Dans la lavande qui s'éveille?
Passe votre roi serviteur.
Il est aveugle et s'éparpille.
Chasseur il fuit
Les fleurs qui le poursuivent.
Il tend son arc et chaque bête brille.
Haute est sa nuit; flèches risquez vos chances.

Un météore humain a la terre pour miel.[m] (AC,27)

Thus the swarm becomes the constellation, as the poetic work follows a meteoric path. For Orion, unlike that other archer captured by beauty in "Front de la rose," is not only pierced by terrestrial radiance but is dispersed as celestial illumination, fragmented as the bees scatter in their flight. Hunter yet pursued, sightless yet shining in a noble darkness ("haute . . . nuit"), Orion is received on high.

[m] Dark bees, whom are you seeking / In the lavender awaking? / Your servant king is passing by. / Blind, he drifts, dispersing. / A hunter, he flees / The flowers pursuing him. / He bends his bow and each beast shines. / High is his night, arrows take your chance. / A human meteor has the earth for honey.

[16a] Discussed in final chapter; for the humanist allegory and the "hieroglyph" of this canvas, see E. H. Gombrich, *Symbolic Images*, New York, Phaidon, 1972, "The Subject of Poussin's *Orion*."

4. The Lizard, The Spider

To the whitewashed wall or ceiling of the poet's mental dwelling there corresponds an exterior wall intensely white, standing, like the cracked wall of Francis Ponge ("Le Lézard"), to show its fault: "Le sourire du lézard sur la fleur de chaux s'affiche au même instant que la convulsive toile. / The lizard's smile on the limestone flower attracts the gaze at the same instant as the convulsive canvas."[17] (RBS,97) The words Char addresses to Miró, quoted in part above, are not far in spirit from these: the wound in a wall suggests the crossing of dimensions, the revelation of a depth and a secret, even a convulsive joining. The sensual links remain elusive, as the lack and the excess (RBS,35) of the poet-artist are translated into white spaces on the page and in the lines of the textual canvas, in the down- and up-strokes of writing seen as a visual act:

> Its completion does not suppose an ending, but rather an indentation—the most serious slash naturally rectilinear and not indictable, permitting a glimpse of the secret seams between two things and, therefore, of certain essential relationships unperceived before, the primary identity of the real before the word, that we call poetic. . . . Such an aspect of the real proceeds by pure ellipsis, superposes, intertwines images of which each reveals itself at the moment it plunges into the other. Thus the end becomes beginning, appetite, and Miró's form a chain of advents, of prenuptial lust. (RBS,90)

The changes made in this text clearly indicate the development of the poet's thought, which is less often the case for René Char's prose than for his poems. Looking only at a few of the corrections made in proof,[18] we see that instead of central terms like "échancrure" and "déchirure" (roughly,

[17] André Breton, Nadja, Gallimard, 1963, p. 155: "La beauté sera CONVULSIVE ou ne sera pas."
[18] Flux de l'aimant (printer's proofs No. 817, AE-IV-7).

indentation and slash), there was originally the more neutral word: "ouverture," less precise and more innocent. In place of the adjective "rectiligne," hard and implying a kind of un-puritanical purity despite the nuptial theme, there was origi-nally the word "droite," where the two senses of moral and linear directness or uprightness led to an expression con-trasting by a detour: not indictable ("non inculpable") and, further on, to these "pures ellipses" which were originally called "ellipses essentielles." When the original indication of extreme attractiveness: "d'énormes appâts" is altered to "de prénuptiales luxures," the most familiar thread appears once again, that of a whole system of contraries and warring di-mensions, linked in the series of textual encounters, leading us from the age of reindeer and caverns ("Transir") up to the future confrontation of the "Biens égaux."

5. *The Phoenix, The Salamander*

"Anneau tard venu, enclavé dans la chevalerie pythienne saturée de feu et de vieillesse, quel compagnon engagerais-je? Je prends place inaperçu sur le tirant de l'étrave jusqu'à la date fleurie où rougeoiera ma cendre. / Ring lately-come, linked in the order of the oracle, saturated with fire and age, what companion might I engage? Unseen I take my place on the brace of the prow until the beflowered date when my ashes will redden." (FM,38) The phoenix implicit in this fiery passage is coiled, snake-like, in the ring of rebirth: will the one to whom the myth attaches be reborn with the memory of a former knowledge or in the oblivion of Lethe? Might this passage or that of the salamander through the fire instruct in any way the poet and the reader, as they pass among the fragments of a verbal archipelago? Animal commitment seems more extreme than does human: "Flamme à l'excès de son destin, qui tantôt m'amoindrit et tantôt me complète, vous émergez à l'instant près de moi, dauphine, salamandre, et je ne vous suis rien. / Flame in excess of its destiny, now dimin-ishing and now completing me, you emerge in this moment

near me, dolphin, salamander, and I am nothing to you."
(LM,126) However, were we to believe in the actualizing
power of metaphor, would not the verbal gesture of comparing be already one of transfer, as in the emblem of the
bee between boundaries? Then the metaphor would effectively
annul the disclaimer: "Je ne vous suis rien."

But the exchange is made in the true dimension of a poetic
language, where the ambiguous is to be chosen above the
certain, for the future plurality of readings: "DEMAIN LE
MULTIPLE."

6. The Serpent, The Wolf, The Lamb

"Il m'offrait, à la gueule d'un serpent qui souriait, mon impossible que je pénétrais sans souffrir. / He offered me, in
the mouth of a serpent smiling, my impossible which I penetrated without suffering." (FM,193) So this future "lord of
the impossible" learned that he was not to side with the partisans of the facile, of whom he will say later: "No precious
viaticum embellishes the mouth of their uncoiled snakes."
(NP,13) The impossible source of the least approachable
and therefore most seductive poetry is perceived as a rare
danger. At best, the enigmatic snake will appear as a marginal
being,[19] belonging to no hearth: at worst, he will appear murderous, like the viper. The thin rifle, menacing the swift in
flight above the familiar, menaces the snake also, resembling
him mortally in its interior bores or coils.

Equally marginal, the wolf in honor of whom "Marmonnement" was written, and whose profile we have seen before,
haunting the text from its center, will clarify the image of
the poet without betraying his mystery à côté:

"MARMONNEMENT"

Pour ne pas me rendre et pour m'y retrouver, je t'of-
fense, mais combien je suis épris de toi, loup, qu'on dit à

[19] For the marginality of the snake, see note 6, p. 45, on Turner,
The Ritual Process.

> tort funèbre, pétri des secrets de mon arrière-pays. . . .
> Loup, je t'appelle, mais tu n'as pas de réalité nommable.
> De plus, tu es inintelligible. Non-comparant, compensa-
> teur, que sais-je? . . .
> Continue, va, nous durons ensemble. . . .[n] (LM,131)

Now the poet names his marginal companions, certain of whose qualities he shares: he chooses for himself the solitude of the wolf,[20] lending himself no more easily to appearances: "non-comparant."[21] He will not present himself, nor his poem, directly.

And yet it is evident that the concept of marginality works in two senses: the word implies not only a situation on the edge of society, but a positive demand for a margin sufficient to assure his free path in a breathable space, suited to a being bare in his lack of heritage and heritors.[22] Moreover, the poet would never identify himself only with the victim: "It is not worthy of the poet to mystify the lamb, to glorify his wool."

[n] Not to surrender and so as to take my bearings, I offend you, but how in love with you I am, wolf, wrongly called funereal, moulded with the secrets of my back country . . . Wolf, I call you, but you have no nameable reality. Moreover, you are unintelligible. By default, compensating, what else could I say? / . . . / Go on, we endure together. . . .

[20] (For a discussion of the wolf and the outsider, of Rimbaud and Char—in particular, the poems "Marmonnement" and "L'Inoffensif," Mechthild Cranston, "L'Homme du Matin et . . . celui des Ténèbres," *Kentucky Romance Quarterly*, Fall 1974, pp. 195-214.) See also "Sommeil aux Lupercales" (NT), for a further implicit presence of the wolf and of his moment, although there is evident in the poem a convergence of the Saturnalia and the exchange of roles taking place during that festival with the image of the Lupercalia.

[21] This sentence was added to the manuscript after it was typed (No. 690, AE-IV-8); and is of a particular importance. In the major appearances of this image, there is a clear departure from the modesty, timidity, and herd instinct of the sheep and, in its place, a noticeable attraction to heights, rocks, and summits. Part goat, part bird, as the nest of wool indicates, the lamb and its brother animals are "concordants" of the mountain—obstinate, difficult, and enduring.

[22] "Déshérence" (NP,44): the absence of inheritors again evokes the marginal being.

166

(FM,198) At each appearance, the lamb will have something of the wolf or the snake—the long threads or traces of his suffering, either visible on the slopes, or alluded to, could just as well be pulled from the tail of a wolf. For the wool ("laines") which lines the rocky nest and the mountain lair in these poems suggests the haughty refusal of the poet, the spirit of a conqueror, or that of a conqueror pursued; but never a lament. More closely associated with the cave of Lascaux than with a sheep-fold, whether the latter be seen as deserted or in flames (in "Vivre avec de tels hommes"), this poetry calls not for sympathy—a generally passive senti-ment—but for a continuing action: "The poet does not grow angry at the hideous extinction of death, but, confident in his particular touch, transforms each thing into prolonged wool." (FM,74) The prolongation is that of the poem.

A brief text in correspondence with "Marmonnement," comments on the trace carved out on the mountain's surface by the wolf's claw, and within the poet by that ancient flee-ing, like an exterior mark now become interior. Its double hero and its dual struggle represent the mortal partners pitted against each other, playing also the legendary against the real: "Il y a Ouranos l'actuel dévalant avec les loups, et il y a Orphée. Tous deux au coude à coude, crachant la terre de leur captivité. / There is the present Ouranos descending with the wolves, and there is Orpheus. Both set against each other in close combat, spitting out the earth of their captiv-ity." (NT,39) This spot marks the convergence of the lyric poet and of earth's husband, set against each other in their rebellion, leaving their tracks in the early text and the later one, superposed on it.

The marginal poet remains, like the wolf, hunter and hunt-ed; a "bestower of freedom," he resides in a country of the future that is empty of everything except poetry. Fleeing or simply returning upland, he is the noblest prey of his own images, the victim of the illuminating dart he places at the true center of his song: "la flèche de leur bouche dont

167

le chant venait de naître / the arrow of their mouth where
the song was just born." (FM,40)

7. *The Unicorn*

At moments the poem's tapestry holds the memory of another, its medieval precursor in which the unicorn rests by
a fountain, purifying the waters by his single horn. Elsewhere,
he is hunted like a white stag, tracked and followed by the
hunters, whose lances eventually pierce the innocent and miraculous beast. This hero is betrayed too by friendship, or
here, taken in a trap of beauty. Finally, the unicorn is enclosed by a circular fence, a circle of stars, or by the ring of a
poem, which itself forms "l'anneau de la licorne."[23] The
singular animal exemplifies a singular tragedy:

> Il s'était senti bousculé et solitaire à la lisière de sa con-
> stellation qui n'était dans l'espace recuit qu'une petite ville
> frileuse.
> A qui lui demanda: "L'avez-vous enfin rencontrée? Êtes-
> vous enfin heureux?," il dédaigna de répondre et déchira
> une feuille de viorne.° (NT,83)

The "viorne," or guelder-rose, is called a "boule de neige"
because of its virgin color; so a virginal flower is torn apart
by the teeth of the animal, whose insatiable love is as brutal as
it is tragic. The unicorn chases his own image through a series of maidens holding up a mirror for it.[24] In an infinite

[23] For instance, the unicorn tapestries in the Cluny museum in
Paris, and the Cloisters of New York's Metropolitan Museum.

° He had felt jostled and lonely at the border of his constellation,
only a little town shivering in tempered space. / To the questioner:
'Have you finally met her? Are you happy at last?' he did not deign to
reply, and tore a leaf of guelder-rose.

[24] Rilke describes the last scene of the unicorn tapestries in *The
Notebooks of Malte Laurids Brigge*: "But here is yet another festival;
no one is invited to it. Expectation plays no part in it. Everything is
here. Everything for ever. The lion looks round almost threateningly:
No one may come. We have never yet seen her weary; is she weary?
or has she merely sat down because she is holding something heavy?

ring, at once a prison and a recurring promise, the water of rebirth like a fountain in its resurgence is linked to the texts of pursuit—either by another, as in a Christ-deer imagery resembling that of Jean de La Ceppède or Pierre-Jean Jouve, or like the arrows which the flowers aim in their turn toward the bees at the end of *Aromates chasseurs*, or then, in an interior pursuit: "chasseur de soi. / hunter of himself."

Several passages in *Le Nu perdu* show a "Jeu muet," in which both the game and the self playing ("jeu/je") are silent. "Avec mes dents / J'ai pris la vie / Sur le couteau de ma jeunesse. / Avec mes lèvres aujourd'hui, / Avec mes lèvres seulement. . . . // With my teeth / I have seized life / Up against my youth's knife. / With my lips today, / With my lips only." (NP,75) (JG) The young animal, always fierce in his singularity, destroys easily, as with "his lips only" he stabs the other's life on the single horn of his youth. At the conclusion of this brief game of a text, the disquieting imagery is mute no longer: "Le dard d'Orion, / Est réapparu. // Orion's dart / has reappeared." (JG) The entire network of images from bee-sting to knife, to the beam of

---

A monstrance, one might say. But she curves her other arm towards the unicorn, and the flattered animal bridles and rears and leans against her lap. It is a mirror that she holds. See: she is showing the unicorn its likeness—." (SO,154) And in the Unicorn sonnet of the sonnets to Orpheus: "O dieses ist das Tier, das es nicht gibt. / . . . / Zwar *war* es nicht. Doch weil sie's liebten, ward / ein reines Tier. Sie liessen immer Raum. / Und in dem Raume, klar und ausgespart / erhob es leicht sein Haupt und brauchte kaum / zu sein. Sie nährten es mit keinem Korn, / nur immer mit der Möglichkeit, es sei. / Und sie gab solche Stärke an das Tier, / dass es aus sich ein Stirnhorn trieb. Ein Horn. / Zu einer Jungfrau kam es weiss herbei— / und war im Silber-Spiegel und in ihr. // O this is the creature that does not exist. / . . . / Indeed it never *was*. Yet because they loved it, / a pure creature happened. They always allowed room / And in that room, clear and left open, / it easily raised its head and scarcely needed / to be. They fed it with no grain, but ever / with the possibility that it might be. / And this gave the creature such strength, / it grew a horn out of its brow. One horn. / To a virgin it came hither white— / and was in the silvermirror and in her." (SO,76-77)

stars and the arrows of the hunters, crueler still in the probing iron and the dart of Cupid, reappears with the modest
flower of the Vaucluse called "le dard d'Orion," for its scattering of seeds into the air like so many arrows: the amatory
imagery of the horn needs no elaboration. The pursuit takes
on a calmer resonance near the fountain at which the hunted
hunter rests: "Permanent invisible." The title of his poem is
also that of a rose's predicted density, like the red mark of
an erotic wound spreading, marking the prey of the "desired
hunting." The desire for a battle to the death is laid open, as
in the cycle of "Le Visage nuptial" and "Le Mortel partenaire," a battle at one with the quest for a source redeeming
and restoring:

.   .   .   .

O mon distant gibier la nuit où je m'abaisse
Pour un novice corps à corps.

Boire frileusement, être brutal répare.ᵖ (NP,82)
.   .   .   .

For the "jours heureux" of the fountains are those in which
the legendary animal, already wounded by the future spear,
betrayed and wild, yet never betraying, comes quietly to take
his own nourishment: "celui qui vient en secret, avec son
odeur fauve . . . sans fausseté, et pourtant trahi par ses plaies
irréparables / The one who comes in secret with his wild
scent . . . without falsity, and still betrayed by his irreparable
wounds." (NP,104)

Human and legendary, an Orion pursued and pursuing, at
once desiring, wounding, and wounded: the poet or the unicorn takes his strength from the mortal struggle predicted,
as distance and time are suppressed beside a fountain. The
tapestry before us now shows at last the entire cycle of the
work.

ᵖ Oh my far-off prey the night where I stoop / For a novice wrestling. / To drink shivering, to be brutal restores you.

D. CYCLE OF THE WARRING COUPLE: "LE VISAGE NUPTIAL"

L'homme et la femme rapprochés par le ressort de l'amour me font songer à la figure de la coque du navire lié par son amarre à la fascination du quai. Ce murmure, cette pesanteur flexible, ces morsures répétées, la proximité de l'abîme, et par-dessus tout, cette sûreté temporaire, trait d'union entre fureur et accalmie.[q] (RBS,169)

The series of meditations on the marriage of the poet with the poem called "Le Visage nuptial," and the central text in particular, express the refusal to separate an outer visage from an inner one; the most difficult elements of language are here wedded to the simplest perceptions of love. The return upstream, a primitive task turned into a complex poetry, is carried out under the shelter of an ambiguous veil already perceived: "Essaime la poussière / Nul ne décèlera votre union." (MM,146) The encounter of these poems is at once profoundly natural and intensely verbal.

We shall follow three different paths along the central poem: the first a fragmentary sketch along the lines of our initial study of forms and fragments; the second following the motifs of desire, possession, and freedom in their clear yet wonderfully difficult expression; and the third extending beyond the individual joining toward a convergence of the natural with the human: that is, from the singular to the universal. The entire surface of the poem is marked by the signs of several readings, implicitly superposed, resulting in a complex concision where the "art bref" is superbly reconciled

[q] Man and woman brought together by the spring of love remind me of a boat's hull anchored to the fascination of the wharf. This murmur, this flexible weight, these repeated bitings, the proximity of the abyss, and above all, this temporary certainty, a joining between furor and calm.

171

with a harmonic enduring, the intermittent flash with a sustained radiance.

. . . .

"LE VISAGE NUPTIAL" (1938)

A présent disparais, mon escorte, debout dans la distance;
La douceur du nombre vient de se détruire.
Congé à vous, mes alliés, mes violents, mes indices.
Tout vous entraîne, tristesse obséquieuse.
J'aime.

L'eau est lourde à un jour de la source.
La parcelle vermeille franchit ses lentes branches à ton
front, dimension rassurée.
Et moi semblable à toi,
Avec la paille en fleur au bord du ciel criant ton nom,
J'abats les vestiges,
Atteint, sain de clarté.

Ceinture de vapeur, multitude assouplie, diviseurs de la
crainte, touchez ma renaissance.
Parois de ma durée, je renonce à l'assistance de ma largeur
vénielle;
Je boise l'expédient du gîte, j'entrave la primeur des survies.
Embrasé de solitude foraine,
J'évoque la nage sur l'ombre de sa Présence.

Le corps désert, hostile à son mélange, hier, était revenu
parlant noir.
Déclin, ne te ravise pas, tombe ta massue de transes, aigre
sommeil.
Le décolleté dimunue les ossements de ton exil, de ton
escrime;
Tu rends fraîche la servitude qui se dévore le dos;
Risée de la nuit, arrête ce charroi lugubre
De voix vitreuses, de départs lapidés.

Tôt soustrait au flux des lésions inventives
(La pioche de l'aigle lance haut le sang évasé)
Sur un destin présent j'ai mené mes franchises
Vers l'azur multivalve, la granitique dissidence.

O voûte d'effusion sur la couronne de son ventre,
Murmure de dot noire![25]
O mouvement tari de sa diction!
Nativité, guidez les insoumis, qu'ils découvrent leur base,
L'amande croyable au lendemain neuf.
Le soir a fermé sa plaie de corsaire où voyageaient les
fusées vagues parmi la peur soutenue des chiens.
Au passé les micas du deuil sur ton visage.

Vitre inextinguible: mon souffle affleurait déjà l'amitié de
ta blessure,
Armait ta royauté inapparente.
Et des lèvres du brouillard descendit notre plaisir au seuil
de dune, au toit d'acier.
La conscience augmentait l'appareil frémissant de ta per-
manence;
La simplicité fidèle s'étendit partout.

Timbre de la devise matinale, morte-saison de l'étoile
précoce,
Je cours au terme de mon cintre, colisée fossoyé.
Assez baisé le crin nubile des céréales:
La cardeuse, l'opiniâtre, nos confins la soumettent.
Assez maudit le havre des simulacres nuptiaux:
Je touche le fond d'un retour compact.

Ruisseaux, neume des morts anfractueux,
Vous qui suivez le ciel aride,
Mêlez votre acheminement aux orages de qui sut guérir
de la désertion,

[25] Compare the smaller but related canvas of the last stanza of
Rimbaud's "Soleil et chair" ("credo in unam"), in its visual and verbal communion with Char's epic poem: for instance, the lines: "Et
tandis que Cypris passe, étrangement belle, / Et, cambrant les ron-
deurs splendides de ses reins, / Étale. . . . / Et son ventre neigeux
brodé de mousse noire. . . ." Like the entire space of "Le Visage
nuptial," this stanza is stretched from one standing figure to another:
"Debout . . . / . . . / Majestueusement debout. . . ." (OR,45) Cf.
also in relation to the phrase: "la peur soutenue des chiens," Rimbaud's allusions to "dogues" in his "Nocturne vulgaire" and "Les
Douaniers." (And see Cohn, op.cit.: as if a certain oblique angle
were often to offer another perspective on the texts one chooses to
dwell in.)

Donnant contre vos études salubres.
Au sein du toit le pain suffoque à porter coeur et lueur.
Prends, ma Pensée, la fleur de ma main pénétrable,
Sens s'éveiller l'obscure plantation.

Je ne verrai pas tes flancs, ces essaims de faim, se dessécher,
s'emplir de ronces:
Je ne verrai pas l'empuse te succéder dans ta serre;
Je ne verrai pas l'approche des baladins inquiéter le jour
renaissant;
Je ne verrai pas la race de notre liberté servilement se
suffire.

Chimères, nous sommes montés au plateau.
Le silex frissonnait sous les sarments de l'espace;
La parole, lasse de défoncer, buvait au débarcadère an-
gélique.
Nulle farouche survivance;
L'horizon des routes jusqu'à l'afflux de rosée,
L'intime dénouement de l'irréparable.

Voici le sable mort, voici le corps sauvé;
La Femme respire, l'Homme se tient debout.[r] (FM,58-60)

[r] (Now let my escort disappear, standing far off into the distance; /
Numbers have just lost their sweetness. / I give you leave, my allies,
my violent ones, my indices. / Everything summons you away, fawn-
ing sorrow. / I am in love.)
(Water is heavy at a day's flow from the spring. / The crimson
foliage traverses its slow branches at your forehead, dimension reassured. / And I, like you, / With the straw in flower at the edge of the
sky crying your name, / I cut down the traces, / Stricken, strong in
clarity.)
(Ring of vapor, many made supple, dividers of fear, touch my renewal. / Walls of my enduring, I renounce the succour of my venial
breadth; / I timber the device of the dwelling, I thwart the first fruits
of survivals. / Afire with itinerant solitude, / I summon the swimming
on the shade of her Presence.)
(The desert body hostile to an alloyage, had returned yesterday,
speaking darkly. / Decline, do not halt your movement, let fall your
bludgeon of seizures, acrid sleep. / Indentation diminishes the bones
of your exile, of your sparring; / You freshen constraint self-devour-
ing; / Gust of the night, halt this grim cartage / Of glazed voices,
departures pelted with stones.)
(Soon subtracted from the flux of contriving lesions / The eagle's
matlock flings high the flaring blood / Across a present destiny I

1. *First Reading: Outline and Formal Structures*

Standing at the first and the last lines of the poem, the two instances of "debout" resound like a summons called from one pole to another, whose terms are inverted: ("Now disappear, my escort, standing off into the distance / . . . / Woman breathes, Man stands upright.") Distance and leavetaking are resolved into presence and continuity: "This the body saved. . . ." The entire course of the poem is directed toward this redemption of the body of poetry itself, toward this declaration of its own active stance: for it is also an "être debout," and an "être du bond."

---

have led my exemptions / Toward an azure multivalved, granite dissidence.)

(Oh vaulted effusion upon the crown of her belly, / Murmurings of dark dowry! / Oh the exhausted motion of her diction! / Nativity, guide the unyielding, may they find their foundations, / The almond believable in the fresh day to come. / Evening has closed its corsair's gash where the rockets soared aimlessly amid a dogged fear. / Past now the micas of mourning on your face.)

(Unquenchable pane: my breath was already grazing the friendship of your wound, / Arming your hidden royalty. / And from the lips of the fog descended our joy with its threshold of dune, its roof of steel. / Awareness increased the quivering array of your permanence; / Faithful simplicity spread everywhere.)

(Tone of morning's adage, slack season of the precocious star, / I rush to the term of my arch, interred coliseum. / Long enough embraced, the nubile hair of grain: / Oh carder, stubborn one, our reaches force your submission. / Long enough condemned the haven of nuptial semblance: / I touch the depths of a compact return.)

(Streams, neuma of craggy deaths, / You who follow the arid sky, / Mingle your going with his tempests, who could heal desertion, / Striking against your saving studies. / At the roof's center bread suffocates carrying heart and light. / Take, oh my Thought, the flower of my penetrable hand, / Feel the dark planting waken.)

(I shall not see your sides, those swarms of hunger dry up, be overrun with brambles; / I shall not see the mantis replace you in your greenhouse; / I shall not see the minstrels approach, disquieting the reborn day; / I shall not see our freedom's lineage servile in self-sufficiency.)

(Chimeras, we have climbed upland. / The flint was shivering under the vine-shoots of space; / The word, tired of battering, drank at the angelic wharf. / No savage survival: / The horizon of roads until the abounding dew, / Intimate unfolding of the irreparable.)

(This is the sand dead, this the body saved: / Woman breathes, Man stands upright.)

As a prelude to the interior substance of the poem, the poet's definitive dismissal of his violent friends and past companions—of an exterior escort—composed of superficial witnesses, no longer necessary—prepares the interior radiance whose herald the poem is. The poet is to be reborn in a privileged space where time has slowed down with the solemnity of language: "L'eau est lourde à un jour de la source. / La parcelle vermeille franchit ses lentes branches à ton front, dimension rassurée." The weight of the water, removed from its origin, calls into being the heavy branches sweeping across the path of this encounter. Then the poet speaks his love in the simplest and briefest way, the verb in its monosyllabic strength devoid of qualifier and even of object. Yet the sentence is complete, as the formulation is sufficient: "J'aime." In its wide context, this word stands out sharply, clearing the path toward the destructive action exercised in one long breath throughout the poem against the forms of the past and the vague, passive surroundings of the present.

A first reading stresses only a few words carrying at least a double sense in their sonority, valid only as an opening; they are italicized throughout this discussion.

J'abats les vestiges
Atteint, sain de clarté.
Ceinture de vapeur. . . .

The term "atteint" can be interpreted as an elliptical indication of a goal attained, permitting the double deciphering of a heroic theme, or read as the first element of a paradox: stricken with an ambiguous malady, but nevertheless healthy because of this clarity conferred by love on this love. In either case, it is girded like Thor, like Orion, by a belt of brightness, already predicting the following line where the "ceinture" is explicit:

Atteint, sain de clarté

$$\begin{bmatrix} \text{sein} \\ \text{saint} \\ \text{ceint} \end{bmatrix}$$

Or again, allowing for a slightly altered appearance—since all precise indications of an exterior escort have been dismissed by the poet—we might read the word in apposition with the ruins over which the hero stands finally triumphant:

J'abats les vestiges
Atteint(s), sain(t) de clarté.

Situated, by his rebellious nature, at the other pole from the passive "vapeur" and the quiescence so-far unaroused, the renascent poet, always "insoumis," will acquire from the very strength of the poem all the uncompromising hardness or permanence of the almond shell. The single horn of the legendary animal is predicted, like the future source of another abundance: "Touchez ma renaissance. / Parois de ma durée . . . Je boise . . ." The emphasis falls on the erotic preliminaries to a positive creation, personal as well as poetic.

The drops now evoked on the other's forehead take up the water from the spring, growing heavier in their abundance, together with the gentle almond rain from the poem directly preceding this one in the nuptial series ("fine pluie d'amande mêlée de liberté docile / a fine rain of almond mingled with gentle liberty"). Again, like the horn, this series of images suggests a quite explicit sexual violence: ("La pioche de l'aigle lance haut le sang évasé") and predicts the possibility of a fresh morrow and a rebirth in brightness for those refusing to resemble the many and the meek—that is, for those clear-visaged lovers who have bid farewell to their too-numerous escort, the multitude parasitic on the energy of the unyielding few: "Nativité, guidez les insoumis . . . / L'amande croyable au lendemain neuf."

Trying out his new freedom, the lover summons the "simplicité fidèle" of his partner in its flowing response—a calmer double for the blood spurting high, or then spilled out, "évasé" in either sense—which will spread everywhere with the irreversible progress of the poem. Certain of his own direct openness ("J'ai mené mes franchises"), the poet hastens to the term of his action ("Déclin, ne te ravise pas . . . ta massue de transes") within the text he constructs as a build-

177

ing, where the threshold and the roof are made of the couple's joy ("notre plaisir au seuil de dune, au toit d'acier"), illumined and fed by the bread of effort within the heart of a grief to be dwelled in: "Au sein du toit le pain suffoque à porter coeur et lueur." In the universe of René Char, the poet, like the partisan, "makes his bread of suffering"; it is finally the nourishment of this suffering that calls forth the streams from the rocks to redeem the "desert" body and sterile sand. (Compare in *Moulin premier*: "Le feu se communique au son du pain des cuisses. / Ô touffe élargie! Ô beauté / Instable longtemps contrariée de l'évidence, Main d'oeuvre errante de moi-même!")[8] (MM,142) "Au sein du toit: ["Ô saint / Ô ceint / Ô sain"]—this syllable picked up once more underlines the accretion analyzed above, of which the later expression "ces es*saims*," is only another hidden indication, a distant echo. The menace hanging over the heroic-erotic universe is further aggravated by a double reading of the concluding word in the following passage:

. . . ce charroi lugubre
De voix vitreuses, de départs *lapidés*.

These voices are also paths ("voix/voies")—as in "la voix du météore"—glazed over like the other songs, those of the greater multitude. The term "lapidés" replaces the term "lynchés" from a first version, bringing to the poem a lapidary hardness, a concision, and a brilliance from which danger is never absent. Still the poem is, like a stone, opposed to temporal fluidity: "tôt soustrait au flux / soon removed from flux. . . ."

The supreme realization of Char's poetics, this majestic text condemns every evidence of a too-easy marriage between contraries, every false or falsifying pact between words and things. Char describes the aspect of the true nuptial countenance, as it is turned toward the inner "retour amont,"

[8] Fire spreads at the sound of the bread of thighs. / Oh widened tuft! Oh unstable / Beauty contradicted at length by evidence, / Wandering handcraft of myself!

the true and difficult *compacité* which he will always have chosen: an attitude we might compare to that of poets like Francis Ponge or Marianne Moore, in favor of what the latter called "contractility":

Assez maudit le havre des simulacres nuptiaux:
Je touche le fond d'un *retour compact.*

The depths of this return can be read in parallel with the heights, with the summit climbed and the roof of joy—yet within this text the descent preceding the return upstream or upland is evoked only in an oblique reference. *"Prends, ma pensée, la fleur de ma main pénétrable, / Sens s'éveiller l'obscure plantation."* By the suppression of a single comma, and a semantic divergence under a phonetic similarity, the first line reads: ["Prends ma pensée, l'affleure. . . ."]. The instrument of poetic awakening is glimpsed here in profile, and then again, in a multiple perspective on the arousing of a sensibility to the point of a secret effusion: the "obscure plantation" of the seeds for a future growth, not only in the body of the mortal partner, but within the poem itself in its central moment of waking between verbal walls as hard as those of an almond: [sens s'éveiller / sens éveillés]. And yet, the opposite result is equally possible, the continued passivity of a sand dead may retain its passive hostility, still "parlant noir . . .": ["sans s'éveiller"]. Amorous combat would seek in vain an easy outcome; tragedy and cruelty are inseparable from Char's major love poems. Yet the whole sweep of this epic is marked by a tone of confidence, the metallic substantives for the sonority of the ascending song serving as the metaphoric and verbal support for the upland climb: "Le silex frissonnait sous les sarments de l'espace," made with instruments hard as the flint found under the earth of the actual hill whose rise the form and the tone of the poem approximate, this flint that might still give forth a flame.

With each fresh redemption of a desert and a dune, the amplitude of a lyric chorus is heard, and a dominant faith in poetry is rediscovered: the repetitions are particularly moving for the reader because their use is so limited in Char's work:

> Je ne verrai pas. . . .
> Je ne verrai pas. . . .
> Je ne verrai pas. . . .
> Je ne verrai pas. . . .

The defiantly repeated refusal determines the ground for the final stance and the definite gesture, where man standing brings the poem—that other partner breathing freely now— to its uphill rise.

2. *Second Reading: Nuptials*

Certain of the innumerable texts of nuptial and "prénuptiales luxures," charged with an evident and complex eroticism remind us of that mysterious series of poems traced like drawings on the walls of Lascaux, which open with a hymn in honor of an ancient and amorous battle between a beast about to die and a man half-animal, dead also: "Homme-oiseau mort et bison mourant." (LM,101)

> Long corps qui eut l'enthousiasme exigeant,
> A présent perpendiculaire à la Brute blessée.
> O tué sans entrailles!
> Tué par celle qui fut tout et, réconciliée, se meurt;
> Lui, danseur d'abîme, esprit, toujours à naître,
> Oiseau et fruit pervers des magies cruellement sauvé.[t]
> (LM,101)

As a primitive and pitiless force, this "exigent enthusiasm" will pass into the poems of love, a lyric charge transmitted across the centuries, from the wounded stone-age beast to the present struggle between mortal adversaries. From another angle, those lines might read: ["Ô tu es sans entrailles!

[t] Thin body that had imperious enthusiasm, / Now perpendicular to the wounded Brute. / O killed without any pity! / Killed by what was all and, reconciled, is dying; / He, the abyss dancer, spirit, yet to be born, / Bird and perverse fruit of magics, cruelly saved. (JG)

180

/ Tu es par celle qui fut tout . . . // O you are without pity! / You are by her who was all . . ."]. The phoenix will be born and reborn, dancing over danger, like a spirit pierced yet saved, like a victim redeemed throughout the cruelest of rituals, having traversed oblivion, death, and death by pleasure or "la petite mort." In a passion as exigent as it is murderous, an animal fury is the sudden and brutal source of light; the text also is stabbed, as if wounded doubly by the horns of a bull or singly, by a unicorn: "Il ne fait jamais nuit quant tu meurs / . . . Fauve d'amour, verité dans l'epée, / Couple qui se poignarde unique parmi tous" ("Le Taureau," LM,106).[26]

Not to succumb to the abyss, but rather to traverse it, joyously, perversely, to watch over it—this would be the true proof of victory, of the intellect remaining voluptuous even at the peak of lucidity. Loyal to their battle, the partners sink and wake always within this self-perpetuating ritual. In the "very perfect" victory of a shared love still vital while submerged, a double recreation will be made from the ruins

[26] To the furrow or the amorous wound, the mortal wound responds, and to the moment of pleasure, a time obsessive, destructive, and interior, as in the line quoted elsewhere: "Temps, mon possédant et mon hôte. . . ." (NP,104) Love as a passage to be traversed, shared, and suffered is an agent of reversal and of elevation: "Le doute remonte l'amour comme un chaland le courant du fleuve. C'est un mal d'amont." (S) Jean Starobinski, in his article "René Char et la définition du poème," (*Liberté*, Hommage à René Char, juillet-août, 1968, vol. 10, no. 4) speaks of the heart's freedom and its risk, of which, he says, Char's bestiary is "le symbole foisonnant." The beings chosen by the poet are, as he expresses it, "exposés à la mort du fait même de leur souveraineté"; soaring and peril stand to each other in a relationship *amoureux-agonique*. Greta Rau describes Char's poems written after 1937 as works "ouvertes comme des plaies, et tournées vers les hommes." (*René Char ou la poésie accrue*. Corti, 1957, p. 30.)

The peculiar and resplendent nature of the deadly conflict finds its perfect metaphor in the sun pierced through by the horns of the bull, himself pierced by the sword of the matador: "la rencontre du taureau et de l'epée, ces deux pointes mortelles qui s'unissent comme les amants prédestinés," the concepts "verité" and "amour" stabbing like twin blades: "lames jumelles d'une confrontation fatale," James Lawler, "René Char: 'Le Taureau' et 'La Truite,'" *Le Siècle éclaté*, no. 1 (Minard, Paris, 1974). Cf. English version, note 13, p. 156.

of the poem shattered by its very violence, that is, from "le poème pulvérisé." As the action of love is double, so is its expression ambivalent: the poem's density is increased by a wide range of images applicable to both partners, such as "l'obscure plantation," which can be, on the one hand, taken as a parallel to the gentle spreading of the "simplicité fidèle," or then, as a hidden action corresponding, on the man's part, to the glimpsed obscurity of his partner's "murmure de dot noire." Similarly the multiple aspects of the almond can be seen singly and doubly: the expression "parois de ma durée" joins the concept of duration to that of a shell's hardness while the evening's "plaie de corsaire" and the "amitié de ta blessure" would correspond to the natural joining and painful separation of its two parts. The image represents above all the delicate opposition of those rigid walls within one lover, and yet repeats their structure on the contrary sides of the warring couple, whose partnership is itself repeated outside and in, with no necessary end set to the relation of parts.

However, the difference that subsists on all levels, as the most fertile source of continuity, remains in and between the texts. Some passages of profound calm echo not with the strains of a mortal passion in its fight to the death but rather with a shared presence:

.   .   .   .

Nous nous aimons aujourd'hui sans au-delà et sans lignée,
Ardents ou effacés, différents mais ensemble.[u] (NP,25)
.   .   .   .

For his going, the poet needs a password, like all of us. The poem "Conduite" grants a safe-conduct to him, so he may transmit it to his reader:

Passe.
La bèche sidérale
autrefois là s'est engouffrée.

---

[u] We love each other today with no beyond and no issue / Ardent or effaced, different yet together. . . . (JG)

Ce soir un village d'oiseaux[27]
très haut exulte et passe.[v] (FM,55)
. . . .

In one version of the collection *Le Visage nuptial* (PPC)
the texts "Hommage et famine" and "La Liberté" precede
"Gravité" (a title alchemically resonant), "Conduite," and
"Le Visage nuptial" itself, in what is perhaps the chance of
an order "insurgé," or perhaps instead the proof that the poet
consents to help us pass between the fragments. Thus we
proceed from the free marriage of contraries to the recognition, both serious and silent, of the union mirrored in the
poem's ambivalence. Fifteen years later, "Le Mortel partenaire" (1953), in which the adversaries seek their opposition,
expresses a love of conflict as secret as it is vital, depicts a
related struggle, whose resolution is different. These beings
"for whom it is difficult (complicated) to find a name and
an homage," as the poet says in one of the first versions of
the text, are lost in the labyrinth of their own intensity, like
the poet at desperate odds with, and amorous of, his poem:
"Ô dédale de l'extrême amour! / Oh maze of extreme love!"
(LM,122) In "Le Mortel partenaire," the surface stretched
taut where the combat is held and the "rosy streak" slashed
on the partner's cheek are indications of the conflict also between poet and possessed reader, between poet and text. It
is not by pure chance that the poet modifies in his textual
work the word "minuscule" to yield a white surface ("blanche
surface") seemingly made of sheets, serving as the backdrop
for a violent and interior spectacle the height of whose pitch
is attained in a crescendo of effort. "Nous sommes montés
au plateau," reads a triumphant line from "Le Visage nuptial," applicable also to the passion of the page.

As an entry to this latter series, we take once more the

---

[27] Could we not inscribe all these texts under the emblem of the
passereau, this bird with a particular resonance to his name? (I am
grateful to Micheline Tison-Braun for this suggestion.)

[v] Pass. / The sidereal spade / Long ago struck in there. / Tonight a
high village of birds / Exults and passes.

example of the almond. In light of the suggestion "amande/ amante," we read in "Gravité" the tragic but radiant story of this fruit enclosed to be opened and destroyed for a joy never devoid of cruelty ("morsures répétées," RBS,169):

"GRAVITÉ"

L'Emmuré

. . . .

Tu vas nue, constellée d'échardes,
Secrète, tiède et disponible,
Attachée au sol indolent,
Mais l'intime de l'homme abrupt dans sa prison.

A te mordre les jours grandissent

. . . .

J'ai pesé de tout mon désir
Sur ta beauté matinale
Pour qu'elle éclate et se sauve.

. . . .

Un parfum d'insolation
Protège ce qui va éclore.ʷ (FM,56)

More than the beauty loved, the freedom of that beauty will blossom from the surrounding shell ("l'amande palpite, libre . . . ," FM,101) and the freedom it in turn confers. A similar generosity is seen in "Marthe": "Je veux être pour vous la liberté et le vent de la vie . . . / I want to be freedom for you and the wind of life. . . ." (FM,191) In the struggle, vital yet mortal, there is not one victim, or one survivor, but two, the couple whose love is victoriously "éclaté" as its own fountain and its own source: "L'arc des eaux jaillissantes, quelle beauté! Quelle victoire! / The arching waters surging forth what beauty? What a victory!" (AHPP)

The path is made almost clear in a poem entitled "Con-

ʷ You go naked, bestarred with splinters, / Secret, warm and at leisure, / Attached to the indolent soil, / But the close friend of man abrupt in his prison. / Biting you the days grow longer / . . . / I have weighed with all my desire / On your matinal beauty / That shining forth it might escape. / . . . / A sun-drenched perfume / Protects what is to blossom.

duite," where the softest of rains suggests the gentlest of transitions, leading finally to the rushing flood:

.　.　.　.　.　.　.

Par une fine pluie d'amande,
mêlée de liberté docile,
ta gardienne alchimie s'est produite,
Ô Bien-aimée![x] (FM,55)

In a recent edition of *Fureur et mystère* (coll. Poésie, 1967), "Conduite" precedes the other texts, signaling the passage, as if the poet had now chosen to go before: "Passe . . . passe." The poem of "Le Visage nuptial" furnishes both password and key ("loquets pour la chambre d'amour") for the "labyrinth of extreme love." Detached from the other texts, of which it is nevertheless the dense concretion, this deeply cut passage opens at the center onto the new birth of the image:

Nativité, guidez les insoumis, qu'ils découvrent leur base,
L'amande croyable au lendemain neuf.
Le soir a fermé sa plaie. . . . (FM,59)

The wound, seen in its most atrocious lighting in the years 1940-44, at the moment when "La Liberté" was written, is healed only by a saving destruction ("If you must destroy, let it be with nuptial weapons.") In "La Liberté," what appears at the edge of the wound: "par cette ligne blanche" (FM,52) is not made precise. The exterior situation merges thereby with the interior. The boundary-marks of division and of fusion, such as the white line, the wall's fissure, the line of verse, the "lips of the wound," the red streak on the cheek of the mortal partner, signal not only a *partage* but also a *passage*. Thus the importance, previously discussed, of the image of the bee of boundaries.

Under the sign of this fine almond rain the greatest poems of Char take their place, to the sounds of a "lyre nuptiale," which one might re-read as a text of union: ["lire nuptial"].

[x] Through a fine rain of almond / mingled with gentle liberty / your guardian alchemy has done its work, / oh Beloved!

185

Here passion and possession meet in a corridor exposed and obscure, bounded between the hard walls of the book and open in the wound of the page. The poem as erotic weapon is redeeming and yet irremediably destructive:

L'horizon des routes jusqu'à l'afflux de rosée,
L'intime dénouement de l'irréparable.[28]

["L'horizon déroute"]: the poem is unsettling in its relentless course, toward the initial releasing of sources and the eventual saving of the body from the sand.

Later, the "vertes avenues libres"—those paths green in their renascent freedom, whose emblem is the iris ("iris plural, iris d'Éros") the flower of "gravity" in the *Lettera amorosa*—are changed to an "eau verte, et encore une route. . . . Fleur vallonnée d'un secret continu. / Green water, and still a road. . . . Flower valleyed by a continuous secret." (NP, 14) The valley or gorge is at once the calmest and the most tortured aspect of the mortal wound. This series of texts opened as a passage forms a conduit, only mentioned here, between the image of the unicorn and the cycle of waters. The triple motif composed by the legendary force of the pursuing and redemptive animal, the curative fountain, and the hidden mortality of the ephemeral and heroic being, is embodied in a text responding, in its own quiet resonance, to the most interior aspect of the encounter, as it is inserted in time.

. . . .

Temps, mon possédant et mon hôte, à qui offres-tu, s'il en est, les jours heureux de tes fontaines? A celui qui vient en secret, avec son odeur fauve, les vivre auprès de toi, sans fausseté, et pourtant trahi par ses plaies irréparables?[y]
(NP,104)

[28] See the following text on time: the irreparable act of passion is closely allied to the other irreparable wound, its dark and passive double in this understated version of the *liebestod*.

[y] Time, my possessor and my host, to whom do you offer, if there be any, the happy days of your fountains? To the one coming in secret, with his wild scent, to live them out near you, without any falseness, and yet betrayed by his irreparable wounds?

This host is also a guest, both meanings included in the term "l'hôte," since time is sheltered like a wound within the couple and within the page. The "irreparable" closing of this passage, like the conclusion of "Le Visage nuptial," leaves nevertheless a furrow which, once recognized, cannot be covered over. The works of passion are not to be repaired.

3. Third Reading: Present Encounter

But seen from another angle, the series of poems passes beyond the song of an individual love to another kind of triumph. Between the word "passe" which opens the passage and its recurrence, the poem "Conduite" implicates all the texts within the most vital present: "Ce soir, un village d'oiseaux / très haut exulte et passe // Tonight a town of birds / high above exults and passes," and in a presence which opens also the chant of "Le Visage nuptial": "A présent. . . ." The poem "Conduite" plays itself out between earth and sky: the falling of the meteor in its streaking trail forms a vertical balance with the flock of birds passing far above, as if certain poems were to be situated higher than the rest.

Of the contradictory, vertiginous movements of the period when this group of poems was written, the poet says (in his commentary on the poem "Biens égaux," a poem begun in 1937, a year before the publication of "Le Visage nuptial," and reworked later) that he was seeking in others about him "these contrasts and these vertigos without which the sovereign look would not exist." In its definitive version, as well as by its alterations, "Biens égaux" offers an invaluable insight into the double period of its writing and into the group of poems we consider as dwelling at the center of Char's work.[29] There are found the two major themes of the poem

[29] There is a proliferation of complex prose poems during this period: "Force clémente," "Léonides," "Fenaison," "L'Absent," "L'Épi de cristal. . . ." It seems that certain privileged themes are the foci for these dense concentrations: thus the hunter, the fire, the harvest, the threshold would be the real centers of the work in its most durable moments—together with the cluster of poems on the nuptial countenance from almost the same period as the poems listed above. Later,

187

"Le Visage nuptial"; first, that of the vision once lost and then lit anew, holding the poet in its sway: "un visage perdu . . . par instants s'éclaire et me regagne." And, by the necessity of this unique dominance, an inner and outer freedom from the trivial and the evident "indices," from all that is not the union of contraries, in its deepest significance: "Je n'ai retenu personne sinon l'angle fusant d'une Rencontre. . . . / L'espace pour toujours est-il cet absolu et scintillant congé? . . . // I have retained no one except the fusing angle of an Encounter. . . . / Is space for ever this absolute and sparkling vacancy?. . ." (FM,174)

The meeting itself, spiritual and yet specific, situated at the heart of things, bears witness to a poet's encounter with an absolute, shared with the reader, when all else is finally turned away. "Conduite" draws attention to the system of essential truths, complex and mobile in its approach to us:

. . . .

Vois bouger l'entrelacement des certitudes arrivées
près de nous à leur quintessence[z] (FM,55)

. . . .

However, these certainties will not always have the massive and almost optimistic force which attaches to them in this moment. Compare, for example, in "Plissement": "Vers ta frontière, ô vie humiliée, je marche maintenant au pas des certitudes, averti que la vérité ne précède pas obligatoirement l'action. / Toward your boundary, oh humiliated life, I now walk with the step of certainties, aware that truth does not necessarily precede action." (FM,50) And elsewhere, these certainties are said to be "distracted."

This group of poems has a profile distinct from that of any

---

the songs of refusal and resistance: "Chant du refus: *Début du partisan*," "Vivre avec de tels hommes," "Hommage et famine," and, a decade later, the texts from *Le Poème pulvérisé*: "Biens égaux," "L'Extravagant," "J'habite une douleur."

[z] Mark the moving of the interwoven certainties / that beside us have attained / their quintessence.

other. The characterization of an attitude first appearing here in a natural context: "Et le gravier debout sur l'algue / And the gravel standing upon the seaweed" ("Gravité") reappears at the beginning and the conclusion of "Le Visage nuptial," whose reach extends from the initial escort dismissed into the distance, to the final image of man saved and standing,[30] as if sculpted against the mass of the last two redemptive verses like another celebration of a couple, formally removed from the remainder of the text. Confrontation, elevation, and a double victory determine the tone of the epic poem, in its quiet depth, its extreme tension and solemn orchestration. Within the entire passage of the series, nothing belonging to man or to the things he loves will be definitively vanquished: this realization is finally the moral victory of Char's greatest work.

Taking another point of view on the broad lines of the central passage, we now recognize a radiance conferred not only on man but also on the earth. A cry of recognition and of resemblance is heard as prelude to the resurrection of the final luminous statement:

Et moi semblable à toi,
Avec la paille en fleur au bord du ciel criant ton nom,
J'abats les vestiges,
Atteint, sain de clarté. (FM,58)

The long resounding clarity of the second line spreads everywhere in the poem, in its own "simplicité fidèle," denying any contradictory vestiges as it does every future threat to openness: "Je ne verrai pas les ronces. . . ." From the first encounter with the fusing angle of the sky in "Conduite" to the universal convergence of the entire body of poems, the text welcomes and concentrates a unity rediscovered, in the fitting celebration of the four elements.

The element of water first appears as a fountain or a stream

---

[30] On the being-standing, see Georges Blin's preface to *Commune présence*, Gallimard, 1966. And we hear Rimbaud: "Majestueusement debout. . . ." (OR,45)

189

in joyous apposition with and as encouragement to human love. Nevertheless, as has already been apparent, it is through this element also that the most searing grief and the quietest suffering appears, as if it held within it all the glorious and tragic sides of our nature, of our connection with the universe, of nature or of men. In the universe of "Le Visage nuptial" itself, the water is already heavy, at a single day's distance from the spring where it takes its origin in purity, and yet it grows still heavier by absorbing the weight of these "lentes branches" as they mark the rhythm of the poem. By the route of water, we are led to the irreparable moment of effusion, signifying the "retour compact" and to its parallel in the classic invocation, where the distant sound of a Gregorian chant is heard, although muffled:

Ruisseaux, neume des morts anfractueux,
Vous qui suivez le ciel aride (FM,60)

Then the path leads to a water, where the word is nourished in silence:

La parole, lasse de défoncer, buvait au débarcadère angélique (FM,60)

"L'afflux de rosée": the coming of dew, beyond the physical manifestations of erotic effort, signals the new body's resurrection after the old shall have perished. As in an alchemical or religious tradition, man is saved by means of water, wherein the gold sleeps or from which the new man rises afresh, abandoning a former enclosure or outgrown shell to begin again. The arid sand here is cast off like the almond shell elsewhere, so that the inner kernel, living, can grow once more. It is this principle of resurrection or regrowth whose fertile freedom the water mirrors.

The element of fire calls to itself the flint, trembling here "sous les sarments de l'espace" as if indicating the stone of the "muet silex de midi écartelé / mute flint of quartered noon" of the poem "Évadné" which follows. Fire reflects also the crystal, whose traces are seen everywhere, in these vitreous or glazed voices and their corresponding image, the "vitre inextinguible"; from this visage the sorrow has disappeared, leaving only a morning radiance. Nonetheless, the poem is placed under a metaphysical sign rather than a visual one. Formerly, says the poet in "Post-scriptum," his poetry was too clear: "Mes feux ont trop précisé leur royaume / My fires made their kingdom too precise." (FM,62)

In the desert, another figuration of the element of earth, and a scene of an indistinct burning, the sand dies and the flint trembles: but the poem will be victor over all aridity and even over all harvest of a merely seasonal kind. "Nulle farouche survivance," we read in "Le Visage nuptial," and, in "Évadné": "La faucille partout devait se reposer. / Everywhere the sickle must have been at rest."

In this wider reading, the word itself shivers like the flint, in space or then under the light cover of clouds ("nage/ nuage") surrounding and interweaving signals half-effaced the dispersed elements of the word: ["paro—le"]. These are italicized here, as are the vapor and the airiness of the clouds, and their repose: thus we read ["des airs"].

Ceinture de vapeur, multitude assouplie, diviseurs de la crainte, touchez ma renaissance.
*Paro*is de ma durée, je renonce à l'assistance de ma largeur veniel*le* [see suggestion above]
· · · · · · · · · · ·
J'évoque la *nage*. . . .
Le corps *désert*. . . . (FM, 58-59)

Removed now from the restrictive limits set by an interpretation of the poem as nuptial in only the most specific sense, the images of the breath as an agent of vitality ("mon souffle affleurait déjà l'amitié de ta blessure, / Armait ta royauté inapparente") may be read in apposition with the "vitre inextinguible" and also with the "lèvres de brouillard," and not only as the source or provocation of the lovers' joy ("notre plaisir"). Moreover, in a gradually enlarging cycle, the word is the instrument of consciousness and of knowledge: "La

191

conscience augmentait . . . ," before becoming that of silence and of transcendence in a decreasing volume matched to an increasing depth:

effusion → murmure → mouvement tari de ta diction!

Although these allusions obviously follow the same line as that of other love poems, for example: "ton cri qui me donne ton silence / your cry which grants me your silence," the massive harmony of "Le Visage nuptial" transports them now to another level, and with them, all the other images and poems their mortal equals. Yet the epic encounter is protected by a margin; its very interiority impresses us first, reinforced by the other evocations of the poem, which, self-determining, refuses an outward vision: "Je ne verrai pas. . . . Je ne verrai pas. . . ." For the inner path offers no compromise with the outer: the concluding poem, added as a "Post-scriptum," dismisses everything that is not the poem and its making, not this passion going beyond the "fer" of the hunter's lance or the unicorn's weapon, or even beyond the poet's "faire." The poem finally realizes a love less for an individual than for the union of contraries, in a universal correspondence. All the exterior traces are merged, at last, with an acute consciousness of inevitable fragmentation and disappearance, within time, of even this convergence, also passing:

Écartez-vous de moi qui patiente sans bouche;

  .   .   .   .

Le trèfle de la passion est de fer dans ma main.

Dans la stupeur de l'air où s'ouvrent mes allées,
Le temps émondera peu à peu mon visage,
Comme un cheval sans fin dans un labour aigri.[ax] (FM,62)

[ax] Draw away from me awaiting mouthless; / . . . Passion's trefoil is iron in my hand. / In the stupor of the air where my goings open, / Time will hone away my countenance, bit by bit, / Like a horse ceaseless in an embittered ploughing.

192

E. CYCLE OF THE HARVEST AND THE FRUIT

Notre rareté commençait un règne. (FM,62)

Within Char's universe, celebration is "without lineage." Love is neither possessing nor restricting, burdened neither by prediction, nor afterthought, nor regret. Prosaic abundance of production runs counter to poetic survival: "Il y a des feuilles, beaucoup de feuilles sur les arbres de mon pays. Les branches sont libres de n'avoir pas de fruits. / There are leaves, many leaves, on the trees of my country. The branches are free to bear no fruits." (LM,42) In similar fashion, to clarity and "usefulness" in the prosaic sense, the unlimited cloud which makes no effort to continue, and the tools of pruning are preferred: "Restez près du nuage. Veillez près de l'outil. Toute semence est détestée. / Stay near the cloud. Watch over the implement. All seed is hated." (LM,149) (*) This ascetic attitude is in keeping with the bareness chosen later in the work as a spiritual country toward which the poet will "roll his chances," and to the "nordique visage des confins / the Nordic countenance of boundaries." (AC,34) Exterior restraint corresponds paradoxically to an unlimited and fresh horizon: "Passer sur le chemin nouveau. Ce que nous désirons est vaste. / To pass by on the new path. What we desire is vast." (AC,39)

And yet the land and the fruits of the land, transfigured by the poet's own work, recur in Char's writings with a revealing frequency. The fullest human participation is included within the natural cycle of work upon the land, for example, within a sunlit field corresponding to the radiant work of the natural elements:

. . . .

Pleine sera la vigne
Où combat ton épaule,
Sauf et même soleil.[bx] (LM,175)

[bx] The vine will be full / Where your shoulder struggles, / Safe and same sun.

Char's poems of harvest[31] and of fruit thus become the loyal adversaries for the ashes and the fragments, redeeming the partial, refusing failure except as an ephemeral moment within a larger cycle:

"REDONNEZ-LEUR . . ."

Redonnez-leur ce qui n'est plus présent en eux,
Ils reverront le grain de la moisson s'enfermer dans l'épi et
s'agiter sur l'herbe.
Apprenez-leur, de la chute à l'essor, les douze mois de leur
visage,
Ils chériront le vide de leur coeur jusqu'au désir suivant;
Car rien ne fait naufrage ou ne se plaît aux cendres;
Et qui sait voir la terre aboutir à des fruits,
Point ne l'émeut l'échec quoiqu'il ait tout perdu.[cx]
(FM,165)

Natural presence is recaptured after natural loss, as each action is begun afresh, reinserted within a temporal cycle of sparseness and plenitude. To participate in the cycle involves also a psychological correspondence, so that human seasons appear as the answers to natural seasons, stretching always from the falling to the rising. Emptiness succeeds to fruit, and fruit to emptiness. An identical goal permits the passage by the flowing of time across all the dry periods (those of ashes, of the desert sand) toward an end which will compensate even for cyclical loss, but will then pass as well. So the traditional images found here, such as the wheel of history, the

---

[31] In a first version of AUSC, we find: "L'obsession de la moisson, l'indifférence à l'Histoire," (No. 124) which then becomes: "L'obsession de la moisson et l'indifférence à l'Histoire sont les deux extrémités de mon arc." (AUSC,19) A negative observation on actual events was added later in proof: "L'ennemi le plus sournois est l'actualité." (RBS,164)

[cx] Restore to them what is no more present in them, / They shall see again the harvest grain shelter in the ear and sway on the stalk. / Teach them, from fall to soaring, the twelve months of their face, / They shall cherish their heart's emptiness until the next desire; / For nothing suffers shipwreck or contents itself in the cinders; / And a man who can watch the earth through to its end in fruit— / Failure does not shake him though he has lost all. (JG)

194

setting sun, the rose offering itself, and the grape in its ripening, correspond to the more specific and personal imagery of the watermill, or, transformed, to that of the sun-mill ("moulin à soleil").

The poet will extol the gestures of the wheat-gatherer together with those of the initiator: they are interdependent and together describe the role of the "poet, the great beginner." According to the revolution of the cycle—whose formal parallels we have seen, together with its images—there will be nothing "frankly unfruitful" in man's undertakings (as Char maintains, speaking of his "pulverized poems," AHPP). Scaling the mountain, a poet or his chosen companion only loses "ce qu'il se plaira ensuite à rechercher / what he will take pleasure in seeking again." Poetry's own guardian, the man on watch ("en attente") knows a changing and enduring scene.

Even the round form of some fruits, or of what the fruits represent, seems to respond to an affection for the circle and the cycle, their shape seen as both sensual and psychological:

"ALIÉNÉS"

De l'ombre où nous nous tenions, les doigts noués, sans nourriture, nous discernions le globe coloré des fruits les mieux dotés se glissant hors des feuilles. Leur maturité jaillissait du volume des arbres. . . . Ces fruits, comme dédaignés, s'abaisseraient jusqu'à leur pourriture finale devant notre amour immodeste auquel ils n'avaient su ni pu succéder.[dx] (NP,110)

Yet at the same time the cycle interior to the fruit completes its turn: the full makes its inexorable way toward the rotted.[32]

[dx] From the shade where we were, our fingers gnarled, without nourishment, we saw the colored globe of the most fully endowed fruits slipping out from the leaves. Their maturity burst forth from the trees' volume. . . . / These fruits, if despised, would sink to their final rotting in the face of our immodest love to which they had neither known how to, nor been able to succeed.

[32] Heidegger on fruit and ripening: "What we have in view is the fruit itself in its specific kind of Being. . . . The ripening fruit . . . not only is not indifferent to its unripeness as something other than itself

Furthermore, just when the fruit might be possessed, it appears in a distance about which nothing sure can be known: "La poésie est ce fruit que nous serrons, mûri, avec liesse, dans notre main au même moment qu'il nous apparaît, d'avenir incertain, sur la tige givrée, dans le calice de la fleur. / Poetry is that matured fruit which we grasp gladly at the same moment as it appears to us, with an uncertain future, on the frosted stem, in the calyx of the flower." (LM,194)

The poet's double perception, of agent and acted upon, of blade and bough, of presence and distance, is heightened by a temporal awareness in its promise and its threat: compare, in the *Sonnets to Orpheus*, "weil wir, ach, der Ast sind und das Eisen / und das Süsse reifender Gefahr // for we are, alas, the bough and the blade / and the sweet of ripening danger." (SO,114-115) A pervasive feeling of cyclical reassurance underlies the harvest of the fruit—and of the word—in both Rilke and Char. The latter's brief and yet full poem "Redonnez-leur . . . ," quoted in this chapter, might have as its center Rilke's own "Die Erde *schenkt*. / The earth *bestows*." (SO,38-39) Fruition goes beyond the seasonal cycle to em-

---

but it is that unripeness as it ripens. The 'not-yet' has already been included in the very Being of the fruit, not as some random characteristic, but as something constitutive. Correspondingly, as long as any Dasein is, it too is already its 'not-yet.' " (BT,288) Hölderlin, in his "Mnemosyne," associates the ripening of fruits with the prophecy of the serpents, the image of renewal: "Reif sind, in Feuer getaucht, gekochet / Die Frücht und auf der Erde geprüfet und ein Gesez ist / Dass alles hineingeht, Schlangen gleich, / Prophetisch, träumend. . . . // Ripe are, dipped in fire, cooked / The fruits and tried on the earth, and it is law, / Prophetic, that all must enter in / Like serpents, dreaming. . . ." (FH,498) In a note to this poem, Hamburger explains that mourning for the past (thus the title, "Memory") "is not permitted to the poet, who must 'collect his soul' for a different task, that of interpreting 'the signs of day,' all that is present and actual." (He refers us to the conclusion of *Patmos.*) This "cooking" of the opening line indicates natural ripening, as opposed to roasting and burning— the same distinction as in ancient sacrificial rites. Hamburger continues, quoting Paracelsus: "The ripening of fruit is natural cookery: therefore what nature has in her, she cooks, and when it is cooked, then nature is whole." (FH,611)

brace all the scope of human experience, in its deepest entirety: "Wir gehen um mit Blume, Weinblatt, Frucht. / Sie sprechen nicht die Sprache nur des Jahres. // We have to do with flower, vine-leaf, fruit. / They speak the language not only of the year." (SO,42-43)

For the universe of poetry includes all the correspondences.[32a] To this intermediate cycle between that of the mortal partners or loyal adversaries and that of the self-pursuing hunter, three texts in particular stand witness to a free ordering. They sustain intimate relationships with other cycles, with "matinal" themes and poems such as "Le Tout ensemble" for example, ("Faucille qui persévérez dans le ciel désuni / Malgré le jour et notre frénésie; / Lune qui nous franchis et côtoies notre coeur // Sickle persevering in the sky disunified / Despite the day and our frenzy; / Moon crossing through us and grazing our heart," LM,49) and with meditative ones, like "La Faux relevée," quoted above. All these other correspondences lend strength to the tensions and resolutions of this changing surface of the text which weds the natural cycle to the poetic one. In the edition *Fureur et mystère*, the three texts follow one another—except that between the first two "L'Absent" serves as a defense, as an assurance of presence even at the heart of apparent absence ("il occupe le fourneau dans l'unité," FM,39). So "Fenaison" (FM,38) leads directly to "L'Épi de cristal égrène dans les herbes sa moisson transparente" (FM,40), and to "Louis Curel de la Sorgue." (FM,41) Some links remain open, explicit even in the title concerning the harvest, whether of hay or of the "crystal ear" of wheat.

"Fenaison," the first poem of the three, revolves around a few clear images, set at the boundaries of perception, and luminously expansive. An "anemone lamp" and a "pollen hand," for example, indirectly summon the presence of the bee, as an image of traversal, of steering between boundaries:

[32a] "Nos vergers sont transhumants." ("Faire du chemin avec. . . ," 1976) The fruit trees of poetry, in an *âge cassant*, change their orchards—as bees do their meadows—according to the season.

"frontalière." Thus the anemone and the pollen each suggest the flower from which the bee makes the eventual honey of the poem, as the poet, like a human meteor, "has the earth for honey." The poem summons also the image of the phoenix reborn from ashes, within the cycle designated by the ring and the circular light, lunar or solar or each in its turn:

"FENAISON"

. . . .

Je m'appuie un moment sur la pelle du déluge et chantourne sa langue. Mes sueurs d'agneau noir provoquent le sarcasme. Ma nausée se grossit de soudains consentements dont je n'arrive pas à maintenir le cours. Anneau tard venu. . . . (See p. 164.)

Ô nuit, je n'ai pu traduire en galaxie son Apparition que j'épousai étroitement dans les temps purs de la fugue! Cette Soeur immédiate tournait le coeur du jour.[ex] (FM,38)

. . . .

The presence of the cycle is continually signaled, phonetically and conceptually, by a chain of images:

chan*tourne* → *anneau* → *tournait* le coeur
↓
ma nausée

The pure past time of carefree ventures is opposed to the presence of a day in its immediacy. All that has been retained from the night and the adventures of early dawn will be just as fleeting ("je n'arrive pas . . ."). But the poet's companion, chosen for his upright stance, holds firm in the path leading upland, opposed to the facility of passive content, of all involvement which is not that of the most difficult

[ex] I lean for a moment on the spade of deluge and cut around its tongue's curve. My black lamb sweat provokes sarcasm. My nausea swells with sudden consenting whose course I cannot maintain. Ring lately-come. . . . / Oh night, I could not translate into a galaxy its Appearance whose intimate spouse I became in the pure escapade moments! This immediate Sister was turning the heart of day.

198

poetry: "Salut à celui qui marche en sûreté à mes côtés, au terme du poème. Il passera demain DEBOUT sous le vent. / My greeting to the one who walks safely by my side, to the term of the poem. He shall pass tomorrow UPRIGHT under the wind." (FM,38) He is, as the reader would hope to be, one of the "quelques êtres" whose real dwelling is the largest sense of the poem.

The three poems are set at an affirmative angle. Central to the trilogy is a denial of defeat and an assertion of freedom:

"L'ÉPI DE CRISTAL ÉGRÈNE DANS LES HERBES SA MOISSON TRANSPARENTE"

La ville n'était pas défaite. Dans la chambre devenue légère le donneur de liberté couvrait son amour de cet immense effort du corps, semblable à celui de la création d'un fluide par le jour. L'alchimie du désir rendait essentiel leur génie récent à l'univers de ce matin.[fx] (FM,40)

. . . .

The lightness of the morning suits the freshly born love with whose hope and desire the future is impregnated. Like a distant *continuo*, sonorous even over city noise, the roar of the sea renews the lovers' faith in multiple possibilities, laying open its "grands espaces du voyage" for other new births. When the bestower of freedom and of matinal possibility finally takes his leave, the strains of his hunting song will continue to sound: "La flèche de leur bouche dont le chant venait de naître. / The arrow of their mouth where the song had just been born."

The last poem of this group presents in unornamented fashion an act we consider to be surrounded with wide margins, like the spacious work of the poem itself—these margins necessary to the development of the poem as almond, enclosed, whether by walls or spaces, against the temptation of

[fx] The town was not undone. In the room become weightless, the bestower of freedom covered his beloved with this immense bodily effort, akin to a fluid's creation by the day. Desire in its alchemy rendered essential their recent genius to that morning's universe.

facility and the levelling influence of the air which might render too clear. (See the above commentary on "J'habite une douleur.") Here, the work of the harvest in its regular and forceful rhythm encourages a tone heroic yet modest in its order:

"LOUIS CUREL DE LA SORGUE"

Sorgue qui t'avances derrière un rideau de papillons qui pétillent, ta faucille de doyen loyal à la main . . . quand pourrai-je m'éveiller et me sentir heureux au rythme modelé de ton seigle irréprochable? Le sang et la sueur ont engagé leur combat qui se poursuivra jusqu'au soir, jusqu'à ton retour, solitude aux marges de plus en plus grandes. L'arme de tes maîtres, l'horloge des marées, achève de pourrir.[gx] (FM,41)

.   .   .   .

The sickle, a privileged weapon taken from the field of a personal landscape and as cutting as poetry—pruning toward productiveness—triumphs even over time, as we have the habit of counting and dividing it, so that the natural cycle of a work effectively entire negates the fragmentation that a uniquely human culture might have chosen.

Standing victorious, imposing his own mark even on the seas of waving wheat, sensed in the preceding poem under the distant immobility of the sea behind the lovers, this man integral with his field will share in its movements and its redemption: "Sorgue, tes épaules comme un livre ouvert propagent leur lecture. . . . / Il y a un homme à présent debout, un homme dans un champ de seigle, un champ pareil à un choeur mitraillé, un champ sauvé. // Sorgue, your shoul-

[gx] Sorgue advancing behind a curtain of flickering butterflies, holding your sickle of loyal elder . . . when may I waken joyous at the graven rhythm of your irreproachable rye? Blood and sweat have joined their combat which will last until evening, until your return, solitude, with ever greater margins. All but rotted now, the weapon of your master, the clock of tides.

ders propagate their reading like an open book. . . . / There is a man now standing, a man in a field of rye, a field like a machine-gunned chorus, a field redeemed." (FM,41) The images of shoulders and the back—for the bearing of burdens, for the execution of work and its continuation through others, recur in a frequent expression of potential force and its extension, as if it were the only metaphoric fruit borne, characteristically, by this poet's tree. In a lasting fruition the reader is renascent from his reading, or more exactly, from the poet's work and his word, as in "Les Trois soeurs":

. . . .

Cet enfant sur ton épaule
Est ta chance et ton fardeau
. . . .
Violente l'épaule s'entr'ouvre[hx] (FM,172)
. . . .

In a powerful conclusion to the text "Louis Curel de la Sorgue" and to the cycle where we situate it, the man standing upright in a field to be harvested answers the attitude of the poet standing against the wind. The common stride of the harvester and his companions toward the end of the poem corresponds now to a collective moral preparation for the poem. In the same way, the bestower of freedom and the savior of the field are unified in their calling, that is, to defend the new song of refusal or any song of spiritual victory against the heart machine-gunned or mowed down by the butcher, whether of wartime or peacetime ("L'Épi"), or by the divisive motion of the clock, a temporal persecutor.

Finally we might read, by an implicit joining, the separate but corresponding poems as parts of the same whole, so that the season of harvest and that of the verbal fruition are seen to meet in the dominating presence of the cyclic passage from poem to poem:

[hx] This child on your shoulder / Is your fortune and your burden / . . . / Violent the shoulder parts, asunder.

"Fenaison"	"L'Épi de cristal égrène dans les herbes sa moisson transparente	"Louis Curel de la Sorgue"
DEBOUT sous le vent	ils précédaient le pays de leur avenir	il y a un homme à présent debout
. . . .	. . . .	. . . .
aux approches du désir	le chant venait de naître	dans un champ sauvé
	. . .	
	une nouvelle fois	

Thus the song is saved by this cycle, as, in "Le Visage nuptial," the desert body was redeemed, each time afresh, from the sand. "Man stands upright" now, as in that poem.

F. CYCLE OF THE HUNTER

L'aigle voit de plus en plus s'effacer les pistes
de la memoire gelée
L'étendue de la solitude rend à peine visible
la proie filante[ix] (MM,67)

Throughout the central works one profile is seen constantly passing. The future task appears, already luminous, to the boy in "Le Devoir" who strengthens his sight and his determination near a forge and a smelting hearth as a fiery and always difficult testing ground: "Dans la constellation des Pléiades, au vent d'un fleuve adolescent, l'impatient Minotaure s'éveillait. / In the constellation of the Pleiades, in the wind of an adolescent stream, the impatient Minotaur was waking." (FM,43) The combative figure is aroused, Orion developing his sight as if for an ultimate blinding.

[ix] The eagle sees the tracks of frozen memory growing ever fainter / The stretch of solitude renders scarcely visible the fleeting prey.

Localized in the hearth, where the iron is tempered the trial must be passed through, as in the testing of metal, or as in the medieval "Ordalie,"[33] ordeal for the hero's *passage* by fire, proving his endurance: he merits thereby the opening of an interior way. So the young hero is reinforced in what will later be his "refusal song," negating any exterior ordinance contrary to his inner necessity:

"L'ADOLESCENT SOUFFLETÉ"

Les mêmes coups qui l'envoyaient au sol le lançaient en même temps loin devant sa vie, vers les futures années où, quand il saignerait, ce ne serait plus à cause de l'iniquité d'un seul. . . .

Il recommencerait ainsi jusqu'au moment où, la nécessité de rompre disparue, il se tiendrait droit et attentif parmi les hommes, à la fois plus vulnérable et plus fort.[jx] (LM,58)

The youthful hunter always defines himself by his ardent thrust toward what lies ahead of him, "a feverish forwardness" (FM,190), representing the impulsiveness of his character, exemplified by these ventures ("fugues") in the early dawn that reappear in several of the poems associated with him. As his particular nature and singularities grant him his independence from others, the adolescent "upright and attentive" will gradually take on the features of his brother and absent comrade, whose memory is unforgettable, dominant

---

[33] From Yves Bonnefoy's "L'Ordalie II": "Je ne sais pas si je suis vainqueur. Mais, j'ai saisi / D'un grand coeur l'arme enclose dans la pierre. / J'ai parlé dans la nuit de l'arme, j'ai risqué / Le sens et au-delà du sens le monde froid." (*Du Mouvement et de l'immobilite de Douve*, Gallimard, 1970, p. 179.) The text is marked with the images of the passage through trial: the "feu rouge," the breaking of bread "où l'eau lointaine coule," and the ship entering its port.

[jx] The same blows that cast him to the ground projected him at once far ahead into his life, toward the future years when, wounded, he would no longer bleed from the iniquity of one being. / . . . / Thus he would start again until, no longer needing to break off battle, he could hold himself upright and attentive among men, more vulnerable and stronger.

even at a distance. He is one of the constant figures in Char's work whose very presence is sensed precisely in his standing apart: he is himself the moral hearth for the testing of character, like an alchemical crucible for the burning of contraries into a paradoxical unity, even his most exterior features representing the conflicts of extreme and opposing forces. He might be considered a spiritual portrait of the poet, at once absent and present.

"L'ABSENT"

Ce frère brutal mais dont la parole était sûre, patient au sacrifice, diamant et sanglier, ingénieux et secourable, se tenait au centre de tous les malentendus tel un arbre de résine dans le froid inalliable. . . . Comme l'abeille quitte le verger pour le fruit déjà noir, les femmes soutenaient sans le trahir le paradoxe de ce visage qui n'avait pas des traits d'otage.

J'ai essayé de vous décrire ce compère indélébile que nous sommes quelques-uns à avoir fréquenté. Nous dormirons dans l'espérance, nous dormirons en son absence, puisque la raison ne soupçonne pas que ce qu'elle nomme, à la légère, absence, occupe le fourneau dans l'unité.[kx]
(FM,39)

Within the space created about him by the intensity of his desire for it, this companion remains unrepentant and brutal: "être brutal répare." It is his shadow, seen by the harshest light, that will haunt our reading in its admittedly passionate

---

[kx] This brutal brother but whose word was true, steadfast in the face of sacrifice, diamond and wild boar, ingenious and helpful, held himself in the center of all misunderstandings like a resinous tree in the cold admitting of no alloy. . . . As the bee leaves the orchard for the fruit already black, women withstood without betraying it the paradox of this face which had none of the lineaments of a hostage.

I have tried to describe for you this indelible companion whose friendship some of us have kept. We shall sleep in hope, we shall sleep in his absence, reason not suspecting that what it names, thoughtlessly, absence, dwells within the crucible of unity.

involvement, a shadow already perceived, as if he were the true mortal partner for the reader and for the composite figure of the poems chosen here. Situated at the summit of the cycle—as we see it—"L'Extravagant" reveals the hunter with an "active heel," as he walks with an uncompromising gait (an image found elsewhere: LM,49). This figure, placed in a lonely altitude, is destined to transcend the limits of an individual personality as he strides through the space of the poet's work:

"L'EXTRAVAGANT"

Il ne déplaçait pas d'ombre en avançant . . . ce marcheur que le voile du paysage lunaire, très bas, semblait ne pas gêner dans son mouvement. Le gel furieux effleurait la surface de son front sans paraître *personnel*.[ix] (FM,182)

. . . .

Of the same heroic stature as the absent brother whose contradictory aspects are difficult to accept, this extreme personage chooses never to be seen in his totality. The poet has himself opted for a certain protective mystery within his work: "Tu es reposoir d'obscurité sur ma face trop offerte, poème. / You are, poem, a resting-place of obscurity upon my too exposed face." (LM,134) Having learned the lesson of the bird in self-containment (see "Le Martinet"), he presents himself only in profile:

. . . .

Personne n'aurait à l'oublier car l'utile ne l'avait pas assisté, ne l'avait pas dessiné en entier au regard des autres. Sur le plafond de chaux blanche de sa chambre, quelques oiseaux étaient passés mais leur éclair avait fondu dans son sommeil.
Le voile du paysage lunaire maintenant très haut déploie

[ix] He displaced no shadow in his advance . . . this man whose walking the low-hanging veil of the lunar landscape appeared not to hinder. The raging frost brushed his forehead lightly without seeming *personal*.

205

ses couleurs aromatiques au-dessus du personnage que je dis. Il sort éclairé du froid et tourne à jamais le dos au printemps qui n'existe pas.^mx (FM,183)

The lunar landscape is now absorbed by the dreamer's white ceiling; elsewhere the poet refers to: "Le mur de chaux de la pièce où je travaille / The whitewashed wall of the room I work in." (FM,133) The rooms adjoin, as the poetic figures passing in profile make up several aspects of a same personality. And the poet hunter, extravagant in the strictest sense of wandering outside (extra-vaguer) founds his anguished wisdom here on a cold and lucid solitude, striding along under the luminous veil of these aromatic colors that will guide his final ascent to the place, no longer of the Minotaur, but of Orion, as the labyrinth takes on at last its true depth, or its true height.

---

^mx No one would have to forget him, for self-interest had never aided him, had never sketched him whole to the others' gaze. Across the whitewashed ceiling of his room, some birds had passed, but their flash had melted into his sleep.

The veil of the lunar landscape, now lifted high, unfolds its aromatic colors above this personage of whom I speak. He comes forth lit by the cold and forever turns his back on the springtime that does not exist.

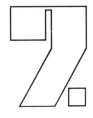

THE WAYS OF THE WORD: "CES HAUTS VOYAGEURS"

A. BREATH AND FREEDOM

Il nous faut une haleine à casser des vitres. Et pourtant il nous faut une haleine que nous puissions retenir longtemps. (RBS,172)

Although it gives the first indication of life, human breath proves an efficacious agent in the destruction of its noblest traces: in the cave of Lascaux, man has almost eliminated the art of his ancestors by his own presence there, as it were, simply by breathing: "L'âge du renne, c'est-à-dire l'âge du souffle. Ô vitre, ô givre, nature conquise, dedans fleurie, dehors détruite! / The age of the reindeer,—that is, the age of breathing. Oh pane, oh hoarfrost, oh conquered nature, in flower within, outside destroyed!" (LM,105) (JG) To breathe on a cold glass is to make the crystal flower, but this new blossoming cannot recreate the pictures left on the cavern walls. That art could have illuminated our future. "Insouciants, nous exaltons . . .": careless and profane, we kill our past that we should have put before us. "Space man," says Char in 1959, "will be a thousand times less luminous and will reveal a thousand times fewer hidden things than the granite man of Lascaux, recluse and reclining. . . ." (LM,200)

Breath, this sign of life, and, by implication, of knowledge and intelligence ("le souffle de la connaissance," FM,177) reveals our kinship with the energy of animal forces. According to a statement in *Partage formel*, "Every breath proposes a reign: the task of persecuting, the decision to maintain, the ardor to liberate." (FM,79). The peak effort is similarly marked: "Le sommet du souffle dans l'inconnu. / The summit of breath in the unknown." (LM,80): the poet recognizes himself only in his extreme, aggressive breathing, as he climbs a slope representing the eternal image of marginality

207

and risk. After his long walk upland (or, in the interchangeability of the two images, upstream), he lays down his possessions, even the sweat earned by his own toil, and casts aside even prudence. "Debout, croissant dans la durée, le poème / Standing erect, growing in duration, the poem" (FM,80): choosing an identity with his poem, the poet is granted a "souffle nouveau." (LM,85)

Often the most intensely concentrated force, recognized in man or in what resembles him, is compared to the vital rhythm of respiration. For instance, in Georges Braque, it is "the eye which breathes and inflames the trace." (RBS,65) The intuitive being senses the joining of correspondences, not in daylight but rather under a nocturnal sky and by the path of the nostrils. Such a primitive union of men and universe demonstrates an unbroken continuity with the Lascaux man in his struggle with the bison: "In the night, the poet, the drama and nature are only one, but ascending and breathing each other." (LM,168) Within the poet always troubled by an ethical concern, this moral anger—avid for even the cruelest justice—is expressed by a harsh intake of air. The poems of the partisan are marked by a fierce and unforgiving energy.

Any rebel against a constraining system shows his mutinous nature by "breathing more strongly than the lungs of the executioner." (FM,137) It is in this sense that one should interpret, from the political, the economic, and the psychological viewpoints, this "land which had only its breath with which to scale the future." (PPC,227) Every rising path will require a dynamism sufficiently haughty, represented by an intense respiration. (Cf. Valery: "BREATHING. Freedom is a sensation. It is to be breathed." *Regards sur le monde actuel.*)

For breathing, although an ordinary and automatic function of the body, is considered inextricably linked to freedom, either from exterior circumstances or from the self. "La Liberté," last of the "Neuf poèmes pour vaincre," describes the liberated work as "the canvas where breath is inscribed" ("la toile où s'inscrivit mon souffle" FM,52). The two cycles where this image predominates are turned toward an identical problem, although differently. In *Arsenal* (MM), liberation from the confines of reality is won either by a natural breathing magnified or by an alchemical transformation. But the language of this transformation is not stressed, so that the allusion finds the lightest of inscriptions. The cloud which was to play a minor role ("Le rôle effacé") according to the first version of *Arsenal* (A,11) goes first of all ("passe devant") in "La Torche du prodigue." It is a

. . . . . .

Nuage de résistance
Nuage des cavernes
Entraîneur d'hypnose.[a] (MM,17)

The poem is a convincing example of the foreboding of the period from 1937 to 1944 of which the poet speaks in the preface to the second edition, that of 1945. These allusions to resistance, to caves and to hypnosis might surprise the reader of the *Feuillets d'Hypnos* were it not precisely one of the functions of poetry to predict. This "cloud of the caverns" is equally a premonition of the destruction of the art of the Lascaux cave.

The title of the last text of *Arsenal* underlines precisely the organs connected with the breath: "Les Poumons." And the following remark on the poem "Le Solitaire" (found in *Le Tombeau des secrets*, another part of the manuscript of *Arsenal*), casts its own light on the entire system of interlocking images: "This poem is not commemorative but contradictory, spiritual but respiratory." Breathing is matched to the regular rhythm of the hammer or to that of the heart, both represented in the title: *Le Marteau sans maître*, indicating steadiness together with freedom. The heart's rhythm determines that of the lungs, but this regularity later perceived in the graven rhythm of the harvest ("Louis Curel de la Sorgue") also points the way to escape from system, toward the rebellious path that will later be that of the marginal

[a] Cloud of resistance / Cloud of caverns / Trainer of hypnosis.

and the mutinous personage. His individuality develops here, even before the more evident portraits of the child learning an exceptional duty, of the adolescent boy, of the absent brother, and of an extravagant or extreme being ("Le Devoir," "L'Adolescent souffleté," "L'Absent," "L'Extravagant"). Poems of escape stand out in relief among this collection: "Le sphérique des respirations pénétra dans la paix / The balloon of breathing penetrated into peace" (MM,87) or again: "Poitrine en avance sur son néant / Chest ahead of its nothingness." (MM,89) The most illuminating text in this connection explains the title of the series and its basic theme — that strength depends on the possibility of escape as well as on that of isolation, specifically here, on the bridge to be crossed or lifted:

"TRANSFUGES"

Sang enfin libérable
L'aérolithe dans la véranda
Respire comme une plante

L'esprit même du château fort
C'est le pont-levis.[b] (MM,22)

The hammer without a master serves as a theme for several texts of the first version of *Arsenal*, such as "La Guerre sous roche" ("On libère le bras qui tombe sous les sens") and "La Délivrance naturelle," where the verse boils in its chrysalis as it does in the poem "Robustes météores," already discussed. One of the first versions appears in "Bonne aventure," from *Arsenal*:

Dans le bois on écoute bouillir le ver
La chrysalide tournant au clair visage
Sa délivrance naturelle[c] (MM,21)
. . . .

[b] Blood able at last to be freed / The aerolith in the veranda / Breathes like a plant / The very spirit of the fortress / Is the drawbridge.
[c] In the wood we listen to the worm boiling / The chrysalis turning toward a clear face / Its natural deliverance.

210

One of these texts could be interpreted as the refusal of a prison too bookish, as a mute and impulsive appeal again based on the image of a bodily tempo, and running counter to any deciphering of the mystery of love:

. . . .

Le sang muet qui délivre
Tourne à l'envers les aiguilles
Remonte l'amour sans le lire.[d] (MM,18)

Understood in these lines is a desire for definitive freedom; chains of any sort impede the free going of the naturally elusive being. (Compare the mood of "Deshérence," for instance.)

The second and related leit-motif, of what we might call a heroic or exceptional breathing, includes the entire cycle of poems on love, in which one is doubly freed: "Nous nous faisions libres tous deux." (FM,42) *Le Marteau sans maître* envisions, before the fact, this singular cycle. A nomadic wanderer falls asleep on the poet's mouth:

"SINGULIER"

. . . .

Volume d'éther comme une passion
Délire à midi à minuit elle est fécondée dans le coma de
    l'amour arbitraire
La pièce de prédilection de l'oxygène.[e] (MM,26)

The poem already provides a sketch of "La Chambre dans l'espace" where the lover, whose attachment to his partner's freedom is absolute,[1] admires the delicacy of her breathing as it takes flight: "l'aile de ton soupir met un duvet aux

[d] The mute blood liberating / Turns the hands counter-clockwise / Winds up love without reading it.

[e] Volume of ether like a passion / Delirium at noon at midnight she is impregnated in the coma of arbitrary love / The favorite room of oxygen.

[1] Compare this poem to "Marthe," where the poet insists above all on free departure and fresh beginning.

211

feuilles / the wing of your sigh lays a down upon the leaves."
(LM,138)

Within the cycle of the nuptial countenance already discussed, the three titles "Gravité," its sub-title: "L'Emmuré,"
and "Le Visage nuptial" taken as a whole, accentuate the
solemn aspect of the meeting destined finally to deliver the
couple from its former egoism. For the poet's generosity
works against possession, as it does against self-satisfaction:
what is enclosed, like the almond, will have to break forth:
"emmuré"→"éclore." "Gravité" begins with the words: "S'il
respire," and it is by this probable respiration that the still
center is reached. It is then transcended by all the passion
of encounter ("Vitre inextinguible. Mon souffle. . . ."), moving from rapid ardor to the tranquil conclusion, where a regular breathing of the still warring adversaries determines the
extreme oppositions: sand/body, and dead/saved. The two
partners occupy the same space, seen from this angle: "La
Femme respire, l'Homme se tient debout."

In the center of these poems, whose rhythm corresponds
so closely to it, human breath will endure, aggressive in its
invocation of a definitive freedom, whereby "la maison sera
delivrée de son enclos / the house will be freed from its enclosure." Man both prey and hunter, whose harsh breathing
expresses his difficult nature, steps past all the limiting en-
closures and compartments of human constructions toward a
dwelling always built higher up in the stream, its angles
thrusting against the current ("Recours au ruisseau").

B. Dream and Speech

Nous sommes des malades sidéraux incurables.
. . . (FM,106)

The "Argument" placed as a warning to the collection
L'Avant-monde (inserted in Fureur et mystère) presents in
a brief space several themes essential to our present traversal
of these pages. Situated at the exact center of the text, the

212

argumentative Word opposes everything which is not the unique concern of the poet: "nothing obsesses me but life." (FM,203) Written after *Arsenal*, along the same lines, and bearing the same weapons toward the same goal, it still argues the history of limits transcended—thus the continuing importance in the work of René Char of the verb "franchir." In absolute opposition to bonds passively accepted, a "being of the leap" can function only in freedom, toward a harvest of the invisible: *"L'homme fuit l'asphyxie. / L'homme dont l'appétit hors de l'imagination se calfeutre sans finir de s'approvisionner, se délivrera par les mains, rivières soudainement grossies. // Man flees suffocation. / Man, whose appetite for what is beyond even imagination becomes airtight still laying in supplies, will find freedom by his hands, rivers suddenly swollen."* (FM,19) The hands kneading the bread of poetry, in the "transhumance du Verbe" as it changes pastures with the seasons, are here, significantly, clasping a ring instead of putting it on to be encircled by it: "Nous tenons l'anneau." They hold it in evidence. This sign of freely-chosen yoking and an association, the iron links of which one must forge, as with a *Marteau sans maître*, beyond the visible form: *"Déporté de l'attelage et des noces, je bats le fer des fermoirs invisibles. // Deported from the yoke and from the nuptials, I strike the iron of invisible hinges."* (FM,13)

Everything in this text is excessive: increased rivers swelled by a mental springtime, a natural economy flooded by excessive consciousness and a haughty refusal, all limits transgressed, and gestures aggrandized, in an August light too brilliant: *"Déborder l'économie de la création, agrandir le sang des gestes, devoir de toute lumière. / . . . / Aoûtement. Une dimension franchit le fruit de l'autre. Dimensions adversaires. // To overflow the economy of creation, to increase the blood of gestures, a duty of complete illumination. / . . . / August ripening. One dimension traverses the fruit of another. Warring dimensions."* (FM,13) This text is already impregnated by the perceptions evident in a text of thirty years later—as if the later "dimensions" had traversed the

213

earlier. "Espace couleur de pomme. Espace, brûlant compo-tier. / Space, apple-colored. Space, burning fruit-dish." (NP, 116) Here, under an intensely consuming yellow light, the limits of normal vision are exceeded, the excess and the ex-ception preparing the uncommon conjunction of elements (yet never as mere *alloys*: the term "inalliable" recurs with a notable frequency in Char's writings).

In this invocation to August light we might hear an al-chemical allusion: the ring, the key, ("la clé angélique") the adversaries, the tempered iron, thrusting for an invisible goal. By the force of the Word at its work, its resources enlarged as if by miracle, rivers suddenly swell as if to confer life, and multiply it: they run over, their banks increase, their flow surging past the fragments. But the text "Possessions exté-rieures" in *Le Nu perdu* raises to the cosmic level the problem of an exterior vision over which we have no sway, to which, however, we respond, creating a common resonance: "Parmi tout ce qui s'écrit hors de notre attention, l'infini du ciel, avec ses défis, son roulement, ses mots innombrables, n'est qu'une phrase un peu plus longue, un peu plus haletante que les autres. / Among everything that writes itself beyond our notice, the infinite of the sky, with its challenges, its rum-bling, its innumerable words, is only a sentence slightly longer, of a quicker breath than the others." (NP,68)

To the distant Word, (like some summit or ideal for our landscape), we confide our moments of emptiness to give them a full sense and our hesitations so that they might be resolved ("Nous . . . donnons à son sens ce qui nous semble irrésolu et en suspens dans notre propre signification / We . . . give to its sense what seems to us irresolute and sus-pended in our own meaning"). The nocturnal inscription rep-resents all we could not write, compensating for our insuf-ficiency, from a daily moderation toward a radiant and excessive space, fit for heroes or poets. The night, affected by our imaginings, now writes its story in a shining sentence, sleep conferring on it a corporal change similar to ours: "Ainsi trouvons-nous la nuit différente, hors de sa chair. . . . /

Thus do we find the night different, outside its flesh. . . ."[2] Like the stars of a constellation, a swarm of bees dispersed, or the scattered fragments of a poem burst apart, the luminous fragments of sense serve as a path traveled by the dreamer who listens, clothed in his dream: *"Enchemisé dans les violences de sa nuit."* (NP,101) Responding to one another, these starry fragments in correspondence feel themselves linked as if by choice and not yoked by necessity, called but not summoned to a stellar conformation, resembling a bunch of grapes ("Fontis"), a swarm of bees ("Réception d'Orion"), a cluster of pebbles ("La Nuit talismanique"), or even an archipelago of texts, "La Parole en archipel" transported upward.

The hesitation once felt by Char as to the origin of the poetic work: whether an interior arrangement of the unconscious or a necessity, "Commandement interne? Sommation du dehors?" (FM,82) is no longer felt in this warning against a belief in the purely spontaneous, no matter how appealing: "Let's be careful not to imagine an automatic transcription." (RBS,86) The paradox of the situation is no longer a subject for anguish; even if the matching of fragments is necessarily significant, the responsibility visible in the verbs "we read," "we give," "we find"—weighs now on the poet and his perceptive powers rather than on some exterior marvelous chance that he might have accepted during his brief surrealist period. A previous text announces this one, forming an inner chain of an ordering rebellious rather than simple ("ordre insurgé"). "La Bibliothèque est en feu" offers a brief meditation on the individual will and on invisible determination,

---

[2] See the epigraph of Paul Éluard for *Le Tombeau des secrets* (privately printed, 1930): "Dormons, mes frères. Le chapitre inexplicable est devenu incompréhensible." *Arsenal* is closed, explicitly, even in its "justification de tirage": "Qu'on le veuille ou non, 'Arsenal' a été tiré. . . . Il est réconfortant de penser que les imbéciles n'en sauront rien." It is interesting that the most cursory examination of the style of purely "automatic" writing as it appears on Char's manuscripts kept in the Bibliothèque Doucet from his surrealist period shows it to be far removed in spirit and style from Char the poet (in the manuscript no. 685, AE-IV-5). Nothing reveals more clearly his innate distance from that movement.

where the convergence of desire and correspondence illuminates us: "Désir, désir qui sait, nous ne tirons avantage de nos ténèbres qu'à partir de quelques souverainetés véritables assorties d'invisibles flammes, d'invisibles chaînes, qui, se révélant, pas après pas, nous font briller. / Desire, desire aware, we gain advantage from our darkness only with the support of certain true sovereignties matched with invisible flames, with invisible chains which, revealing themselves, step by step, make us glitter." (LM,149) (JG) Nostalgia for a continuous constellation, or for a cavern fire, or then a revealing premonition?

A suggestion of adequate mystery must be left to dream and to the poem ("Un poète doit laisser des traces et non des preuves . . ."). The poet of *L'Age cassant* (1963-65), with his distant gaze fixed on the bird-crossed land ("terre croisée des oiseaux"), on this *auspex* of the invisible future, easily perceives the farthest contraries from which he will form his own work, both durable and slipping by: "L'inclémence lointaine est filante et fixe. Telle, un regard fier la voit. / Distant inclemency is shooting and fixed. Thus does a proud look see it." (RBS,184) But—like André Breton telling his daughter, and by implication telling us, that he could not dwell in the sublime point forming the resolution of all extremes— Char describes the least attainable as the surest of guides: "L'impossible, nous ne l'atteignons pas, mais il nous sert de lanterne. / We don't attain the impossible, but it serves us as a lantern." (RBS,180) In *Le Nu perdu*, "le oui et le non" are shown to be, in their very opposition and excess, a salutary origin for the word which is thereafter free to take on its proper nuances. (NP,127)

The extreme may be realized, but its verbal expression will be veiled: obscurity facilitates the leaving of a margin, the developing of a space around the poem and the poet, propitious for their expansion "dans la durée." A sense perhaps optimistic converges with a desire perhaps unrealizable: "Ah! le pouvoir de se lever autrement. / Oh! the ability to rise in another fashion." (LM,153) Exclamation in which we read:

216

"Ah! (this is then) the ability . . ." or "Ah! (if only I had) the ability. . . ." Or again, an ambiguous gesture may correspond with words of varied sense as the context is various: "Lorsque je rêve et que j'avance, lorsque je retiens l'ineffable, m'éveillant, je suis à genoux. / When I dream and move forward, when I hold back the ineffable, awaking, I am on my knees." (LM,153)

Finally, and still related to the dream, a short text, formulated as a question, offers a possible if paradoxical response to the serious question of men as murderers of their own past: "Qui oserait dire que ce que nous avons détruit valait cent fois mieux que ce que nous avions rêvé et transfiguré sans relâche en murmurant aux ruines? / Who would dare to say that what we have destroyed was a hundred times better than what we had dreamed and ceaselessly transfigured murmuring to the ruins?" (RBS,181) There might still be time to place all that we have behind us in our past before us to guide our dream.

C. SUPPORT AND RETURN

. . . dans la stupeur de l'air où s'ouvrent mes
allées (FM,62)

The poet suffers at seeing "the unreal still existing, scarcely touched by events, in a world half destroyed by the forces of history": perhaps he was never to give himself over to the dream, whose existence he would choose to return to men, beyond the horror surrounding them. For his marginal stance in no way implies the abandoning of the work in common, the harvest and seasons shared, even if the poet must eventually shatter that in which he has participated.

"Quoi que j'esquisse et j'entreprenne, ce n'est pas de la mort limitrophe, ou d'une liberté hasardeuse et haussée qui s'y précipite, que je me sens solidaire, mais des moissons et des miroirs de notre monde brûlant. / Whatever I may project and undertake, it is not to a bordering death or to a risky

217

and elevated freedom which rushes toward it, that I feel myself committed, but rather to the harvests and the mirrors of
our burning world." (RBS,182) The title of the collection
Recherche de la base et du sommet indicates a double necessity: history and participation or work in common taken as
a point of departure for the road to the summits—recognized
as both interior and exterior, human and natural. A double
equilibrium never lost even in the trackless immensities of
time, those "immenses étendues que nous n'arriverons jamais
à talonner." (LM,194)

The second poem in the series *Neuf poèmes pour vaincre*
(1940-44) tells of an inner voyage that will take place long
after the moment of its composition, although the events of
the Resistance furnish the most evident elements such as
hunger, volleys of gunfire, crimes, remorse, and above all,
companionship in danger:

"Vivre avec de tels hommes"

Tellement j'ai faim, je dors sous la canicule des preuves.
J'ai voyagé jusqu'à l'épuisement, le front sur le séchoir
noueux. . . . On tuait de si près que le monde s'est voulu
meilleur. Brumaire de mon âme jamais escaladé, qui fait
feu dans la bergerie déserte? Ce n'est plus la volonté elliptique de la scrupuleuse solitude. Aile double des cris d'un
million de crimes se levant soudain dans ses yeux jadis
négligents, montrez-nous vos desseins et cette large abdication du remords!

. . . . *(sic)*

Montre-toi; nous n'en avions jamais fini avec le sublime
bien-être des très maigres hirondelles. Avides de s'ap-
procher de l'ample allégement. Incertains dans le temps
que l'amour grandissait. Incertains, eux seuls, au sommet
du coeur.

Tellement j'ai faim.[f] (FM,45)

[f] So hungry am I that I sleep under the dog days of ordeals, I've
traveled to exhaustion, my forehead pressed against the knotted dry-

The poem of this temporal passing is cyclical in form, like the year, beginning in the dog-days of August. The month recurs frequently in Char's writings, perhaps as if in correspondence to a particular ardor of expression, whose exemplary image might seem to be the burning August fruit-bowl: but the proofs of August here differ greatly from those in the bowl of *Contre une maison sèche*, where seasons and cycles mingle, as in another crucible. To the violence of the fire of autumn, a reply must be prepared, according to the cyclic nature here represented. The realization of that correspondence, moral by implication, covering space as well as time, brings sweat to the forehead, like the sweat which the mountain-climber of the barest texts must leave behind him as a part of his riches (*Partage formel*) and the sweat of the workers' foreheads and the poet's hands in "Lutteurs." Although the literal expression of the image is suppressed here on the surface of the text, the knotted drying-beam replaces it by suggestion. For the mountain, the most unforgettable and most enduring of all images in Char's poetry, is in its deepest interpretation interior, not only to the poet, but also to the text. "Voici l'époque où le poète sent se dresser en lui cette méridienne force d'*ascension* / This is the time when the poet feels lifting in himself this meridian force of *climbing*." (FM, 129) The form of the mountain, present in or only suggested by the text, dominates the action, the conception, and the expression.

When every mark of evil has disappeared and every "number" is effaced from those hunted and penned-up (the politi-

---

ing-rack. / . . . / Killing came so near that the world willed itself a better one. Brumaire of my never-scaled soul, who is firing in the deserted sheep-fold? No longer is it the elliptical desire of a scrupulous solitude. Double wing of cries of a million crimes looming up suddenly in eyes once negligent, show us your purpose in this wide abdication from remorse! / . . . / Show us your presence; we had not done with the sublime well-being of the thinnest swallows. Avid to move toward an ample assuaging. Irresolute within the time of love's growing. Irresolute, they only, at the heart's summit. / So hungry am I.

cal events leave their trace within these poems, even when they seem to have withdrawn) only hunger and a dear memory of the innocent remain.[3] From this sheepfold emptied by a collective criminal force and not by an individual will, there will come later the strands of wool like traces of a past suffering with which the poet, remembering, will line his "craggy nest," within a chosen solitude. As we have seen, however, he does not place himself with the lambs whose cries provoke only a fleeting reaction in the remorseless gaze of the other, to whom memory and conscience are lacking. The double wing of swallows figures here, perhaps, the necessary complexity that is the contrary of the look turned in a single direction, against which oversimplification the poet protests elsewhere: "Anticyclops! Anticyclops!" Naked with the essential purity of the moral traveler, the swallows actively participate in what Char will call the width and breadth of upstream ("amplitude d'amont"). In the light spaciousness of the summit, and the exhilaration of the counter-current, the ascetic of mind alone will survive, choosing a meagerness ("minceur") like the swift's, abandoning wealth and certainty for the sake of moral risk.

The circling of swallows ("Dans la boucle de l'hirondelle un orage s'informe, un jardin se construit," FM,194) indicates their insertion into cyclical and seasonal nature ("l'hirondelle successive"). This poem imitates by its form a circular flight, proving by its own profile that the return upstream is based on a continual and difficult desire, passing from the initial proliferation of the word toward the summit of silence—for instance, in local and specific images, from a Fontaine de Vaucluse at the source, up toward the divergence of the Sorgue at its "partage des eaux," finally toward the Mont Ventoux, whose crest is bare of all but eagles ("miroir des aigles").

[3] The sheepfolds resemble the concentration camps with their fences forming another sort of "anneau" or ring. (Thence the "mark" of evil in its remorseless trace.)

D. Silence

Parole d'aube qui revient chaque jour. Lieu qui
tourne et ne s'use pas.[4]

At the summit, silence replaces breath.[5] In the poems of *Le
Visage nuptial*, silence is accompanied by an extraordinary
depth of feeling, or by a noticeable cessation of ordinary work
during a moment observed as more intense, more violent or
more luminous than others.

. . . .

La parole, lasse de défoncer, buvait au débarcadère angélique.
Nulle farouche survivance

. . . .

"Le Visage nuptial," (FM,60)

La violence des plantes nous faisait vaciller

. . . .

---

[4] "Faire du chemin avec . . ." (1976).

[5] Maurice Blanchot speaks most eloquently of Char's silence, of
his language always at the origin of this "parole future, impersonnelle
et toujours à venir, où, dans la décision d'un langage commençant il
nous est cependant parlé intimement de ce qui se joue dans le destin
qui nous est le plus proche et le plus immédiat . . . elle nous parle de
ce loin, mais avec une intime compréhension qui nous la rend si
proche. . . ." (*La Bête de Lascaux*, GLM, 1958, pp. 17-24). For
Char's language, see also Blanchot's essay in *Critique*, 1947, p. 396:
"Un tel langage où nous nous sentons entièrement engagés et dont
la plénitude est si grande qu'elle semble exiger notre participation . . .
un langage capable de nous énoncer nous-mêmes, en même temps que
nous le lisons. Voilà ce que Char propose au lecteur pour l'unir au
poème. Ce langage est le plus présent qui soit. Il est impossible de s'y
soustraire. La souveraineté du ton en est extrême." But his essay
should be read in entirety. On Char's language also, Jacques Barelli,
L'Écriture de René Char, La Pensée universelle, 1973.

Jean Starobinski speaks also of the silence from which the poem
tears itself, observing "qu'après s'être accomplie chaque phrase laisse
derrière elle un silence comparable à une eau dormante et noire, où
se forme la vie naissante" (article cited above).

221

Sur le muet silex de midi écartelé

. . . .

La faucille partout devait se reposer
Notre rareté commençait un règne.

. . . .

"Évadné."[g] (FM,61)

The angelic wharf, associated by implication with the image
of the ferry linking the fragments, joins language to silence.
"L'intelligence avec l'ange, notre primordial souci. / (Ange,
ce qui à l'intérieur de l'homme, tient à l'écart du compromis
religieux, la parole du plus haut silence, la signification qui
ne s'évalue pas.) // Understanding with the angel, our primordial concern. / (Angel, that which, in man's inner being,
holds itself aside from religious compromise, the word of this
highest silence, the meaning we cannot evaluate.)." (FM,90)
But the angel entering here is at once human and beyond the
human: "Connaît le sang, ignore le céleste. Ange: la bougie
qui se penche au nord du coeur. / Knows the blood, is unaware of the celestial. Angel: the candle leaning to the north
of the heart." (FM,90) Akin to the gods within our own
being ("Des dieux intermittents parcourent notre amalgame
mortel . . .") Char's angel links, as does Rilke's,[6] the visible

[g] The word, tired of battering, drank at the angelic wharf./ No
savage survival. The violence of plants made us reel. / . . . / On
the mute flint of quartered noon / . . . / Everywhere the sickle must
have been at rest / Our rarity was opening a reign.

[6] Rilke's angel dwells in another realm like Char's "third realm":
"there is neither a here nor a beyond, but the great unity in which
those creatures that surpass us, the 'angels,' are at home." (SO,133)
"The angel of the Elegies is that being which stands securely for recognizing in the invisible a higher level of reality.—Therefore 'terrible'
to us because we, its lovers and transformers, are still clinging to the
visible." But our role is also a mediating one: "All the worlds of the
universe fling themselves into the invisible as into their next-deeper
reality; *some stars heighten directly in intensity . . . others are dependent on creatures who slowly and laboriously transform them, in
whose terror and ecstasy they reach their next invisible realization.
We are . . . these transformers of the earth; our whole existence, the
flights and downfalls of our love, all capacitate us for this task.*"
(SO,135)
The various degrees of silence, and of its depth, and the privileged

222

to the invisible toward which we tend, setting also into vibration the diverse rhythms of man's respiration and gilding the lure of his dreams: "Accordeur de poumons qui dore les grappes vitaminées de l'impossible." The silent angel responds to man, but uniquely to the watchful man, "en attente," who speaks little to listen all the better, as does the poet to his household gods, located on his own interior summits. "Lorsque nous parvenons face à la montagne frontale, surgissent minuscules, ceux dont nous disons qu'ils sont des dieux, expression la moins opaque de nous-mêmes. / When we come to face the frontal mountain, there emerge those minute beings of whom we say that they are gods, the least opaque expression of ourselves." (NT,84)

"Qui appelle encore? Mais la réponse n'est point donnée." (NT,74) Rilke speaks of "the incessant message" of the breath as it is formed by silence. Heidegger, speaking also of the call, unpredictable and involuntary, maintains, as would Char, that it comes from the self and yet from beyond the self. (BT,320) "The call discourses in the uncanny mode of *keeping silent*," calling man back "*into the reticence of his existent*" potentiality-for-Being." (BT,328) The poet dedicates himself finally to a silent battle ("For these dearly won victories which stop speaking") where an attitude he has mentioned previously reappears: "Whether I observe myself in my lacks or in my excess, in drunkenness, in torment, I discover no *ambition* in me." (RBS,172) The sentence on the silence of victories dates from 1948-49. Its reply was added, later, between parentheses,[7] setting apart the moment where the poet

---

image of the bird-call in all its understatement mingle within certain texts of the authors of René Char's region: "On y jouissait de deux privilèges: et d'abord du silence. Non pas silence désertique, mais silence de bon pays délicatement habité . . . privilège si précieux qu'il créait aussitôt un autre privilège: celui des oiseaux." (HB,84)

[7] Appears in different versions of AUSC, No. 724-730 (AE-IV-14). Or again, speaking of a particular visionary moment on a trip to Spain, Rilke summarizes the relation between poet and angel: "Everywhere appearance and vision came, as it were, together in the object, in every one of them a whole inner world was exhibited, as though an

will choose a quiet departure over a modest crepuscular threshold, causing the dimensions to pass over into one another: "I am not at present far from the line of intermingling and of the final moment when, everything in my mind, by fusion and synthesis, having become absence and promise of a future which does not belong to me, I shall ask you to grant me my silence and my leave." (RBS,173)

This leave-taking will be double: leave is given to the reader as it was to the nuptial escort, and it is taken by the poet; both are loyal and both, free: "Je ne vous dénoncerai pas, je vous précède / I'll not denounce you, I precede you." (NP,53)

---

angel, in whom space was included, were blind and looking into himself. This world, regarded no longer from the human point of view, but as it is within the angel, is perhaps my real task, one, at any rate, in which all my previous attempts would converge." (DE,10) The lesson taught by Char's inner gods is not so distant from that taught by Rilke's angel. (see also Heidegger's comments on Hölderlin's use of the terms: "Angel of the year," and "Angel of Light," EB,273).

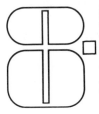

SEEING: "TON DUR SECOND REGARD"

A. NETWORK

Dans notre errance il faisait beau (LM,110)

1. *Parapet and Landscape*

The traveler destined for a "return upland" takes a path which is never that of others— which, however, resembles theirs at first sight: ". . . toward the totality of men and women mourning for an interior country . . . wandering so as not to be similar. . . ." (LM,161) For a series of steps apparently straying (in "errance"), may, by its invisible attachments deserve the name of "passage." There is often another network beyond the evident one: if the reader sees only a fragment or a peak where there is, as the poet's titles indicate, a series or a mountain range, an island where there is an archipelago, a few dispersed enumerations where there is a network, a few scattered volumes of an entire library to set afire, or finally, one twig when there is a construction of branches, his lack of perception in no way hinders the poet's vision which transcends the sum of the elements added.[1]

Although it has been altered in the definitive version of the title *Le Rempart de brindilles*, Char's original "parapet de brindilles" remains the culminating point of the path in which its presence is suspected. As an overlook, occasionally difficult of access, from which the gaze opens onto a network only suggested, this parapet interior to the text includes in its con-

---

[1] Such as in the following titles listed in order of reference: *La Parole en archipel; Recherche de la base et du sommet*; "Sept parcelles de Luberon," "Pyrenées," "Sur les hauteurs," "Les Dentelles de Montmirail," "Tables de longévité," "Cotes," *La Bibliothèque est en feu; Le Rempart de brindilles*. Hölderlin exclaims precisely in the ode called *Der Archipelagus*: (H,2,103) "Deiner Inseln ist noch . . . keine verloren. / Not one of your islands . . . has been lost."

struction both a sense of necessary elevation and of distance overcome by clear vision. The viewpoint it offers permits a multiple series of re-readings and thwarts neither the irregular wandering of the text nor the recurrence of interweaving thoughts and themes. In the complexities of the fragments (or "éclats"),[2] of the multiple readings and perspectives ("Lyre"), the most essential line must not be lost: the correspondence between the interior parapet or the lookout of the reader onto the text—from his own rampart—and the poet's advancing gaze, described as "en allant"; nor, above all, the intimate correspondence between the conceptual spaces within and the exterior motions and structures.[3]

2. *From Twigs to Fire*

A sufficient margin for interpretation and reinterpretation is created inside the word by the resonance of the concepts and their verbal expression, which sometimes transcends them. As an example, we take the first radiant twigs or "brindilles" from which the fire of books draws its aphoristic nourishment.

"LA BIBLIOTHÈQUE EST EN FEU"

Par la bouche de ce canon il neige. C'était l'enfer dans notre tête. Au même moment c'est le printemps au bout

[2] The distance, felt instinctively by the reader, between Char and Pierre Reverdy, a great one in spite of the several themes in common and in spite of their mutual tributes, Reverdy's to Char, published in *L'Herne*, and Char's to Reverdy (in RBS, 106, 122), is nowhere better exemplified than in their attitude toward the single concept of the flash of exterior brilliance. For Char, the *éclat* is always to be valued, as it always corresponds with an interior illumination. Reverdy takes the opposite position: "Rien n'est plus dangereux pour l'oeil que les éclats. La couleur de la matière apparaît alors et non plus celle qui vibre sous nos paupières." A perfect illustration of the intense tonal contrast between their writings and the gulf between their attitudes.

[3] A remark made by Char on the branches of Picasso's tree could in its turn be applied to the poet's own work in its multiple ramifications and its basic unity: "Il n'y a pas d'oeuvre séparatrice dans l'oeuvre de Picasso: il y a certes, des rameaux survenus par excès de sève. Qui s'en plaindrait?" (P)

de nos doigts. C'est la foulée de nouveau permise, la terre
en amour, les herbes exubérantes.

L'esprit aussi, comme toute chose, a tremblé.

L'aigle est au futur.

Toute action qui engage l'âme, quand bien même celle-ci
en serait ignorante, aura pour épilogue un repentir ou un
chagrin. Il faut y consentir.

Comment me vint l'écriture? Comme un duvet d'oiseau
sur ma vitre, en hiver. Aussitôt s'éleva dans l'âtre une ba-
taille de tisons qui n'a pas, encore à présent, pris fin.[a]
(LM,145)

.　　.　　.　　.　　.　　.　　.　　.　　.　　.

The present participle phonetically implicit in the title prepares a surface wide open to expansion and retraction: ["La
Bibliothèque étant feu . . . / The library being fire . . ."],
the hidden conflagration coexisting with the evident: "is on
fire." Hugo Ball also wanted to burn all extant books so that
the age of the image might begin; we might say that the texts
of René Char or those of any great poet are situated in the
moment after an initial destruction.

The first observation refers to a *feu-acte*, both a "fire-act"
and a "former-act": "From this cannon's mouth" there came
the fire in our own head. But the snow falls in this very moment[4] and spring weather imposes itself, while the mental fire

[a] *THE LIBRARY IS ON FIRE* / From this cannon's mouth it is
snowing. Hell was there in our head. At the same moment it's Spring
at our finger-tips. To stride again permitted, the earth in love, grasses
overflowing. / The spirit too, like everything else, has quaked. / The
eagle is in the future. / Every action that commits the soul, even
though unawares, will have as its epilogue a repenting or a sorrow.
One has to consent to that. / How did writing come to me? Like a
bird's down on my window-pane, in winter. At once there arose in the
fireplace a battle of embers that has not, even now, come to an end.
(JG)
[4] Compare "Le Doux défunt" (RBS,171), part of *A une Sérénité
crispée*: "Il a neigé jusqu'à la chaleur et personne n'est venu le sou-
lever."

227

retreats to the past. The seasonal series is marked by the revolution from the present to the imperfect and again to the
present, preparing a logical and temporal unfolding: winter
—summer—spring, from which series the second season, by
its ardor, sweeps away the others, so that spring may arrive
"at the same moment" as snow. The four following aphorisms
or flashes are held in an intimate relationship with the violence of the first, convulsive in their tone as well as in their
temporal tensions. The explosive action of both the fire and
the grasses suggest the past spiritual quaking successful in
destroying all the present which trembles at its contact, in
an impulse toward the future.

Once more the signs of division appear within the poem,
in the distance stretching between this element and that, a
distance also translated into a metaphoric difference between
first and second versions—a verbal slippage of instants, like
a temporal fault—and then, in the second version, between
action and its later consequences: 1° "Toute action qui engage l'âme, quand bien même celle-ci en aurait été tenue
ignorante, aura pour *corollaire* un châtiment ou un chagrin /
Every action that commits the soul, even though it was kept
unawares, will have as its corollary a punishment or a sorrow."// 2° ". . . quand bien même celle-ci en serait ignorante, aura pour *épilogue* un repentir ou un chagrin." This
gap between action and result is troubling as if the inevitable
separation between all our moments were to be moral as well
as temporal. Immediately afterward, a contrary couple of
elements reappears under the guise of snow and fire, down
and burning brand, as a textual and thematic incorporation
of distance. From this implied battle there will be no other
issue than the snow's "gentle defunct" touch, the soft effacement of a feather disappearing in its inscription and in a
dangerous hush.

Throughout the struggle of the word in convulsion or
"afire," the images of hearth and brand prepare the scene
for the single candle of *La Nuit talismanique* and for an
observation of wide reach, no less destructive than creative,

resonant in its certainty: "Le feu est en toute chose. / The fire is in everything." (S) And this ["feu étant toute chose / fire being everything"], would it not be the close neighbor of a Pascalian fire, like the title "L'Effroi la joie"?[5] In that simple word there echoes another vocabulary, a certain elliptical rhythm where the cry: "Le silence éternel de ces espaces infinis m'effraie" joins the cry "joie joie pleurs de joie," the fire of that memorial text finding its present response in Char's anguished meditation.

"From this cannon's mouth": an apparent verbal destruction provides a real and interior illumination. This bundle of twigs set aflame lights the passage from book to fire, from fire to night, and for the encounter of *Artine* with Mary Magdalen before her mirror in *La Nuit talismanique* at whose source this text is still seen burning.[6]

[5] Char speaks also for every poet, speaking of Picasso: "Dans la possession de soi, dans l'effroi intérieur. . . ." (P) See our preceding comment on the title "L'Effroi et la joie." Reading René Char's account, in poetry, of his stroke in 1968, we think again of Pascal's own meditation in front of the silent spaces of the night, of the candle and the star in their silence. See also Pascal's *Mémorial*, quoted in note 19 of this section.

[6] The comparison made by Michel Serres between Pascal and Georges de La Tour in the essay "Pensées d'un provincial" (*Critique*, no. 302, juillet 1972, 644-645) lends support to the net of correspondences we are sketching here: "tout gommer, tout déraciner, abolir le monde, l'entourage, les objets, et le corps même. . . . Tout le malheur de l'homme, ne savoir pas demeurer en repos, dans une chambre. . . . Madeleine. La sécheresse solitude. Le miroir, le flambeau et la mort. Non pas l'Utopie, mais l'alibi. Dehors, c'est l'alibi. Dedans, c'est le recentrement, autour du flambeau pauvre, la mort reconnue, découverte, pleurée, trahie, espérée, la reconnaissance du néant, la tête de mort se refusant à voir, de ses yeux vides, son image au miroir noir. Pascal, Georges de La Tour illustre *les Pensées*, quasi contemporaines." To each text illumined by this candle in its silence we could assign the quality that the poet admires in Heraclitus and Georges de La Tour, those who show us the place our mind might inhabit; but it is also the place of "L'Effroi et la joie." Heidegger quotes the words of Hölderlin: "Was bleibet aber, stiften die Dichter/ But what is lasting, the poets provide" (HB,490-491), and then he continues the thought: "But this very permanent is the transitory." (EB,304) The theme of the *mental dwelling* is essential to the thought of René Char, from the earliest texts of *Le Marteau sans maître*, where we find "la tête habitable." (MM,28)

229

B. VIGIL AND INTERIOR LIGHTING

> Regarde, mon coeur. . . . (note added in the
> margin of the manuscript for *Le Rempart des
> brindilles*)

Here, in a vigil faithfully kept, the hopeful surrealist waiting changes to a watchful state, their "attente" to a constant
"attention."[7] The place of interior presence, like the "interior
country, sought by the wanderer, will be transferred, as is the
mountain perceived far off, to the real center of the gaze
itself.

"I touch the expanse and I can inflame it. I restrain my
span, I know how to use it." (LM,160) Although the poet's
capacities can be deployed to other ends and in circumstances
relatively exterior, their description applies equally to his
prowess in verbal restraint and verbal variation. Certain moments, visibly set apart, exteriorize his greatest inner tension.
One of these renders the experience of a poet who no longer
shares either happiness or easy language. The tragic intensity
of this personal confession of a solitiude not always sought
is stressed by italicization in the series of aphorisms called
"Tables de longévité." The moment thus removed from the
ordinary current of the text weighs on all the subsequent
textual experience of the reader whose own vision will be
haunted by that solitude. The inexorable apparition of the
poet's presence forces the moral recognition of a transparent
and obsessed being, "fascinating" in his willful destitution,
who is refused the easiest satisfaction of the approximate and
the virtual, whose words—themselves obsessive to the highest degree—are destined to be read both outside and inside.

In Char's perception, outer and inner are reversed: the
man, poet or not, who has "a mountain in his gaze" has only
on occasion, to turn his eyes toward a certain space in order
to behold the most profound inversions taking place there.

---

[7] To be attentive, to be *en état d'attente*: the correspondence with
Heidegger is particularly marked here: see note 11, pp. 283-85.

Neither perspective nor limit, neither parapet nor rampart, will have any real sense outside of this vision itself. From the injunction: "Look, my heart . . ." to the correspondence reflected in the image of the heart as a sheaf-gatherer, a whole path can be seen extending, in an always widening scope: "De toujours plus grandes fiançailles du regard. / Always broader espousals of the gaze." Only a passionate intuition, which René Char claims as the essential characteristic of poetry, will bind together all the twigs in view of an ardent interior presence—a fire to which the August fruit bowl, burning, will form the natural counterpart.

Only in the inner light of the poet's attentive look do the contraries mingle, for the duration of his glance, never losing their difference, their distinctive and separating weight. In the following text, already mentioned, a will to lightness becomes the primary moving force:[x]

"L'ALLÉGRESSE"

Les nuages sont dans les rivières, les torrents parcourent le ciel. Sans saisie les journées montent en graine, meurent en herbe. Le temps de la famine et celui de la moisson, l'un sous l'autre dans l'air haillonneux, ont effacé leur différence. Ils filent ensemble, ils bivaquent!

. . . .

Saurons-nous, sous le pied de la mort, si le coeur, ce gerbeur, ne doit pas précéder mais suivre?[b] (LM,205)

The initial transfer of vision in this text proves its efficacy at joining elements, at fitting dimensions into each other, as, upon two different occasions in the sparse prose of *Contre*

[x] Rimbaud's "Aube" has the same lightness: the rhythmical patterns in the prose poems are often similar.

[b] Clouds are in the rivers, torrents course through the sky. Unpicked, the days arise and seed, perish in the green. The time of famine and the time of harvest, one beneath the other in the tattered air, have wiped out their difference. They slip by together, they encamp! / . . . / Shall we know, under the heel of death, if the heart, binder of sheaves, should not precede but follow?

une maison sèche, one fruit is said to mingle with another. To the separate dry stones of a house and to every building of individual "sparse" elements (as the ends are scattered, in "le terme épars") the poetic vision might apply its metaphoric assembling power, assembling the diffuse stalks of wheat into a bundle or a "gerbe." In any case, the exact moment must be determined for gathering the dispersed elements, whether into a simple conjunction or a complex interweaving.

An initial impulse for the fresh beginning of the path illumined by this particular light is given by one brief text of invocation, absolutely negating a temporal and spatial distance: "Prête au bourgeon, en lui laissant l'avenir, tout l'éclat de la fleur profonde. Ton dur second regard le peut. De la sorte, le gel ne le détruira pas. / Lend to the bud, leaving it the future, all the radiance of the profound flower. Your hard second look is capable of that. Thus the frost will not destroy it." (LM,152) According to our first reading, the intensity of the look already lends to the sign of the coming flower the radiant future beauty which is potentially found there. Therefore the winter has no effect on the spring and its *reviviscence*.[9] But this future-granting gaze can also deepen, reversing the direction of temporal effects: the flower ready to bud will be on the point of regaining its youthfulness, in a state of virtual rejuvenescence, for its radiance renders all else profound. The harsh look of the poet, used at certain moments as a weapon or the "fer": aggravating, probing, and deepening, can modify the verbal syntax or the course of time, reversing all order if he so chooses.[10]

[9] On this word and its association with the motif of the fountain, see above.

[10] The elliptical impulse is sufficient for the reversing of vision and language: the wasp's sting seen within the star, as if the ray of its own light had stung it, like the rose, used to invoke the rain which has already made it flower; to those examples might be added this title: "Le dard dans la fleur," (RBS,69) in which the bee has encountered the flower in his passage, leaving there only his wounding *éclat*, which will in its turn wound the passer-by prey to beauty, as in "Front de la rose."

In such a way, the poem reaps its own harvest: the poet sees, and the reader with him, the fructification of his text after the gathering of the word: "Pourtant la grappe, qui a suivi la moisson, au-dessus de son cep, boucle. . . . / However, the grape cluster, following the harvest, curls above its stock. . . ." (LM,152) The slow beginning of the latter sentence builds up momentum so that this meteoric work may find at last its fullest force. However, this lasting response precedes, by the very strength of its affirmation, the question concluding *Le Nu perdu*: "Qui, là, parmi les menthes, est parvenu à naître dont toute chose demain se prévaudra? / Who, there, among the mint, has managed to be born, over whom, tomorrow, all things will prevail?"* (NP,131) We might envision the poems as one text clairvoyant in its continuity: for the Pleiades, who enter this poetry later will take the form of a grape cluster, or of a group of words like islands in an archipelago, finally lifted skyward.

To the lucid and anguished observation opening the last text of *Contre une maison sèche*—"Tout ce que nous accomplirons d'essentiel à partir d'aujourd'hui, nous l'accomplirons faute de mieux / / All we accomplish from today on, we shall accomplish for want of something better." (NP,131) (JG)—there has already, long before, been the reply: "Pourtant, la grappe. . . ." And now there returns to the continuous memory of the reader, "Fontis," the poem of the vine harvest, closing the collective volume *Les Matinaux*, while opening it once more to another system of images, wherein the grapes are assimilated to the setting sun and the star:

. . . .

Le rosaire de la grappe;
Au soir le très haut fruit couchant qui saigne
La dernière étincelle.[c] (LM,206)

Explicit proximity and implicit network reinforce the significance of certain privileged moments, such as the juxtaposition

[c] The rosary of the cluster; / At evening the lofty fruit setting bleeding / The last spark.

in *Commune presence* of this poem with the title poem, "Le Nu perdu," directly following it: "Porteront rameaux ceux dont l'endurance sait user la nuit noueuse qui précède et suit l'éclair. Leur parole reçoit existence du fruit intermittent. . . . / They will bear boughs, whose endurance has learned to wear out the gnarled night which precedes and follows the flash. Their speech receives existence from the intermittent fruit. . . ."* (NP,31) Within the cluster, the grape is still intermittent, each island of its "très haut fruit" related to the others in the archipelago as the flash of one text is related to that of another: by this implicit conjunction, the poet's word and his understanding receive their analogous deepening. The branches carried by the most enduring companions will reappear, with the reeds and the mint leaves of the final text in *Contre une maison sèche*, like the mental juxtaposition of fruit side by side in a bowl, finally transfigured into the knots of stars clustering in a radiant conflagration against the night.

In *Being and Time*, Heidegger explains the profound metaphoric correspondence between fruit and the human being. "Ripening is the specific Being of the fruit. It is also a kind of Being of the 'not-yet' (of unripeness)"; and, as such, it is, like human existence, "already its 'not-yet'. . . ." (BT,288) This fruit sometimes called contracted—like the intense contraction of the aphoristic text, which bears its form—this "unfinished prelude," verbal and conceptual, is best considered against its appropriate and tragic temporal backdrop. For we shall perhaps die, says the philosopher, without having seen the fruits ripen, before having "traversed this maturity" to complete our specific being.[11] "Mon amour préférait le fruit à son fantôme. / J'unissais l'un à l'autre, insoumis et courbé. // My love preferred the fruit to its phantom. I

---

[11] Cf. note 6, p. 29. "Mit der Reife *vollendet* sich die Frucht. / With ripeness the fruit *fulfills* itself." The editors point out that "Reife" applies to almost any kind of maturity, even that of Dasein, that the verb "vollenden" involves also the verb "enden": it means not only "to bring fully to an end," but also "to complete" or "to perfect." (BT,288)

joined them together, I was unsubdued and bowed." (JG)
(NP,121)

Marked by time, whose guest and whose host we are, even
by the inseparability of terms: "Temps, mon possédant et
mon hôte. . . ," the poet nevertheless refuses the idea of
incompletion. Pushed to the maturation of thought, the text
or this fruit of meditation will explode like a grenade and a
pomegranate, will be disaggregated, even lost—but will never
rot under the constant *faire* of the poet in revolt, who, like
the land, is often oppressed but never reduced:

> La terre ruinée se reprend
> Bien qu'un fer continu la blesse.[d] (LM,25)

C. Source and Night: Artine and
La Nuit Talismanique

> Il ne fallait pas embraser le coeur de la nuit.
> Il fallait que l'obscur fût maître. . . . (NT,16)[11a]

To leave the darkness in unchallenged mastery, while uncov-
ering the obscure radiation of a possible source. . . . The following reading of two major texts of René Char—written
more than forty years apart and seemingly opposed in tone
and attitude—would choose to cast the most discreet and
flickering of illuminations, befitting an unhurried gaze toward
a luminosity completely interior, toward a poetry of contemplation.[12]

[d] The ruined land begins again / Although a continual iron wounds
her.

[11a] "Utilité du mystère." (V,I,562)

[12] The following account of contemplation as it goes beyond the
need for discourse is given by the Jesuit Louis Richeome: "Contemplation is more than meditation, and as it were the end thereof, and
it floweth and springeth upon it many tymes, as the braunch doth
upon the body of the tree, or the flowre upon the braunch. For the
understanding having attentively, and with many reasons to and fro
meditated the mystery, and gathered divers lights togeather, doth
frame unto her self a cleere knowledge, whereof without further discourse, one way or another, she enjoyeth (as I may say) a vision
which approcheth to the knowledge of angells, who understand with-

For the inner work is carried out in silence, in a dwelling whose walls may or may not be of that glass that Breton would have chosen for his house of salt crystal: here even the glass is deepened and interiorized. As the paintings of Georges de La Tour are lit by an inner and paradoxical source, the more profound texts of René Char are only visible in the shadow of that "impossible solution" glimpsed by candle-light at the conclusion of "Madeleine à la veilleuse," the poem responding to de La Tour's canvas. From this *Nuit talismanique*, the candle flame will not be lost, even in the brightest sunlight of the most open day. The realm of Char's poetry is often hidden, at least in part; but its reach extends beyond any inner dwelling that could be specified. Yet the outer resonance retains a muted tone, recognizable as coming from another source, not to be identified. In the canvas sketched out or completed, there appear strokes made by "another hand."

If, at certain times, the reader believes himself admitted to the inner dwelling itself, he will perhaps see that interiority has other reaches beyond this one, other dwellings still more interior, and other deeper sources. Like Mary Magdalen's fin-

---

out discourse." (Translated E. W., Paris, 1629, quoted in Louis L. Martz, *The Poetry of Meditation*, New Haven, Yale University Press, 1954, p. 17).

On the dust jacket of *The Poetry of Meditation* is "La Madeleine au miroir" by Georges de La Tour. Inside, facing another reproduction of the same painting, a poem of Yeats (from *All Souls' Night*, in *The Collected Poems of W. B. Yeats*, Macmillan, New York, 1933): "Such thought—such thought have I that hold it tight / Till meditation master all its parts, / Nothing can stay my glance / Until that glance run in the world's despite / To where the damned have howled away their hearts, / And where the blessed dance; / Such thought that in it bound / I need no other thing, / Wound in mind's wandering / As mummies in the mummy-cloth are wound." As the painting of de La Tour is constantly present in the writing of René Char, so we take from another source than his—in one more oblique correspondence— the winding, and the circle of a dance within the flame of the mind as the talisman for our study. Char's contact with de La Tour is of course *direct*; our oblique passage here through Martz's work is of the same kind and toward the same end as that taken through Heidegger's study of Hölderlin and Mallarmé's homage to Rimbaud.

gers touching the skull, or like the image of the ox flayed which haunts the last text of *Contre une maison sèche*, the innermost thought is not necessarily visible, as the names of Georges de La Tour and Rembrandt do not need to be cited in order for their presence to be felt. Then through the glass walls occasionally permitted to the poem, which on occasion become glass doors, one might well see no source and no canvas: the most profound art does not announce itself. But the image dominates, in silence, like a source inexhaustible in suffering renewed and mortally resurgent, a well which has become at last a fountain.

Artine (1930), a dream meditation, recounted in a dozen parts, represents one of two summits of *Le Marteau sans maître* (1934), the other being that dense group of prose poems hermetically sealed and yet thrown open to the future by their title, *Abondance viendra* (1933). "Au silence de celle qui laisse rêveur": *Artine* is dedicated explicitly to silence and implicitly to the imagination—not only does she encourage reverie by her own verbal restraint, but she is simultaneously the figure at the source of the dream, who might, by her appearance, leave one dreaming. Unlike a "real" model of the ordinary kind, an object of direct and exterior contemplation, akin to Breton's "modèle extérieur" which he would have us reject for an interior vision, Artine, who is herself also the dream, is placed nevertheless at some distance from the onlooker: "l'appareil de la beauté d'Artine," (MM,42) as if it were to be constructed, or prepared. Although she is never to be other than silence, she represents the interiority of the discourse always sought, like the inner landscape. She is absolute transparency and an unceasing current. Her freshness, allied now with coolness, as in the word "fraîcheur," and then again with an intense ardor, is a word which will not cease, an unending stream.

The one whose imagination runs through the driest of lands, Artine penetrates each part of the text by her name, with the significant exception of those two paragraphs more explicitly erotic, until the final murderous statement, terse in its

237

ambiguity: "Le poete a tué son modèle. / The poet has slain his model." It is not, or so we would maintain, Artine who is eliminated here, but rather the exterior pattern of the real, rejected in favor of motion inward, as an "interior model" at once transparent and all-encompassing.

Assembling in its own dense fabric many of the threads dominant in the changing canvas of *Arsenal* throughout its several versions (1927-1929) and predicting many subsequent works, *Artine* appears at the center of Char's poetic inscape. *La Nuit talismanique* (1972) opens with an allusion to the same nocturnal stream by which a matinal language is watered: "Je sus alors que la nuit était eau, qu'elle seule abreuve et irrigue. . . . / I knew then that the night was water, that it alone quenches and gives drink. . . ." (NT,11) Deprived of this obscure oneiric nourishment, the poet meditates in times of insomnia on the light of a candle held by a hand other than his own, "une main autre." As Artine brings, paradoxically, a "monumental drought" to the minds she visits, an aridity such that it can be quenched only by dream, so the candlelight enforces an obscurity all the deeper by contrast with its gleam and its restlessness. And might not the spot of oil left in the poet's bed in the beginning of *Artine* be identified with the drop of oil ("un peu d'huile") spreading through the dagger of the flame in the prose poem "Madeleine à la veilleuse?" Like a talisman of the poem's night, an emblem of our deepest meditations and of that inner silence we rarely mention, this painting is lit by the same candle that leaves also and only this trace of an "impossible solution," a watchfulness never deceived by an easy response.

"La plupart de ces étoiles s'éteignaient après quelques minutes, mais il y en avait une qui étincelait au milieu de sa poitrine et qui s'y enfonçait, s'y enfonçait toujours, et Bella ne pouvait pas en détacher les yeux. / Most of these stars faded out after some moments, but one remained brilliant, plunging deeper and deeper into the center of that breast, and Bella couldn't take her eyes off it." This epigraph originally marking the text of *Artine*, taken from Achim von Arnim's "Isabelle d'Egypte," disappears like an exterior model rendered finally unnecessary, in an inward motion. The pruning exemplifies Char's method of *enlèvement-embellissement*, that is, the elimination of excessive discourse for a beauty more intense. The text opens with a catalogue of elements marked as oneiric by their accompaning props: "in the bed prepared for me were: . . ." Forceful precisely in its incongruity, yielding in advance the dispersed elements of Artine's "body," this initial and abundant source waters the subsequent expansion by the cavalier rhythm of its headlong rush: "Offrir au passage un verre d'eau à un cavalier lancé à bride abattue sur un hippodrome envahi par la foule suppose, de part et d'autre, un manque absolu d'adresse; Artine apportait aux esprits qu'elle visitait cette sécheresse monumentale. / To offer a glass of water to a horseman as he passes, hurtling headlong on a racetrack invaded by the mob takes an absolute awkwardness, on both sides; Artine brought to the minds she visited this monumental drought." (MM,41) Offering only this "verre," or this ["vers"]—and in whose passing?—she arouses the thirst for dream that has been prepared in the flux of the catalogue, apparently so disordered.

The list of props is announced in a straightforward statement: "Dans le lit . . . il y avait. . . ." A formal reflection of the flux and yet structurally cohesive, whether deliberate in its order or accidental, this catalogue seems to us to contain the elements essential to the subsequent writing. Without entering once more into the debate about the possible structuring of the unconscious and the extent to which spontaneous writing mirrors this structure, we will simply sketch, in as unadorned a manner as possible, some of the more salient interrelations. For all such discussion, it must be borne clearly in mind that the reading, like all the others in the present essay, purports only to be an individual interpretation, and never (unless it is so stated) a declaration of the poetic intentions of René Char—a point that cannot be made too

239

often.[13] Bound to the text and to the possible interpretations it may be meant to convey, we are nevertheless detached from them, freed into the moment of our reading which is different from that of the author's own: the readings may coincide, or they may differ. Ideally, as in Char's conception, they form the two wings of the text for its "envol" or flight.

Even if the elements of this catalogue were never to reappear, in this identical form or in another guise, the prolonged enumeration would be worth examining. There are but few examples of this extended listing in Char's later work, where the juxtaposition of elements is usually compressed into a form so terse as to rivet the attention. Furthermore— and here the answer is already implicit in the posing of the question—is not this very abundance the adequate source of the future poetic word? A sure prelude to *Abondance viendra, Artine* is nonetheless the spring, "source" and resource of the *Fureur et mystère* to come. To all appearances, the stylistic difficulty seals off forever "dans les serres bien closes," this passage from the invasion by a crowd. Nevertheless, the text of Artine is expansive here, at the outset:

> *Dans le lit qu'on m'avait préparé il y avait: un animal san-guinolent et meurtri, de la taille d'une brioche, un tuyau de plomb, une rafale de vent, un coquillage glacé, une cartouche tirée, deux doigts d'un gant, une tache d'huile; il n'y avait pas de porte de prison, il y avait le goût de l'amertume, un dia-mant de vitrier, un cheveu, un jour, une chaise cassée, un ver à soie, l'objet volé, une chaîne de pardessus, une mouche verte apprivoisée, une branche de corail, un clou de cordonnier, une roue d'omnibus.[e]*

(MM,41)

---

[13] René Char points out that some omissions and additions in his works correspond to presences or absences in his life. But the reader's chance awareness of these holes, or these additions, and the reason for them can serve his reading implicitly, while not intruding upon it openly.

[e] In the bed prepared for me were: an animal bruised and slightly tinged with blood, no larger than a bun, a lead pipe, a gust of wind, an icy seashell, a spent cartridge, two fingers of a glove, a spot of

At the risk of interrupting the "silence . . . qui laisse rêveur," and thus betraying "an absolute awkwardness," let us consider the catalogue to be divided into two parts, preceding and following the sole negative phrase: "Il n'y avait pas. . . ." There are then corresponding elements and subdivisions, as if in prediction of the following statement, placed directly after the first presentation of Artine: "L'impatient se rendait parfaitement compte de l'ordre des rêves qui hanteraient dorénavant son cerveau. . . . / The man of impatience took full account of the order[14] of dreams which would henceforth haunt his brain. . . ." (MM,41) The juncture between the two parts is properly ambiguous: the alliterative repetition of the plosive "p" marks the center of the structure: "il n'y avait pas de porte de prison." Are we to read: there was no prison? or no escape from it?

il y avait / il n'y avait pas de porte de prison / il y avait

Through the enumeration there runs a possible connotation of violence: on both sides of the catalogue, we are first aware of a crime or a pain inflicted, of a reduction, a resentment, or a suffering, and then of an alternation with more utilitarian objects, represented often by their smallest denominator, an emphasis on the partial found also in the poetic expansion: one hair, one day, a coral branch. We sense, although obscurely, the alternation of the reductive and the useful; but through the more lyric grouping, the catalogue itself transcends its apparent structure to attain its cumulative effect.

In more detail then, the implicit suffering pictured in the first element of the catalogue ("l'animal sanguinolent et meurtri") finds an emotional reflection in the first image of

---

oil; there was no prison door, rather the taste of bitterness, a glazier's diamond, one hair, one day, a broken chair, a silkworm, the stolen object, an overcoat chain, a tame green fly, a coral branch, a cobbler's nail, a bus wheel.

[14] The word "ordre" here can also mean "kind" or "sort." We have tried to retain both meanings later, in referring to *the order of the dream.*" But this is an example of the way in which each reading is already, necessarily, an interpretation.

the second part ("le goût de l'amertume") directly following the mention of imprisonment, while its negative force is echoed in the natural world by the gust of wind, then in the human world by the shot ("cartouche tirée") and later by the broken chair, a cultural object, and by the tamed green fly, a natural phenomenon taken out of context, thus marked by a trace of previous violence as in the "objet volé" (linked implicitly to the prison) and also, perhaps, of an erotic transgression. The conceptual correspondence of the transgression suggested in the three last-named images (including, of course, violence done to the human law as well as to the creations of human work and of nature) and the results of that transgression are underlined by the sharp phonetic stress laid on the past participle: "tirée," "cassée," "volé." To these three participles there can be added the "glacé" of "coquillage glacé," directly following the image of a sudden wind, since the chill is its natural echo. Thus, in the first part and in the second, the images occupying roughly the same position can be seen in a relation at once temporal (a result of past action), conceptual (violence, "wrongdoing," suffering inflicted), and even sonorous.

The reduction of the initial image ("de la taille d'une brioche") as if to modify the negative presentation, finds an echo in the subsequent partial images of utility and in the synecdochal process apparent in them. Thus the lead pipe is oddly matched to the "diamant du vitrier," itself an instrument of violence—even if the attack should be carried out only on glass. (Here we are reminded of Baudelaire's "mauvais vitrier," of Tzara's transparent creations on the mountains of crystal, of his crystal corridors, and of Breton's praise of the cube of rock salt and of glass houses in his "Éloge du cristal.") The simple and single elements of the lyric chorus succeeding the diamantine image—a hair, a day, and, eventually, a branch of coral—participate also in the imaginative power of extension from the partial to the whole. On the natural level, the coral branch corresponds to the ice shell, as the silkworm (related to the hair by the cliché omitted here:

"silken hair") in its implicit future usefulness and luxury redeems both the suffering (by a reconstruction) and the utilitarian quality of the lead pipe, the spot of oil, the cobbler's
nail, and two fingers of a glove (affording, like the overcoats,
a partial protection against the "rafale de vent"). Finally, the
fly now tamed, caught in an unnatural and incongruous situation, a useless relative of the captive silkworm, assumes the
suffering of the "animal meurtri," but again as a weaker
counterpart, and the possible imprisonment. Yet the coral
branch follows upon that image, as if to emphasize the natural beauty of the green fly, whose vibrant color in the enforced abnormal immobility of the normally beating wings—
as of a fly in amber—will be glimpsed again in the brief but
profound space of *Artine*. If we abstract the elements of what
we have called the lyric expansion, then the parts of the
catalogue are seen facing each other in an order more convincing than we would ordinarily expect to find in a "random" text. This is perhaps *the order of dream*, luminous and
sensed as necessary, like a glasscutter's diamond, an "absolute
transparency" situated at the heart of the deepest interior
night.

"Artine traverse sans difficulté le nom d'une ville. . . . /
Artine traverses effortlessly the name of a town." (MM,42)
Effortless in her silence, which sets sleep loose ("qui détache
le sommeil") clarifying and purifying, the stream removes the
stains ["dé-tache"] from the residue of sleep, and it frees that
force, like that of the horseman hurtling along, "lancé à bride
abattue." Unleashing the oneiric imagination in its optimistic
headlong rush, the stream remains a major source for language. In one of the texts of *Le Nu perdu*, Char speaks of
rendering to man the night of dream; he has not forgotten
Artine, ". . . épopée quotidienne et nocturne. / an epic daily
and nocturnal." (MM,42) The daily epic is never to be opposed to the nocturnal catalogue in its apparent fragmentation; rather, they are complementary forces, like the "Biens
égaux" of a later text, companion witnesses to the "extraordi-
naires bouleversements," that *vertige* at the center of Ara-

243

gon's *Le Paysan de Paris*, of the writings of Breton and Desnos, that is, then, at the center of surrealism, and occasionally at the center of poetry itself.

". . . édredon en flammes précipité dans l'insondable gouffre de ténèbres en perpetuel mouvement. / . . . eiderdown aflame cast into the unfathomable abyss of shadows in perpetual motion." (MM,42) To throw off the guilt is a crucial act, signaling the intense discomfort felt by, indeed and almost necessarily, chosen by, the reader of this poetry, itself in perpetual motion like the title of one of Aragon's early volumes, *Le Mouvement perpétuel*. Participating in shadows, this language retains still the same "intarissable fraîcheur . . . la transparence absolue . . . / inexhaustible freshness . . . absolute transparency . . ." (MM,42) as that which Artine retains, in spite of the animal and the natural worlds ("en dépit des animaux et des cyclones"). (MM,42) The wounded animal whose presence opens the list of objects in the bed, and the gust of wind—sweeping not only through that list but through many of Char's greatest texts in a compendium of suffering, anger, and a burning impatience—are at the source of those most extraordinary upsets. Fanned by the wind, the sheets are aflame: "Les apparitions d'Artine . . . évoluaient dans les plis d'une soie brûlante peuplée d'arbres aux feuilles de cendre. / Artine's appearances . . . evolved in the folds of a burning silk peopled with ashen-leaved trees." (MM,43) With the sheets of that bed, containing all the elements of this poem and of others ("Dans le lit qu'on m'avait préparé"), there are burning also the leaves of a book ("les feuilles"), in an extension of the silkworm or the result of the tree's destruction, implying the erotic, intellectual pleats of a Mallarméan unfolding. This premonition of a subsequent image ("le visage de bois mort") serves also to recall the poem "Robustes météores" from *Arsenal*: "Dans le bois on écoute bouillir le ver / In the wood we listen to the worm boiling." (MM,21) Originally the line read: "Dans quelle forêt bout le ver? / In what forest does the worm boil?"[15]

[15] Version of *Arsenal* presented to Paul Éluard. (AE-IV-4, no. 684)

until the concrete expression of the wood itself and the act of listening replaced the indefinite questioning and the general image of the forest. Like the term "bois" (where the homonym ["bois"] for the imperative: ["drink"] prepares the corresponding homonym: ["verre"] for ["glass"]), the other echo: ["vers/ver"] (for a line of poetry and a worm) responds to the verb of listening, as the verb "boiling" continues to represent the always implicit danger of burning wood or of liquid heat. So the phoenix is reborn through the flame as a worm, then winged, like a butterfly from its chrysalis.

Arsenal, Artine—these opening syllables of arson singe the page behind them: "L'énorme bloc de soufre se consumait alors lentement, sans fumée, présence en soi et immobilité vibrante. / The enormous block of sulphur consumed its substance slowly and smokelessly, presence in itself vibrating motionless." (MM,43) No better definition than this has been given of Char's own poetry of this period. As the "soufre" consumes within itself the memory of that initial suffering [or "souffre"] implicit in the image of the bleeding animal, or, more distantly, in the trace of the emptied cartridge, so the slow burning of this presence echoing ["soie" / "soi"], a self always inflammatory, leads to another presence, motionless, a force captured like the green fly tamed, still alive after its consumption. It is not unlike the final quivering of a leaf aflame, long after its substance has been burned out by this passion of the page and of the dream. The "serres bien closes"[15a] now yield to their opposite, the open book, an inanimate victim spread out on the knees of Artine, an object immobilized and still vibrant. Here the heroes come to read their fate; they prefigure those exceptional beings who people the later poems, when, on the "burning silk" of the bed and the page, there will be traces other than just those of the trees consumed. On somber days (thus at once "quotidiens et nocturnes") they see their future only there ("les voies multiples et terrifiantes dans lesquelles leur irreprochable destinée allait à nouveau s'engager" [MM,43]), as the book of Artine

---

[15a] "Very hot houses," or "tightly closed claws," with even the echo of a brothel ("maison close").

itself opens out only into the exceptional poet's future with its "voix multiples."

In sum, the separate paragraphs of this prose poem seem united in a constant flow of separate appearances, those "apparitions d'Artine," her own moments of dreaming, and what she sees. Galloping through the whole, the image of the horseman, in all its transpositions, could be compared to that of the dreamer himself—or, and more ambiguously, to that of the poet. For his dashing gait prepared at the outset by the gust of wind ("rafale de vent"—"lancé à bride abattue") hurtles on to the following statement of impatience and lucidity joined: "L'impatient se rendait parfaitement compte," and, more distantly, to the "voiture à chevaux lavée et remise à neuf / the horse-drawn chariot washed and renovated," (MM,43) where the washing and the rejuvenation remind us of the cleansing action silence has upon sleep (by a homonymic extension of the word "détache," as we have pointed out, "le silence détache le sommeil"). A continuum of poetic feeling is favored by the verb attached to the horse-drawn vehicle: "l'emportait" (where we read, by a faint echo ["emporté"] or the recurrence of the impatient and headstrong hero), as well as by the image of the stream.

And so the exceptional is readied: the horseman prepares the hero, in his opposition to the state of lethargy that precedes Artine's appearances. The anonymous crowd in the hippodrome, like passive attendants at a heroic spectacle, finds a subsequent incarnation in the throngs of Artine's nameless opponents, "la multitude des ennemis mortels d'Artine." (MM,43) As for the violence heard so clearly in the italicized prelude, it far exceeds the simple warring of combative parties: "Les apparitions d'Artine dépassaient le cadre de ces contrées du sommeil, où le *pour* et le *pour* sont animés d'une égale et meurtrière violence. / Artine's appearances went past the border of those countries of sleep, where the *for* and the *for* are endowed with an equal and murderous violence." (MM,43) This also surpasses the suffering of the small animal, as the violence perpetrated on the page by

Artine and the poet easily surpasses the more ordinary struggle between the opposed terms any *for* and any *against*.

The linguistic violence of the poetic word can be qualified
as one of the goals toward which this dreaming is directed,
culminating in the final murder. "Le poete a tué" . . . ("Tuer
m'a decuirassé pour toujours," *L'Age cassant*, XIX). To be
sure, the violent change wrought in the poet by the Resistance
had no real precedent on the moral or the personal level. But
is it not already here a case of the deadly responsibility of
the exceptional being, whose attentions are always *mortal*—
who, from necessity, kills his model by an "irreproachable
destiny"?

In *La Nuit talismanique* (1972), the penetration of the
candlelight throughout the series of nights it illuminates might
be compared to that of Artine through the corpus of her
texts, although it must be inscribed under the sign of free
order rather than under that of violence. But the contradictory tendencies are marked in the poet and in his text. "La
Flamme sédentaire" and its sequel, "Don hanté," betray an
impatience in all its ferocious potential: "Précipitons la rota-
tion des astres et les lésions de l'univers / Let us hasten the
stars' revolution and the lesions of the universe." (NT,84)
The response comes shortly after, wisdom following upon
desire: "On a jeté de la vitesse dans quelque chose qui ne le
supportait pas. Toute révolution apportant des voeux, à
l'image de notre empressement, est achevée, la destruction
est en cours, par nous, hors de nous, contre nous et sans recours. / They have cast speed into something that could not
stand it. Every revolution bearing hope, the image of our
eagerness, has been accomplished, destruction takes its course
through us, outside us, against us and without recourse."
(NT,85) Patience and impatience mingle in their depth and
their verticality, flame and night, opposite and fitting elements.

In this essentially contemplative poetry, where the relations of fire to water, of consumption to continuation direct
the verbal flow, the rhythm of the text, uneven but unrushed,

247

should not be disrupted, nor should the essential, paradoxical silence of the discourse in its own passage. Ideally, we would intend only to cast an additional flame into *La Nuit talismanique*, for its shadow as for its illumination.

Under the picture of a dull orange sun, a circle standing out against a slightly lighter yellow-orange background, where only the date 1957 appears in black, we read: "Beauté, est-il encore des mains discrètes pour dérober ton corps tiède à l'infection de ce charnier? / Beauty, are there still new hands discreet enough to hide your body, slightly warm, from the stench of this charnel-house?" (NT,44) As is true of the love poems of Char, it is unnecessary to be acquainted with the exact setting or origin; for instance, we do not have to ascribe any specific content to the "beauté." Part of the discretion and certainly part of what we might call the radiation from the text depend precisely on its not being delimited in such a manner. We might say this of any poetic text, but particularly in the case of René Char, or in this reading of his work, it is essential to acknowledge this intentionally non-specific—or discreet—reading from the start.

Free order, patience with impatience, discretion: all these qualities loosely grouped together may be implied in the first two lines of the prose poem entitled (again with a Mallarméan slant) "Volets tirés fendus": "Lenteur qui butine, éparse lenteur, / Lenteur qui s'obstine, tiède contre moi. // Slowness reaping, dispersed slowness, / slowness persisting, tepid against me." (NT,61) "Corps tiède," "lenteur . . . tiède": a measured warmth contrasted with the heat of impatience and the cold of a patience too passive, or, at worst, lacking in interest, this modest temperature corresponds to the more restrained heat and light of a candle compared with the harsh glare of electricity, two lightings that Char opposes at the beginning of *La Nuit talismanique*.

Meditation—of beauty, of poetry—should not be forced in its pace. The gait of the headlong horseman cannot be ours; the contemplative poet and the reader following him in a

248

chosen fidelity will not be among those cursed with "la malé-
diction d'atteindre," where we might read, as a suppressed
link, cursed with the desire for attainment. For the thrust
toward accomplishment, toward a more direct understanding
of the mysteries of beauty and obscurity, is an impulse of
daytime, inimical by its nature to the flickering light of solitary contemplation whose outcome is often uncertain, always
indirect. "Je ne suis pas seul parce que je suis abandonné. Je
suis seul parce que je suis seul, amande entre les parois de
sa closerie. / I am not alone because I am abandoned. I am
alone because I am alone, an almond between the walls of
its enclosure." (NT,41) Char's picture and poem of the almond is itself an object of contemplation, poetic rather than
mystic. The patient yellow oval encased in a green shell is
placed diagonally on the page, as if to halt too rapid a reading (and facing another picture placed diagonally, as if to
stress the angle). The image appears to represent not only
the almond, like a slow fruit of the imagination and corresponding to the double enclosure of the lovers in one shell,
but also the candle flame, in its "greening circle."[16] The poet
enters into a solitary dance not because he is deserted (a
passive description ill fitting the poem in its contemplative
making) but because he chooses that isolation: "nous nous

[16] The poet's active contemplation of the almond and the flame has
a particular depth and richness, illuminating the rest of his work. Tranquillity is often seen to spring from motion: thus, in one of Rilke's
Sonnets to Orpheus, the final steps of a dance whirl into the blossoming stillness of a tree around which the movement is said to "swarm."
This tree "of ecstasy" and warmth—standing outside the motion
—then bears fruits of quiet and of fullness: "Aber er trug auch, er
trug, dein Baum der Ekstase. / Sind sie nicht seine ruhigen Früchte:
der Krug, / reifend gestreift, und die gereiftere Vase. // But it bore
too, it bore, your tree of ecstasy. / Are these not its tranquil fruits: the
pitcher, / streaked as it ripened, and the still riper vase?" (SO,104) For
a further relation between the spiral of the dance and the fruit: "Tanzt
die Orange." (SO,44) The recurring image of the fruit bowl, itself a
still condensation of movement and mingling in Char's poetry, can be
compared to Rilke's own image: "Schalen mit rühmlichen Früchten"
("bowls with fruits worthy of praise").

249

suffisions / we were sufficient for each other."[17] The trail of
the meteor, unlike any other, creates a space about itself,
as here, the trees hold their distance apart. Compare, in "Je
veux parler d'un ami," Char's words about Camus and a
friendship, shared as two swallows share "the sky's infinite":

> L'amitié qui parvient à s'interdire les patrouilles mala-
> visées auprès d'autrui, quand l'âme d'autrui a besoin d'ab-
> sence et de mouvement lointain, est la seule à contenir un
> germe d'immortalité. . . . Dans la constance des coeurs
> expérimentés, l'amitié ne fait le guet ni n'inquisitionne.[f]
> (RBS,109)

Withdrawn in his evident presence, solitary[17] in every gesture
of his friendship—the poet's contradictions are more apparent in this volume than previously. Now his own talismans
for his most silent contemplation, the records of his night,
are held out to our gaze. How, in respect and in discretion, is
the reader to share the poet's contemplation and its private
space?

The last text of *La Nuit talismanique* insists, as do the
first texts, and the epigraph for this chapter, that, above all,
the obscure be maintained. The candle flame or the after-
light of a day overcast and following on a night of vision will
not set afire the dark preceding and surrounding. Like friendship, like love, the heart of night—as was apparent from the
start—must not be lit by any light other than its own wavering
clarity. The other hand protecting the oval flame protects also
the heart of this rose and its beauty, even from the "oiseau
spirituel" associated by juxtaposition with the snake and
bird, transcending, surpassing all contradictions: "Hirondelle,

[17] Rilke writes in 1903: "Loneliness, vast inner loneliness. To walk
in oneself and to meet no one for hours on end,—that's what one
must be able to attain." (*Briefe an einen jungen Dichter*.) (DE,99-100).

[f] Friendship that forbears from those unwise patrols near the other
when his soul needs some absence and distant movement is alone in
having a seed of immortality. . . . In the constancy of practiced hearts,
friendship neither spies nor questions.

active ménagère de la pointe des herbes, fouiller la rose, vois-tu, serait vanité des vanités. / Swallow, active house-keeper of grass tips, to search the rose, you see, would be the most futile of futilities."[18] (NT,95)

To join patience with impatience, desire with discretion. In "Nous tombons," the clash of opposite forces and their joining—in particular that of the "profondeur d'impatience" and the "verticale patience"—are so strong that the text might bear comparison with "Le Visage nuptial" of 1938. As it un-folds, the implicit reversals, renderings, and returnings ("O mon avalanche à rebours!"; "Toute liée. Rendue à l'air"; "La danse retournée"; "La mort nous bat du revers de sa fourche") stress the correspondence of contrary elements, the partners not only amorous but warring, not only man and woman but also all they represent. We sense here how the illumination cast against the night corresponds to the shadows appearing in the daylight, as the scene shifts toward the interior.

As elsewhere, the text immediately announces the brevity of its own fragments (or to borrow a phrase from the poem, its "parcelles dispersées," those scattered elements apparently free in their ordering.[19] In the undoing of the text—as the

[18] Thus *La Nuit talismanique* ends on an image of privacy and of interior space: Rilke conveys the same feeling, by the same image: "Outside was the park: everything was in tune with me—one of those hours that are not fashioned at all, but only, as it were, held in reserve, as though things had drawn together and left space, a space as undis-turbed as the interior of a rose, an angelical space, in which one keeps quite still." (DE,126). We may be reminded of the interior life of nature in Provence as described by Bosco: "au royaume de la grâce intérieure, dans l'un de ces jardins du monde où l'on sent partout le génie du lieu." (HB,115) A darkened room, signaling the mystery of the scene, a meditation on a candle-flame, a breath, and on a page momentarily open, with the old gods storming outside: we are re-minded of Mallarmé's *Igitur* and *Les Dieux antiques.*

[19] See Virginia La Charité, "Beyond the Poem: René Char's *La Nuit talismanique*," in *Symposium*, Spring, 1976, for a study of the interrelations of the written word and the illustrations, in whose con-vergence the aphorisms "emerge as poem" and of Char's pebbles as a "starry constellation in reverse."

251

initial statement can be seen to provide the threads, which are then unraveled the length of the fragmentary discourse—the line seems contradicted and then reaffirmed, in a reversal formally stressing the underlying pattern of the poem:

Ma brièveté est sans chaînes.

. . . .

Toute liée.

. . . .

Toute liée. Rendue à l'air.[g] (NT,48)

The complexity of a binding and liberating relationship, which links without enchaining, provides the emotional and structural background for much of Char's writing, and necessarily for any reading of his work, which will also be, as we stated at the beginning, tied and free, determined by what we know of the poet and loosed by his own acknowledgement of the freedom of each reader.

"Tel un chemin rougi sur le roc. Un animal fuyait. / Like a path reddened on the rock. An animal was fleeing." The trace left by the setting sun, by the passion or the animal fearful in its going reminds us of the red streak or the jagged surface left on the cheek of one of the sparring partners in the earlier poem of deadly ambiguity called "Le Mortel partenaire," a "raie rose" slashed raw like the reddening of the horizon and, at the same time, the red tinge of the small wounded and captive beast in the poet's bed at the outset of *Artine*.[20] As is always true for René Char, the animal world is not a simple reflection of the human, but rather an extension of it, deep in its possible implications because it is more readily subject to our vision and our discourse. Here, the fleeing is prepared by the path traced out, the suffering or fright incited by the reddening, as if branded into the rock. The path ir-

[g] My brevity is without chains. . . . Completely bound. . . . Completely bound. Rendered to the air.

[20] And also, of the "brisant de rougeur." Compare with Rilke's Second Duino Elegy: "Höhenzüge, morgenrötliche Grate / aller Erschaffung // ranges, summits, dawn-red ridges / of all beginning. . . ." (DE,28-29)

revocably burned out, incised and inscribed, absorbs a verbal intensity from the flight of the animal, and of the text, each sentence isolated in a rapid expiration down the page.

The poem itself is retraced and reinforced, inserted here, like its companion texts dating from an earlier period, for the nourishment of this later night—like so many talismans. Each of these texts acquires a double strength from our re-reading of it: first a return to the original context, and then a repetition against the present backdrop of the sleepless night shared now by poet and reader.

Framing "Nous tombons"—that is, on the page before and the page following—are two texts of passage. Preceding it, "L'Issue" begins by the extinction of outer and inner illumination and a sense of loss:

Tout s'éteignit:
Le jour, la lumière intérieure.
Masse endolorie,
Je ne trouvais plus mon temps vrai,
Ma maison.[h] (NT,45)

.   .   .   .

But, by a swerve in direction, the tone suddenly changes to its opposite, so that fullness replaces loss, as work replaces suffering, and the intensity of the sunlight now compensates, physically and morally, for the extinction and exhaustion of the first lines. The instantaneity of the harvest is now recaptured as a sufficient ground for hope, for an illumination both exterior and interior, a fruit glimpsed on the other side of failure. The moment of this text is also that of another, more universal time, where the seasons fill out the space of the man growing with them, in the cycle of their poetry. "Redonnez-leur ce qui n'est plus présent en eux / . . . . / Apprenez-leur, de la chute à l'essor, les douze mois de leur visage / . . . . / Et qui sait voir la terre aboutir à des fruits, / Point ne l'émeut l'échec quoiqu'il ait tout perdu. // Restore to them what is

[h] Everything was extinguished: / The day, the interior light. / Grief-stricken, / I no longer found my true time, / My dwelling.

no more present in them / . . . / Teach them, from fall to soaring, the twelve months of their face / . . . / And a man who can watch the earth through to its end in fruit— / Failure does not shake him though he has lost all." (JG) (FM, 165) As elsewhere, the images of the shoulder and the work in the vineyards are inseparable from the energy of the sun, so the poet circling solitary in the dance of his candlelight shares in a more general time of fire and of obscurity, of an idea tempered in a flame and a vision reaching past the oval burning toward another mystery beyond this room and this text. "Une autre main. . . ."

On the far side, in this triptych of dark and light—whose central panel is marked by arrows pointing in both directions: by verbs of giving back, of reversing, by images turned around, seen backward—there stands a poem of hesitation. In "Éros suspendu," the night half-gone is sliced, suddenly, by the blast and the color of a red trumpet, as of a sun blaring through a place of cruelty. "Nous volons," cries the poet, as if this flying were to supply the other half of the cry in its falling: "Nous tombons," which directly precedes it in the center panel. The flight in its "espace cruel" responds to the human subjection to gravity, and to the grave art of love. Falling, like the meteor, or flying, like "l'oiseau spirituel," at once a bird and a serpent, the poet keeps his force and his mystery.

Nevertheless, *La Nuit talismanique* is preceded by its source, as if the poet consented to direct our reading. The texts of 1955-1958, grouped under this title and, as the poet says, dating from a difficult period of insomnia, are the prelude and the source for the night of the talisman. If sleep is absent, then the bark of the tree must suffice, the outward appearance of the talisman for an inner motion: "Faute de sommeil, l'écorce. . . ." Here the reader of *Artine* thinks of that wood burned out in the page consumed, in its passage. It is of these texts that the almond-flame discussed above forms the center, and the primary and shifting object of contemplation, "mobile comme le regard"—unlike the unmoving stare of the electric light. The uncaptured gaze of meditation refuses the immobile as it refuses the indiscreet fixity of an answering look; thus the source may retain its mystery, and the poet, or the reader, the freedom of his contemplation. "L'eau nocturne se déversa dans le cercle verdoyant de la jeune clarté, me faisant nuit moi-même, tandis que se libérait *l'oeuvre filante.* / The nocturnal water flowed into the verdant circle of the young clarity, making night of me, while *the work streaking by* set itself free." (NT,12) The circle of solitude is again reflected in the title image of one of the last texts of this volume, "L'Anneau de la licorne," where the poet—set apart, marginal, like the unicorn in his circular fence—refuses, to the questions of the indiscreet, any answer other than the destruction of a virgin leaf: "il dédaigna de répondre et déchira une feuille de viorne." (NT,83)

The green is restored to the dry sands, as in the image of the almond (where the "ver" or "verdoyant" still echoes with the "vers" of poetry), the round of light thrown by the flame setting apart the space of the dance. So the solitary and "votive" song of the meteor (NT,62) is prepared by the freeing of the work, fleeting as a shooting star ("l'étoile filante") streaking past into the night, and by the slipping away of time ("le temps file") and its metaphoric signal of the flowing of the oil of a lamp ("la lampe file"). We remember, from *Artine* ". . . there was no prison door," and it is in that light that we read here, in this other night, of the poet's reluctance to tarry, which leaves both parties free: "Ma brièveté est sans chaînes / My brevity is without chains." (NT,48)

The transcription of the images of insomnia and their insertion here like so many way-stations of the poem fourteen years later, bring to completion the "solitary gesture of raising the candle." But it seems to us that these nocturnal meditations respond also to the glass of water brought in *Artine* just that many years before the onset of the insomnia

255

and to her "monumental drought," setting this cycle of flame and water, of contemplation and vision into a larger circle still:

$$1930\text{——}1955\text{–}1958\text{——}1972$$

Dates are of little interest except insofar as they describe the flow of a poet's life work: Artine continues to assure the existence of the poet as a creative force. Sometimes the other hand holding the flame seems to be that of the Magdalen glimpsed in a previous meditation, still keeping watch over the vision, like an interior model ever present.

Neither is Pascal absent from the night of this volume:[21]

FEU

The candle holds firm against the storm, when old gods become beggars, says the poet. The multiple deities coursing through us, intermittent and flickering like the flame, are in correspondence with them, and can remain so, as long as we do not consider them to be divine. "L'éclair me dure. / The flash lasts me." (NT,24) "L'éclair," "l'effroi. . . ." Engraved in yellow against a ground of midnight blue, this text describes both the storm and the candle, insofar as a lightning flash can be made constant by its interior absorption and its flash or exterior clarity—dagger-sharp as in "Madeleine à la veilleuse," durable in its transcendence of any one problematic moment: "Luire et s'élancer—prompt couteau, lente étoile. / To shine and to shoot forward—quick knife, slow star." (NT,13) On this active meeting of the simple and the stellar illumination, of the relatively transitory and the relatively eternal, rests the strength of the meteoric work, nocturnal and clarifying in its obscurity, the deepest thought of the poet enduring, like night itself.

Facing this text of the durable flash on the opposing page

[21] From the "Mémorial" of Pascal, written on the 23rd of November, 1654: "Depuis environ dix heures et demie du soir jusques environ minuit et demi, / FEU / . . . / Certitude. Certitude. Sentiment, Joie, Paix. / . . . / Joie, joie, joie, pleurs de joie." (Blaise Pascal, *Pensées*, ed. Brunschvicg, Garnier, 1951, p. 71).

—as in the mirror of the canvas behind the poet, into which the penitent Magdalen gazes—is a reminder of poetic impenitence and unforgiving impatience: "Obéissez à vos porcs qui existent. Je me soumets à mes dieux qui n'existent pas. / Nous restons gens d'inclémence. // Obey your swine who exist. I submit to my gods who do not. We remain men for inclemency." (NT,25) Only these lines of the inscription are lit in the image, as if the candle had chosen its text. . . . These gods, exclusive and discreet, explain, perhaps, the distant foreboding of the night, that "inclémence lointaine," as Char entitles a group of poems. The old gods rave outside: the intolerance of the poet is no less terrible. But the submission, the severity, and the impatience are a matter of choice, on the part of the poet and of his reader, following still: "La lumière a un âge. La nuit n'en a pas. / Light has an age. Night has none." (NT,34) As the star is finally transformed into a dark abyss, in a reversal as complex as that of Mallarmé's night sonnets, only the nocturnal streaming remains, having become the source that we can only question in its obscurity—complete and limitless. It is into this ageless darkness that the former texts are now inserted, each an emblem of meditation, a picture, and a flame: "Nourri par celui qui n'est pas du lieu. . . . / Nourished by the one from elsewhere." (NT,46)

These initial texts are durable "illuminations," a word we take here in its Rimbaldian sense, as many of Char's own words can be taken—the title "Pour nous, Rimbaud" is not just a title but a relationship chosen and acknowledged. The passage leading from them toward the texts of 1972 is a reversible one, unlike the movement of *Artine*, which works only from the source toward a burning. Furthermore, *La Nuit talismanique* goes past the oppositions apparent in *Artine* ("verre d'eau / sécheresse" . . . "silence / intarissable") to a nocturnal world apparently characterized less by ambiguity than by anguish. Following the text and drawing of "L'Oiseau spirituel"—itself a joining of artist and poet, Georges Braque and René Char—and accompanying a double image of birds, one labeled "Le Serpent," we read

257

the underlying inscription that explains the apparently contradictory joining of snake and bird: "Au-dessus des contradictions partielles sont apparues les identités antagonistes qui,
elles, mettent fin. Plus d'attente prospère. / Above the partial
contradictions there have appeared hostile identities who put
an end. No more prosperous expectation." (NT,36-37) As
the almond flower appears within the flame, the identities are
finally revealed: the other three elements, according to Char,
whose poetry privileges the land, its "first silt" and its continuing and contrary harvest.[22]

But the place of meditation is already, and necessarily,
one of torment. From any individual absence where the
source of the appeal is unknown ("Qui appelle?") a universal
presence or calling may be summoned, all signs now appealing to us: "Chacun appelle." Or again: "Tu es celui qui
délivre un contenu universel en maîtrisant ta sottise particu-
lière. / You are the one who delivers a universal message
by overcoming your particular foolishness." (NT,71) An
anguish unspecified and unlimited remains within the interior model of our contemplation. The steps of "the muti-
lated giant" through these pages, his reason shamed like that
of Pascalian man conscious of his disproportion and remark-
able precisely in his anguish, will lead eventually to those of
the "disaggregated giant" in the constellation of Orion. Some
of the radiance of the flame lit here will be lost in the surrounding obscurity; some of the signals of the correspondence
will go unnoticed, as if the call—in Heidegger's sense of the
term, close to that of Char—could not always be answered.

. . . .

Qui appelle encore? Mais la réponse n'est point donnée.
Qui appelle encore pour un gaspillage sans frein?[i] (NT,74)

. . . .

[22] For a close study of the four elements in Char's work, see the
chapter "The Elements of the Poem," in our *René Char*, Twayne,
forthcoming.

[i] Who is calling now? But the answer is not given. / Who is calling
now for a waste without limit?

Indeed the lesson of the night is all in nuances. The poet contemplates the birth of shadows from the shadow, instructed by the sudden backward sputter of the flame: "D'elle j'appris à me bien pencher et à me redresser en direction constante de l'horizon avoisinant mon sol, à voir de proche en proche une ombre mettre au monde une ombre par le biais d'un trait lumineux, et à la scruter. / From it I learned to stoop over and to straighten quickly in the constant line of the horizon bordering my land, to see, nearing, a shadow giving birth to a shadow through the slant of a luminous shaft, and to scrutinize it." (NT,87) This close perception blossoms forth as another flower arising from the flame, opposing the winter in the poem's title: "Éclore en hiver."

And still the flame depends on the water, as in *Artine*. Without the night, the candle would have no place, nor would its contemplation hold us. The dreamer remains one with the night as a source, still or running, silent or sonorous in all its contradictions:

    .   .   .   .

Parvenu à l'arche sonore, il cessa de marcher au milieu du pont. Il fut tout de suite le courant.[j] (NT,71)
Mon lit est un torrent aux plages desséchées.

    .   .   .   .

J'inventai un soleil et je bus sa verdeur sous l'empire de l'été.[k] (NT,86)

Yet on the screen ("l'écran rêveur") of the poet's sleep or the pages of his poetic contemplation one shadow never ceases to fall: "Le roi des aulnes se meurt. / The elder-king is dying." (NT,82).[23] The figures flicker: Mary Magda-

[j] Arrived at the resounding arch, he halted at the center of the bridge. He was at once the current.

[k] My bed is a torrent with dried-up banks. / . . . / I invented a sleep and drank its greenness under the sway of summer.

[23] See Goethe's ballad, "Der Erlkönig" ("Le Roi des aulnes"), and a ballad of Wordsworth; the same subject and title are found among Herder's *Volkslieder*. The original source is an old Danish song. My thanks to Jean-Jacques Demorest and to Henri Peyre for help on

len, her fingers on a skull by the candle flame, before a mirror; Pascal in his night of fire; the other hand holding the candle. We think then of the frailty of the hand grasped in "Le Gaucher" (NP), and of that finger placed on the lips of the dying woman in the poem "Faim rouge" (NP,40) as if to signal the silence of another country, when we read here: "Sa main froide dans la mienne j'ai couru, espérant nous perdre et y perdre ma chaleur. Riche de nuit je m'obstinais. / With her cold hand in mine I ran, hoping to lose us and to lose thereby my warmth. Rich in night I persisted." (NT,89) The profound night of the talisman, described in a slower and more elliptical style than that of *Artine*, is haunted always by a spectre of death unfamiliar to the earlier volume. To the poet, here an "amnesiac of lands warmed to life again," (NT,90) this memory returns once more, near a statue of a smiling Eve: the text "Relief et louange" is carved out, its presence temporarily renascent, like the past.

"A faible distance, Eve d'Autun, le poignet sectionné. . . . / Not far away, Eve of Autun, her wrist cut off. . . ." (NT, 91) Some instinct leads us to look again at the longest prose poem inserted here, as the most singular talisman of this night of the text. In the sunset of "L'Inoffensif," an unwanted solitude is suddenly imposed: ". . . soudain tu n'apparais plus entière à mon côté; ce n'est pas le fuseau nerveux de ton poignet que tient ma main mais la branche creuse d'un quelconque arbre mort et déjà débité." (NT,22) Against the

---

this point. Because he would not dance with the queen of the fairies, King Olaf is struck dead, and his body is returned to what was to have been his own marriage-feast on the saddle of his horse. The line is preceded here by the image of a white scorpion (an animal whose sting is often mortal), so that the unearthly purity of the weapon is placed in relief: in the Vaucluse, René Char's country, white scorpions are found mostly in ruins of buildings: the image carries with it much the same aura of past mystery as the night-time forest of the *Erlkönig*, which is set apart from the daily present. As the horn of the unicorn, found on the facing page (NT,81-82) is deadly in its single thrust, so is the scorpion's tail; within both images, the erotic merges with the menacing.

unforgettable background presence of that skull and that mirror, and in response to the gesture of Heraclitus summoning our silence, the poet here takes in his own hand the hand holding the candle, to burn the page.

And the final text of *La Nuit talismanique* moves from the poet alone to a word shared, from the solitary vigil to the midday sun, from the anguish of a dreamer or a seer to an ineluctable and sufficient human suffering: "Nous nous suffisions, sous le trait de feu de midi, à construire, à souffrir, à copartager, à écouter palpiter notre révolte, nous allons maintenant souffrir. . . . / We sufficed for each other, under the shaft of midday fire, in our constructing, in our suffering, in our sharing, listening to the throb of our revolt; now we shall suffer. . . ." (NT,92-93) The "sedentary" oval flame gives way at last to memory, to these brilliant "flashes of our youth," like bright lizards called forth from their sleep to accompany the poet, redeeming the red trace of the animal bruised, now fleeing past the night of the talisman into another day. Always moving past us, "the fundamental traveler" cannot be seen constant by his candlelight, not even in profile, nor against the screen of his sleep and its apparitions.

The questions asked in this night of semi-darkness are not to be answered, nor are they to be forgotten. Their double summons, paradoxical and sufficient to nourish all feeling, haunts the entire work of René Char:

Mais pourquoi la joie et pourquoi la douleur?[l] (NT,84)

Mais quel fut l'instant de cette source entière?[m] (NT,34)

Over the canvas of the nocturnal creation stretched out, there passes from time to time a circle of light thrown by an interior flame. Circle illuminating and endlessly exigent, obscure clarity of texts which remain for our own contemplation, talismans against a future drought, and for a future night.

[l] Why joy? Why suffering?
[m] But which was the moment of that integral source?

MOUNTAIN: "UNE POURSUITE CONTINUE"

Wir sind nichts; was wir suchen, ist alles.
Hölderlin, *Hyperion*

The three series included in *Le Nu perdu* (1972) gather once more all the themes dispersed in the preceding works, moving past this scattering to attain a massive coherence; together with *La Nuit talismanique* (1972) and *Aromates chasseurs* (published in 1975, preliminary version, 1974), they complete this study. The themes binding those fragments into sheaves, or tying the separate twigs into bundles of kindling for the ancestral fire, have been themselves gathered into cycles; now we follow only the moments marked, in our private reading, as way-stations up the mountain, in the order of their appearance, no longer fragmentary instants but instances of the entire return, seen whole in each moment, as each contains them all.

A. Retour amont

Où passer nos jours *à présent*? (NP,51)

Our path through this collection opens with "Sept parcelles de Luberon," the title already indicating the conscious partitioning of a landscape and a poetry of mountainous singularity within its universal range. Here the word particles ("parcelles")[1] recalls the preceding declaration, which we attribute less to the poet than to the poem—"the quantity of fragments tears me to pieces" (FM,32)—and the majestic crossing of dimensions: "La parcelle vermeille franchit ses lentes branches à ton front, dimension rassurée" (FM,58)—

---

[1] Elsewhere: "Il est des parcelles de lieux où l'ame rare subitement exulte. Alentour ce n'est qu'espace indifférent." (LA,42)

predicting, at the same time, the infinity of "parcelles lumi-neuses" with which the poet will finally be clothed in the constellation of Orion.

1. *Division*

"SEPT PARCELLES DE LUBERON"

. . . .

Dans un bel arbre sans essaim,
Vous languissez de communion,
Vous éclatez de division,
Jeunesse, voyante nuée.[a] (NP,11)

. . . .

From the actual absence and the implied presence of the swarm—for the "nuée" resembles a large cloud of insects separate but flying together—there arises first a mountain range like the Luberon and later, as in the poem "Réception d'Orion," a constellation, in which each bee is changed to a star, part of a swarm flying together, and composing the dis-aggregated body of a hero. If the wolf is marginal, the bee is "frontalière," flying between distant elements to fuse them into one another, crossing "dimensions," transporting the pol-len until there is—as Anaxagoras pointed out—a portion of everything in everything. The insect of boundaries mediates between the star's ray and the probe of the poet's *fer*, between the unicorn's purifying horn and the walking stick piercing the side of the mountain—for the pierced rose is also beauty triumphant, the wounded mountainside finds a positive par-allel in an abundant waterfall, the source of a resurgence, and the texts find their separate flashes changed to an endur-ing series of illuminations. In the stanza above, the morning slope shines transparently, a light diaphanous cloud, on the opposite side from the opaque configurations of the dense prose poems: the poem about the Luberon serves as a portal to a mountainous range, a "massif central" for the work of

[a] In a handsome swarmless tree, / You yearn for communion, / You shatter with division, / Youth, farseeing cloud.

René Char. Combining a surface separation with an underlying unity, even a single text suffices for a model of the range. The lines of undoing—"De mon logis, pierre après pierre, / J'endure la démolition. // Of my lodging, stone after stone, / I endure the demolition." (NP,12)—provoke in turn an apparently contrary massive structure, these next lines responding in as if a partnership of opposites, or of enemy brothers: "Massif de mes deuils, tu gouvernes / Massive range of my mourning, you govern." (NP,12)

2. Mourning

> . . . il est grand temps de nous composer une
> santé du malheur. Dût-elle avoir l'apparence de
> l'arrogance du miracle. AUSC (PPC,231)

The following poem is deeply carved, as if into a mountainside of grief, a moment of mourning complete in its brevity:

"TRACÉ SUR LE GOUFFRE"

Dans la plaie chimérique de Vaucluse je vous ai regardé souffrir. Là, bien qu'abaissé, vous étiez une eau verte, et encore une route. Vous traversiez la mort en son désordre. Fleur vallonnée d'un secret continu.[b] (NP,14)

The valley, a wound dug out of the mountain, a mark of suffering dividing the landscape, is green here like the plants over which the Sorgue streams, as it is nourished by the Fontaine de Vaucluse for a future renascence. Yet the renewing spring is of no avail against temporal demolition: the flower is penetrated by death, undone from the inside as the dwelling is undone, stone by stone. This image at the heart of all Char's work, sensed—although in silence—throughout the moments of calm, is felt retrospectively in the *Lettera amorosa*. Even the iris is subject to the incursion of pain, the

---

[b] In the chimerical wound of Vaucluse I watched you suffering. There, although subsided, you were green water, and yet a road. You traversed death in its disorder. Flower valleyed by a continuous secret.

latter not to be redeemed by suffering as is the nuptial countenance by a final triumphant stance.

And once perceived, the image runs like a tragic current under every path. Many of the poems in this collection have their own source in the themes of water, time, and death undermining life, in particular "Dansons aux Baronnies" and the poem following it, "Faction du muet." This thought and its image are secret and incessant, a profound counterpart to the "incontinent" boat, bearing the poet with his companions, passing above the individual divisions of a time as divided as that in "Allégeance." The continuous wound is revealed only at certain moments, for a few beings.

"Chérir Thouzon"

Lorsque la douleur l'eut hissé sur son toit envié un savoir évident se montra à lui sans brouillard. . . . L'ensorcelant désir de parole s'était, avec les eaux noires, retiré. Ça et là persistaient de menus tremblements dont il suivait le sillage aminci. Une colombe de granit à demi masquée mesurait de ses ailes les restes épars du grand oeuvre englouti. (NP,16)[c]

.   .   .   .

High like a mountainous mourning, reminiscent in its mood of the haunting poem: "J'habite une douleur," and, in its architecture, of the mental dwelling called a "tête habitable," this poem represents a culmination of pain and thus a perspective clear by its distant knowledge.[2] Like the summit of silence perceived at the climax of *Le Rempart de brindilles*, from where the landscape is observed in a progressively wider view, the hill on which the abandoned abbey of Thouzon lies

[c] When grief had hoisted him onto its coveted roof, an obvious knowledge appeared to him with no mist. . . . The captivating desire of the word had withdrawn, along with the black waters. Here and there slight disturbances persisted whose narrowed wake he followed. A granite dove half-masked measured with its wings the scattered remains of the great work engulfed.

[2] A number of Char's poems are built with explicit architectural references: a study of these appears in our *René Char, op.cit.*

in ruins, confronts and accepts the disappearance of an ideally total poetic work, assimilated to the remainder of a past civilization. Of Thouzon, only a fresco remains, enclosed in a museum.[3]

The "restes épars" of the texts also, like the final moment of the "terme épars," reach as wide as the wings of the granite dove half-hidden—a sign of the early martyrs, a bas-relief left in a niche and visible only from a certain angle, turned toward the landscape in ruins.[4] Now this narrow furrow of suffering will guide our passage until the reeds and the mint of *Le Nu perdu*, like the narrowest of traces open in the word until the moment of final joining. From this time of destruction there will spring a new resurgence: "Dans l'ère rigoureuse qui s'ouvrait, aboli serait le privilège de récolter sans poison. . . . Dans le creux de la ville immergée, la corne de la lune mêlait le dernier sang et le premier limon. / In the rigorous era commencing, the privilege of harvesting without poison would be abolished. . . . In the hollow of the town immersed, the horn of the moon mingled the last blood and the first silt."

In the cycle of the harvest still continuing, the bread is suffering, as yet unhealed: the part of pain the sickle carries with it has now become visible and collective. Related to the horn of the unicorn—that is, the legendary container of a curative magic—the horn of the waxing moon, an alchemical symbol and the sign of another "abundance to come," mingles past and future, using what has preceded as a land to cultivate in preparation for the other work implicit in that of the word, yet transcending it. Again the past is put before us, as in the "Pause au château cloaque," (NP,22) a text explicitly furnishing a moment of respite. As we turn back to the past where our "eroded memories" are sleeping, the present is preparing its attack upon us: man is prey to other things exterior to his own conscience and to the butcher he bears in himself, according to the poet.

[3] A Pietà from Thouzon has been preserved in the Louvre.
[4] This statue has since been destroyed.

In the commentary on enigma, a warning was heard against the partisans of facility, of platitude, against those for whom rings should be opened, margins eliminated, and the mystery of the snake uncoiled. To the observer who has climbed by many paths toward the peak of anguish, the enigmatic, silent, and deeply serious game, a "jeu muet," played after the recession of the dark waters, reveals itself. The half-open countryside is propitious to love, but that love will be seen only as pain, like this wound always present, whose cruel red resembles the setting sun. Many of the most difficult poems are underlined, as if with an impersonal cruelty, by a mark of the same red: these poems are rendered dense not only by their textual matter but by the suffering they transcribe and in their turn inflict: the brutal perception given as a source for the living. The "mirage of the peaks" remains etched in the consciousness throughout this later traverse: "Dès lors fidèle à son amour comme le ciel l'est au rocher. Fidèle, méché, mais sans cesse vaguant, dérobant sa course par toute l'étendue montrée du feu, tenue du vent; l'étendue, trésor de boucher, sanglante à un croc. // From then on faithful to his love as is the sky to the rock. Faithful, fused, but ceaselessly wandering, concealing his way through all the sweep revealed by the fire, held by the wind; the sweep, the butcher's hoard, bleeding on a hook." In its extreme transformation and its continuation of pain, this "massacre d'archers" can be taken in its cruelest sense, as the animal's head detached from his body and placed above the skin, in a garish disjuncture—as in a fox's mask awarded after the hunt. Like Rembrandt's flayed ox, finally taken as the poet's "only sun," this violent image illuminates the epic struggle upward, against the current.

By a violent contrast, the next poem, "Aux portes d'Aerea," (NP,19) opens with the quest for a high and lost city, an expression of nostalgia for a golden age that can, by its lack of an explicit temporal framework, be carried over into our own present: "L'heureux temps." During the collective work of the harvest, fear and fatigue were rulers of the field and of the workers' singing, in a repeated convergence of the scene and the song: "champ/chant."[5] But the poet, participating in the collective task, again implicitly compared to that of the bee,[5a] keeps nevertheless to the side: "Le pollen de l'esprit gardait sa part d'exil / The pollen of the mind kept its part of exile," the distant suggestion of the insect reminiscent of the absent swarming in the "Sept parcelles de Luberon." The absence felt in the text, as if a poem might itself be in a state of expectation, is cured only when the sting of the bee, become a star, returns at the conclusion of the passage toward a series of metaphoric terms, occasionally scattered, perhaps sparse ("le terme épars" in two of its senses), and of an apparently meager yield. But this text, ferocious and seasonal, closes on the image already glimpsed, here and elsewhere, of passage, of a beauty pierced, whose tears may eventually water a fresh beginning: "Marche forcée, au terme épars. . . . Visée par l'abeille de fer, la rose en larmes s'est ouverte." The iron bee is the bitter opposite of the poet.

The image will return, its pain ever increased by its recurrence, as the furrow carved out in the landscape by suffering, "traced on the abyss," is gradually deepened within the work.

3. *Fig Tree, Rock, and Oriole*

"DEVANCIER"

> J'ai reconnu dans un rocher la mort fuguée
> et mensurable, le lit ouvert de ses petits com-
> parses sous la retraite d'un figuier.[d] (NP,20)

This crack in the rock where the abyss is recognized and even measured, compared to the open bed of death, is a still more anguished manifestation of the furrow traced in the preceding

---

[5] The double resonance "champs/chant" is present in a number of passages where it is heard only by association: "Champs, vous vous mirez dans mes quatre moissons. / Je tonne, vous tournez." ("Captifs," *Cinq poésies en hommage à Georges Braque*). Compare Reverdy: "Mais, par-dessus les refrains et les champs. . . ." (*La Liberté des mers*, Maeght, 1959, p. 44) "Champ" has also the sense of an electromagnetic field; the strength of the question is not only rhetorical.

[d] I have recognized, in a rock, death fugal and measurable, the open bed of its small assistants under the seclusion of a fig-tree. (JG)

poems, while the fig tree[6]—whose fruit contains in its interior structure seeds like those of the pomegranate—prepares the way phonetically for the "Lied" a few steps later ("Fuguée-figuier"). In the "Lied," the presence of love is inextricably united with the reminder of the disaster whose memory a bird song recalls. For in a further recognition, the song of a former oriole announcing a cataclysm hovers over the later text, so that the two passages are joined, by a triple image: dawn, bed, and bird are gathered in a peril announced under the surface of the last line in the later poem:

"LE LORIOT"   *3 september 1939*

Le loriot entra dans la capitale de l'aube.
L'epée de son chant ferma le lit triste.
Tout à jamais prit fin.[e] (FM,33)

"LIED DU FIGUIER"

.   .   .   .

Le figuier demanda au maître du gisant
L'arbuste d'une foi nouvelle.
Mais le loriot, son prophète,
L'aube chaude de son retour,
En se posant sur le désastre,
Au lieu de faim, périt d'amour.[f] (NP,34)

---

[6] Rilke's Sixth Duino Elegy opens with a similar tree: "Feigenbaum, seit wie lange schon ists mir bedeutend, / wie du die Blüte beinah ganz überschlägst / und hinein in die zeitig entschlossene Frucht, / ungerühmt, drängst dein reines Geheimnis. // Fig tree, how long it's been full of meaning for me, / the way you almost entirely omit to flower / and into the seasonably resolute fruit / uncelebratedly thrust your purest secret." (DE,54-55) (See note on our "contracted fruit"; we bloom too early and thus waste the strength we might have lent to our fruit.) One year, when the fig trees had frozen in his garden, René Char purchased dried figs from the grocer and soaked them in milk so that the birds could be nourished.

[e] The oriole entered the capital of dawn. / The sword of his song closed the sad bed. / Everything forever ended.

[f] The fig-tree asked the master of the recumbent one / For the bush of a new faith. / But the oriole, its prophet, / The warm dawn of its homing, / In alighting on the disaster, / Instead of hunger, perished of love. (JG)

The oriole too is a "oiseau spirituel": in the second text, his still piercing song recalls the time of disaster, in some sense redeeming it by his future hope. Thus the tragic ending of the first song, heard again in the hunger of the second ("fin/faim"), is replaced by a note of triumph, resounding even as the bird perishes. As to a possible renascence, it is uncertain here.

The poet of an art at its most concise, always the forerunner of other texts in a massive series, carves out his own destiny, but not in the stone; he digs his tomb rather in the air hard as rock, sundered by the lightning of the word, near the habitable summit of his mountain. "J'ai creusé mon retour:" his definitive return will be made under the sign of the bird of prophecy, another "concordant" of the mountain, and thus of the inner text as it makes its own return upland.

4. Convergence

From a parapet, distinct views are seen to combine: in what might be called a "convergence des multiples," as in the title of one of the poems in this same series, a central instant or a central poem concentrates the major themes already present and predicts the others about to appear. As in the case of all readings, the *pause* may seem differently located at different moments, as the parapets are different: from the particular path we follow here, "Les Parages d'Alsace" (NP,25) appears to contain such a convergence. After a brief allusion to clouds like those among the branches of the first text on the "Sept parcelles de Luberon," the images of mountains, trees, of birds, and man the hunter of himself merge; the very abundance of images like a dowry displayed marks the initial step for an eventual rise toward the bare summit. Here fire/flower and forest are designated, as well as the bee and the phoenix which remain implicit in the pollen and the blazing forth of the bloom:

> Je t'ai montré La Petite-Pierre, la dot de sa forêt, le ciel
> qui naît aux branches,

L'ampleur de ses oiseaux chasseurs d'autres oiseaux,
Le pollen deux fois vivant sous la flambée des fleurs. . . .[g]
(NP,25)

. . . .

The fertilizing principle lives doubly within the flame of the flowers and in the potential conflagration of the forest, a massive *materia prima* for the poem or, by metonymic substitution, the *vers*: "Dans le bois on écoute bouillir le ver. . . ." Closely linked to the abundant natural landscape, to the birds of prey as "ample" as the wide spaces across which they fly (thus the opposite to the "thinness" of the swift flight circling about his home: see "Le Martinet") and to the flowers flamboyant in their display, human love chooses its own freedom and its nature, *concordant* in its oppositions, and without a continuity enforced beyond this present: "Nous nous aimons aujourd'hui sans au-delà et sans lignée / Ardents ou effacés, différents mais ensemble."

Now the tragic dwelling of the summit is transformed, at least momentarily, into a lodging "en-avant," into the image of a ship in whose existence we must believe, summoned, like the poem, to be the proper vessel for our return upstream to the peaks. The seascape once more emerges with the mountain landscape, as in "Fastes"; from this height the waters of the word are seen to recede, as in "Chérir Thouzon." The return voyage, upstream and upland, will last as long as the faith in its possibility:

. . . .

Le navire fait route vers la haute mer végétale.
Tous feux éteints il nous prend à son bord.

. . . .

L'appelé, l'hôte itinérant, tant que nous croyons à sa vérité.[h] (NP,25-26)

[g] I showed you La Petite-Pierre, the dowry of its forest, the sky born at the tips of its branches, / The compass of its birds hunters of other birds, / The twice-living pollen under the flare of the flowers. (JG)

[h] The ship is bound for the high sea's vegetation / With all lights

5. *Juncture by Water*

The ship image in "Les Parages d'Alsace" inaugurates a group of poems obliquely focused on the images of water. In "Dansons aux Baronnies," the amorous wound of a valley —open like the Sorgue—is juxtaposed to a ring designating fidelity in its circling: a luminous pain covered by a living water prepares a metaphoric path toward a poem whose name is already suggested here: "le vif de l'eau" ⟶ "Eau vive," in its ancient form "Aiguevive." The path shows a visual marking also: the final line bears above it the typographic alternation of the preceding lines, placed on one side and the other, so many steps of the dance led up the mountain, as in the little town of Buis-les-Baronnies, the lime-blossom harvest calls for festival.

> une vallée ouverte
> > une côte qui brille
> un sentier d'alliance
>
>   .   .   .   .   .   .   ,   .   .   .
>
> > > ont envahi la ville
> où la libre douleur est sous le vif de l'eau.[i] (NP,27)

The following poem, "Faction du muet," finds a more concentrated expression as if the ellipses visible between the elements in the poem of the dance were to be absorbed again under the surface. Individual sentiment yields to a feeling both collective and continuous: "Je me suis uni au courage de quelques êtres, j'ai vécu violemment, sans vieillir, mon mystère au milieu d'eux, j'ai frissonné de l'existence de tous les autres, comme une barque incontinente au-dessus des fonds cloisonnés. / I have joined in the courage of a few beings, have lived violently, without growing older, my mystery in their midst, I have trembled at the existence of all the others like an incontinent boat above the partitioned

---

dowsed she takes us aboard. / . . . / The travelling host while we believe in her truth. (JG)

[i] an open valley / a gleaming coast / a path of assent / have invaded the town / where free pain is under the quick of the water. (JG)

depths." (NP,28) This boat, not watertight and still continuing in time, will transport the poet and his chosen fellow
passengers—whom an isolated destiny does not prevent from
sharing the common work—above temporal discontinuity
and the fragmentation of separate existences.

The title poem describes the raging night wind, a natural
fury attacking the mind and the body, unclothing the chosen
beings for a spiritual bareness like that of the doomed and
magnificent bird. "Le Nu perdu" seems a descendant of those
ancestors scratching with a flint on the walls of their caves
the story of the struggles we call primitive, marking out our
history too with notches and signs we cannot understand,
"l'entaille et le signe" of their language, the source of our
own, as they lift to the rim of the well the bucket of "ralliement," a potential restoring force, causing the ripples to spread
outward in a "flowering circle," (NP,31) toward the poem
itself. The downy softness of the dark ("duvet de nuit noire")
protects them in their mystery as it protects each star and
every poet after his naked exposure in a primitive ritual by
that cavern fire: "Enchemisé dans les violences de sa nuit."
He will be reclothed by the stars reflected like the flowers of
the well's waters in its own green blackness, intermittent in
their flash as the projections from Char's poetry are intermittent.

The circle spreading outward—like the wedding ring in
"Dansons aux Baronnies" or like a rose blooming wider and
wider—around the water as it is lifted, repeats the generosity
and the gesture in the poem "Yvonne," directly preceding it.
The mortal risk conveyed by the image of the recumbent
water ("l'eau gisante") will never again be absent from the
poems making their way upstream from this source:

. . . .

Qui a creusé le puits et hisse l'eau gisante
Risque son coeur dans l'écart de ses mains.[j][7] (NP,30)

---

[j] Whoever has dug the well and raises recumbent water / Risks his
heart in the disjoining of his hands. (JG)

[7] In one of the Sonnets to Orpheus, Rilke allies the water of re-
covery and the flower with the touch of girls' hands: "Blumen, ihr

273

The cycle of water we are following responds both to the cycle of fountains and springs previously described and to the widening circle left by the lifted bucket; it is climaxed by a poem whose optimistic title suggests the rebirth of the waters themselves; here, the waters of springtime increase in their resurgence:

"AIGUEVIVE"

La reculée aux sources. . . .
Revers des sources: pays d'amont, pays sans biens, hôte pelé, je roule ma chance vers vous.
M'étant trop peu soucié d'elle, elle irriguait, besogne plane, le jardin de vos ennemis. La faute est levée.[k]
(NP,35)

The return upstream from the spring and the source of language in its profusion is chosen in large part for its difficulty and for the meagerness of the resources it procures; this "pays sans biens" and this "hôte pelé" having the ascetic bareness of the marginal being, of a famished wolf, an ambiguous snake, or of the "badly clothed birds" in "Dans mon pays. . . ." The upstream country, like a land stripped bare, will be irrigated only by the rarest water; its spiritual lot is cast upward, like that of Sisyphus. Refusal of the uphill task would enforce the ease of a "besogne plane," a moral reduction parallel to that which men accept once the enigma is exposed, its serpentine coils released, its circle opened out-

---

schliesslich den ordnenden Händen verwandte, / (Händen der Mädchen von einst und jetzt), / . . . / wartend des Wassers, das sie noch einmal erhole / aus dem begonnenen Tod. . . . // Flowers, kin in the end to those arranging hands, / (girls' hands of then and now) / . . . / awaiting the water that once more was to recover you / from death already begun. . . ." (SO,82-83) Understood in the title of Char's play "Le Soleil des eaux" is also this curing illumination for the ills of a suffering, in the frequent association of the two elements.

[k] The going back to sources. . . . / Reverse of the springs: land of upstream, meager land, stark host, I roll my fortune toward you. Since I cared too little for her, she watered, level task, the garden of your enemies. The fault has been lifted.

ward. But by the more difficult choice, the dead waters of the *terre gaste* will change to quick and living waters: "revers des sources."

The real town of Aiguesmortes and its "dead waters" are present only by suggestion, transformed into the living waters of "aiguevive" when the choice is made, against the current. The undefined fault is removed, lifted like the pail of water itself, by virtue of the difficult upstream tasks assumed. "I speak, a man without original sin, on a present land." (RBS, 151) And from now on, the texts will be the stations of ascent for the lifting of this fault.

6. *Steps*

The first poem reached on the upward way offers a particular severity for the poet, materially destitute like the wolf, furtive like the snake—"on exile une lyre" ("Déshérence," NP,44). He has attained his vertical deliverance:

"Le Village Vertical"

Tels des loups ennoblis
Par leur disparition,
Nous guettons l'an de crainte
Et de libération.[1] (NP,36)
. . . . . .

Under a future said to be snarling with a menace far greater than his own, the animal in exile awaits the possible fullness of an "amplitude d'amont," moral rather than material.

The text transcends its exterior references, such as the "loups" (the young inexperienced fighters of the Maquis), the fear and the "liberation" of the time of the Resistance. Although the initial framework leaves room for this image of snow-covered wolves, the vertical village takes on a definite metaphysical cast, regardless of all the "villages perchés" in Provence and even of the "village of birds" passing high above, exulting in the poem "Conduite." These parallel lines

[1] Like the wolves ennobled / By their vanishing, / We lie in wait for the year of / Dread and liberation. (JG)

add to, but are not essential to, the poem, whose reach is never limited by its origin.

Only this naked, essential upland permits the joining of extreme perspectives: "Nous savons que les Choses arrivent / Soudainement, / Sombres ou trop ornées. / We know that things do happen // Suddenly, / Sombre or too ornate." (NP, 36) (JG) But one might see them together, in a union exemplified by a wooded valley where a green water flows in a rocky silence—a contrast striking in the title *L'Effroi la joie*, and subtle in the image of two roses linked by a ring in "Jugement d'octobre," the next poem. The two countries of downstream and upstream, or uphill and down, like two covers of a bed, or two slopes of a mountain, are henceforth met in a radiant arch, visible to the "future" eyes of a poet setting out on this vertical road:

Le dard qui liait les deux draps
Vie contre vie, clameur et mont,
Fulgura.[m] [8]

Thus the sting of the frontier bee in his mediating task returns with the amplified song of the bird or the poet, in this concluding line, pointed, dazzling like a flash or a dart, against the slow preparation of the future. "Lenteur de l'avenir" begins with the warning: "Il faut escalader beaucoup de dogmes et de glace pour jouer de bonheur et s'éveiller rougeur sur la pierre du lit. / You have to scale many dogmas and a mountain of ice to happen on good luck and awaken, a blush on bed rock." (NP,38)

This country deprived of all riches but sun, rock, and wind

---

[m] The dart joining both sheets together / Life against life / clamor and mountain, / Flashed. (JG)

[8] Rilke describes a bird's cry in its joining of inner and outer realities: "He remembered the hour . . . when, both outside and within him, the cry of a bird was correspondingly present, did not, so to speak, break upon the barriers of his body, but gathered inner and outer together into one uninterrupted space, in which, mysteriously protected, only one single spot of purest, deepest consciousness remained." (DE,125)

prepares itself slowly for sunrise as well as for night and death, its path already marked with mortuary signs:

. . . .

Cet obstacle *pour le vent* où échouait ma pleine force, quel était-il? Un rossignol me le révéla, et puis une charogne.

La mort dans la vie, c'est inalliable, c'est répugnant; la mort avec la mort, c'est approchable, ce n'est rien, un ventre peureux y rampe sans trembler.[n] (NP,38)

. . . .

A passage scaling upward has been prepared by two major images of linking: a boat passing timeless above temporally partitioned depths, and the repeated homage paid to the bee joining borders. Elsewhere, the vigorous rejection of compartments is seen as a stride outward past the walls of a closed dwelling: "sans solennité, je franchis ce monde muré. . . . / Without solemnity, I crossed this walled-up world." (NP,46)

This entire rampart of poems, whose intensity and breadth combine the "lenteur de l'avenir" with the "amplitude d'amont," opens the way for the succeeding series: *Contre une maison sèche* and *Aromates chasseurs*. It becomes clear that no definitive stopping-point is to be reached on the peaks. Even the vertical village, no less a text than an image, is to be traversed (NP,36). In the latter poem, the hunter who is at once the wolf "enneigé" with a snowy pelt, a snow-capped peak, or a foam-crested wave—in a convergence of mountain and sea, reminding us of "Fastes"—is both murderer and victim, guilty and innocent, even "ennobled," since the fault has been effectively erased, for us all. The twin fates of the animal and the poet meet in exile, according to the "portrait pensif" of the wolf in the poem "Déshérence." (NP,44) Yet a trace of guilt remains, like the trace of the claw scratched

[n] This obstacle *for the wind* where my full strength failed, what was it? A nightingale revealed it to me, and then a carcass. / Death in life can admit of no alloy, it is repugnant; death with death can be approached, is nothing, a cowardly stomach crawls over it without trembling.

across the conscience and across the barren mountain swept by the night wind of the Mont Ventoux. In the poem, a house is half-opened at nightfall, and in this house there is a fault of construction, disguised as if under a mask of black velvet, that other sense of the word "loup" here associated with the "down of black night" confronting the "man naked and lost."[9] Pursued and pursuing, the hunter speaks of the path that continues: "Notre figure terrestre n'est que le second tiers d'une poursuite continue, un point, amont. / Our earthly face is only the second third of a continuous pursuit, a point, upstream."

7. *Juncture by the Hand*

At this moment there begins what might be seen as another cycle of the hand, repeating, as does the circle of water, an earlier one. These images of work and of nourishment lie at the very basis of Char's most active poetry. A human palm makes a poor and touching canvas, where the story of a humble life is read in all its various traces, accompanied by the inescapable presence of death. In "Le Banc d'ocre," the hand opens and exposes itself, like the already recumbent prey of the poet, who has now become reader and interpreter in his turn: "Tu ouvris ta main et m'en montras les lignes. Mais la nuit s'y haussait. Je déposai l'infime ver luisant sur le tracé de vie. Des années de gisant s'éclairèrent soudain sous ce fanal vivant et altéré de nous. / You opened your hand and showed me its lines. But night was rising there. I laid the tiny glowworm on the line of life. Years of recumbency lit up suddenly under that living lantern thirsty for us." (JG) Those ochre slopes, like Roussillon's cliffs, whose red is more visible still in the setting sun, mark the hand or the poem with a definite hue. The glowworm like a luminous line of poetry ["vers luisant"] lights up once more the rosy trace on the cheek or the trail left by the bleeding animal across

[9] See *Lettera amorosa* (Gallimard, 1953): "Lunes et nuit, vous êtes un loup de velours noir, village, sur la veillée de mon amour." (Quoted in *Exposition Georges Braque/René Char.*)

278

the rock—as if a poem stressing personal pronouns could be the least sentimental and most reserved. In "Faim rouge," a quiet death ["fin"] takes for its own gentle sorrow the silencing gesture Char associates with Heraclitus, an act of sharing in understatement:

.   .   .   .

Tu mourus, un doigt devant ta bouche,
Dans un noble mouvement,
Pour couper court à l'effusion;
Au froid soleil d'un vert partage.

Tu étais si belle que nul ne s'aperçut de ta mort.
Plus tard, c'était la nuit, tu te mis en chemin avec moi.°
(NP,40-41)

.   .   .   .

Moreover, the *vert partage* bears in this case all the force of division as well as of sharing: it is the color of hope and resurgence, all the while suggesting the ambiguous division inflicted by the poem as agent ["un vers partage"], the two readings converging like the memory of green water tracing in the heart the most profound valleys of its secret and common destiny, from "Médaillon" to "Tracé sur le gouffre."

A summit of this cycle and perhaps even of the entire path called *Retour amont* is composed of only one sentence.

"LUTTEURS"

Dans le ciel des hommes, le pain des étoiles me sembla ténébreux et durci, mais dans leurs mains étroites je lus la joute de ces étoiles en invitant d'autres: émigrantes du pont encore rêveuses; j'en recueillis la sueur dorée, et par moi la terre cessa de mourir.ᵖ (NP,43)

° You died, a finger held before your mouth, / In a noble motion, / To cut effusion short; / In the cold sun of a green sharing. // You were so lovely that no one perceived your death. / Later it was night, you started out with me. (The title applies also to the Resistance.)

ᵖ In the sky of men, the stars' bread seemed to me shadowy and hardened, but in their narrow hands I read the joust of these stars

Joining stars and men, celestial joust and earthly travail in a gesture heroic yet infinitely simple, the sentence-image has its origin in the sky of men. Conversely, the lowliest symbol of human toil is raised to the noblest level, as this radiant bread is shadowed with care like the forehead of man, shares the hardness of his hand. Dense in form like "Le Mortel partenaire," which it resembles in its theme, "Lutteurs" bears within its title a phonetic recall of the lute ["luth"], the partner of the *lyre* in the early pages of this essay. The text read in these hands—as fate in the guise of a glowworm is read from the text of a hand in the poem "Le Banc d'ocre"—integrates a stellar with a terrestrial landscape. And by the image of sweat, this text is joined to its brother, "Le Mortel partenaire" in its own struggle: the two poems are, more than mortal partners sharing the same destiny, witnesses of an incorruptible existence. Each is heavily creased by the weight of a work, equivalent to the signs cut into the wall by the artists of Lascaux or of Font-de-Gaume; each is finally as bare of ornament and as deeply incised. Some of the anonymous and heroic beings invoked at the conclusion of the earlier text will reappear in the pages of the *Nu perdu*: these are, as in those poems of an earlier epoch, "extravagant" and extreme beings, from whose number the immigrant workers of "Lutteurs" are not excluded, nor the heroes of *Artine*.

The conclusion of "Le Mortel partenaire" was added after the first draft of the poem, and intensively *worked*, as we have seen: a sign of its importance for the poet and also for us.

Certains êtres ont une signification qui nous manque. Qui sont-ils? Leur secret tient au plus profond du secret même de la vie. Ils s'en approchent. Elle les tue. Mais l'avenir qu'ils ont ainsi éveillé d'un murmure, les devinant, les crée. O dédale de l'extrême amour![q] (LM,122)

---

calling others: emigrants from below deck still dreaming; I gathered their golden sweat, and through me the earth ceased to die.

[q] Certain beings have a meaning which escapes us. Who are they? Their secret dwells in the depths of the very secret of life. They approach it. It kills them. But the future which they have thus awakened

To this exalted portrait of exceptional beings another answers, whose setting is no longer that of a primordial struggle but rather, of a moral and psychological isolation.

> Quelque êtres ne sont ni dans la société ni dans une rêverie. Ils appartiennent à un destin isolé, à une espérance inconnue. Leurs actes apparents semblent antérieurs à la première inculpation du temps et à l'insouciance des cieux. Nul ne s'offre à les appointer. L'avenir fond devant leur regard. Ce sont les plus nobles et les plus inquiétants.[r] (NP,64)

Thus the poetic work they serve, in its return upland, is illumined by an unfailing and anterior light: "non-fautive" and disquieting. It is signaled by the image of the rainbow, suggested in "Lutteurs" and evident in "Le Requin et la mouette," Char's most celebrated poem of correspondence: "Ô vous, arc-en-ciel!" (FM,190) In "Lutteurs," human sweat is given the luster of gold, as it is transfigured into the liquid of stars: through this alchemical liquid, the "last blood" and the "first loam" (mixed in advance by the horn of the moon) will join history to harvest, the past of men and the sky's future, as a rainbow ("arc-en-ciel") joins all within its reach.

Finally, from the working hand to the hand linked with the heart: "Le Gaucher" (The Lefthanded) opposes bodily weakness to emotional strength. As the next-to-last poem of *Retour amont*, the fragile moment directly precedes the highest point. But placed in the emphatic title position, the image of the ordinarily weaker becomes a source of strength to the marginal being, so that this hand protecting from nothing, neither ravine nor thorns, clarifies the mortal peril and the

---

with a murmur, finding them out, creates them. Oh labyrinth of extreme love!

[r] A few beings are neither in society nor in a state of dreaming. They belong to an isolated fate, to an unknown hope. Their open acts seem anterior to time's first inculpation and to the skies' unconcern. It occurs to no one to employ them. The future melts before their gaze. They are the noblest and the most disquieting.

privilege of a chosen companionship: "where we are increased." The sharing of fragility and strength makes a fitting culmination to the poems of forging and of bread-making, of guiding and of mediating, all the while keeping the silence initially promised: "On ne se console de rien lorsqu'on marche en tenant une main, la périlleuse floraison de la chair d'une main . . . cette main préférée à toutes, nous enlève a la duplication de l'ombre, au jour du soir. / You find consolation in nothing when you walk with a hand in yours, the perilous flowering of a hand's flesh . . . this hand preferred to all others, removes us from the duplication of shadow, from the evening's day." (NP,47)

Shadow, like an evening of daytime, is transmuted into its contrary, this day risen higher than twilight, through the poet's command to the sun: "Je dirai: 'Monte' au cercle chaud. / To the hot circle I shall say: 'Rise,' " (NP,45)

At present, the entire series of poems has mounted the slope of the return, "to the evening's day."

8. *Upland*

In the last poem, the land that should have been lost at sunset is rediscovered. The sun rises to join the supposed absence to the real presence. What has been crumpled in the setting agony of a red sky ("froissé son seuil d'agonie") reappears intact, to merge all slopes in a path upland:

"L'Ouest derrière soi perdu"

L'ouest derrière soi perdu, présumé englouti, touché de rien, hors-mémoire, s'arrache à sa couche elliptique, monte sans s'essoufler, enfin se hisse et rejoint. Le point fond. Les sources versent. Amont éclate. Et en bas le delta verdit. Le chant des frontières s'étend jusqu'au belvédère d'aval. Content de peu est le pollen des aulnes.[8] (NP, 48)

[8] The west lost behind you, assumed to have been engulfed, affected by nothing, out of memory, breaks away from its elliptical bed, rises without losing breath, hoists itself up at last and joins again. The point melts. The springs pour out. Upland bursts forth. And below, the delta turns green. The frontier song reaches to the vantage point of downstream. Easily contented is the alders' pollen.

Seen from above, the brevity of the flash would correspond
to its rapid verbal expression, extreme in its taut compactness: "Le point fond. Les sources versent. Amont éclate."
The force of the sun's hot circle is absorbed in the ardor and
the abundance of the verbs, from the point of view of those
noble and disquieting beings before whose gaze the future
is said to melt. "Être du bond":[10] for the observer who has
been chosen to see, and by the light of that "anticipatory
force" of which Heidegger speaks (QM,164), a temporal and
spatial compression will correspond to the grammatical compression and ellipsis discussed above in connection with this
triple statement. From the summit, like a final parapet, high
above the rampart of twigs, the countryside is seen, renascent
in a "greening delta."

A complete landscape can be glimpsed in the two words
of one simple sentence, which makes a poetic observation
of the first order: "amont éclate." Here at the highest point
of an upstream "éclatant," the lightning flash and a brilliant
vision coincide in a meeting of outer spectacle and inner perspective. The momentary flash, summit of the poetic vision,
discovers, corresponds, illumines, and endures.[11] To return

[10] Compare, with this implicit procedure of making a verb into a
noun while keeping it a verb, the parallel procedure of making a
noun of an adjective: in one of the manuscripts of *La Bibliothèque
est en feu* (no. 792, AE-IV-29) there is an asterisk after the word
"profond" in the following sentence: "Enfin toute la vie (la vie
heureuse, le rare délice), l'éclair sincère, quand j'arrache la douceur
de ta vérité amoureuse à ton profond!" Here the punctuation draws
attention to discretion, yet also to suggestion. But in the Gallimard
edition of 1951 we read: "à ton profond."

[11] Plato attributes an astonishment (*thaumadzein*) to the "pathos"
characteristic of the philosopher; Descartes speaks, in the *Traité des
passions*, of admiration; but it is Heidegger who gives to the word
"astonishment" or "amazement" an unusual weight incontrovertibly
justified in this poetry. For he shows the relation of this attitude
to those of suffering, waiting, bearing, enduring, letting oneself be
carried away: "In astonishment we are made to halt. . . . Astonishment, while it is a drawing back and a ceasing, is at the same time
pulled towards and so to speak enchained by that before which it
retreats." (QP,44-45)

Heidegger speaks in particular of responding to a call of something
beyond the conscious self, but which is at once the self, as if one
were summoned to one's own possibility. "The call dispenses with

upland is finally to return toward this height of irregular brilliance. The dweller of space summons his margins all about him once more in a visual condensation, as if the "mental habitation" had been finally attained, as if the lost town of Aerea had been found again.

---

any kind of utterance. It does not put itself into words at all. . . . *Conscience discourses solely and constantly in the mode of keeping silent.* In this way it not only loses none of its perceptibility, but forces the Dasein which has been appealed to and summoned, into the reticence of itself." (BT,318) The notion of correspondence, on which much of Char's work relies, means, according to Heidegger's essay on philosophy, "to be summoned and to be disclosed"; in *Sein und Zeit*, he says of "disclosedness" that it is "constituted by state-of-mind, understanding, and discourse, and pertains equiprimordially to the world, to Being-in, and to the Self." (*Being and Time*, London, SCM Press, 1963, tr. MacQuarrie and Robinson.)

To show us what links thought and poetry in the correspondence of one summons and one unique language ("this corresponding is saying") Heidegger explains: "Correspondence which . . . speaks according to the being of being-here ("L'être de l'étant") this is philosophy. . . . Between . . . thought and poetry, there reigns a kinship in the depths of being, because both give themselves to the service of language and expend themselves for it." (QP,48) (See also EB, 391, on the guardianship of language.) But, and here Heidegger quotes Hölderlin, poetry and philosophy "dwell near to one another on mountains farthest apart." But in Hölderlin's *Patmos*, the context is different: "Und die Liebsten nahe wohnen, ermattend auf / Getrenntesten Bergen. . . ." (FH,478) Yet within this *correspondence*, thus within a still broader context, the image stands true, and is strengthened by the eagles and the mountain bridges, by the water and the traversal: "Im Finstern wohnen / Die Adler, und furchtlos gehn / Die Söhne der Alpen über den Abgrund weg / Auf leichtgebaueten Brüken. / Drum, da gehäuft sind rings, um Klarheit, / Die Gipfel der Zeit, / Und die Liebsten nahe wohnen, ermattend auf / Getrenntesten Bergen, / So gieb unschuldig Wasser, / O Fittige gieb uns, treuesten Sinns / Hinüberzugehn und wiederzukehren. // In gloomy places dwell / The eagles, and fearless over / The chasm walk the sons of the Alps / On bridges lightly built. / Therefore, since round about are heaped, around clearness, / The summits of Time, / And the most loved live near, growing faint / On mountains most separate, / Give us innocent water, / O pinions give us, with minds most faithful / To cross over and to return." (FH,478-479) Here the themes of innocence and clarity, of water "without fault" and mountain chasms, of crossings and bridges already meet within the heights and chasms of this other poetry. About these distant peaks, between which separate flashes may be intercepted like signals linking two stars in the same constellation, Heidegger quotes Aristotle on the "flash of ap-

In conclusion, the barren trees seen at the outset are themselves refertilized, modestly sufficing after the abundant "dowry": "Content de peu est le pollen des aulnes. / Easily contented is the alder's pollen."

B. DANS LA PLUIE GIBOYEUSE

Là, nous ne souffrirons plus rupture. . . .

(NP,51)

To the anguished question opening this collection of poems, like a *memento mori*, "where shall we spend our days at present?" the title poem responds: "Let us stay in the quarried rain and knot our breath to it." (NP,51) The quarry here is the hunter's prey, and our own. The breathing of *Le Marteau sans maître*, aggressive and liberating, is now that

---

pearance" (QP,51) and refers us to his own *Sein und Zeit* (section 78) concerning the concept of Logos. Finally the true sense of the instantaneous flash is explained, as it reveals an element in its togetherness ("Beisammen") with another, thus *discovering* it in its appearance. Heidegger claims for man a "tendency toward seeing," as by a natural light ("lumen naturale"). What we call here the interior parapet is situated in the *disclosedness* of the world, and in the clarity of relations between seer and seen. Speaking of "Dasein," Heidegger explains: "To say that it is 'illuminated' ["erleuchtet"] means that *as* Being-in-the-world it is cleared ["gelichtet"] in itself, not through any other entity, but in such a way that it *is* itself the clearing." (BT, 171; see also BT,214) For the translations of Heidegger, we have used, where possible, those of Robinson and MacQuarrie just quoted. The translators explain, in a note to this passage: " 'Lichtung.' This word is customarily used to stand for a 'clearing' in the woods, not for a 'clarification'; the verb 'lichten' is similarly used. The force of this passage lies in the fact that these words are cognates of the noun 'Licht' ['light']." (BT,71) But in many cases Char's text has closer affinities with the French translation than with the German original: a case in point is the expression "parmi" in his essay on the artist Sima ("Je ne suis pas séparé; je suis parmi.") although Heidegger writes "sein bei," meaning simply "alongside of." In some cases, therefore, we refer to the French translations of Jean Beaufret rather than to the German original or to the translations in the Regnery edition, *Existence and Being* (Chicago, 1949), of "What is Metaphysics" and the two essays on Hölderlin. Thus the varied styles: our concern here is not with Heidegger, but rather with Char, for whose texts the "correspondences" are meant to serve as chorus and as backdrop.

of the pursuer and the pursued united in the sport, as the wolf of "Marmonnement" and the marginal poet are finally one, beyond the track and the pursuit. The contradiction lying at the center of this poetry will continue its conflict under the cover of a fertile storm renewed and renascent until the moment when the mortal partners in word and idea, "drinking at swollen springs . . . may fuse in an inexplicable loam." (NP,51) Thus the source is seen to engender the harvest.

The union between hunter and prey transports to another level of metaphor the opposed elements in convergence. The deathly and amorous conflict between poet and poem, those mortal enemies and partners often exchanging roles, is long. Boxing-ring, bed, prehistoric wall, closed alembic, hermetic page, mountainous landscape, stream, valley, and well of suffering, so many scenes where the same contradictory profiles pass, fraternally similar, in an order Char terms "hallucinated." (NP,54) A necessary ritual transcends the purely aesthetic for a deeper necessity: "L'art qui naît du besoin. . . ." (NP,109)

The grave narration is guided by a simple waterside plant, a "buveuse" (so-called for its inexhaustible thirst), implying the primary gesture of offering water, and the myth of a bacchante with "burned fingernails," as if the *soror* of the alchemists were to have her nails singed by too bright a flame from the work.[12] In the outward path of a "successive flowering," (NP,63) a clear margin is finally given to the epic gesture as it endures: "ce chant qui dure / Toute la nuit. . . . // this song lasting / The whole night long."

"TABLES DE LONGÉVITÉ"

En la matière sèche du temps qui avant de nous anéantir déjà nous décime, ceux qui ont donné la mort expient en

---

[12] We think of the burning fingers in Breton's first Surrealist Manifesto: "L'esprit . . . va, porté par ces images qui le ravissent, qui lui laissent à peine le temps de souffler sur le feu de ses doigts" (André Breton, *Manifestes du surréalisme*, Pauvert, 1962, p. 53). In the Kabbala, the fingers are burned to regenerate the life of the soul. My thanks to Anna Balakian for her information on this point.

donnant le bonheur, un bonheur qu'ils n'éprouvent ni ne partagent. Ils n'ont à eux que le feu d'un mot inaltérable courant dans le dos de l'abîme et mal résigné à la fantasque oppression. La balance d'airain consentirait-elle à les remettre à l'innocence, que l'hôte auquel ils appartiennent les distinguerait encore là, nus, destitués, fascinants, dans l'incapacité de jouir du mot virtuel.[t] (NP,61)

Through a conscious confession, the man of past violence, to whom there can remain at present nothing but the solemn, burning, and unchanging word, the man possessed by death—as in "Hôte et possédant" of *L'Effroi la joie*—works out his own preparation in the "dry matter of time" for the later meditation on the dry house that is at the end of the long path followed by the *Nu perdu*. The poet is to be counted among those few isolated and exceptional beings, ill at ease and disquieting, who appear in the texts of this period after the early figures who were no less disturbing. On the scales of justice a harsh sentence is meted out, by fate, to the man of past actions, strong in his verbal brutality and his moral ardor, henceforth incapable of sharing in happiness and in the common word. He will be silent. For each act accomplished, Zarathustra asked: "Is it hunger or abundance that is the creator here?" Hunger creates, in these texts, this terrible silence that delights in its own paradox.

The last flash of these "tables" is at once an exhortation and a reminder: it suggests a statue of Orpheus in lamentation, a composite figure with elements of the decapitated man-bird, of the snake and the angel: a being who fascinates. "Souvenez-vous de cet homme comme d'un bel oiseau sans tête, aux ailes tendues dans le vent. Il n'est qu'un serpent à

---

[t] *In the dry stuff of time that before annihilating us decimates us, those who have dealt death expiate by dealing happiness, a happiness they do not experience or share. They themselves have merely the fire of a resistant word running along the back of the abyss and imperfectly resigned to the whims of oppression. If the brazen balance did restore them to innocence, the host they belong to would pick them out still there, naked, destitute, casting a spell, incapable of enjoying the word's potential.* (JG)

genoux. / Remember this man as a fine bird with no head, its wings outstretched in the wind. He is only a kneeling serpent." (NP,62)

Although the snake returns to haunt these new fragments ("Mistrust me as I mistrust myself, for I am not without recoil"), the heroic isolation of the naked and enigmatic beings rivets the gaze. These uneasy beings struggle through the most difficult battles toward a triumph seized from the dark self. ("True victories are only won over a long period, one's forehead against the night.") This interior struggle takes place, as the title indicates, on the slope of a mental mountain. ("To walk in oneself," said Rilke. . . .)[13]

The harshness of the battle will be prolonged into the image of a "flint moon" in a following poem, where one quarter of the moon strikes against the next (NP,66) and, farther along the path, into the "torn sides" of a river within a mental dwelling falling into ruin.[14] (NP,69) The crumbling of this dwelling leads to the severest construction of the dry house, like a winter mountain one might scale, arduous, bare, and unchanging, similar to the spiritual habitation of "J'habite une douleur" or like the dwelling of the mind, lasting.[15]

[13] "Ce moment d'apparence vide, ce moment de tension où l'avenir vous pénètre est infiniment plus près de la vie que cet autre moment où il s'impose à nous du dehors, comme au hasard et dans le tumulte. Plus nous sommes silencieux, patients et recueillis dans nos tristesses, plus l'inconnu pénètre efficacement en nous. Il est notre bien. Il devient la chair de notre destinée. . . . Nous *sommes* solitude." Rilke, *Lettres à un jeune poete.* (Ed. Poètes d'aujourd'hui, 192-193) And again: "La grande solitude intérieure. Aller en soi-même, et ne rencontrer durant des heures personne—c'est à cela qu'il faut parvenir." (R,189) See also Valéry's "solitude portative."

[14] The title of this poem, "La Scie rêveuse," and its sister title, "Même scie," outdistance the simple pun by their symbolic extension: for the saw divides as this dense text is itself divided.

[15] From Hölderlin's "In Lieblicher bläue": "Voll Verdienst, doch dichterisch, wohnet der Mensch auf dieser Erde. / Full of acquirements, but poetically, man dwells on this earth." (FH,601) But this often-quoted statement—on which Heidegger bases part of his major essay on Hölderlin—comes precisely from the poem whose authenticity is most in doubt. See Hamburger (FH,612), on Wilhelm Waiblinger's novel *Phaeton* (1823), in which Waiblinger gives "a few pages

The lines of the two following texts demonstrate a contrast, the first one beginning with an infinite nocturnal word writing itself beyond us ("ce qui s'écrit hors de notre attention" NP,68) and the other, with the active daylight language, at first a quiet murmur, then openly flowering ("S'assurer de ses propres murmures et mener l'action jusqu'à son verbe en fleur" NP,69). The contraries converge, however, in a chiaroscuro[16] where two distinct elements remain intact, unalloyed, in a luminosity conjoining and penumbral. The texts could be said to be situated, according to the poet, as are the next two under discussion, "sur un même axe," where the components of twilight and threshold are seen to retain their difference even in their merging.

"Justesse de Georges de La Tour" (NP,73): we recognize again a flickering but sufficient candlelight coming from within the canvas. Our path not only through *La Nuit talismanique* but through all the deepest texts is ideally to be lit in such a fashion, as if all our meditations on silence, following the more fragmented although perhaps clearer ones on the word, were to have been guided by that image of Mary Magdalen, of her candle and her mirror. To each text so lit, and so shadowed, we might attribute the quality Char admires in Heraclitus and in de La Tour, who show us "what house a man should inhabit . . . at once a dwelling for the breath and meditation." (PNR,12) To approach one of Char's deeper poems is to renounce a diurnal clarity for a tormenting scene rich in shadings, to whose center only the fascination of an

---

from" the papers of the mad poet, which he may have adapted, adding and omitting.

16 From Hölderlin's *Hyperion*: "Meinem Herzen ist wohl in dieser Dämmerung. Ist sie unser Element, diese Dämmerung? Warum kann ich nicht ruhen darinnen?" (HSW). The question and response in echo would be the formal parallel to this duo and duel of the mortal and amorous couple: "Nous avions allongé puissamment le chemin. Ne menait nulle part. Nous avions multiplié les étincelles. Enfin où menait-il?" (NP,103) Such counterpoint plays on ellipsis and on litanic recall. On voice, dialogue, and echo: Mechthild Cranston, "René Char 1923-28: The Young Poet's Struggle for Communication," *PMLA* Jan., 1972.

impossible solution draws us. The poet sings no loud victory —the odes of this "fils de l'ode fervente" (NP,79) are among his briefest poems—but rather, in a muffled voice, the refusal to retreat from the realm of ambiguity into the straightforward light of day: "L'unique condition pour ne pas battre en interminable retraite était d'entrer dans le cercle de la bougie, de s'y tenir, en ne cédant pas à la tentation de remplacer les ténèbres par le jour et leur éclair nourri par un terme inconstant. // The unique condition for not admitting an interminable retreat was to enter the candle's circle, to keep therein, without succumbing to the temptation of replacing the shadows by daylight and their full flashing by an inconstant term." (NP,73)

In the other text situated on this same axis, "Ruine d'Albion," (NP,74) the poet declares himself to be in search of a site. We imagine it on an elevation: an interior dwelling lit by contemplation and rendered intact by silence. Correspondingly, we make our present way through these canvases and through this dwelling when possible, only by allusion to the first, where one flame and one glass of water serve as a corridor. Around this site, and these texts, we leave an untouched margin; if some of the exterior summits of Provence have been ruined by atomic installations, as in this title, at least the interior presence retains its indomitable mystery.

To the "peu dire" of a condensed poetry, there responds a "Jeu muet" (NP,75); beyond the phonic play on the "e muet," a mute letter or then a muted self ["je muet"], an allusion to Orion the hunter appearing in the modest guise of a flower ejecting its petals into the air, like so many arrows, or like the novae, bursting in their brilliance. Here the bee returns with his weapon, the animal figuration of man carrying the word in a quiver of arrows and transfigured into a celestial hunter: "La fleur des talus, / Le dard d'Orion / Est réapparu. // Flower of the roadside, / Orion's dart / Has reappeared." (JG) At this point the dynamism of the metaphoric voyage is stressed by a title of mechanical measurement, as if to connote the energy necessary to the climb.

290

"DYNE"[17]

Passant l'homme extensible et l'homme transpercé,
j'arrivai devant la porte de toutes les allégresses, celle du
Verbe descellé de ses restes mortels, faisant du neuf, du
feu avec la vérité, et fort de ma verte créance, je frappai.
Ainsi atteindras-tu au pays lavé et désert de ton défi. . . .
Mais qui eût parié et opté pour toi, des sites immémoriaux
à la lyre fugitive du père?[u] (NP,78)

Leaving the primitive cave, the scene of struggle between the
moral partners—the unnamed Beast transfixing the man-bird
mortally, as did the man-bird the bison—the poet, young in
his faith, makes from his "vert partage" a fresh credence,
green like a new sharing in spite of the millennial struggle:
"sa verte créance." Making a significant traditional gesture,
an assertion of commitment and hope, he knocks at the door
of the tomb beyond which there lies a country of challenge,
a Word newly washed. The individual quest, no longer a
mute or egotistic "je muet" or "jeu muet," is transformed into
a collective ritual, into an epic search for a language we might
all speak. "Thus will you attain": so the voyage is given
heroic direction, even certainty of outcome.

"Dyne" indicates a transposition of linguistic force, a conflict hammering—like another *Marteau sans maître*—one element against the other in an even-numbered rhythm, "père"
against ["pair"], father against peer, partners equal in the
arena of the page where a poetic wager is played out. Of
the page swept clean there are premonitions and echoes: for
instance, in the double poem of love and death called "Redoublement" (NP,80): "Le visage de la mort et les paroles

[17] The title, a unit of mechanical measure, indicates the force of
the water, its energy exactly measured.
[u] Passing man expandable and man pierced through, I arrived at the
door of all gladness, that of the Word unsealed from its mortal remains, making afresh, making fire from truth, and strong in my green
credence, I knocked. / Thus will you attain the cleansed and desert
country of your challenge. . . . But who would have wagered and
chosen for you, from the sites immemorial to the father's fugitive lyre?

de l'amour: la couche d'une plage[18] sans fin avec des vagues y précipitant des galets—sans fin. / Death's visage and love's language: the bed of a beach endless with waves throwing pebbles onto it—endlessly," (NP,80) and in the following collection a text whose title shows an obsession with the thought of death: "Couche." The title could indicate another bed ambivalent in its nuptial and mortuary repose, or it could be interpreted in the imperative, marking the reversal from the voyage out, from the times of psychological inclemency ("Nous restons gens d'inclémence") and intemperate weather, to the time of return: "L'heure est venue pour moi de rentrer, ô rire d'ardoise! dans un livre ou dans la mort." (NP,106) Elsewhere, "slate-quarrying tasks" summon the voyager home to set his roof in order, preparing against future inclemency.

And this shelter battered by the elements as well as by the injustice of men, this "abri rudoyé" (NP,81) of a house dry yet passing over the waters of time like the boat in "Faction du muet," will enclose both the falling rain and the interior prey, when the "quarried rain" is transferred into the mental dwelling of the poem itself. To the title image of the bed in the preceding poem, this other text of habitation responds, in a further doubling or "Redoublement"—in the landscape where we can always start afresh, this is only one of the duets [or "pairs"] opted for. The sentence of this poem falls ceaselessly, like rain pursuing its own fertile trace from a slender thread to a massive downpour: "De tout temps j'ai aimé sur un chemin de terre la proximité d'un filet d'eau

---

[18] Reminder of that maxim in *A une Sérénité crispée*, worked over, thought out, which began thus (no. 724, AE-IV-14): "Phares, tueurs d'hirondelles," to which the poet added, in a different color of ink: "cependant que la mer moutonne," which becomes (no. 726, AE-IV-14): "Phare, tueur d'hirondelles, alentour la mer moutonne, les rivages sont couchés. Moi qui veille te remercie de balayer ma page. (Exemple d'image jactée qui ne me satisfait pas. Je la rapporte pour *m'alerter*. Profit du phare!)" The three last words were added after the others. Although the entire section between parentheses, concerning the insufficiently worked image, was suppressed in the final publication, so that the watchfulness and the warning are finally interior, the work of the text remains to alert the reader also.

tombé du ciel qui vient et va se chassant seul et la tendre gaucherie de l'herbe médiane qu'une charge de pierres arrête comme un revers obscur met fin à la pensée. / From time immemorial I have loved on an unpaved road the proximity of a stream of water fallen from the heavens that comes and goes in pursuit of itself and the tender awkwardness of the single median grass that a weight of stones stops as a dark underside puts an end to thought." (NP,81) The poem seems one single description, a single phrase applicable to poet and to poem, each a dwelling harshly tried by the simple, that "éprouvante simplicité" given as a title to a poem in *La Nuit talismanique.* A major source of nourishment and illumination, the night "quenching and watering" (NT,11) forms the permanent but only half-visible background for the texts to come, for the candle and the river of *La Nuit talismanique,* where a glass of water induces the arrival of fire and encourages the stream running by, or "filante," and the parallel work streaking by, *l'oeuvre filante.*

The two final texts are placed like mortal partners, face to face in the volume of *Le Nu perdu,* whose title replies to the question implicit in each. In structure and in image, they are opposed and reciprocally perpetuating, not unlike the ancient flints called "bifaces" because they were made with two cutting edges, "à double trenchant"—these texts too are trenchant.

"Permanent invisible"

Permanent invisible aux chasses convoitées,
Proche, proche invisible et si proche à mes doigts,
Ô mon distant gibier la nuit où je m'abaisse
Pour un novice corps à corps.
Boire frileusement, être brutal répare.
Sur ce double jardin s'arrondit ton couvercle.
Tu as la densité de la rose qui se fera.[v] (NP,82)

[v] Coveted hunts enduring invisible, / Near, near invisible and so near my hand, / Oh my far-off prey the night where I stoop / For a novice wrestling. / To drink shivering, to be brutal restores you. / On this double garden arches your cover. / Yours is the density of the rose in its making.

"NI ÉTERNEL NI TEMPOREL"

Ô le blé vert dans une terre qui n'a pas encore
sué, qui n'a fait que grelotter! A distance heureuse
des soleils précipités des fins de vie. Rasant sous la
longue nuit. Abreuvé d'eau sur sa lumineuse couleur. Pour garde et pour viatique deux poignards
de chevet: l'alouette, l'oiseau qui se pose, le corbeau,
l'esprit qui se grave.ʷ (NP,83)

The seven lines of the left page, opening by a verbalized
adjective, are reflected in the seven lines on the right, as if in
a mirror image or then a double garden, referred to in the
text. The garden has the tranquillity of new springtime wheat
before the summer sweat, corresponding to a heated struggle
between a distant prey and a partner close by, a hand-to-
hand fight become a ritual as noble as it is primitive. Under
the cover of night a restorative water saves the being at fault
from his fault, as his brutality restores him to his innocence,
within the mortally luminous cruelty of this poem, partaking
still of the strength of the Lascaux beast and of his human
partner. By a traditional gesture of drinking: "Boire frileusement," a former celebration returns: ". . . admis dans le
verbe frileux." An ardent struggle refreshes itself by the chill
of the water and of the word, an interior spring whose sound
is muffled, difficult to recognize at moments.

"The spirit engraving itself" chisels its own inscription
deeply into the tomb wall, giving a new substance to the
stone. "Fer" and "faire," the two daggers of the double combat, cross and unite above the double bed of death and erotic
undoing described earlier in this series ("Tradition du météo-
ore," NP,71-72) where there is a somber reminder of the
catastrophe as the source of the oriole's poem and the blade

ʷ Oh the green wheat in earth which has not yet sweated, which
has only shivered! At a fortunate distance from the precipitated suns
of life ends. Sparse under the long night. Watered on its luminous
color. For guard and viaticum two swords for the bedside: the lark, the
bird who settles, the crow, the spirit engraving itself.

294

of his song stabbing together the mortal partners on their tragic bed: "L'epée de son chant ferma le lit triste, / The sword of his song closed the sad bed," (FM,33).

"Tradition du Météore"

. . . .

Pale chair offerte
Sur un lit étroit.

Aigre chair défaite,
Sombre au souterrain.[x] (NP,71-73)

. . . .

Nevertheless the garden reappears, not of paradise, but rather the reminder of the long friendship between the poet and those with whom he chooses to walk: "Les compagnons dans le jardin." Will not every faithful reader be also possessed? A double garden and a double tomb where the flash, finally transfigured, nourishes a simple blossom even in the sharp angle of its sounds (as in the quadruple "i" of the line itself): "Qui convertit l'aiguillon en fleur arrondit l'éclair. / Who changes the sting to a flower rounds off the flash." (NP,55) From cave to garden to grave, a mortal combat forms the poem.

C. CONTRE UNE MAISON SÈCHE

Mentons en espoir à ceux qui nous mentent: que l'immortalité inscrite soit à la fois la pierre et la leçon. (NP,79)

Typographically, this series of texts is presented on two levels: the upper one serves as a starting point, a statement to be examined, and the lower, set in italics—is its echo, its elaboration, or its interrogation: "l'examen." The dry house itself, perhaps one of the ancient "bories" in Provence—a dwelling made of stones without mortar, set together in a dry

---

[x] Pale flesh tendered / On a narrow bed. // Sour flesh surrendered, / Sink below ground. (JG)

295

season and watertight in the rain—is also the poem. These stones will hold in the absence of any mediating element, their own integral coherence keeping them joined. Thus an evident relation with Char's own texts, constructed in a series of *pierres-éclair* like an extraordinary archipelago whose elements hold only because of the interior identity and cohesion of their separate fragments, each summoning the others toward a collective response. Since the houses are of a thicker construction toward the top, their form might have inspired that of these double texts, where the upper line dominates, occasionally by its length, but more often by its density. After the initial draft, the echoing texts were added to the first ones, whose answer they become in the time of reading as well as in that of writing. The thematic relationship between the two textual levels, frequently ambivalent, is finally seen to be necessary, for the second texts are like the fruits quenching the thirst of the tree from which they come—an image which is found in the first flat stone or illuminating summit ("sommet éclairant"), the keystone of this series. These magnet-words, "des mots-aimants," attract the gaze, to guide the thought:

> S'il te faut repartir, prends appui contre une maison sèche. . . .
> *Levé avant son sens, un mot nous éveille, nous prodigue la clarté du jour, un mot qui n'a pas rêvé.*[y] (NP,115)

The voyage begins once more, explicitly, and maintains a rapid pace. The distances between its stages may appear insurmountable at times; a singular suggestion moves to the potentially plural realization, so that the reading must leap over or burn the space between the two: "Espace couleur de pomme. Espace, brûlant compotier. / Space apple-colored. Space, burning fruit-dish." (NP,116) What is lacking within the exiguous space of this text is the substantial presence of

[y] If you must set out again, prop yourself against a dry house. . . . / *Risen before its meaning, a word wakes us, lavishes on us the brightness of day, a word that has not dreamed.* (All translations of *Contre une maison sèche* by JG). Cf. also AC,22.

the apple. It is suggested; subsequently, this suggestion is multiplied by all the possibilities within its ideal or potential container, although the contained is not actually in sight. The answering text comments exactly on the abruptness of the leap with a description applicable in varying measure to all the explosive effects of condensation and ellipsis, most apparent for the observer of the "anticipatory forward thrust" of which Heidegger speaks (QM,161): "*Aujourd'hui est un fauve. Demain verra son bond. / Today is a wild beast. Tomorrow will see its leap.*" (NP,116) The conceptual space between the suggestions is thus marked out in time itself, becoming a reservoir of an energy accumulated at high tension, proper to the "Être du bond." (FM,138)[19] The texts are written "against a dry house," leaning on its walls, as the second text leans against and is a reflection of the first, or as a climber leans against the side of the mountain, itself another and more monumental "maison sèche." But they are also written against a mortal partner, as if their vitality were to challenge even the dryness of the tomb.

Profiting from the lessons of pruning so well learned and practiced in *Le Marteau sans maître, Contre une maison sèche* is compact in the extreme. Nevertheless, an epic impulse is revealed in the theme, and in the development of these texts, which themselves stretch out by additions on the proofs or after:[20]

[19] In Rilke's First Duino Elegy, this "être du bond" finds a correspondent: "Ist es nicht Zeit, dass wir liebend / uns vom Geliebten befrein und es bebend bestehn: / wie der Pfeil die Sehne besteht, um gesammelt im Absprung / mehr zu sein als er selbst. Denn Bleiben ist nirgends. // Is it not time that, in loving, / we freed ourselves from the loved one, and, quivering, endured: / as the arrow endures the string, to become, in the gathering out-leap, / something more than itself? For staying is nowhere." (DE,22-23)

[20] No. 830 (AE-IV-7bis). This manuscript carries other variants important for the conclusion, which slowly rises toward a lyric summit. The definitive version eliminates a commentary on the "dimensions" sharing their fruits, like another version of the fruit bowl in its explosion of colors mixing in the August heat, and of the dimensions traversed by the summer and in the convergence of love. The eliminated sentence is between parentheses: "Une simplicité s'ébauche:

1° (original version): N'émonde pas la flamme,
n'écourte pas la braise en son printemps.
Ordonne un peu de vie future là où tu n'es
pas parvenu.

2° (modified) N'émonde pas la flamme, n'écourte
pas la braise en son printemps. Les migrations,
par les nuits froides, ne s'arrêteraient pas
à ta vue.

3° (added later) Nous éprouvons les insomnies
du Niagara et cherchons des terres émues,
des terres propres à émouvoir une nature à
nouveau enragée.

4° (added still later as the second text, a supporting
wall) *Le peintre de Lascaux, Giotto, Van Eyck,
Uccello, Fouquet, Mantegna, Cranach, Carpaccio,
Georges de La Tour, Poussin, Rembrandt, laines de
mon lit rocheux*[z] (NP,123)

The italicized commentary includes the chosen ancestral lineage for the mountain poet, who builds a marginal lair, of
difficult access. From his elevation, the view now takes more
within its reach, of the past and, implicitly, of the future.

This increasing range is accompanied by a fierce refusal
of any opposition to a natural and irreducible force, requiring
its own space. "Nos orages nous sont essentiels. . . . / *On ne
peut se mesurer avec l'image qu'autrui se fait de nous, l'ana-*

---

le feu monte, la terre emprunte, la neige vole, la rixe éclate. (Aucun
n'a son terme en l'autre)." Cf. also Valéry's "fruits ennemis," at once
opposed and mutually sharing.

[z] 1° Don't prune the flame, don't curtail the ember in its springtime. Arrange a little future life where you haven't yet arrived. /
2° Don't prune the flame, don't curtail the ember in its spring-time.
The migrations, on cold nights, would not stop at the sight of you. /
3° We are going through the insomnias of Niagara and searching for
stirred lands, for lands fit to stir a nature once more enraged. /
4° *The Lascaux painter, Giotto, Van Eyck, Uccello, Fouquet, Mantegna, Cranach, Carpaccio, Georges de La Tour, Poussin, Rembrandt,
wools lining my rock nest.* (JG)

logie bientôt se perdrait. / Our storms are essential to us. . . .
/ *One cannot measure oneself with the image someone else
adopts of us, analogy would soon get lost.*" (JG) (NP,124)
Mortality reduces us: it must be "lived" nakedly. "Death,
in the largest sense of the word, is a phenomenon of life,"
explains Heidegger. (QM,133) One's own death (*eigenst*) is
uniquely appropriate to this individual: "being for death, this
being possessed absolutely in his own right."[21] (QM,145) The
"hôte et possédant," at once the guest possessing his host in
mortality, and the host possessing his own death, proper to
himself, is pure in his always absolute specificity; the "nu
perdu" lost and yet face to face with the steepest and most
naked of his interior mountains, may represent precisely this
extreme bareness, where nothing superfluous will ever again
have a place. Within the following sentence, from its variants
as from so many wool strands ("laines de mon nid rocheux")
left on the rocky land of the work, there appears finally one
single modest element endowed with a transforming power.
It is not immediately revealed against the stark background:

   1[o] Nous passerons du monde de la mort imaginée à celui
      de la mort vécue nûment.[22]

[21] In *Sein und Zeit,* Heidegger explains the crucial importance of
the consciousness of Being-towards-death, seen as waiting yet as actu-
ality. "To expect something possible is always to understand it and
to 'have' it with regard to whether and when and how it will be actually present-at-hand. Expecting is not just an occasional looking-away
from the possible to its possible actualization, but is essentially a
waiting for that actualization." And he comments further: "By the
very nature of expecting, the possible is drawn into the actual, arising out of the actual and returning to it. . . ." Anticipation turns
out to be the possibility of understanding one's *ownmost* and utter-
most potentiality-for-Being—that is to say, the possibility of *authentic
existence.* . . . Death is Dasein's *ownmost* possibility. Being towards
this possibility discloses to Dasein its *ownmost* potentiality-for-Being,
in which its very Being is the issue." (BT,306-307)
[22] On the same set of proofs we have just cited. Compare in Char's
"avant-poème" for Guy Levis Mano's *Loger la source* (Gallimard,
1971): "Soudain nous passâmes à l'effroi supérieur." And further
on in the same poem, there appears the theme of the passerby, a
poor and naked worker, in correspondence with the "rocky silence"
of this text: "En ce monde du ressentiment on nierait toute révélation

2° Nous passerons du monde da la mort conjecturée au travesti de la mort vécue nûment.

3° Nous passerons de la mort imaginée aux roseaux de la mort vécue nûment.[ax] (NP,125)

The reeds are linked by the most delicate thread of suggestion to the image of the "mint"—added in a final stage to the last sentence of the volume—and to the lavender, an image omnipresent in the inner landscape of these poems, as in Provence, their outer countryside. In the present text, these "reeds of death lived nakedly" bring several strands of illumination to the poem, in a convergence at the level of the deepest sensibility.

First there is a suggestion of fragility present in all the images associated with this one, which summarizes them all: "Oiseaux qui confiez votre gracilité, votre sommeil périlleux à un ramas de roseaux, le froid venu, comme nous vous ressemblons! / Birds confiding your gracefulness, your perilous sleep to a thatch of reeds once the cold has come, how like you we are!" (LM,148) A biblical resonance: what will be saved, in its innocence, because it has been hidden; and finally, a possible reminder of Ophelia, whose body is half-suggested in the poem "Septentrion" (a poem of the north, of the star, of a madness, and a bunch of reeds): "Je me suis promenée au bord de la Folie. . . . / La Folie se coiffait de longs roseaux coupants//I have been out walking on the bank of the Folie. . . . / The Folie wore in her hair long cut-

---

puisqu'on se refusait à imaginer quelque chose, quelqu'un, un Passant nu et outillé, de plus miraculeux que soi!" (pp. 8-9) Together, with a prediction of the bareness expressed in the title: *Le Nu perdu*, there appears a foreboding of Orion blinded: "Et qu'importe les yeux aveugles! / Il y a toujours un éclat de la fin qui affecte la naissance d'un successif commencement; / et c'est le plus indéchiffrable, et c'est, violent, le plus aimé!"

[ax] 1° We shall pass from the world of imagined death to death lived starkly. / 2° We shall pass from the world of conjectured death to the travesty of death lived starkly. / 3° We shall pass from imagined death to the reeds of death lived starkly.

ting reeds."[23] (NP,33) (JG) A Pascalian resonance is heard and not only in the reeds ("un roseau pensant"); for, here also, "les extrêmes se touchent": the contraries present in the following texts resemble trains always leaving in opposite directions from this central meeting-place. "Je suis né et j'ai grandi parmi des contraires tangibles à tout moment, malgré leurs exactions spacieuses et les coups qu'ils se portaient. Je courus les gares. / I was born and grew up among contraries tangible at every moment, for all their spacious exactions and the blows they gave each other. I haunted railway stations." (JG) (NP,126) Here the upper level of one construction finds its answer in the bottom level of the next one, as if leaving space for absorption or for meditation: *"Le oui, le non immédiats, c'est salubre en dépit des corrections qui vont suivre. / Immediate yes or no is healthy in spite of the corrections that will follow."* (JG) (NP,127)

The cutting edge of the text, this acute-angled flint, works *against* while leaning *on*. In this instant as of a lightning flash, its distinct profile stands out in relief against the white of the page, holding even in an inclement season. "L'éclair trace le présent, en balafre le jardin, poursuit sans assaillir, son extension, ne cessera de paraître comme d'avoir été. / The lightning tracks down the present, slashes its garden, chases, without assailing, its extension, will no more cease to appear than to have been." (JG) (NP,128) From the cave man or the inhabitant of the Ligurian "bories" to the future man we shall not know, the poet's word is pursued, whether in a dwelling of stone or of glass. The unrest of this work extends toward the most distant and the most poetically aroused of lands: "les terres émues."

The evident theme, on which the entire construction is based, reveals a single irony as cutting as its tragedy, that of life killing us through our living, by an erosion already present in the "Post-scriptum" of the cycle "Le Visage nuptial": "Dans la stupeur de l'air où s'ouvrent mes allées, / Le temps

[23] La Folie is a tiny stream near the river Sorgue: its name means madness.

émondera peu à peu mon visage. . . . // In the air's amazement where my ventures open, / Time will prune away my visage. . . ." The most destitute of conditions is preparatory to the definitive liberation of the "nu altérant" and of the emptiness to which alone he is answerable: "La liberté, c'est ensuite le vide, un vide à désespérément recenser. / Liberty, *next*, is emptiness, an emptiness to be desperately counted." (NP,118) (JG)

Accepting, even seeking, the gaping fault and the painful enigma, we might finally rejoin the radiant heart of a future severity: above all, we must return to bareness rather than perfection. (NP,130) After the dwelling is lost to our sight, its wall having ceased to send back the clairvoyant words in echo, the last text, dense and simple, is inscribed against the tomb. Like the fruit nourishing the tree where it appears, this product of all the past breaks with it, and the rupture lights a tragic future: "Tout ce que nous accomplirons d'essentiel à partir d'aujourd'hui, nous l'accomplirons faute de mieux. Sans contentement ni désespoir. Pour seul soleil: le boeuf ecorché de Rembrandt. / All we accomplish from today on, we shall accomplish for want of something better. Neither contentment, nor despair. Our only sun: Rembrandt's flayed ox." (JG) (NP,131) Without any absolute truth, we have only the choice of temporary certainties and emblems sufficiently violent to bear our conviction. The flayed ox reminds us of that other massacre in "Mirage des Aiguilles," compared to a treasure of meat-dealers stretched out. The butcher hidden in the self stalks from the pages of *Le Marteau sans maître* through the later texts to become finally the "hunter of himself," as the flayed animal inserts itself horribly in the individual consciousness. Many of the strongest texts have at their center a similarly shocking image: from the poem "Domaine" we remember the ox tongue turning at the center, dominant over the text, the dreadful and appropriate source for its linguistic energy. Later the language has a different control, and the personages of later poems pursue by a different rhythm

302

their differing goals. But that violent center remains, as if by choice. The rasping cruelty present in some of Char's poems calls for no commentary, begs no excuses, is, precisely, unpardonable as it chooses to be. (See for instance, "Assez creusé," LM,218.)

By contrast, a profound resignation, muffled and rarely evident, strikes us here: "faute de mieux." In the face of an absolute destiny, we have during the working out of our limited time only instruments whose strength is of an uncertain efficacy. We should permit ourselves no nostalgia for the age of the reindeer, when magic was possible: in a simple and touching homage Char renders to Picasso after his death, he explains—and not just so that we might understand the painter—the unique attitude possible for the creator: "To assure one's own morrow requires, in art, the brutalization of everything sacred, admitted or not. . . . Miracles are the fruit of an unbelieving attitude." As for knowledge, radiant but impotent, it imposes not a useless regret for the stone age, but rather a melancholic assurance: "Picasso felt himself sometimes a prisoner, but a prisoner with no jailer, of the perfect knowing which lends existence to sadness and melancholy. But never to nostalgia." (P) In Char's essay we hear an undeniable echo of that measured observation at the end of *Le Nu perdu*: "Neither contentment nor despair," so that the two moments remain joined. The rhythm of the alexandrine in which Char describes the artist's discovery, also his own, sets apart this particular text, at the same time indicating the eventual in its occasional duration and the essential in its passing: "Everything remains possible in the succession of days. The account that Picasso gave of it is neither an approbation, nor a disavowal. We have to pass. He passes." (P)

The last sentence of this longest test in the series opens with a cry that by its rhythm and tone is neighbor to Rilke's tragic question ("Wer, wenn ich schriee, hörte mich denn aus der Engel / Ordnungen? // Who if I cried, would hear me among the angelic / Orders?" DE,21). It is at the same moment a vivid testimony of present triumph in a strong poetic presence, and a lucid forewarning of the defeat that will, of necessity, follow on that presence, in its passing:

> Qui, là, parmi les menthes, est parvenu à naître dont toute chose, demain, se prévaudra?[24] (NP,131)

This sentence, the climax of the collection, took its time in attaining that grave rhythm which remains as if suspended. A first version of the question, added to the preliminary draft, was slightly less sustained and far less touching:

> Mais qui, là, est parvenu à naître, dont toute chose demain se prévaudra?

Between these two expressions there lies a distance to which only a prolonged reading can render us sensitive, a gap refusing reduction and objectifying, like the word of the poet itself: "But poetry, going naked on its feet of reeds . . . is not to be reduced anywhere." (FM,74) It is also to those reeds that the mint responds, and to a searing unrest sufficiently declared now even in its brief expression.

The mint leaves, latecomers to the elaboration of this last sentence, preside retrospectively over the birth and death of everything written against a dry house. Their scent suggests also by association the lavender's, prepares the presence of the burning herbs in *Aromates chasseurs*, and redeems, while retaining it, Rembrandt's flayed emblem of the passage

[24] Moments of heightened intensity often share this characteristic rhythm, a breathlessness betraying the presence of an unspoken encounter. "Le sommet n'est qu'un instant, où l'inconnu, le futur, le silence se manifestent par leur retrait même. . .". (Starobinski, *op.cit.*) And René Ménard: "Le *sommet*, c'est aussi une foi intransigeante dans les forces de la vie, dans les réverbérations du sacré sur les circonstances de notre condition. . . . Cette beauté, qui est *sommet*, est aussi privilège." ("Cinq essais pour interpréter René Char," *La Condition poétique*, NRF, col. Espoir, 1959, p. 132.)

For a discussion of the summit, and of the images of fire, flash, abundance, and fig-tree, among others, see the article of Jacques Kerno on "L'Oeuvre de René Char en 1966," *Promesse*, no. 17, Spring, 1967.

through fire, as well as the other canvas of a skull and a mirror.

For the mint must be boiled so that the fragrance might be reborn in its alchemical power. The implicit image of the phoenix serves as a reminder of a modest but efficacious fire, leaving only a ring, as if this trace were in correspondence with the track of wolf-claws scratched on the mountain slope, and pictured in *La Nuit talismanique*, a circular signal of the ancient convergence of Ouranos and Orpheus. The passage upland is guided by an invocation to an emptiness provoked and already resounding in these pages: "Faire la brèche, et qu'en jaillisse la flambée d'une herbe aromatique. / Make the breach and from it may there spring the flaming of an aromatic herb." (NT,67)

D. AROMATES CHASSEURS

.　　.　　.　　.　　.　　.　　.　　.

Un aromate de pays
Prolongeait la fleur apparue. . . .

.　　.　　.　　.　　.　　.　　.　　.

Le chasseur de soi fuit sa maison fragile:
Son gibier le suit n'ayant plus peur.

Leur clarté est si haute . . .

.　　.　　.　　.　　.　　.　　.　　.

"Les Trois soeurs" (FM,171)

The road marked out here is at once familiar to us and different from those we have already traveled. It participates perhaps in the third space that the poet envisions as a future correspondence of the two others present for us, the intimate and imaginary one within, and, surrounding us, the circular or the real.[25] The major themes whose individual resonance

[25] Robert Cohn explains Rimbaud's "Soleil et chair" ("Credo in unam") as a long Lucretian poem picking up the theme of the "third" realm of history in the utopian sense in which the German Romantics used it: Herder, Schiller, Hölderlin, and Novalis. In the light of his

we recognize from their previous diverse appearances now appear linked in a peculiar harmony preparatory to the traversal described in one of these texts as taking place under the "flanged gaze of the gods." It is as if the "commune présence" of 1937 had been realized at last, in this renewed encounter of all former elements.

These poems move from an initial falling, in which even the idea of the book seems to break in its downward passage, the poet himself writing "en cours de chute," to the concluding elevation of giant pontoon bridges cast across the sky for a traverse far above the prosaic. The path appears thus to ascend once more, although not without difficulty. The way of Orion's return to his tomb, dug in the air, is groping and yet sure.

1. *Circle and Valley*

Certain connections previously only suggested between the images of ring, wheel, well, and circle on one hand and, on the other, human love in its various stages of desire and suffering, are made clearer in these poems, of a more universal scope than those of the "talismanic night." An entire series of statements can be seen in its progressive pessimism, as in the following examples ranging over a great span of years:

. . . .

Sur notre plaisir s'allongeait l'influente douceur de la grande roue consumable du mouvement, au terme de ses classes. (FM,24)

. . . .

Ce soir, la grande roue errante si grave du désir peut bien être de moi seul visible. . . . (FM,36)

---

suggestion that the original Golden Age was perhaps an inspiration for Baudelaire's line: "J'aime le souvenir de ces époques nues," might we sense, as does René Char, in his own phrase "Le Nu perdu" a memory, not just of Hamlet, as Georges Blin points out, but also of an age of the unornamented, bare, and simple, now lost—but perhaps not irremediably? Compare the pure labor described by one of Char's compatriots: "J'ai semé, labouré, moissonné nu (je veux dire pur de souillures passionnelles). . . ." (HB, 416)

. . . .

J'appelle les amours qui roués et suivis par la faulx de l'été, au soir embaument l'air de leur blanche inaction. (LM,140)

. . . .

La roue du destin tourne à l'envers et ses dents nous déchiquettent. Nous prendrons feu bientôt du fait de l'accélération de la chute. L'amour, ce frein sublime, est rompu, hors d'usage.[bx] (first version by AC, *Argile* no 1, 7)

. . . .

The ring, which gave its apparently simple form to the most subtle poems of rejoicing mingled with a grave acceptance of cyclic destruction and rebirth, such as "Grège" and "Invitation," and was related to other circular images such as the wheel and the watermill, betrays an inescapable certainty; historic, as in the above quotation, or legendary, as in the fence surrounding the animal on a ground of flowers in the Unicorn tapestries ("L'Anneau de la Licorne"). It now appears also as a prison determined by our moment (the "anneau nuptial du désert" here, like the barbed wire around a concentration camp ironic in its circular form, placed like a wedding ring around a finger to symbolize fidelity and permanence). The erotic implications of the image in its associations and juxtapositions are not infrequent, as in this attenuated form—"J'aimais ton visage de source raviné par l'orage et le chiffre de ton domaine enserrant mon baiser / I loved your face of a storm-ravined spring and the number of your domain enclosing my kiss," (FM,22) and, as if it were the portrait of the ravaged water, the poem in the form

[bx] Over our joy there stretched out the influential gentleness of motion's great consumable wheel, at the end of its classes. // This evening, desire's great wandering wheel, so serious, may be visible only to me . . . // I summon the loves which, racked and followed by summer's scythe, embalm the evening air with their white inactivity. / Destiny's wheel turns backward and its teeth tear us to bits. // Soon we shall take fire from the acceleration of falling. Love, sublime brake, is broken, out of working order.

of a "Médaillon": "Eaux de verte foudre qui sonnent l'extase du visage aimé . . . eaux saccagées d'un proche sacre. . . . / Waters of green lightning sounding the ecstasy of the loved face . . . waters plundered by a nearby consecration." (FM, 30) The understated poems of love find a well's depth for their *restoring*—"Qui a creusé le puits et hisse l'eau gisante / Risque son coeur dans l'écart de ses mains" (NP,30), a passage to be read in apposition with the page facing it, each deepening the other: ". . . qui élevèrent aux margelles le cercle en fleurs de la jarre du ralliement / who lifted to the rim the flowering circle of the restoring vessel." (NP,31) Wound and rebirth are both present in *Aromates chasseurs*; first in the "sensual lightning" of the water's circular dance, as it is aroused by the bucket: "(Hisser, de jour, le seau du puits où l'eau n'en finit pas de danser l'éclat de sa naissance.) / (To lift, in the daytime, the bucket of the well where the water never ceases to dance the ripple of its birth.)." (AC,12) The description of this birth is placed between parentheses as if to protect the secret of the inward extension corresponding to the outward bright motion as it widens. And then, even more quietly, there is partly revealed the darkened place of suffering and its reflowering, carved out like the road of the dolorous green water, another "valleyed flower" in the Vaucluse of the mind: "Le trèfle obscurci . . . La cicatrice verte. / The darkened trefoil . . . The green scar." (AC,17) In the dark trefoil, an image from "Le Visage nuptial" returns, the "murmur of black dowry" extending beyond its erotic referent to provide a source for a flow as renewing to poetry as it is to love. In like manner, another image from that poem: "Faithful simplicity spread everywhere," re-read in a wider setting, suggests the convergence of many images of time, love, and flux: the suffering of the Sorgue, a valleyed road, a restoring well, and a victorious fountain. We bring with us all these readings superposed and these memories of readings from the accrual of "black events" into the space of the later texts, like so many reeds entangled in the water of the river, in whose depths we perceive a sorrow as the deepest source in the deepest silence.

2. *Understanding, Dwelling*

"Tandis que la moisson achevait de se graver sur le cuivre du soleil, une alouette chantait dans la faille du grand vent sa jeunesse qui allait prendre fin. / While the harvest was finishing its inscription on the sun's copper, the lark sang in the fault of a great wind its youth which was to end." (AC,31) This text is itself inscribed firmly in the page by its measure, as if the "graven rhythm" of the scythe held by Louis Curel de la Sorgue in the poem of his name were here to strike on a resounding solar brass. And pictorially, by the color of wheat responding to the color of the sun, on a canvas whose brightness would seem to include also a memory of the flayed ox, his crimson hue providing the "only sun" for the poet's future action in its own blood-red ardor.

Like the poet, the reader is meant not merely to listen as this lark sings, in all the lightness conferred on the poem by its title, but to comprehend the song. Whereas in the earlier texts of *Le Marteau sans maître* the more passive listening predominates, in the verb "écouter": "Dans le bois on écoute bouillir le ver / In the wood we listen to the worm boiling." (MM,21) "J'écoute marcher dans mes jambes," literally "I listen to the walking in my legs" (MM,28); here an inner comprehension or "entendement" takes precedence over a passive listening to exterior or interior phenomena, a listening nevertheless included in the broader understanding. It is, however, in moments of rest that the most profound and inward perception is granted, within a tranquility more active than passive; thus the recurring image of the shoulder, bearing with it the latent potential of strength matched with a timeless patience: "Le contraire d'écouter est d'entendre. Et comme fut longue à venir à nos épaules la montagne silencieuse. / The contrary of listening is hearing. And how slow was the silent mountain in coming to our shoulders." (AC,16) Yet that silence, though it refuses an easy verbal flux of the *parole*, is unmistakably allied with the poetic word about which the all-important "Argument" preceding *Seuls demeurent* of

1938 is written. The portrait is plainly of the same poet as the one pictured in *Le Marteau sans maître*, his being infused with the need for a free respiration; the man fleeing suffocation, maker of bread, poetry, and life, holds but is not bound by a ring representing the ring correspondences, and cycles. To the ones not called to be his companions, his own mountainous ascent and descent—described here as the moving of flocks from high pastures to low—will be forever unfamiliar: "Aux uns la prison et la mort. Aux autres la transhumance du Verbe. / To some, prison and death. To others, the migration of the word." (FM,19)

In the title poem of *Aromates chasseurs*, a crossing is explicitly effected, away from the world of action toward the mental dwelling that has as its prefiguration the "tête habitable" sought long before, in "Bel édifice et les pressentiments" of *Le Marteau sans maître*. "Maison mentale. Il faut en occuper toutes les pièces, les salubres comme les malsaines, et les belles aerées, avec la connaissance prismatique de leurs différences. / Mental habitation. We must occupy all its rooms, healthy and unhealthy, and the beautiful airy ones, in the prismatic knowledge of their differences." (AC,12) This prism might be compared to the sun shining into the mental dwelling through tiny particles of dust, for we remember the similar conclusion of "Commune présence," also directed toward an inner unity of the poet and a life found to be inexpressible:

Essaime la poussière.
Nul ne décèlera votre union.[cx] (MM,146)

The dwelling situated in the "third space of the future"— a space on which the introductory text of *Aromates chasseurs* is based—will hold no prisoner. In "La Dot de Maubergeonne," a poem in honor of a mistress held captive (thus, badly lodged: "mal hébergée"), the poet bestows on her the grace of all the aromatic herbs of his own country, from which this collection acquires a particular and local fra-

[cx] Let dust swarm / None will divulge your union.

310

grance not to be lost in their final burning:[26] "Un bouquet de thym en décembre, une griffe de sauge après neige, de la centaurée dès qu'elle aimera, un échelon de basilic, la renouée des chemins devant sa chambre nuptiale . . . / Que le ciel, lorsqu'elle sortira, lui donne son vent rapide. // A bouquet of thyme in December, a snatch of sage after the snow, some centaury as soon as she is in love, an echelon of basil, the knot-grass of paths before her bridal chamber . . . / May the sky, when she goes out, give her its rapid wind." (AC,28) In the swiftest wind, freedom is regained and convergence, verbal and conceptual, restituted after the imposed limits. Just as the term "basilic" joins the ordinary herb, "basil," to the mythological lizard or "basilisk," the herb "renouée" is itself another linguistic meeting—by its homonym "renouer," to join again, as in the title of one of the texts from *La Nuit talismanique*: "Pour renouer."

The image of the "tête habitable" might then have served as an advance signal of the inner voyage now to be made.

3. *Ship and Bridge*

> Ils construisirent une barque avec l'écume de la mer afin de se saisir du rivage le plus lointain. Cette chaîne de récifs, c'est eux![dx] (AC,24)

The gods, whom Char never considers to be exterior to us or

---

[26] "La terre, en produisant des aromates, produit donc quelque chose de supérieur à la mort, quelque chose qui confère aux êtres périssables par son oeuvre une certaine possibilité de ne pas passer." (*Paul Claudel interroge le Cantique des Cantiques*, Egloff, 1948, 263. Quoted HB,147.) And one statement in *Aromates chasseurs* replies in condensed form to multiple images of fire, of suffering, and of language as they appear from *Artine* and *Abondance viendra* through *Contre une maison sèche*: ". . . nous sommes une étincelle à l'origine inconnue qui incendions toujours plus avant. Ce feu, nous l'entendons râler et crier, à l'instant d'être consumés? Rien, sinon que nous étions souffrants, au point que le vaste silence, en son centre, se brisait." (AC,34) Joining herbs and flame in one image, Char's aromatics are set afire for the final passage to the summit, made in silence. "Nous faisons nos chemins comme le feu ses étincelles." ("Faire du chemin avec . . ." (1976).

[dx] They built a boat with seafoam so as to grasp the furthest strand. They are that chain of shoals.

strangers to the *mortal* ("ils sont le fruit de la seule de nos pensées qui ne conquiert pas la mort / they are the fruit of the only one of our thoughts which does not conquer death"), choose their companions as the poet chooses his (in first version of AC). They finally adopt those travelers who risk the most extreme sites for their poetic initiation: "Plus les montagnes sont hautes, plus les initiés ont droit à la foudre dans leur bâton / The higher the mountains, the more right have the initiate to lightning in their stick." (*ibid.*) All former distinctions between sea and mountain are rendered unnecessary, the foam peaks of the poem "Fastes" having become, in their simple merging with the mountains, the place for this ultimate voyage, undertaken only by those beings ("quelques êtres") who have earned the right to suffer and to impose suffering by their uncompromising nature: "cruels, opposants, hôtes indésirables. . . ." These frail ships that bear in themselves those other prows of the anvil ("nacelles de l'enclume," MM,56) and that other vessel ("barque incontinente," NP,28) seem to be resting only on the slime found in earlier works: "la vase profonde / the deep mire" ("Poètes," MM,56), "la vase sur la peau des reins / the mire on the skin of loins" ("L'Éclaircie," MM, 99), "la vase" beneath the reeds of "L'Adolescent souffleté." (LM,58) To the fireflies' gleam—to which the boats are compared in the poem—there responds an image of the bees waking in the lavender and waking with them the impenetrable depth of one unfinished line in "J'habite une douleur," from many years before: "Tu crois voir passer la beauté au-dessus des lavandes noires. / You think you see beauty passing above the black lavender." (FM,178) The entire network of ray and dart, sting, star, arrow, and flower is rejoined. For Orion, king and servant of the bees, a human meteor fleeing the flowers pursuing him, has the earth for his honey, in the description of his celestial reception already quoted. Blinded and noble, a hunter still caught by the chase of his own being, he confers on the celestial bees at whose starry

radiance he aims his arrows, their own most lasting brilliance
by his enduring pursuit:

Il tend son arc et chaque bête brille.
Haute est sa nuit; flèches risquez vos chances. (AC,27)

In this "ennobling superstition" of Orion's return to his constellation, risk is implicit: the texts of *Aromates chasseurs*
extend the brief span of their intensity like the bow outstretched, in the form of a pontoon bridge suspended high
above the preceding texts.

Now, in the poems: "Pontonniers" and "Orion Iroquois,"[27]
the preceding images of ship, suffering, and salvation are
joined like so many crossings as the builder of bridges res-
cues the frailest of vessels in the iciest of waters. The pontoon path, constructed by an Iroquois as the legendary
scaler of heights, stretches high above the water, joining all
the texts: "Orion, charpentier de l'acier? Oui, lui toujours; et vers nous. / Orion, builder in steel? Yes, him still;
and toward us." (AC,37) The "constellated" construction
from a former poem (MM,144) also lends its support to this
giant bridge under which—or across which—the whole human adventure, once broken on the falling wheel of the first
text in this collection, can pass resoldered and reborn.

Aromates chasseurs is a work of physical age, says the
poet, but is destined for a youth renewed and a spring to
come. Under this bridge we see an unspoken foundation laid
in an earlier correspondence, a former song of bridging,
where a fresh moment hastens forward in all its brief and
hopeful brightness:

.   .   .   .

C'est de cela seul qu'il faut tirer richesse immédiate et
opérante. Ainsi, il y a un jour de pur dans l'année, un
jour qui creuse sa galerie merveilleuse dans l'écume de la

---

[27] See the final lines of Rimbaud's "Bateau ivre": "Je ne puis
plus . . . nager sous les yeux horribles des pontons." (R,131) See
also Edmund Wilson, *Apologies to the Iroquois.*

mer, un jour qui monte aux yeux pour couronner midi.[ex]
(FM,190)

.   .   .   .

In this "pulverized" poem, "Le Requin et la mouette," written almost thirty years before *Aromates chasseurs*, the days
previous to that one clear day of vision were said to permit
a distance between branch and bud, between what swims beneath the surface and what flies above it: "Hier, la noblesse
était déserte. . . . / Yesterday, nobility was deserted. . . ." But
in one ephemeral and possibly unconscious instant of joining, the arch of the rainbow forms a bridge, and it is the presence of that arch that we see within the semi-circle of Orion's
bow, a bridge stretched out for the meeting of age and youth,
vessel and shore, suffering and desire. Now the poem of the
present takes within itself that former hope, under the arching of a chosen constellation, already predicted in its innocence:

.   .   .   .

O Vous, arc-en-ciel de ce rivage polisseur, approchez le
navire de son espérance. Faites que toute fin supposée
soit une neuve innocence, un fiévreux en-avant pour ceux
qui trébuchent dans la matinale lourdeur.[fx] (FM,190)

[ex] From that alone can be drawn immediate, operative wealth.
Therefore there is one pure day in the year, one day that digs its
marvelous tunnel in the sea's foam, a day rising to the eyes in order
to crown noontime. (JG)

[fx] Oh You, rainbow of this polishing shore, bring the ship close in
to her hope. Make every supposed end be a new innocence, a feverish
forward march for those stumbling in the morning heaviness. (JG)

314

ARCHIPELAGO TO CONSTELLATION: "VICTOIRE ÉCLAIR"

Notre ciel est une veille . . .
(RBS,173)

The poet, recognized by the gods, risks their fury, as a sign of their predilection for him. Heidegger quotes Hölderlin, "the poet's poet," writing a year before the onset of his madness: "The sacred father of old with a calm hand shakes benedictions from the crimson clouds." (EB,308) And a year later: "The mighty element, heaven's fire and human stillness, their life within nature, and their limitations and their satisfaction have constantly impressed me, and as it is said of the heroes, I can finally claim that I have been struck by Apollo."[1] (EB,309) Heidegger notes that too intense a brightness destines the poet to obscu-

[1] (Translations here adapted from EB and the German original.) An initial fascination with lightning leads to the *éclat* and the *éclair*, part of poetry. Hölderlin's letter to Casimir Ulrich Böhlendorff, from the autumn of 1802, after the onset of his illness, could serve as the counterpart to the Pascalian "effroi," as a distant correspondent to Char's *L'Effroi la joie* and the candle flame we have placed at the heart of our own essay. "Nature in these parts moves me more powerfully, the more I study it. The thunderstorm, not only in its extreme manifestation, but precisely as a power and shape, among the other forms of the sky, light in its workings . . . its urgency in coming and going, what is characteristic in forests and the convergence in one region of different kinds of nature, so that all the holy places of the earth come together around one place, and the philosophic light around my window—these are now my joy; and may I bear in mind how I came here, as far as this place!" (FH,14) The forest of "Pénombre" and "L'Inoffensif," the dwelling of "J'habite une douleur," and the brief intensity of "Contrevenir": these elements converge in this natural and intense image of the poem.

René Char points out that he had read Hölderlin extensively before knowing the story of his life, to which his own bears a certain resemblance—for we could also say that René Char had been "struck by the gods."

rity, in a juxtaposition of extremes characteristic of the nature of poetic language, whose peril he calls a marvelous and terrible neighbor to its power of rendering innocent, as a mountain is juxtaposed to a reassuring valley. One of the rare allusions in Char's writings to the event serving as their point of departure—an origin outgrown with varying degrees of rapidity, but usually missing from the surface of the text—introduces *Le Chien de coeur*, a group of poems in *Le Nu perdu* unlike the others. Lightning struck within the head of the poet, who was given to understand in a flash of comprehension that "lightning and blood . . . are one." Thus the convulsive blood said to shine within the body of the poet, himself the bare and the lost, clarifies from the inside what the brightness of the sky illuminates from without.[1a] This moment is marked by the perception of the *entre-deux*, a space stretched between gods and men, before the mortal partner of the gods is returned, scattered, to the universe forever.[2] The space is lit now and from now on by a twilight unfailing, "non fautive," to which the poet will be faithful. This odd light coming from a time before the fall pits its bright intensity against our often opaque sensibility, confronts its stark nakedness with our own: "a light that . . . remained there, naked, increased, peremptory, breaking with all its arteries against us." (NP,97) The warring couple is no longer equally matched.

The cycle of fault and of climbing is briefly recounted within *Le Nu perdu*, from the offending gaze in "Mirage des aiguilles" to the lifting of the guilt in "Aiguevive," a prelude to Orion's own revolutionary insurgence (AC,7) and his insertion in the upward line of *Aromates chasseurs*. After he is received into his constellation, he will again be reincarnate in the world of men as a legend transformed: "Orion Iro-

[1a] For at full moon, say the alchemists, the mad and earthbound dog of death changes to a soaring eagle.

[2] The term can be pejorative: "Celui qui invente, au contraire de celui qui découvre, n'ajoute aux choses, n'apporte aux êtres que des masques, des entre-deux, une bouillie de fer." (LM,149)

quois." A blameless illumination shone in "Seuil," where the poet-host hastened toward the outcome of a "diluvian night" to await us in the wavering dawn, with a bright circle of seasons sparkling as his belt, (FM,81) like an Orion who had not yet been named but whose ring already girded him. Now the cycle of return includes him in its completion and its brightness, a ring forming also a constellation of texts.[3] "L'influx de milliards d'années de toutes parts et circulairement le chant jamais rendu d'Orphée. / The influx of thousands of years from everywhere and, circular in its singing, the never rendered song of Orpheus." (SP,34) Orpheus, bearing in his voice all the strength of tradition, in a text of 1974 meets Orion, who is traveling a dreadful and interior path, as if a poet were to give chase to himself and to his song: ". . . suivre le sentier qui ne mène qu'au coeur ensanglanté de soi, source et sépulcre du poème. / . . . to follow the path leading only to one's own bloodied heart, source and sepulchre of the poem." (SP,33) Orpheus too is dismembered into a constellation, his lyre as lonely as a unicorn's single weapon: "La Constellation du Solitaire est tendue / The constellation of the solitary is taut." (LM,146)(TG)

The being who has chosen his own myth also chooses its limits. The marginal poet is finally, like his reader, not "apart," but "a part of." Refusing the narrow boundaries of a purely mental task, he has rendered himself tragic and vulnerable. The significance of his destiny and the possibility of our participation in it depend also upon his irrefutable insertion alongside us. "The combat of the spirit separates. Feeling is a plunge within the fray. . . . I am not separated. I am *among*. From that comes my torment without hope." (S) Of all the paradoxical themes and ambiguous expressions found within the canvas of this work, this is perhaps the most essential. For the poet willing himself "en avant," stretched toward the future, is already, like each of us, alone by his

---

[3] Already the title "Septentrion" (the Little Bear, or the north, by extension, the North Star) indicates, in *Retour amont*, this stellar preoccupation.

thought-toward-death, in the uniquely impassioned freedom of the rebellious.[4] However, as part of his chosen project and his self-inflicted anguish, he will always exist together with (*Sein bei*) what exists alongside him: " 'project' of a being existing who, from the beginning, is simultaneously the being *among* . . . existing things, the being *with* . . . the human-reality of others, and the being *in relation* to himself." (QM, 96) The presence of the poet will be felt among us; yet he is turned toward his future, and is thus essentially alone. Heidegger's thought often underlies the poetry of René Char: the absolute possibility the philosopher defends becomes the very ground of the poem, to which the poet, and with him the reader, renders himself attentive. Heidegger's essay "The Principle of Identity" speaks of the precipitous "homing" or leap ("être du bond") into the belonging together of man and being, seen as a "Konstellation." This is the unique concern of the watchful man, his "Ereignis."[5] In fact, the four considerations listed as characteristic of his state of Being—disclosedness, thrown-ness, projection, and falling (BT,264) —can be seen to have exact equivalents in Char's thought and imagery, closely associated with the constellation of meteoric figures: illuminating, passing in a flash, hurtling downward, fated and yet soaring.

But the watchful being always "*en attente*" is exposed to the lightning of the gods within. *L'Effroi la joie*, a series of poems whose title recalls Pascal's fearful night, opens with a vision of stars as violent as mortuary flashes then crystallized: "The solstices transfix, diffuse sadness into a hard diamantine

---

[4] "Let the term '*dying*' stand for that *way of Being* in which Dasein *is towards* its death." (". . . *Seinsweise*, in der das Dasein *zu* seinem Tode *ist*.") (BT,291) And see also Heidegger on the unique possibility posed by death and its anticipation as quoted in chapter IX, C, note 21.

[5] "Hence we must leap in order that we may experience in our own person the *belonging*-together of Man and Being. This leap is the precipitous homing without benefit of bridges into that belonging-ness which alone Man and Being as mutually related and, hence, their pattern ['die Konstellation beider'] can provide." (EM,23)

jewel." (NP,79) Experience is shattered, as the word and the vision are fragmented into luminous particles, stellar and tragic: "Enchemisé dans les violences de sa nuit, le corps de notre vie est pointillé d'une infinité de parcelles lumineuses coûteuses. / Clothed in the violence of its night, the body of our life is dotted with an infinity of costly luminous particles." (NP,101)

Within *Partage formel*, perhaps the most coherent group of Char's poetic reflections, one of the exploded texts describes an obligatory passage by contraries; it has been quoted before, at the beginning of this essay, and now the spiraling re-passage returns it to its proper place within the constellated night of poetry, extended far beyond the single poem or the single series:

> Traverser avec le poème la pastorale des déserts, le don de soi aux furies, le feu moisissant des larmes. Courir sur ses talons, le prier, l'injurier. L'identifier comme étant l'expression de son génie ou encore l'ovaire écrasé de son appauvrissement. Par une nuit, faire irruption à sa suite, enfin, dans les noces de la grenade cosmique.[a] (FM,76)

Now the luminous fragments of a "pulverized poem," these islands of the poem's way, have found their final setting, like so many bees transformed into the shining flowers of a celestial ring, or so many swallows circling in another orbit after their meteoric plunge ("météores hirondelles") and their upward flight of return, a "retour amont" toward a constellation formed along the highest path of a work. The presence of Mallarmé, already felt in the introduction, now returns by this vertical passage.

The reader called to be one of the "high travelers" on a

---

[a] Traversing with the poem the pastoral of deserts, the gift of oneself to the furies, the fire of tears as it moulds. Running after it, imploring it, insulting it. Seeing it as the expression of one's genius or again, as the smashed ovary of one's impoverishment. Finally one night, to irrupt in its following, in the nuptials of the cosmic pomegranate.

319

path lit by the most intermittent of guiding beacons will not be laden with baggage.[6] Rather, he will share the fate of the denuded beings like the swift, or like the "nu perdu" against whom there flies the night's blackest down. He remains open to a voluntary correspondence with his destiny, as a moment

[6] And it is here that the poet takes his final leave of us. Although Char speaks of another poet, it is not only "for Rimbaud," but also for us: "Comme Nietzsche, comme Lautréamont, après avoir tout exigé de nous, il nous demande de le 'renvoyer.' Dernière et essentielle exigence. Lui qui ne s'est satisfait de rien, comment pourrions-nous nous satisfaire de lui?" (PNR,15 and RBS,132) Such a drastic leavetaking was already prepared by a severe detachment: "En poésie, on n'habite que le lieu que l'on quitte, on ne crée que l'oeuvre dont on se détache, on n'obtient la durée qu'en détruisant le temps. Mais tout ce qu'on détient par rupture, détachement et négation, on ne l'obtient que pour autrui. . . . Le donneur de liberté n'est libre que dans les autres. Le poète ne jouit que de la liberté des autres." (RBS,132) To give happiness without sharing it: ". . . *en donnant le bonheur, un bonheur qu'ils n'éprouvent ni ne partagent.*" (NP,61) "Nous n'appartenons à personne. . . ." (FM,87) Here the problems of reading meet those of the judgment necessarily rendered, a particularly difficult problem in the case of René Char, as Georges Mounin indicates (*La Communication poetique, op.cit.*). Alain Bosquet, quoted by Mounin: "René Char a désormais un style, un domaine et des habitudes." (p. 124) Compare the opposed attitude of Jacques Dupin, in his preface to the exhibition of René Char, Fondation Maeght, 1971: "Toutes les tentatives pour le presser de questions ne conduiraient qu'à la vaine paraphrase du poème dont il est né, et dont il est exclu, dont il est étranger par excellence, appelé en avant de nous par la très réelle chimère à laquelle il doit une nouvelle fois, donner son sang et accorder son souffle, afin qu'elle devienne visible, demain, dans sa montée au jour. . . . Cette parole nous grandit sans nous attacher, nous rend libres en accroissant nos liens et notre échange. . . ." (n.p.) (Reprinted in René Char, *Le Monde de l'art n'est pas le monde du pardon*, Maeght, 1975.) The great difference between these two judgments is characteristic of what Mounin calls the "extreme attitudes" that Char's critics have adopted, between which he places himself by choosing a third attitude, considering the poet within the history of French poetry rather than as a "sommet voyant." He continues by saying that every profound criticism of Char's work must take into account the idea Char has of poetry, and that for him, "Char poète . . . dépasse de beaucoup Char occasionnellement théoricien d'une espèce de voyance poétique." For our part, however, we would rather consider writing and seeing—*l'écriture* and *la voyance*—to meet precisely within the text as the final and fitting place of a "Convergence des multiples."

320

and a movement, for this meteor's golden voice ("voix d'or du météore") contains implicitly within it the path ("voie") in its fall and its rising. The poet has dug out his own tomb and his own return in the air, and is to become poem, star, and fruit, enduring flash and celestial fragment, when the space and distance he demands are finally accorded to him: "Later they will identify you with some disaggregated giant, lord of the impossible."[7] (FM,178) And still this impossible is closely tied to the most common work of the harvest, to its sheaves and their gathering, to their yellow gleam, as intense as the heaven's own radiance, and to the blue of a human energy to rival the excess of the sky. In "La Faux relevée," Char explicitly joins the color and the light first to the dispersion of his corporal substance and then to the renovating generosity of another source:

> Quand le bouvier des morts frappera du bâton,
> Dédiez à l'été ma couleur dispersée.

[7] "Wunderlich nah ist der Held doch den jugendlich Toten. Dauern / ficht ihn nicht an. Sein Aufgang ist Dasein; beständig / nimmt er sich fort und tritt ins veränderte Sternbild / seiner steten Gefahr. . . . // Yes, the Hero's strangely akin to the youthfully-dead. Continuance / doesn't concern him. His rising's existence. Time and again / he takes himself off and enters the changed constellation / his changeless peril's assumed. . . ." (DE,54-57) ". . . denk: es erhält sich der Held, selbst der Untergang war ihm / nur ein Vorwand, zu sein: seine letzte Geburt. // Consider: the Hero continues, even his fall / was a pretext for further existence, an ultimate birth." (DE,22-23) Thus myth is restored to poetry. The fall of a meteoric presence is seen as the prelude to a rising and an eventual dissolution, disaggregation into the universe of night: "Und jene, die schön sind, / o wer hält sie zurück? Unaufhörlich steht Anschein / auf in ihrem Gesicht und geht fort. Wie Tau von dem Frühgras / hebt sich das Unsre von uns, wie die Hitze von einem / heissen Gericht. . . . / . . . / weh mir: wir sinds doch. Schmeckt denn der Weltraum, / in den wir uns lösen, nach uns? // And those that have beauty, / oh, who shall hold them back? Incessant appearance / comes and goes in their faces. Like dew from the morning grass / exhales from us that which is ours, like heat / from a smoking dish. . . . / . . . alas, / but we *are* all that. Does the cosmic space we dissolve into taste of us, then? . . ." (DE, 30-31) And in Rilke's *Sonnets to Orpheus*, the voice becomes a constellation, guided by lament: "ein sternbild unser Stimme / in den Himmel. . . . // a constellation of our voice / into the sky. . . ." (SO, 30-31)

321

Avec mes poings trop bleus étonnez un enfant.
Disposez sur ses joues ma lampe et mes épis.

Fontaine, qui tremblez dans votre étroit réduit,
Mon gain, aux soifs des champs, vous le prodiguerez.[b]
(LM,184)

. . . .

Among all the others, the constellation of the hunter Orion
assumes the various fragments, however diverse in appearance, of this long trace of writing, opening and concluding in
a clarity enigmatic and obscuring, like the radiance that might
be projected from the philosopher's stone, whose distant presence is felt here and not for the first time. The hunter victim
of his own ardor remains the "prey of destiny," whose blind-
ness is finally as noble as his fate: "Haute est sa nuit." His
reception[8] is not in doubt. As the bees awaken in the lavender, their sting making an arrow of every flower, these flowers themselves set out in ardent and deadly pursuit of their
master, whose weapons are thus directed against his own
being, as the sting of the brightest stars burns even the stars.
These figures already perceived in their metaphoric passage
are in turn the body of the work from which the poet fabri-
cates his own future being, as the tree marking the site of the
dry house bears its own fruit for its own nourishment: "A
human meteor has the earth for honey." Here the poet, "lord
of the impossible," recounts his own destiny as the integral
and violent friend of the most distant bees, whose work and
whose horizons are finally his own.

Aromates, est-ce pour vous? (PPC,142)

In one South American myth, Orion's constellation is

---

[b] When the dead men's drover strikes with his rod, / Dedicate to
summer my color dispersed. / With my fists too blue astonish a child.
/ Arrange on his cheeks my lamp and my sheaves. / Fountain, trembling in your narrow nook, / You will spread my profit toward the
fields athirst.
[8] See the poem "Réception d'Orion," quoted in entirety under the
discussion of the bee and the other Orion poems quoted in foonote 10.

formed by five men who once built a canoe to cross the celestial vault of the country of the dead.[9] Each poet is a ferryman among fragments, for the beings crossing with him, by his choice and theirs, from one island to another of the archipelago of language, transformed at last into a constellation.

On the return journey of the meteor,[10] the legend of an eternal hunter, builder of ships and bridges, converges with that of an absent brother, a brutal and yet "indelible companion," who "dwells within the crucible of unity." (FM,39) The way toward the constellation is marked merely by a smoke of burning herbs: *Aromates chasseurs.* A poetry "non-alliable," admitting of no alloy, makes a traverse not only horizontal— above the partitioned depths of water or of time or across a river "valleyed" by its suffering—but rises upland too, through a prophetic smoke of incense, whose origin might be

---

These four poems are the cardinal points for the construction of *Aromates chasseurs.*

[9] Claude Lévi-Strauss, *L'Homme nu*, Plon, 1971, p. 405.

[10] We might repeat a question posed by Nietzsche, close to the final theme of our study (quoted in *Liberté*, op. cit., p. 169): "Une étoile déclina et disparut, mais sa lumière est encore en route, et quand cessera-t-elle d'être en route?"

Orion was always, as in the first poem of *Aromates chasseurs*, an "Evadé d'archipel," both celestial and terrestrial: ". . . Pigmenté d'infini et de soif terrestre, / N'épointant plus sa flèche à la faucille ancienne, / Les traits noircis par le fer calciné, / Le pied toujours prompt à éviter la faille, / Se plut avec nous / Et resta. / Chuchotement parmi les étoiles." (AC,9) His "réception" begins the second part of the collection, which "Orion Iroquois" ends by the building of the giant bridges "towards us." After the entire aromatic passage, his concluding speech, "Éloquence d'Orion," is all the more eloquent for its conditional form. Rimbaud's own "souliers blessés" find at last their companion image here, as we take our leave, quietly: the poet is speaking only to himself.

. . .

Et à présent si tu avais pouvoir de dire l'aromate de ton monde profond, tu rappellerais l'armoise. Appel au signe vaut défi. Tu t'établirais dans ta page, sur les bords d'un ruisseau, comme l'ambre gris sur le varech échoué; puis, la nuit montée, tu t'éloignerais des habitants insatisfaits, pour un oubli servant d'étoile. Tu n'entendrais plus geindre tes souliers entrouverts. (AC,43)

323

the most modest fire of twigs, set somewhere along a fragile yet definitive *rempart de brindilles*: "Poésie, unique montée des hommes, que le soleil des morts ne peut assombrir dans l'infini parfait et burlesque. / Poetry, unique ascension of men, which the sun of the dead cannot obscure in the infinite, perfected and ludicrous." (LM,195) *Poiesis* signified, from the very beginning, the making of perfumes and of ships. As of an aromatic vessel, for the crossing.

Oeuvre faite, comme on s'extrait de l'épaisseur du son
soir, disparaître de la surface de ses livres pour que s'en
déverse le printemps migrateur, hôte que notre corps non
multiple gênait.

"Faire du chemin avec . . ." (1976)

INDEX

N.B. The following terms, names, and concepts are arranged—in the spirit of this book—by correspondence rather than by the straight alphabetical system, within an "ordre insurgé."

I. Geography

II. Writers, Artists, Philosophers

III. Mythology, Art

IV. Criticism, Essays

V. Ambiguities and Reversals

VI. Terms and Concepts

329

VII. Complete titles referred to in the text

Initials refer to the volume, as in the essay itself, while page numbers refer to the essay; the translations are often rough ones, given only for an idea of the whole, past the fragments quoted. (Titles conform with *Poems of René Char*, Princeton University Press, 1976; titles of poems translated by Jonathan Griffin are marked *.)

Library of Congress Cataloging in Publication Data

Caws, Mary Ann.
  The presence of René Char.

  1. Char, René, 1907-   —Criticism and interpretation.
I. Title.
PQ2605.H3345Z63   848′.9′1209   75-30188
ISBN 0-691-06305-2